ROUTLEDGE LIBRARY EDITIONS: WYNDHAM LEWIS

Volume 3

WYNDHAM LEWIS

WYNDHAM LEWIS
An Anthology of His Prose

Edited by
E. W. F. TOMLIN

LONDON AND NEW YORK

First published in 1969 by Methuen & Co. Ltd

This edition first published in 2022
by Routledge
4 Park Square, Milton Park, Abingdon, Oxon OX14 4RN
605 Third Avenue, New York, NY 10017

Routledge is an imprint of the Taylor & Francis Group, an informa business

© This anthology 1969 Mrs Wyndham Lewis
© Introduction 1969 E. W. F. Tomlin

All rights reserved. No part of this book may be reprinted or reproduced or utilised in any form or by any electronic, mechanical, or other means, now known or hereafter invented, including photocopying and recording, or in any information storage or retrieval system, without permission in writing from the publishers.

Trademark notice: Product or corporate names may be trademarks or registered trademarks, and are used only for identification and explanation without intent to infringe.

British Library Cataloguing in Publication Data
A catalogue record for this book is available from the British Library

ISBN: 978-1-03-205725-5 (Set)
ISBN: 978-1-00-322366-5 (Set) (ebk)
ISBN: 978-1-03-211914-4 (Volume 3) (hbk)
ISBN: 978-1-03-211921-2 (Volume 3) (pbk)
ISBN: 978-1-00-322215-6 (Volume 3) (ebk)

DOI: 10.4324/9781003222156

Publisher's Note
The publisher has gone to great lengths to ensure the quality of this reprint but points out that some imperfections in the original copies may be apparent.

Disclaimer
The publisher has made every effort to trace copyright holders and would welcome correspondence from those they have been unable to trace.

WYNDHAM LEWIS
An Anthology of his Prose

Edited with an Introduction by
E.W.F. TOMLIN

METHUEN & CO LTD
11 NEW FETTER LANE LONDON EC4

First published in 1969
This anthology © 1969 by Mrs Wyndham Lewis
Introduction © 1969 by E. W. F. Tomlin
Printed in Great Britain by
Butler & Tanner Ltd, Frome and London

Other books by E. W. F. Tomlin
LIVING AND KNOWING
SIMONE WEIL
THE ORIENTAL PHILOSOPHERS
WYNDHAM LEWIS
TOKYO ESSAYS

Contents

Introduction 1

1 Sociological and Philosophical Writings 21
Paleface (1929) *The Art of Being Ruled* (1926) *The Doom of Youth* (1932) *The Enemy of the Stars* (1914–1932)

2 Writings on Literature and the Arts 259
The Caliph's Design (1919) *Men Without Art* (1934) *The Diabolical Principle and The Dithyrambic Spectator* (1931) *Madness in Shakespearian Tragedy* (*Preface*) (1929)

3 Autobiographical Writings 319
Blasting and Bombardiering (1937) *Rude Assignment* (1950)

4 Travel 351
Filibusters in Barbary (1932)

5 America 373
America and Cosmic Man (1948)
America, I Presume (1940)

Epilogue: On His Blindness 393
The Sea-Mists of the Winter (1951)

Acknowledgements

My thanks are due to Mrs Wyndham Lewis for granting me permission to use the following passages from her husband's works, and for the interest she has shown in the compilation of this Anthology. I am indebted to my publisher, Mr J. Alan White, for assistance throughout its compilation. My thanks are due to Miss Jane Larkman for her aid in preparing much of the material. I am grateful to my sister, Miss Esther Tomlin, for assistance with proof-reading. Finally, I wish to thank Mr Michael Cullis for much help, the pooling of reminiscence, and that form of advice which, gently but firmly offered, has instructed me in the art of being overruled.

E. W. F. T.
Tokyo – London
  1964–1968

Note

Lewis was sparing with footnotes. Those marked with an asterisk are his: the rest are the Editor's. Where omissions occur in the text they are for the sake of removing material which has no direct bearing on the argument. The introductory remarks to the various excerpts have been kept to a minimum; they are intended merely to provide the reader with information likely to further his appreciation of the text. In most cases epigraphs have been omitted.

The life of the intelligence is the very incarnation of freedom: where it is dogmatic and harsh it is impure; where it is too political it is impure . . . and it is the most inveterate enemy of unjust despotic power . . . It does not exercise power by terror or by romantic pictures of the vast machinery of Judgement and Destruction. It is more humane than are the programmes of the theological justiciary. And its servants are not a sect nor an organized caste, like the priest or the hereditary aristocrat, but individuals possessing no concerted and lawless power, coming indifferently from all classes, and living simply among other people. And their pride, if they have it, is because of something inside themselves which has been won at no one else's expense, and that no one can give them or remove from them.

The Art of Being Ruled

Introduction

The need for some kind of anthology or digest of the work of Wyndham Lewis – one of the most rich and diversified of this century – has long been felt. Lewis is a writer to whom the first approach counts for a great deal, so that any attempt to render it more rewarding would seem particularly worth while. The idea of composing such an anthology occurred to the editor during the last years of Lewis's life, and it had his express approval. In fact, as I have since discovered, the idea did not originate with me. Writing more than thirty years ago, Cyril Connolly observed:

> What is necessary for Lewis is that some of his admirers, or he himself, should make an omnibus Lewis, an anthology of his best and finest passages, applying to his work the selection and compression which in the spate of his original creation have been wanting.[1]

Lewis did not undertake this task; he was far too busy. The necessity remains. But there is also a problem. In so comprehensive an anthology, the great trilogy of his prime, *Time and Western Man*, *The Art of Being Ruled* and *The Lion and the Fox*, would be laid heavily under contribution: the 'best thought' from such works as *Paleface*, *Men without Art* and *The Writer and the Absolute* would provide an important section: and if a selection of the 'finest passages' of the novels and stories were to be added to this *corpus*, the anthology would attain vast and indeed unmanageable proportions. We should have not one but a fleet of omnibuses.

[1] *Enemies of Promise* (1938).

INTRODUCTION

In the interests of economy and in view of the republication of some of the major works, it was decided finally to put together a selection much narrower in scope but, it is hoped, of scarcely less value and interest. The present volume therefore seeks to make a start with preserving as much as possible of work that is unlikely to be reissued.

Nothing that Lewis wrote, or painted, can be considered negligible. If ever an author consistently maintained an attitude of 'high seriousness', in Matthew Arnold's sense, it was Lewis. He could be wilful, playful, irreverent; but he was never facile, and he was never trivial. Behind the light façade of *The Old Gang and the New Gang* (a kind of posthumous offspring of *The Doom of Youth*); behind the fun and games of *The Doom of Youth* itself; behind the gentle satire of *America, I Presume*, behind the blastings and blessings of *Blast* itself, there is manifest the high 'politics of the intellect'. Lewis's attitude of 'solitary schism', an attitude upheld without concession and without compromise over a working-life of fifty years, was the product of an integrity uncommon in any age, and almost unique to our own.

What a great man he was! The younger generation, by which is meant the generation to reach its twenties after the Second World War, can have little idea of the power and impact of his personality. When T. S. Eliot, in his fine obituary notice in *The Sunday Times* (March 10, 1957), observed that 'a great intellect is gone, a great modern writer is dead', he spoke the plain truth. Yet how many readers, even at that level, were made to realize that a great intellect and a great writer had been among them? One speculates, indeed, how many were hearing his name, or at least identifying it, for the first time. Until the last years of his life, he never attained popularity. (The brief and exhilarating episode of the Academy's 'Rejected Portrait' was soon overshadowed by the war.) And apart from a small Civil List Pension, he received no national honours.

It is surprising, to put it mildly, that the author of *Time and Western Man* and *The Lion and the Fox*, books which have exerted wide though often unacknowledged influence, should not have received greater, and very much earlier, acclaim, particularly in academic circles. He was deeply touched by the award of an Honorary Degree by the University of Leeds. A glance down the list of 'distinguished writers' honoured by British universities much older than Leeds would not always make impressive reading. During most of his lifetime Lewis commanded limited recognition. Yet it would be interesting to know how many theses have already been written about him in America alone. Perhaps the United States – a country for which Lewis had great admiration – will be the first to recognize his true stature. For what writer, apart from his contemporaries – Eliot, Yeats, Joyce, and Pound – could boast a literary achievement at once so broad and so original? And if, as is generally agreed, the first three, and possibly the fourth, are major writers, how can we refuse that title to Lewis? Furthermore, Lewis was a painter of whom it may confidently be predicted that his fame will survive many contemporary reputations. On the subject of art, the editor was for some time hoping to be able to include in this volume some specimens of Lewis's art criticism; but the more he sifted the material, the stronger became his conviction that, quite apart from its bulk, this spirited writing deserved a volume of its own. An exception has been made in the case of an article on Picasso. For obvious reasons, another exception has been made of the famous article which, with the celebrated parallel in mind, has been entitled 'On his Blindness'.

When dealing with a writer one has known personally, it is often of interest to mention the circumstances in which one first became drawn to him and his work. By the middle 1930's Lewis was already a legendary figure to a number of us: and one usually heard of the legend before reading a single book or seeing a picture. There have indeed been legends attaching to all periods of his creative life: a pre-war, a post-war, and a post-second-war legend. Some of these legends stand in need of correction: others are of spurious fabrication, and should be exposed.

At this point the editor may be permitted a brief incursion into reminiscence. The first book by Lewis with which I became acquainted was *Paleface*. Because I still consider *Paleface* one of Lewis's best books, I have drawn upon it liberally; and since it likewise contains a good deal of ephemeral material, it provides the best justification for a selective compendium of this nature. The book is unlikely to be reprinted *in toto*: but to allow it to disappear into oblivion would be a misfortune. To read *Paleface* was forthwith to acquire an appetite for the rest.

INTRODUCTION

It is difficult for me to exaggerate the excitement and exhilaration which, in those days, the appearance of a work by Lewis produced. There was first the arresting dust-cover, almost always adorned with one of his designs. Sometimes it was merely a striking ideogram, almost a *cartouche*, the sign of the Enemy. Then, once the pages were turned, there was the immediate impression of the distinctive, the personal, the man apart. The banner-headlines, the unconventional subtitles, the eccentric layout, the liberal and often arcane quotations, the teeming and rich vocabulary, the prodigious learning: these became indelibly associated with even the least of his writings. Finally, once the reading began in earnest (and it could begin at any point), the attention was held by the exhibition of free intellect, the wit, the tough fight-talk, and yet at the same time the urbanity, and the overall style which Eliot, in his Introduction to *One-Way Song*,[1] describes as one of the most original in modern English. Admittedly, the going was not always easy; Lewis rarely wrote smooth, even, *belles-lettres* prose; but all was food for the intelligence, meaty if sometimes gristly, but never synthetic extract.

Lewis's books were displayed at comparatively few shops: his sales at this time were modest. But there were certain areas, the Charing Cross Road for instance, where they were always to be found. The eye would light on them, bright and provocative among the more sober book-jackets, and a kind of mental excitement would gather momentum. Sometimes, or was it only fancy? they seemed to survive change after change of *étalage*, remaining like fixed stars in a shifting firmament; and the same impression was received when, like comets, they returned, as they often did, in second-hand condition.

I do not recall how it was – those days seeming so far distant – that in the spring of 1937 Julian Symons invited me to contribute to a special Wyndham Lewis Number of his periodical *Twentieth Century Verse*.[2] To a very young man this was an attractive proposition. With today's literary world of best-selling youthful messiahs, I remain out of touch; in those days one made one's *début* in the 'Little Reviews'. There were still echoes of the old Bohemia. We would meet in pubs or in people's bedsitters, and sometimes

[1] 1960 edition.
[2] Symons wrote an account of the origin of this issue in *The London Magazine* (October 1957).

drop in at an artist's studio, and find the *maestro* off-duty, often with a serious young woman, her hair plastered back, in silent attendance. On one such occasion, we talked of Lewis, whom Symons knew well, and mapped out the kind of contribution required.

It had been my ambition at the time, being fresh from Modern Greats at Oxford, to write a study of political thought, with particular relation to the development of socialism. Meanwhile, I had been absorbed in *The Art of Being Ruled*, and I had formed the opinion, which I still hold, that it contained more political wisdom, as well as a great deal more entertainment, than most social gospels for which that period was noted. I had already assimilated as much as I was able of *Time and Western Man*. Symons asked me to write on Lewis as political thinker and philosopher.

Shortly after the issue appeared in November 1937, I was much gratified to receive a letter from Lewis (who in that number had said 'I never write a letter', though this was an understatement even in respect of his later years). Dispatched in a registered envelope, it was composed in the incisive, slanting script familiarized by his signature to paintings. He expressed interest in what I had written, and invited me to come and see him. It was a typically courteous letter, and it even contained his telephone number, which 'the Enemy', for security reasons, usually kept secret.

Thus began an acquaintanceship which, with inevitable gaps, continued almost until Lewis's death twenty years later. I well recall that first encounter. It was preluded by a good deal of exploration of obscure doorways near Notting Hill Gate Underground. Finally, the tiny name-plate at the foot of Kensington Gardens Studios was located, and I began the rather unnerving climb up the chilly stone staircase and along the bare passage to the small unpretentious door at the far end. Lewis appeared, as he was thereafter to appear until his blindness prevented him, looming enormous in the small opening, with black sombrero on head, curved pipe in mouth, and gravely proffered hand. This sudden presentation was rendered more dramatic by the fact that an internal flight of stairs, running laterally down to the door, obliged anyone opening it to swivel round suddenly in a confined space to greet the visitor. We went up to what proved to be a pleasant, commodious studio. I was at once impressed by the scrupulous tidiness of the place, as well as by the air of comfort. At the opposite end, but partitioned off, was a

INTRODUCTION

small kitchen, where Lewis forthwith set the kettle to boil. This, by a device novel at the time, would put forth a vigorous whistle when ready, and tea would be served at the low square table.

Despite the great disparity in our ages, Lewis never displayed the smallest air of superiority. He was a man of great simplicity of demeanour. He had no mannerisms. He spoke slowly, with the slightest drawl, in a monotone just above normal pitch, with sometimes a kind of 'hurt' inflection. This provided an appropriately neutral background to some of his more mordant remarks. Yet I recall no epigram, no *bon mot*; he spoke lucid good sense most of the time, and banter for the rest. Even so, I wish I had kept a record of those fascinating discourses. He was a superb mimic: the best example in this *genre* I recall was an impersonation of Roy Campbell. He could also sing but I heard him sing only once, and that was years later in a taxi returning from a performance of Eliot's *Confidential Clerk*. Perhaps that was the last time he did sing, at least in public.

Lewis was a very large man. (The story of T. E. Hulme suspending him from the railings of Soho Square I cannot believe.) He dressed heavily. He once told me that he had tramped the Great Atlas in the hot season in the thick winter suit he happened to be wearing at the moment. He moved as slowly as he spoke, and with great deliberation. When he had guests in the studio, he was accustomed to do business with the Primrose Tea Rooms below; and he had the habit, on mounting the stairs with a milk bottle and a loaf – which, to one sitting on the other side of the room, gave the impression of his emerging magically through the floor – of looking straight in front of him, with almost sphinx-like gravity. This was accentuated by the hat, which covered a balding head of considerable size and majesty, but which he ventured to expose only in his later years. Before the First World War, he tells us in *Blasting and Bombardiering*, he had enough hair for three men. An attack of pneumonia, followed by a course of vibro-massage recommended by a specialist, completed the 'massacre of the follicles'.

One of the privileges I enjoyed at this time was that of watching Lewis paint: that is to say, I was able to survey the scene roughly from the position of the sitter. For he did not permit anyone to observe the picture in the course of composition. On such occasions, he was much relaxed, and always most considerate. Throughout these sessions he would chat pleasantly. There was never a trace of tension or irritation or pose. He was a man of most even temper.

Lewis had a very keen and infectious sense of humour. It was of the quiet kind. When he became blind, his face assumed the aspect of a mask; the lips would be sealed in a liberal mould; he grew more sphinx-like than ever. A picture drawn of him by Michael Ayrton gives a good impression of how he looked at this period. Just when one felt in danger of losing his attention (or perhaps he had grown slightly drowsy), one would glance up to find a look of pleased, quizzical amusement on his face. He would often laugh silently. Perhaps the best description of him was his own, the Soldier of Humour. He enjoyed being read to, apart from its being helpful for his work. I once read him some of his own pieces, and he found them entertaining, though he could no longer remember having composed them.

It was rarely that I saw Lewis except at home. One notable exception was the occasion of a literary lunch, surely one of the last of its kind, which took place at the Café Royal. Ezra Pound was in London, following the death of his mother-in-law, Olivia Shakespear. It was at the initiative of my friend Michael Cullis that the gathering was arranged. Apart from Pound and Lewis, Cullis and myself, the party comprised the late Theodora Bosanquet, one-time secretary to Henry James and Literary Editor of *Time and Tide*, Hugh Gordon Porteus, author of the earliest and perhaps still the best book on Lewis, and Josephine Plummer of the B.B.C., whom he later painted. The meal was an outstanding success. Lewis was in admirable spirits; it seemed to take him back to the old days. I do not recall much conversation between him and Pound. The latter was at his most expansive; his vibrant voice and violent clearings of the throat punctuated, but did not dominate, the proceedings; it is of Lewis that my memories remain. Pound was all energy, fire, fanaticism, and verbal excess; Lewis was quiet and gracious. If he was not the life and soul of the party, he was very much the 'still centre' of it.

The most melancholy of the meetings I had with Lewis took place abroad after the war. I was living in Paris, and Lewis telephoned me unexpectedly one morning, announcing his arrival. I could tell that he was in low spirits. He had lunch with me, and I learnt that the purpose of his visit was to consult, as a last desperate measure, a French doctor about his rapidly deteriorating eyesight. Although he was able to find his way about reasonably well, he was beginning to be much hampered. Once we began conversing, however, he became a changed man. We discussed the predicament of Ezra Pound, whom he had done everything possible to help, and Eliot's *Cocktail Party*, the success of which was proving phenomenal. Alterwards we went to the bank to cash some travellers' cheques, and I observed for the first time that he carried a Canadian passport. I remember vividly seeing him off – a dark super-figure – to a taxi, and observing the happy relationship he struck up with the driver. He was idiomatically at home in French, as in several other languages, and the driver, sympathetic with his plight, went out of his way to be helpful.

The next time I saw him, once more in London, his sight had failed. He rarely spoke of his trouble; and when he wrote of it, it was with courageous objectivity.

Of Lewis's personal kindness I could give many examples. He seemed anxious to help people, even when he was least able to extend material aid. This seems to have been true all his life. He was thoughtful and a fund of encouragement. As the *Letters* show, he would take pains to advise young writers. I recall that it was through him that in the spring of 1938 I met James Joyce. After the war, when our acquaintanceship was resumed, he was repeatedly kind and generous. Indeed, he and his wife were two of the most hospitable people I have known. Perhaps Lewis was never more fortunate than in his marriage. It is not clear whether as a young man he had set much store by that institution, even though he had fitfully contemplated marriage with a German girl he met in Paris, presumably the Bertha Lunken of *Tarr*; but he had come to believe in it (apart from the evidence of *Self-Condemned*) by the time he had known it for thirty years or more. He rarely discussed intimate matters with me, nor I imagine with many others; but he was once moved to say that he thought a happy marriage one of the few blessings in life. He did not add, what was apparent to all, that his own was of this order. I wish likewise to record my belief that Lewis was at heart a religious man. True, he abhorred religious sentimentality, and he never 'talked religion'; but I think he may have contemplated on more than one occasion joining a Church. This would have been the Church of Rome, in which he had been reared. For he believed firmly – and this distinguished him from some of our younger writers, despite their occasional lip-service to religion – that 'life is brutal and empty without the heightening it acquires through metaphysical or religious values'.[1]

The figure of Lewis, the mystery man, is much overdone. On the contrary, he was an 'open person', that which, as he said in *One-Way Song*, 'men fear above everything'. I have elsewhere likened him to Blake. If he was mysterious, the mystery attached to him as it does to all great men: no one really knows how they have come to be what they are, or whence they draw their strength. Lewis claimed to adopt 'the standpoint of genius'; but he did not go out of his way, other than through his art, to expose or to exploit his personality. In the obituary notice published in *The Observer* (March 10, 1957), Geoffrey Grigson, one of Lewis's staunchest champions, remarked truly that he was 'secretive only to keep a space for his autonomy'. If his biography is ever written – and one hopes that it will be – the writer will have some difficulty in coping with certain periods, especially that between 1919 and 1923; for during this time Lewis's life was so isolated as to have been barred from all but one or two intimates. We know he was extremely busy, for there is the enormous output of the next few years to prove it. And the brief surfacing of *The Tyro* and *The Enemy* reinforced the impression of subterranean activity. Indeed, if an artist is not left in solitude, even for very long periods, he will be unable to produce work of the standard which Lewis, for one, set before himself. The mystery behind many major productions is simply hard work.

I set down these matters in view of the impression, so widely circulated, that Lewis was a cold, impersonal character, nihilistic in outlook, and frigid in his personal dealings.[2]

As an instance of the outcoming and warm side of his nature, I do not forget his very touching solicitude when, having sustained a back injury, I was unable to work for several weeks. Lewis was all for ensuring that I received the best possible medical treatment,

[1] *Blasting and Bombardiering*, p. 262. Cf. also *The Letters of Wyndham Lewis:* 'With us – Europeans and Americans – the civilized values are the Christian values.' (To John Burgess, p. 338.)
[2] The picture of Lewis that emerges from Hemingway's book of reminiscences of life in Paris (*A Moveable Feast*, London, 1964, pp. 108–110) is so hostile as to be unrecognizable.

INTRODUCTION

and he even offered to get in touch with a specialist in America in whom he had particular confidence. On another occasion, when I was looking for new accommodation in London, Lewis, though by then almost totally blind, insisted on accompanying me in a taxi round the parts of Chelsea he had known as a young man. This was to me a most memorable experience. I was amazed at the extent to which he recalled every area, every street almost, where a reasonable studio-flat might be available. Here I saw Lewis, that much-travelled cosmopolitan, in a guise I had not hitherto appreciated, that of Londoner. But then Lewis had a highly developed 'spirit of place'. For years, without many of the inhabitants knowing it, he was the first citizen of Notting Hill Gate. Admittedly, he called it, or rather he borrowed the name (from Pound), Rotting Hill; but is there any book which so well conveys the atmosphere of post-world-war-II London than the volume of short stories of that title? The locality of which he wrote has now been transformed beyond recognition owing to the rebuilding of several street-blocks.

My last, and in some ways most abiding, memories of Lewis were of the days when he was finishing the second and third volumes of *The Human Age*, and also thinking about the final volume, though this was never written. In composing that extraordinary work, he set an example of determination and resourcefulness for which there can be few parallels. Seated in his low armchair, his eyes protected by a green shade – he could vaguely make out dark and light forms, even to the extent of knowing where the actors were on a stage – he would spend hour after hour covering large sheets of paper affixed to a drawing board. By moving his thumb down the left margin, he kept to the line. The success of this method depended upon great concentration, patience and a retentive memory. The remarkable fact is that the work he accomplished under these abnormal conditions should contain, as it assuredly does, some of his most powerful and lucid writing. Owing to the pressure of a brain tumour, he would sometimes sink into drowsiness; but on regaining consciousness, he would forthwith resume his labours. Naturally, after the typing and indeed in the course of it, he would make many adjustments, but hardly more than he might have introduced in normal circumstances.

All this work, as indeed most of his waking life, was carried on in the little sitting-room on the first floor of the flat. After the onset of his blindness, he never revisited the studio; nor am I sure whether, even after the repair of damage sustained during the war, it was habitable. The sitting-room, though small, was both convenient and cosy. Lewis occupied a corner near the entrance to the bedroom. Behind him, on the shelf above the books, were a few personal photographs, one being of the degree-giving ceremony group at Leeds. His height, usually impressive, appeared much diminished by the lowness of the chair. A photograph by Douglas Glass, taken about this time, does not convey his stature, but admirably preserves his general appearance, brooding yet peaceful, still full of creative energy. He never looked slovenly, and always wore a smart handkerchief in his breast pocket. Mrs Lewis would usually sit on the couch on his right, perhaps with Agnes Bedford, who helped him so much with his work; and the visitor would occupy the chair opposite Lewis. Behind this chair was the dining-table; and around this board were spent some convivial hours, enhanced by Mrs Lewis's admirable cooking, and more often than not the champagne of which Lewis was so fond. When he was being led – by Mrs Lewis; he did not particularly like anyone else to help him – back and forth across the room, he would wear a playful, slightly arch expression. One cannot say that he enjoyed his confined life; the idea, especially in the case of one so visually endowed, is preposterous; but in bringing out the best in his character, it seemed to release a flood of warmth.

Doggedly at work on a new novel, the scene of which was the Paris of his student days, Lewis failed one day to return from one of the comas into which he increasingly lapsed. I was abroad at the time; but I felt with his death not merely a real personal loss, but a sense that one of the last of the giants had departed.

Towards the end of his life, Lewis's work enjoyed a second merited recognition. This was in a sense a belated revival. In the years prior to 1914, Lewis, like many another artist, moved in circles which today admit few men of his calibre. The divorce between art and the ruling class is of comparatively recent origin. Can we indeed speak today of a ruling class? The attacks launched by young writers on the Establishment resemble shadow-boxing. That expression may be taken literally, because it is the ghost of an establishment that is under fire, and the ammunition is mostly blank. It is a far cry from the time when Mr Asquith, as Prime Minister, could inquire of Lewis, at a diplomatic reception, how his 'movement' was progressing. One hardly imagines the contemporary 'movement', such as it is, being the object of such official solicitude. Nor is it easy to imagine that there was a Vorticist salon at No. 1 Percy Street in the Hotel Restaurant de la Tour Eiffel. Moreover, for Lewis there were aristocratic *soirées*, prolonged stays at palaces in Venice, and Paris Nights.

To gladden Lewis's last years, there was the dramatized version of *The Human Age* on the B.B.C.; the retrospective exhibition at the Tate, the striking appreciation by Eliot in *The Hudson Review*, later broadcast on the evening of a B.B.C. reception in Lewis's honour; the support of critics such as Walter Allen and Hugh Kenner and of fellow-artists like Michael Ayrton. A fine 'profile' appeared in *The Observer* for August 5, 1956. I was glad he lived to see my own tribute.[1] Finally there was the growing volume of appreciation from America, of which Hugh Kenner's own book was typical.

These tributes were amply deserved. It might be thought cynical, but it is not altogether false, to say that the British people tend to accord a man eulogies when he is considered unlikely to be of further embarrassment to them. Few have any conception of Lewis's struggles, not so much for recognition, as for a modest competence; his long illness in the thirties; his wartime difficulties in North America, and his final battle with ill-health: but people began, towards the end, to realize that a single-minded man of genius, despite the uncongenial character of some of his message, may be a national asset.

Lewis has been described as hypersensitive to criticism; but when it is realized that throughout a long career he was the object either of sharp and often wounding attacks or else of total neglect, his feelings in the matter are more easily understood. Some of the neglect was due to a sense of bafflement: a book like *Time and Western Man* fell into no precise category, and the same may be said of *The Lion and The Fox*. Whilst *The Art of Being Ruled* contained some 'muscular' arguments (to use his own term), the in-

[1] *Wyndham Lewis* (1954), published for the British Council by Longmans, Green & Co.

telligentsia preferred the latest piece of sophisticated, or more often sentimental, Marxism from the Left Book Club. Of his literary criticism, *Men without Art* and *The Writer and the Absolute* contained some of the best comment on Hemingway, Faulkner, Sartre, Camus and Malraux that has appeared in English: how often are these books cited? Of the circumstances leading to the withdrawal of that entertaining, and by no means superannuated, book *The Doom of Youth*, it is perhaps best to maintain silence, though it is difficult to resist the conclusion that Lewis was here very badly done by.

Critics like to be able to identify, if not to invent, a school. If there is a group, a coterie, it makes it easier for them to assess relative merits, to trace influences among the *jeunesse dorée*. Lewis was without direct disciples, save perhaps for Roy Campbell. (These words are written when the name of Hemingway is being elevated to the rank of the Titans; but is there not something of Lewis in Hemingway, and is not *The Revenge for Love* vastly superior to the book by Hemingway most resembling it, *For Whom the Bell Tolls*? Is it not a more masculine work?) As Lewis wrote in his 'Essay on the Objective of Art in Our Time': 'He who opens his eyes wide enough will always find himself alone.'[1] And in 'The Code of a Herdsman', he lays down the maxim: 'Yourself must be your own caste.'[2] Finally, writing in 1939 of his early battles, he observed: 'It was not part of a rather bogus battalion but as a *single spy* that I was speaking.'[3] Consequently, whenever Lewis started a movement, or launched a periodical, it was he upon whom all the responsibility devolved. It was he who opened it and he who shut it down. The attempt made recently to demonstrate that, in the case of the Vorticist movement, this was not so, seems rather to have reinforced the original impression. Yet although neither *Blast*, *The Tyro*, nor *The Enemy* survived beyond the third issue, they have already become collector's pieces. As literary reviews, they are unique. Lewis adopted the admirable practice, now unfortunately in desuetude, of bringing out his journal whenever he had amassed sufficient material; and that usually meant his own.

[1] One is reminded of the concluding words of an earlier 'Enemy of the People': 'That man is strongest who stands alone.'
[2] 'Imaginary Letters' (*The Little Review*, July 1917), p. 4.
[3] 'The Skeleton in the Cupboard Speaks': Preface to *Wyndham Lewis the Artist* (1939), p. 69.

INTRODUCTION

Their several suspensions were due not to lack of that, but to the absence or rather to the disintegration of an organized literary *élite*. To unearth the old files is to encounter fascinating as well as nostalgic reading. Concentrated within a few pages, we find the names of many who were to become prominent during the next few decades. Of how many of the larger and more enduring literary reviews can as much be said?

Did Lewis expend too much time on the 'massacre of the insignificants'? He discussed the point in the Preface to *The Diabolical Principle and The Dithyrambic Spectator*. Many people considered that he should have produced more creative work, more books of the stature of *Tarr* and *Childermass*; but, as he explained, he began pamphleteering to defend his work as an artist; hence, for example, *The Caliph's Design*. Secondly, he was engaged throughout in attacking ideas, not persons. The bearer or originator of the idea mattered as little as his calibre. (Jolas, the editor of *Transition*, whom I do not believe Lewis had met, was a man of charm and simplicity.) As he belonged to no set or cell, he was obliged to do his own washing and scavenging:

> He has been his own bagman, critic, cop, designer,
> Publisher, agent, char-man, and shoe-shiner.[1]

If we compare Lewis's pamphlets and polemics with those of Shaw (a writer to whom he once likened himself),[2] we have little difficulty in deciding who was the more profitably engaged. For the first half of his career, Shaw was liquidating a Victorianism already outmoded, and for the long second half he was busy eulogizing the despots of the time, while paying lip-service to socialism. By attacking the Left when it was unpopular to do so, Lewis earned the name of fascist. A close reading of his polemics will show that this was a most unfair description. Even so, Lewis's reputation is supposed to have suffered grievously, some say irreparably, from the publication of the 'Hitler' books. What are the grounds for this imputation? Those who condemned him after reading these works were probably those disposed to label him fascist before their appearance. *The Art of Being Ruled*, when it was understood at all, was construed as an apology for authoritarianism. The ostracism

[1] *One-Way Song*, p. 76.
[2] *Blasting and Bombardiering*.

which he believed himself to have suffered was the theme, or at least one of the themes, of *One-Way Song*, published in 1933. Here the subject is handled with a much lighter touch than that usually employed by the victim of persecution mania. Possibly the political books deterred the new reader from venturing further, instead of alienating those already familiar with the work. If Lewis, like Shaw, was at one time drawn towards the dictators, the attraction was short-lived. (He once told me that he detested the company of those of the Right who, believing they had found an ally, began to shower him with invitations.) Did Lewis at any time belong to any organization of even remotely totalitarian leanings? There is no evidence for it; the same cannot be said of certain of his fellow-writers who, for some reason, have escaped obloquy. The Hitler book and its successors were used, if at all, to distract attention from his real message. People wanted an excuse to be able to say: 'There! We knew it all the time.'

Lewis was one of those writers who are obliged, however unwillingly, to create their own public. Someone has said, Theodore Spencer I believe, that the nineteenth-century novel was written for people scattered in a few thousand armchairs. To envisage Lewis's public is not easy. Some of it may have stood at a factory bench, or gone on a District Commissioner's rounds, or those of a bus inspector. Lewis was far too intelligent and disinterested an author, and preoccupied with too many matters, to have pleased any particular branch of the intelligentsia, such as it was; and although he confessed a liking for women,[1] he made none of the concessions to a female public which tend towards large sales today. He wrote about neither sex nor religion in a manner calculated to ensure a permanently mobilized sisterhood. That is to say, although he wrote about sex, from *Tarr* to *Malign Fiesta*, and about religion, notably in one moving passage in *Time and Western Man*, he never produced that subtle emulsion of the two which ensures the 'raving' of reviewers and the advance purchase of film-rights. His attitude to sex was too astringent, his approach to religion too intellectual. Nor did he ever lend his unrivalled gifts as a painter to the sensational, or the merely clever. Of his versatility there was no doubt.

[1] Preface to the Twenty-Fifth Anniversary edition of *The Apes of God* (1956).

INTRODUCTION

'I move with a familiarity natural to me amongst eyeless and hairless abstractions. But I am also interested in human beings.'[1]

'The hard, the cold, the mechanical, the static': these, as he remarks in his essay, 'The Skeleton in the Cupboard speaks',[2] were the qualities to which he aspired to give expression. I think he underestimated, or failed to exploit, another side to his genius, a kind of incandescent quality of vision. This characterized his prose as well as much of his painting. There is a touch of it already in the early story 'Cantleman's Spring Mate' – a short piece which, even given the stricter standards of those days, seems hardly to have justified the condemnation which visited it (Post Office officials seized the offending number of *The Little Review*). It attained its apogee in *Childermass*; there is much of it in *The Enemy of the Stars*, a piece which would make an admirable surrealist film. It is a dramatic quality. Indeed, one could wish that Lewis had essayed the dramatic form more often; he had a gift for the theatrical. Moreover, he could produce effective and original dialogue, as 'The Ideal Giant' and 'The Tyronic Dialogues' prove.

Some of Lewis's writing is admittedly difficult to place. He was, among other things, an elemental. In an early review of *Tarr*, Eliot likened him to a cave-man, but one with whose energy was combined 'the thought of the modern'. The combination produced a blend rarely found in English literature. Lewis is the only English author, at least within the present century, who could be imagined as writing a work such as *Ubu Roi*. As David Gascoyne observed: 'Jarry's humour is not unlike that demonstrated by Wyndham Lewis in *The Wild Body* – a cold, cerebral humour at the expense of the stupid and clumsy human machine. The laughter it produces performs the moral function of a purge: while at the same time it is antisocial and subversive'.[3] Antisocial and subversive: yes, if by that is meant an over-turning of the comfortable humanist view of man and a revelation of what, bereft of cultural values, he is in stark reality. To quote *Blast*: 'We only want tragedy if it can clench its side-muscles like hands on its belly, and bring to the surface a laugh like a bomb' ('Manifesto', 10). Such chastening,

---

[1] Preface to *Thirty Personalities* (Alex Reid & Lefevre Ltd, London, October 1932). [2] *Wyndham Lewis the Artist* (1939).
[3] *A Short Survey of Surrealism* (London, 1935), p. 17.

INTRODUCTION

medicinal laughter performs a moral function indeed: and so Lewis came to realize when, after contending in *Men without Art* that 'the greatest satire is non-moral', he declared, in the new preface to *The Apes of God*, that the justification of all satire was an underlying moral passion.

One feels of Lewis, what it is difficult to feel of Lawrence, that his vision of human nature, even after the passage of years, will retain its validity. For it is the truth about a permanent aspect of that nature, an aspect which the idealist moralist endeavours to ignore, because it provides cold comfort. What Lawrence dwelt on was, after the first shock, acceptable to all: hence the chorus of enthusiasm at the Chatterley trial, with ecclesiastics ranged shoulder to shoulder with the free-thinker and the immoralist. To write *Lady Chatterley's Lover*, or at least those pages of the novel which provoked the fuss, lies within the reach of a modest talent.[1] Lewis went deeper, and therefore tended to cause greater offence. The 'essays in a new human mathematic'[2] which form his best work, came from an intellect free from sentimentality. Here there was 'no pandering to the mighty vagueness of our hearts'.[3]

At the same time, we have yet to discover why it is that the early masterpieces such as 'Bestre' or 'The Cornac and his Wife', had no later fulfilment. This is the real Lewis problem. Throughout his career, he wrote passages of which the meaning is but faintly adumbrated: it seems to be either too far off or too far down. What, for example, is the real meaning behind the, admittedly unfinished, 'Crowd Master' (*Blast*, No. 1, 1915), and some of 'The Imaginary Letters' (*The Little Review*, May–July 1917)? One receives an impression no less baffling from a piece written forty or so years later, namely 'The Boxer's Confession' in *The Red Priest* (1956). These mysterious communications might have been penned by Mr Zagreus of *The Apes of God*. Much of the conversation between Hanp and Arghol in *The Enemy of the Stars* is strangely recondite. (Are not these two the prototypes of Beckett's clowns, and their successors?) The point is mentioned here for the benefit of future students of Lewis. Such pages have not been drawn upon, even by way of sample, because they would suffer still further by mutilation.

---

[1] This is not to belittle Lawrence's artistry elsewhere.
[2] 'Inferior Religions', *The Wild Body*, published originally in *The Little Review*, September 1917.   [3] *One-Way Song*, p. 19.

INTRODUCTION

In composing a selection of this kind, the question of extract and excision presents formidable difficulties. I have refrained, though with reluctance, from drawing upon the 'puce monster', *Blast* itself. You can blast only once: an explosion cannot be split up into separate detonations. Secondly, there is the question of redundance. There are no extracts from the pamphlet *Satire and Fiction*, first because it to some extent misfired (Roy Campbell's 'rejected review' of *The Apes of God was* in fact published), and secondly because Lewis said all that he had to say on this score in *Men Without Art*. Nor have we drawn upon *The Old Gang and the New Gang*, because it is overshadowed by *The Doom of Youth*. For reasons already given, the editor was in a quandary concerning four topical and controversial works, *Hitler, Left Wings over Europe, Count your Dead: They are Alive,* and *The Hitler Cult*. *Left Wings over Europe*, as a piece of high-speed journalism, remains, together with *The Hitler Cult*, one of the most competent things he did in this field. The pamphlet *Anglo-Saxony: a League that Works*, despite some interesting pages on Marinetti, is likewise covered by *America and Cosmic Man*. *The Writer and the Absolute* and *The Demon of Progress in the Arts* are still in print.

A day may come when all Lewis's works, even the ephemera, will be gathered together, and issued with the appropriate Introduction and Notes. This is unlikely to happen until the Ph.D. aspirants, exercising due academic caution, have worked through most of his inferior, if better known, contemporaries. Some of Lewis's fiction, including early fragments and some later short stories, remains unpublished. There are other papers, including some early poems. Meanwhile, the *Letters*, with their fund of interesting material, are now available,[1] and several full-length studies of Lewis have appeared.[2] Others will surely follow.

This essay, being an introduction, cannot cover the whole man; but since the occasional pieces were designed to support the heavier, and since their significance is such as to lie beyond them, we may

---

[1] Edited by W. K. Rose (Methuen), 1962.
[2] Unfortunately, the most lengthy and recent of these, namely Geoffry Wagner's *Portrait of the Artist as Enemy*, is in some respects the most disappointing, owing to its lukewarm tone and lack of a positive attitude towards its subject.

INTRODUCTION

conclude by touching briefly upon Lewis's place as a writer and an influence in society.

To begin with his particular cast of mind: the neglect of Lewis, especially by the Schools, was, if the paradox may be forgiven, a kind of tacit recognition. *Time and Western Man*, admittedly not an easy work, remains a major essay in metaphysics. The judgement was first pronounced, if I recall, by Michael Roberts; it was confirmed by men so markedly different in outlook as Father M. C. D'Arcy, S.J., and Dean Inge.[1] If the practitioner believes that metaphysics is an effete science, he can dismiss such a work out of hand. This may save time; but it also means that if the tide should turn (as it is now doing), a great many professional philosophers will be hampered by ignorance. Of the details of Lewis's argument I do not propose to speak. Some thinkers give the impression, at least in their published writings, of holding reality up to ransom, while they consider at leisure their attitude to it, as if expecting it to observe a benevolent tolerance of the vagaries and shifts in their thinking. This is due primarily to a loss of the sense of value. Such loss is to be attributed, as Lewis observed in an interesting letter to Charles Whibley,[2] to the 'crushing of the notion of the subject'; for if we abandon the concept of the self or, like Hume, protest that we cannot find it (in which case who are 'we'?), we abandon quality and value as objective. The abandonment of the subject opens the floodgates to relativism, flux and illusion: in short, to what Lewis called 'time worship'. It is the empiricist Hume, resolving the world into a *pointilliste* phantasmagoria, who opens the way to Vaihinger, for whom everything is 'as if' it were itself, and to the relativists for whom nothing is ever quite itself. The sense of objective value perceives that 'the answer is there all the time; we "discover" it':[3] a point which seems to have eluded some contemporary thinkers. Lewis's was an orthodox, almost a Catholic, mind; and it is the measure of the deviation of modern thought from the norm that so many sophists, acute thinkers though they may be, are entrenched in our traditional seats of learning,

---

[1] The first in *The Nature of Belief* (1930); the second as recorded by Adam Fox in his *Life of Dean Inge* (1961). The Dean no doubt remained unaware that he was the object of one of the 'curses' in *Blast* (p. 21).
[2] *Letters*, p. 155.
[3] *Letters*, p. 378.

INTRODUCTION

while Lewis, the man of tradition, continues to be regarded as an aberrant and wayward iconoclast.

It is my belief that Lewis may come finally to occupy a place in English letters far more secure than most people, even some of his friends, are at present disposed to allow. His lone battle for the 'external' standpoint was simply his way of asserting the objectivity of values in a world given over to the worship of flux and arbitrary fashion; and so, like Swift, he stands as a great civilizing force, an opponent of the *via mediocris*, whose tracts for the times, the best of which are here preserved, may be expected to retain their vitality long after the figures they trounce have passed into limbo.

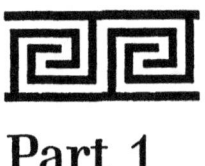

Part 1

Sociological and Philosophical Writings

Paleface 1929

Of all Lewis's sociological studies, Paleface *is the most closely meditated and finely composed. The first draft, like that of* Time and Western Man, *appeared in his magazine* The Enemy *(1927). For obvious reasons, it is more liberally drawn upon here than any other book, save* The Art of Being Ruled. Paleface *was on the whole well received by the critics. The Times, not always friendly to Lewis, described it as 'strong, brilliant, and splendid stuff'. It is a work of maturity, coming after the trilogy of* Time and Western Man, The Art of Being Ruled *and* The Lion and the Fox *and displaying great limpidity of style. And it is still remarkably apt.*

No work better illustrates the breadth, the intelligence, the gusto of Lewis's mind. It also reveals a side not sufficiently appreciated: his public-spiritedness. At the close, he invites his readers to correspond with him on the problems of racial integration. He was so far ahead of his time that even now his concept of the melting-pot seems a trifle utopian.

Throughout his life he was concerned at the dilution of civilized values, though he was no blind worshipper of tradition. The tendency to enthuse over the savage, the primitive, or the coloured races, simply by virtue of their supposed 'nearness' to nature, seemed to him symptomatic of a decadent sentimentalism: and the history of sentiment, he remarked, 'is one of the survival of words, after the fact they symbolize has long vanished'.

Much of the earlier part consists of an appraisal of the American novelist Sherwood Anderson, and of the work of D. H. Lawrence. Although Lewis greatly admired Lawrence's artistry, he deplored his adulation of the 'primitive consciousness'. Lewis makes an interesting point: that Lawrence was really exalting the average man. The more recent attempts to present Lawrence in the rôle of a latter-day messiah would have confirmed Lewis in his view that this gifted and sensitive man has been sadly misunderstood.

Paleface *carries the argument beyond these writers to a consideration of certain inherent weaknesses in Western culture. It was Lewis's belief that the underlying cause of the movement towards primitivism in art, in literature, and in certain educational doctrines, lay in the worship of time, or the flux, conceived as a creative medium. To this extent,* Paleface *represents a prolongation, with a wealth of new arguments, of the central thesis of* Time and Western Man.

The three passages quoted are an extract from Section 16 of Part I, the Introduction to Part II, and the whole of the Conclusion.

In the first passage, Lewis inquires into the meaning of the free personality. He then exposes the true complexion of modern nations, those 'dreamy polyp-organisms'. There follows an analysis of the rôle of genius in contemporary society. He refers to the man of genius as an outlaw, *his word twenty-five years ahead for* outsider. *Finally, he makes a plea for the establishment of a 'world-society'. Since this cause was given fresh emphasis in* America and Cosmic Man, *his references to* America *in* Paleface *are of exceptional interest.*

PART I

SECTION 16

The German philosophers of the beginning and the middle of the last century have perhaps provided us with the best example of 'internationalism' of any people in modern times, that is, such men as Goethe or Schopenhauer. Schopenhauer's father gave him the name or 'Arthur' because Arthur is the same (he argued) in all european tongues – at least it is not exclusively german. (It is interesting to note that the 'Arthur Press' received that name for a reason of a similar order.¹) And Schopenhauer himself never ceased to criticize his countrymen for their german-ness. Nietzsche after him did the same. Goethe before him was quite as confirmed an 'internationalist', in the sense that he always advocated a universal language of Volapuc for Europe, and hoped for a confederacy of states and an abolition of frontiers. — Today we are, with Fascism,² with Irish, Czech, Catalan, Macedonian, Indian, Russian, Turkish, Polish, etc., etc., nationalism (which invariably takes the form of abolishing every local custom and becoming as like everybody as possible), at the other pole to that attitude of mind so common a century ago. This appears to me very regrettable indeed. I should like everybody to be imbued with the spirit of internationalism, and to keep all their local customs.

I have, in addition to my often expressed desire for an international state, another craving, up till now unexpressed (that is publicly). I would, if I were able to, suppress all out-of-date discrepancies of *tongue*, as well as of skin and pocket. I desire to speak Volapuc, to put it shortly. I cannot help it, it is if you like a crank, but I should like to speak and write, some Volapuc, not english — at all events some tongue that would enable me to converse with everybody of whatever shade of skin or opinion without an interpreter—above all that no shadow of an excuse should subsist for a great Chemical Magnate to come hissing in my ear: 'Listen! That low fellow' (magnates always speak in such lofty terms, partly for fun) 'says "ja" — I heard him! Here is a phial of deadly gas. Just throw it at him, will you? He won't say "ja" any more, once he's had a sniff of that!'

But this is not the end of the matter, where my many disqualifications are concerned. I am actually conscious of the many difficulties that must beset any honest Paleface, called to the defence of his skin. Although people of a lightish complexion have overrun the globe, they have, he would be compelled to confess, taken with them, and stolidly, irresistibly, propagated a civilization which is exceedingly inferior to many civilizations found by them in full-swing, possessed by people of dark, or 'Coloured' complexion.

So, confining ourselves to 'skins', if this Paleface is told that he has been foolishly arrogant — his 'superiority' at the best a very

¹ The publishing house which issued *The Apes of God* (1926).
² Lewis was writing in 1929.

temporary material or technical one – he cannot find much to answer. Further, the charge has to be met of having imposed a rotten, materialist civilization upon all sorts of people with great cruelty often, of having wiped out races of very high quality, such as the Indians of North America, in the name of a God who was all compassion: so he is convicted of hypocrisy of the ugliest, of the 'civilized' kind, on top of everything else.

How can the White Man confront these charges? As an Anglo-Saxon he cannot point to America and England today, and claim that spectacle as a justification of his dominion. What is he to do? If a timid man, as the Paleface often is, all those vindictive pointing fingers will put him quite out of countenance.

Now I of course can find him the necessary arguments to dispose of his passionate critics, and I am only too glad to, for his opponents are a stupid crew for the most part – just 'to amuse myself' I would help my Paleface. But all the same I recognize that his case is dangerously open to attack.

Beyond this, as an artist I am convinced that all the very finest plastic and pictorial work has come out of the Orient, and that Europeans have never understood the fundamental problems of art in the way the Indian, Persian, or Chinese have done. These hasty remarks will have served, nothing more, to define the nature of my disqualifications for the rôle of White deliverer.

PART I, CONCLUSION[1]

In Rome what constituted 'abnormality' was the being either a slave, a stranger or a minor (of whatever age) within the potestas of some head of a family. A slave and, originally, a stranger, a 'peregrinus' was legally a 'thing', coming under the 'jus quod ad res pertinet'. The absolute legal roman *persona* was only enjoyed, I suppose, by the eldest male of a roman family. But originally the status of a non-Roman was as 'abnormal' as that of a slave. All animals were naturally 'things' – a lion in the forest or a wild bee was a 'res nullius', but a watch-dog or slave was not 'wild', so could not be affected to another person than his owner by capture – though if you felt like it you could acquire a lion, for *it* (as we still

[1] The first paragraph, referring to a previous argument, is omitted.

say) was a thing not entangled legally with a 'person'. You could then become its unique entanglement, and it would cease to be wild, but would remain a thing.

To be normal was to be free in the roman state, but it is now generally supposed that the 'slave' in Antiquity, although outside the law of persons, was nevertheless not treated as a *thing* by his master to any greater extent than let us say a drapery assistant or a charwoman is treated as a thing. The female slave, of an averagely humane roman citizen, did not call herself a 'lady' but a 'slave'; there probably the difference ended. It is unlikely that there was any contemptuous disability attached to her state to compare with that of the victorian 'skivvy' or 'slavey'. If the choice lay between being a 'slavey' and a 'slave', in fact any rational person would prefer to be a 'slave', I should think – without ambiguity, sentimentality or, in a word, offence.

What I am attempting to get at here is that very important factor of 'sentimentality' in the relations of human beings, especially as that applies to the wholesale reform of those relations, at present in progress all over the world. It is the verbal problem, really; and the history of 'sentiment' is one of the survival of words, after the fact they symbolize has long vanished. It is possible under certain conditions to have a person as a slave in the most effective sense – to make him work himself to the bone, live upon crusts of bread, call you 'sir' or even 'lord', and be in short entirely at your disposal, and yet for you to have no *legal* right whatever over him, indeed for him technically to be 'free and equal' – even for you to be, ostensibly, *his* servant. We are all accustomed to this situation as illustrated in the expression 'servant of the Public', for instance. 'Dictatorship of the Proletariat' affords another example. In such cases a minority governs a majority, often with an iron hand, either telling the majority that it is its 'servant', or, in the other case, telling the majority or Proletariat that it, the Proletariat, is sovereign, paramount, and engaged all the time in ruling itself. These (and many similar instances will no doubt readily occur to you) are all matters simply of *words*: and what I am describing is of course the sort of government that we call today a 'democracy' – either with elective representatives or with a small body of people who are kind enough to 'dictate' to it. But in all cases it is government by words.

Everything that the word 'democracy' implies, however, we get from the Romans and the Greeks. And in spite of the fact that all the circumstances of physical life and of our present society have suffered an absolute change, yet in our institutions we still perpetuate these ultimate distortions of a law framed for a political body in every respect different from our own. The roman body was compact and efficient, if nothing else, and is not to be despised. But either we should retrace our steps and acquire that body (which is impossible) or else adjust our laws for those vast, sprawling, dreamy polyp-organisms we call nations, but so that those laws will enable such degraded organisms to issue once more as a formal structure of some kind, somewhat higher than at present.

If, again, we cannot all be 'free' in the roman sense, or be 'persons' as were all Roman Citizens, then should we use their words? It is impossible not to question the propriety of that: for not until we cease to *call* ourselves free shall we be able to recognize how unnecessarily servile we have become. The word 'free' is merely, as it were, a magical counter with which to enslave us, it is full of an electrical property that has been most maleficent where the European or American is concerned.

But beyond that I suggest that very few people can be 'free' under any circumstances, or equally you may say that very few people can be 'persons', still to employ the roman terminology, but in this case abstractly. It is the 'democratic' conceit that is at fault, is it not? – it seems as though it were the love of fine words that has undone us, as much as anything. That is where the 'sentimentality' comes in and plays its destructive part. (It is that 'lady' in char-lady that has given us a false security and made us blind to the novel facts upon which we must at last concentrate our gaze and recognize that we are beset.) If people managed to resist these verbal blandishments, they would, it is true, be sadder (at first) but also wiser. That is of course the ideal – to be wiser; and no one can accuse me in this of indulging in a verbal blandishment with my word 'wise', for who on earth, in a general way, ever wanted to be *wise?* 'Free', yes: but never wise.

But in saying that very few men are able to be 'free', or very few to be 'persons', one must I suppose be prepared for every hair upon the body of the true democrat (or doctrinaire of the dictatorship of Demos) to bristle. 'Ah! that is very nice indeed, that is charming!' he said: 'in a nation of fifty million people there are to be a handful of "great" *persons* (according to your aristocratic plan and whatever you may mean by your mystic of the *person*) – that is to say, at any one time, a statesman or two, a poet or two, a man of science or two, and so on, and no more. But what of the rest of the community? – where do they come in? Are they not to have an equal share in the statecraft, art, science and all that constitutes a civilized state?'

In the first place the plan is, of course, not mine at all, but nature's. 'Nature' has repeatedly been interrogated, often angrily, upon this very point – it is a burning question. Why does not nature produce a dense mass of Shakespeares or Newtons or Pitts? That has been the idea; and means have been considered and plans worked out for assisting nature in this respect, but it is conceivable that nature after all may usually produce as many as are needed of these 'persons', and that this ratio may be according to some organic law that we are too stupid or too conceited to grasp.

It is always possible that nature may not desire a structureless, horizontal jelly of a society, as does the modern democrat, but a more organic affair. A 'moral situation', it may even be, does not enter into the comprehension of that legislator or creator which we habitually call 'nature'. Just the correct number of Shakespeares, Newtons and the rest may have been regularly supplied to us, and overcrowding at the top (a top and bottom being perhaps part of this hierarchical, non-moral, creative intention) have been guarded against.

But we will return from this region of idle speculation to that of practical politics. It is not disputed by anybody that we have evolved a very mechanical type of life, as a result of the discovery of printing and its child, the Press – the Cinema, Radio and so forth, and the immense advances in the technique of Industry. There is much less differentiation now, that is, between the consciousness of the respective members of a geographical group and between the various groups or peoples, than before machines made it possible for everyone to mould their mind upon the same cultural model (in the way that they all subject themselves to the emotional teaching of a series of films, for instance, all over the surface of the globe).

The more fundamentally alike nations become, the more fiercely 'nationalist' is their temper: but also the more *impersonal* they grow (in the nature of things, in a more intensely organized routine of life), the more they talk of freedom, and of their 'personality'.

Both these paradoxes of the present age are, I believe, the merest habits. There is very little sign that the majority of people desire to be 'persons' in any very important sense: their conversation about 'developing their personality' is a sentimental habit, merely, it would seem. If they were cured of this habit nothing would ever be heard of their 'personality' again. But government on a democratic pattern entails an insistence upon these mythical 'personalities' on the part of their rulers: so the habits remain and flourish. It is impossible to bring them up-to-date, for they are too chronologically absurd to do that with. And the same system requires that some purely sentimental and unreal notion of 'freedom' should, at all costs, be sustained. (It is like the cry *La Patrie est en danger!* There was *once* a 'country' that was culturally and racially intact, and so susceptible of being put in 'danger', and in consequence the martial cry still evokes a situation that is dead, and people flock to defend that grinning corpse or historical spectre.)

Only a *person* can be susceptible of a *right*–that is not a roman law but a universal one. What is 'due from everyone to everyone' (in the words of Green[1]) is either (1) a merely sentimental *cliché* – and that is what it generally amounts to in contemporary democracies; or it is (2) an entirely non-sentimental compulsion – namely that it is due to merit, to personal character or to personal ability. There is nothing else 'due' from one person to another.

Another and more exact way of stating this would be to say – There is nothing 'due' at all from one person to another: but there are persons who attract, or compel those services spoken of by Green, described by him as mysterious debts on account of which all truly moral men are constantly denying and impoverishing themselves (of the things of the mind as well as of the body – in order to be 'the poor in spirit') so that they may adequately render what 'is due from everyone to everyone'. But this something in fact is 'due' not because the object of it is 'human' nor because the skin in question is white or black: it is 'due' because in some way

[1] T. H. Green (1836–1882), the moral philosopher with whose *Prolegomena to Ethics* Sections 3 to 7 of Part I are concerned.

we recognize an entity with superior claims to ours upon our order, kind or system: as I see the matter, that is the only ground for an obligation that exists. The sentimental, or the moral, elements, have no part in it.

This obligation that all men are under to personal power or to the vital principle that resides in *persons*, is apt to be bitterly resented. What the 'puppet' owes to the 'person' (to make use, as in the *Art of Being Ruled*, of Goethe's terminology) is the cause of many heart-burnings and revolts, and is, where that is possible, withheld. This is the case more than ever where an aggravated 'moral situation' exists, as at present. Indeed a 'moral situation' is essentially a revolutionary situation, in the most frivolous sense, when for a time the unreal and purely sentimental values, in a dissolving society, get the upper hand. The Power to whom the direction is being transferred dare not yet openly announce itself (this is, I suppose, somewhat the case in Russia), there is only one Master-principle visible, above the surface, still ostensibly effective, and that is weak. So the pack flings itself upon it, and all for the moment is confusion.

For what is the essence of a 'moral situation'? It is of course, and always has been (since those days when, to be the curse of the West, 'morals' were first invented), a situation in which a society loses its organic structure and disintegrates into its individual components – into its millions of individual units. This may in itself be desirable; but it naturally isolates or disconnects for the time all that is most powerful and exposes it to attack. As this society becomes, instead of an organic whole, a mass of minute individuals, under the guise of an Ethic there appears the Mystic of the Many, the cult of the cell, or the worship of the particle; and the dogma of 'what is due from everybody to everybody' takes the place of the natural law of what is due to character, to creative genius, or to personal power, or even to their symbols.

I do not need to point out how intense this mysticism of the Monad or 'the Many' has become, nor how it has resulted everywhere in the wholesale aggression, aimed at anybody, either in the past or present, possessing those 'great' qualities to which 'something is due' from everybody. (The daily belittlement of or the personal attacks upon, in books or in the Press, the 'great men' of our literary Pantheon is one of the obvious signs of this sansculottist temper.) It is almost as though the duty of the truly moral man was as much to destroy what he regards as 'great' (or possessed of the enjoyment of the powers and delights of the mind) as to deny himself such enjoyment: and a sentimental value for what is little or ineffective, or merely distant, or incomprehensible, must be eagerly professed.

I will now apply myself to the question of how we are to define (1) a person; (2) the term 'human'; and (3) the conception 'the common good', those terms of critical importance that we have been up till now using without much definition.

The idea 'person' I associate essentially with the idea of 'organization'. What we would say was 'due' to what is highly organized on the part of what is less highly organized – that is the principle character of this obligation. If I were working this out more thoroughly here, I should have to go into the question of how I understood this version of the law of persons and the law of things, insisting that in every case our human laws must be in the nature of a 'law of things'. For it is upon this basis that I should naturally think of it.

All that is 'due' from one creature to another is, as I should describe it, in reality due to God, whose 'things' we are—only the fictions as it were of that Person. It would be best for me to recall here (since the existence of a spiritual power or God, or any reference even to that power, is involved for most people with the sickliness of some debased ethical code) the *unsentimental* nature of this obligation I am supposing to exist. And this character of compulsion, this intellectual character, applies as much to what is 'due' to God, as to what is 'due' elsewhere: and what is exacted from us elsewhere is an expression merely of a more absolute dependence.

So our dependence or our independence is, I should say, an organic phenomenon, a matter of concentrations and dispersions, which we familiarly regard as the 'personal' attributes, when they become highly concentrated. As to political independence, or political 'freedom', it has very little to do with personality, and so, in a fundamental sense, very little to do with independence. Political independence is the gift of a society, whereas independence of character, or the being a person, is a gift of nature, to put it shortly. The gift is held for our natural life, irrespective of function. A person can only be 'free' in the degree in which he is a 'person': and if the most potentially effective and the wisest members of a given society are obscured or rendered ineffective, then it can only mean that that society is about to perish, as an organism, for it cannot survive in a condition in which what is most vital in it is obscured or not permitted to function.

How it is that we are able to say that only a *person* can be susceptible of a *right* because no sentimental value is attached here to the word 'right': because, in short, the law we are presupposing is a non-moral law. Every ethical system has those 'rights', infested with sentiment: but such mere systematizing of expansion-impulses is not worthy of the name of law.

Does being *susceptible of a right* mean anything else than being a creature who has recognized his willingness (or whose willingness is assumed) to abide by a set of rules, said to be for the 'common good' of the community, and who so comes to form part of a certain social system? That is all that 'human' meant for an early Roman or a Greek. A stranger was 'abnormal', susceptible of no rights, and no more 'human' than a wild bee or a lion in the forest. – To be beneath the same law – that is to be 'normal', and to be 'human': let that be our definition.

In the modern nation – and this is of course the case particularly with America – the working of this principle is very easy to follow. The 'Frenchman' as the 'American' is a person *beneath the same law* as all other 'Frenchmen' and 'Americans' – though he may by birth and training be a Russian, who emigrated upon the Revolution, a Spaniard or Italian, a Polish Jew or an African ex-slave. 'Human' in the same way is a term describing anybody beneath the same law as ourselves – it is a term of the same order as 'American' or as 'Russian'.

But all the natural leaders today in the White world are strictly speaking *outlaws*. They are in an 'abnormal' position. (Some are intelligent enough to realize this, but others still believe that they are functioning, or that it is still possible to function traditionally.)

I, for example, am an outlaw. I am conspicuous for my clear appreciation of that fact.

What can I possibly mean by saying that the best individuals of the european race are outlaws? I mean of course that we are now in the position of local tribal chiefs brought within a wider system, which has gathered and closed in around us; and that the *law* or *tradition* of our race, which it is our function to interpret, is being superseded by another and more universal norm, and that a new tradition is being born. (Of this more universal norm there are as yet no accredited interpreters – for the Soviet leaders are too involved in opportunist politics to lay claim to that position. I am perhaps the nearest approach to a priest of the new order.)

The reason we are outlaws then is that there is no law to which we can appeal, upon which we can rely, or that it is worth our while any longer to interpret, even if we could. We, by birth the natural leaders of the White European, are people of no political or public consequence any more, quite naturally. Even, we are repudiated and hated because the law we represent has failed, not being as effective as it should have been, or well-thought-out at all, I am afraid; having been foolishly and corruptly administered into the bargain. There is not one of us (except such a venerable and ineffective figure as Shaw, for instance) who is in a position of public eminence; nor will a single one of us, who is worth anything, ever be allowed to attain to such a position. We, the natural leaders in the World we live in, are now *private citizens* in the fullest sense, and that World is, as far as the administration of its traditional law of life is concerned, leaderless. Under these circumstances, its soul in a generation or two will be extinct, as a separate unit it will cease to exist. It will have merged in a wider system.

Speaking, simply in order to make quite clear what I mean, about myself, if I were a politician, like Shaw, a man of platforms and cameras, I should be very disappointed in the face of this situation. But there are many reasons why it suits me quite well to be denied a public life, to be treated as a dangerous outlaw – still to illustrate my argument by means of personal statement: I do not desire personal notoriety (and that is really all that is at stake). I would rather slip a book I had written into the hands of the Public than I would make a thousand speeches: my abilities, and my interests, again, do not lie in the economic or the political field at all, but in that of the arts of expression, the library and the theatre. But, far more important than anything else is the fact that I do not happen to regret the norm that is being superseded and rather find my sympathies on the side of the more universal norm which is (as I see the situation) to take its place. I am a man of the 'transition', we none of us can help being that – I have no organic function in this society, naturally, since this society has been pretty thoroughly dismantled and put out of commission, though, of course, if you ask me that, I would prefer a society in which I was beneath a law, which I could illustrate and interpret. But I have no desire to walk into the Past. I am content to think a world-law will be better than a law for Tooting Bec, and politically speaking to leave the matter there.

But these various circumstances tend to make me a sort of extremist: for since what we have lost was not absolutely to be despised, and should be bitterly regretted if nothing is put in its place as good as it; and seeing how many chances there always are that after wholesale destruction no one will have the genius or the *bonne volonté* even to do anything but batten upon the ruins and call that the 'New-World', I am what is called a 'bitter' critic of all those symptoms of the interregnum that suggest a compromise or a backsliding or a substitution of opportunist romantic policies (prepared to follow every sinuosity of the landscape, rather than build spectacular escapes) for a policy of creative compulsion.

The reasons, then, that I should give for not regarding as a tragedy the fact of the personal eclipse of all that is most intelligent in the Western communities, and the falling apart of those communities in the mass (as they grope their way back to an unconsciousness), are as follows. Our political disorganization is our own doing, is it not? It has been at our own hands, as socialists, liberals, radicals, or artists, and not at the hands of another and hostile organism, that we have been overcome: or it has come about through physical necessity, in the person of our revolutionary Science, all terrestrial societies being called upon to coalesce into a vaster unit – namely a world-society. If this can be effected without more violence and confusion than the human organism is able to endure, it should be the reverse of a misfortune, I think I am right in believing.

But there are extremely few people in the world at this moment who regard the situation in this light. That is a very great pity and likely to involve a great deal of violence and confusion. The remnants of our Western Governments, in the grip of a network of financial groups, or War and Trade Trusts, are behaving as though we were called upon to revert to a super-feudalism and the Dark-Ages, and the Communists tend to play up to every gesture of violence and to allow their doctrine to be converted into a proletarian imperialism (this must be taken as nothing more than an impression of one not more informed than the next and merely judging from report).

How these remarks affect the question to be canvassed in *Paleface* is as follows. The anti-Paleface campaign has all the appearance of attacks upon a disintegrating organism, by some other intact and triumphant organism: it has very much too *human* and personal a flavour. What it seems to imply is that the White World is 'finished', that it is a culture or political organism that is going to pieces under assaults from without and from within, quite on the traditional, historical, *Decline and Fall* pattern. And the *Revolt of Asia*,[1] the *Dark Princess*,[2] and such books, suggest that it is the 'Coloured Races', or the non-European, who have done it or are doing it, and are to be the beneficiaries of a reversal of political power. That is why the tactless assaults of the Borzoi big-guns[3] have to be checked and are certain in the end to cause a disturbance and make it worth somebody's while to take up the cause of the 'Paleface'. That championship is a title that is going begging, but for the moment only.

As good little revolutionaries, at all events, we Palefaces have to claim our revolutionary rights – that is my message in *Paleface*. We ask nothing better than to go over into the reformed world-order, am I not right? But we will not be *pushed* over, no, nor barked at as we go by the big Borzois and other mongrels, or in short, march out to a chorus of Dark laughter.[4] That, if I understand my fellow Palefaces, is the position. We are somewhat touchy about the legend of our despotisms: this is as much *our* Revolution as anybody else's. Indeed, it is we who have made it possible. It is *more* ours, we can claim, than anybody else's. The White component in the world-combination will be of exactly the same importance, as shown by the revolutionary-weighing-in machine, as every other: but we will not be so gratuitously revolutionary as to allow the

[1] Upton Close.
[2] W. E. B. Du Bois, the Negro writer.
[3] A series of books largely on Negro subjects published by Knopf, New York. Borzoi: Russian wolf-hound.
[4] The title of one of Sherwood Anderson's best-known novels.

Paleface interest to weigh less, that is the idea. Even a White revolutionary has his rights, that is my meaning in *Paleface*. But I am 'purely and simply amusing myself', as Paul[1] would say. I have no official position, White, Red, or Black, nor do I covet one.

America has been called the 'Melting-Pot' — it is where more than anywhere else the world-state is being prepared, in a big preliminary olla podrida. I have called this book a *Philosophy of the Melting-Pot*: so there is no occasion to explain how it is that America is the scene I have chosen for my main illustrations.

The outlaws like myself who are preparing the new Law and the new Norm have a very heavy responsibility. It is their business to detach themselves entirely from the specific interests of the human component or group from which they have come, whether Paleface, Negro, Indian or Jew. That is why you find me, in *Paleface*, in a position of defence where my poor downtrodden Paleface brother is concerned. And because a certain short-sighted cockiness in the Paleface makes him sometimes scorn my assistance and causes him to be blind to the novel dangers of his situation, I do not for that reason abandon my impartial ministrations.

The new Law will effectively take shape, it is very likely, in the continent of America, for the same reason that the metropolitan position of Rome caused the *jus gentium* to be developed practically there rather than elsewhere, in the ordinary course of the daily routine of the Praetor Peregrinus. — In Rome the magistrate appointed to deal with the cases in which foreigners were involved (and to whom the roman code was not applicable) was the Praetor Peregrinus. As Rome grew in importance, foreigners from all quarters of the world made their appearance; and the Praetor Peregrinus had forced upon him what was to some extent a constant exercise in comparative jurisprudence. It would be discovered no doubt after a time that, underlying the respective codes of even the most widely separated states (whose subjects the Praetor Peregrinus had before him), there was a sort of rough system common to all. It was upon this more universal system (as it sorted itself out in his daily practice) that the Praetor Peregrinus would base his judgements. In arriving at any decision involving a conflict between one

---

[1] One of the contributors to the review *Transition*, who comes under Lewis's fire in *The Diabolical Principle*.

code and another, he would naturally choose the law that experience had shown him to be of the more universal application.

The main principles of the *jus gentium* were finally incorporated in the roman system, which would benefit by acquiring a more universal applicability. The well-known though disputed identification by Sir Henry Maine of the *jus gentium* with the *jus naturale* ('*jus naturale* is *jus gentium* seen in the light of the Stoic Philosophy'[1]) may serve to emphasize still more the significance of this juristic evolution, consequent upon the meeting and trafficking of nations.

We are in a world in which we are all in some sense outlaws, at the moment, for our traditions have all been too sharply struck at and broken and no new tradition is yet born. Some such process as occurred in the administration of the Praetor Peregrinus is occurring today in every quarter of the globe – there is no country that is not in that sense metropolitan. Meanwhile, we are, technically, in an 'inhuman' situation. This is a very delicate position. It is necessary, I think, in consequence, to insist a little upon the essential (though imperfect) *humanity* of any ill-treated and threatened group – such, for instance, as the Palefaces – who so recently were the rulers of the world, and who are, as a result, looked at somewhat askance, in the new dispensation, and perhaps hustled, on occasion.

As to the 'common good',[2] what can be said briefly on that head, in connection with the things we are discussing, is as follows:

No successful human society could be founded upon a notion of the 'common good' which attempted to weigh out to everybody an equal amount *and* kind of 'good'. The 'pleasures of the mind', for instance (which Green denied himself) cannot be equally distributed unless you have a community composed of standard minds, turned out according to some super-mechanical method. It is exactly that sort of regularity or quantitative fixity that it is necessary to avoid, for the sake of the mutual satisfaction of the members of any social group.

The 'common good' can only mean organic 'good', the functional 'good' belonging to some social organism. There cannot be any 'good' common to an unorganized mob of 'things'. It is only when a mob of things is organized, and has become possessed of *persons*

[1] *Ancient* Law (1861).
[2] The principle dwelt on by T. H. Green.

(interpreting and administering its laws and its tradition) that it can be said to have a 'common good'. A 'common good' is, in short, an expression of the law of 'normal' beings (in the juristic sense of beings beneath a common law), and it reduces itself, in the end, to the proper working of their particular law – where that law is healthy and effective, operating in a naturally closed system.

A society is formed, in the first instance, it might be said, by the secretion of some spiritual quiddity (which is the germ of the norm or law) by some single powerful family, or group of active families. It is this norm, as it matures and acquires the strength of habit, that holds them together. From the start that norm is incarnated in the chiefs and leaders of the group, and becomes *personal*, as it were. It is to those leaders that everything is 'due' on the part of the other members of the group.

For Green, however, the 'common good' would mean something entirely different from the laws of this organic complex of relationships. For him the 'good' had become a (falsely) personal 'good', and human society was conceived as a horizontal egalitarian plane of equal and undifferentiated 'persons'. There were no 'things' in this world at all – except 'lower animals', stones and trees. For him, as a typical nineteenth-century revolutionary moralist, until every man, woman and child (but especially every woman and child), in the entire world, had been accommodated with all the 'pleasures of the mind' of Plato, Green could know no peace. And (to turn from the pleasures of the mind of Plato to things about which there is likely at any time to be more trouble), if one individual had a wireless set, or a Bentley or a Morris-Oxford, then everybody must have them – quite irrespective of the fact that it is evident to any fairly intelligent and observant person today that the possession of these machines is not spiritually of very great advantage to the average man, and so such possessions can hardly be regarded as eligible for a position among that aggregate of things we agree to call the 'common good'.

The 'common good' can, then, only be defined, in a general way, as the law of any social organism. But perhaps *any* social organism is too sweeping: for a society can be so low in the vital scale that it is incapable of realizing anything that can properly be described as a 'good' at all. Most of our Western democracies are rapidly reaching that biologic level. So it must be the law, I think, of a fairly active and *perpendicular* – a well-proportioned, elastic, orderly – society. – As for the indefinite expansion of the idea of the 'good', or of the 'human' without limit of time or place – so that any number of units may be embraced by a law that is unique – there again the emotional or sentimental expansiveness of the protestant moralist seems to me to be at fault, and to provide for us, in place of a well-built society, an emotional chaos. That type of feeling must to my mind result in social ideas that are at once metaphysically impossible and foolish, or, from the standpoint of the engineer or the artist, in structures that will be disgustingly unsatisfactory or else quite meaningless – a sort of rainbow-bridge of crude and stupid tint, stretched from nowhere to nowhere.

I do not wish to seem too severe or even perhaps a trifle roman, but I must pursue my analysis of this type of ethics a step further, or else the word 'human' will be left up in the air, I am afraid, or get mixed up with Green's 'lowest animals'. And yet the 'Je suis Romain – je suis humain' of Maurras[1] is a formula for the provençal countryside – and a very good one – rather than for the american 'Melting-pot', into which we all must slip (and, in my view, *should* slip, although I say so without any dogmatism).

Outside what would popularly be regarded as the 'human' norm, lie all the other forms of the animal creation. In order to know what we really mean by 'human', we cannot escape considering that irrational world; any more than in considering what appears on the face of it the 'human' world, can we help discriminating between the rational and the irrational. There is no question but that a dog, for instance, of a charming character, is more worthy, in the abstract, of our interest and sympathy, than are very many men, both Paleface and Coloured. If you isolate that particular 'lower animal', and that inferior man, then the animal is the more 'human' – gentler, better, and more rational. To that proposition, I am sure, I shall have no difficulty in receiving your assent (though if the Borzois are listening, they no doubt will bark, for they will perceive that this might raise difficulties for them).

A deer or a horse is a nobler creature physically, perhaps, than many men; and some individual horses and deer would be superior spiritually to them. Yet those animals could not be said to come

---

[1] Charles Maurras (1868–1952), the French royalist thinker and moving spirit of the newspaper *Action Française*.

within a human canon, or to be themselves 'human': and therefore there is nothing 'due' from us to them or *vice versa* – or only a sentimental something, which is in its purest state that something that Green, or the primitive Christian, seizes upon, exaggerates, transfers to men, and proceeds to convert into the peculiar property of man, calling it 'love' and the ethical sense. But indeed it is most unreasonable when the 'lower animals' are excluded from such 'human' canons.

Ethics as conceived by the author of the *Prolegomena to Ethics* whom I have chosen for my illustrations in this essay, should be entirely confined, perhaps, to questions regarding our relations to animals, other than men. The science of Ethics altogether might find its true rôle in the regulation of such relationships. Dogs, horses, cats and cows are the natural, and the true, clients of the moral philosopher, I believe. As such, the exercise of ethical emotions would give rise to very grave problems indeed: and they would involve questions very much more difficult to meet than those raised by the purely human variety of ethical speculation: we should immediately be confronted with the problem of the pork-chop and the mutton-cutlet, in fine, or of the draught-horse. And I need not point out to the reader possessed of an acute political eye what repercussions this newly demarcated ethical science would have in the world of revolutionary politics. In a flash everything would be in an uproar.

I believe the problem of the mutton-cutlet will yet come into its own, and become one of first-class political importance. – But of all neglected problems of that order, the *Paleface* problem is to my mind the first on the list – if only because, in that instance, we ourselves are the mutton-chop. I am sorry to terminate this part of my essay upon this sordid animal note.

PART II

INTRODUCTION

The following passage deals with fashions in both art and thought, which at the time of their initiation exercise an imperative social influence. This is one aspect of the time-philosophy in operation, with its emphasis on subjectivity. Despite the attention given to the subject, Lewis raises certain problems which are only today beginning to receive serious study. His chief point is that 'we have been thrown back wholesale from the external, the public world ... into our primitive private mental caves', and he emphasizes the naïvety with which the writer and artist, deprived of tradition and a common body of knowledge, 'accepts what he receives in place of these things'.

In the following essay I quote very fully and examine at considerable length passages from Mr D. H. Lawrence, Mr Sherwood Anderson, and other writers using popular narrative to present ideas and even religions. That so much careful attention should be given to artists in fiction, or to works written, it is felt, in the first instance, to amuse, may seem strange to some people. It is not usual to honour them in this way. Were it the analysis of the conditions favourable to a virus, of some definite 'social problem' (with the accompanying statistics, references to philosophic and sociological treatises, and so on), it would not appear at all strange to devote a great deal of space to a minute examination of things that were in themselves, perhaps, not very important or interesting.

What I wish to stress, then, is that these essays do not come under the head of 'literary criticism'. They are written purely as investigations into contemporary states of mind, as these are displayed for us by imaginative writers pretending to give us a picture of current life 'as it is lived', but who in fact give us much more a picture of life as, according to them, it *should be* lived. In the process they slip in, or thrust in, an entire philosophy, which they derive from more theoretic fields, and which is usually not at all the philosophy of the sort of people they portray. The whole of *Paleface,* in fact, deals with and is intended to set in relief the automatic processes by which the artist or the writer (a novelist or a poet) obtains his formularies: to show how the formulas for his progress are issued to him, how he gets them by post and then applies them.

According to present arrangements, in the presence of nature the artist or writer is almost always apriorist, we suggest. Further, he tends to lose his powers of observation (which, through reliance upon external nature, in the classical ages gave him freedom) altogether. Yet *observation* must be the only guarantee of his usefulness, as much as of his independence. So he takes his nature, in practice, from theoretic fields, and resigns himself to see only what conforms to his syllabus of patterns. He deals with the raw life, thinks he sees arabesques in it; and in fact the arabesques that he sees more often than not emanate from his theoretic borrowing, he has put them there. It is a nature-for-technical-purposes of which he is conscious. Scarcely any longer can he be said to control or be even in touch with the raw at all, that is the same as saying he is not in touch with nature: he rather dredges and excavates things that are not objects of direct perception, with a science he has borrowed; or, upon the surface, observes only according to a system of opinion which hides from him any but a highly selective reality.

The mere fact – with the artist or interpreter of nature – that his material is living, exposes him to the temptation of a drowsy enthusiasm for paradox, since 'life' is paradox (sprinkled over a process of digestive sloth), and all men live, actually, upon the amusement of surprise. 'What man is this who arrives? A beautiful, a wonderful stranger!' they say: and all strangers are wonderful or beautiful. 'What will the day bring forth? There will be some pleasant novelty, at least of that we can be certain! A novelty with whose appearance we have had nothing to do.' 'Life' is *not*-knowing: it is the surprise packet: so, essentially unselective, if nature can be so arranged as to yield him as it were a system of surprises, the artist will scarcely take the trouble to look behind them, to detect the principle of their occurrence, or to reflect that for 'surprises', for the direct life of nature, they are a little over-dramatic and particularly pat. So he automatically applies the accepted formula to nature; the corresponding accident manifests itself, like a djinn, always with an imposing clatter (since it is a highly selective 'accident' that understands its part): and the artist is perfectly satisfied that nature has spoken. He does not see at all that 'nature' is no longer there.

You are merely describing, you may say, the famous 'subjective' character of this time, in your own way and a little paradoxically. If I could surprise anybody into examining with a purged and renewed sense what is taken so much for granted, namely our 'subjectivity' – though who or what is the subject or Subject? – I should have justified any method whatever. But I am anxious to capture the attention of the reader in a way to which he is less accustomed, a less paradoxical way.

In Western countries the Eighteenth-century man and the Puritan man are perhaps the most marked types that survive, disguised of course in all sorts of manners, and differently combined. We have learnt to live upon a diet of pure 'fun', we are sensationalist to the marrow. Ours is a kind of Wembley-life of raree-shows, of switchbacks and watershoots.[1] We observe the gleeful eye of Mr Bertrand Russell and he appears suspended for a moment above some formal logical precipice. Or there is Mr Roger Fry in the company of his friend Mr Bell, sustaining delightedly shock after shock from the handles of some electric machine, or in other words from the unceremonious vigour of some painting which, charged with a strange zeal, outrages in turn all the traditional principles of his English training and his essential respectability. Then there are the roundabouts for the Peter Pan chorus, swings for exhibitionists, mantic grottoes and the lecture-tents of the gymnosophists. Oh, it is a wild life that we live in the near West, between one apocalypse and another! And the far West is much the same, we are told. In a word we have lost our sense of reality. So we return to the central problem of our 'subjectivity', which is what we have in the place of our lost sense, and which is the name by which our condition goes.

Elsewhere I have described this in its great lines as the transition from a *public* to a *private* way of thinking and feeling. The great industrial machine has removed from the individual life all responsibility. For an individual business adventurer to succeed as he could in the first days of industrial expansion, will tomorrow be impossible. It is evidently in these conditions that you must look for the solid ground of our 'subjective' fashions. The obvious historic analogy is to be found in the Greek political decadence. Stoic and other philosophies set out to provide the individual with a complete substitute for the great public and civic ideal of the happiest days of Greek freedom: with their thought we are quite at home. I will take the account of these circumstances to be found in Caird.[2]

> Even in the time of Aristotle a great change was passing over the public life of Greece, by which all its ethical traditions were discredited.... By the victories of Philip and Alexander the city states

---

[1] Much of *Paleface* was written shortly after the Wembley British Empire Exhibition.
[2] Edward Caird (1835–1908), British Hegelian philosopher.

of Greece were reduced to the rank of subordinate municipalities in a great military empire; and, under the dynasties founded by Alexander's generals, they became the plaything and the prize of a conflict between greater powers, which they could not substantially influence . . . we may fairly say that it was at this period that the division between public and private life, which is so familiar to us but was so unfamiliar to the Greeks, was first decisively established as a fact. A private non-political life became now, not the exception, but the rule; not the abnormal choice of a few recalcitrant spirits, like Diogenes or Aristippus, but the inevitable lot of the great mass of mankind. The individual no longer finding his happiness or misery closely associated with that of a community . . . was thrown back upon his own resources. . . . What Rome did was practically to pulverize the old societies, reducing them to a collection of individuals, and then to hold them together by an external organization, military and legal . . . its effect (that of roman power) was rather to level and disintegrate than to draw men together. (*The Evolution of Theology*.)

There is not much resemblance, outwardly, between the pulverization by one central power, such as that of Rome, and the pulverization of our social and intellectual life that is being effected by general industrial conditions all over the world. But there is, in the nature of things, the same oppressive removal of all personal outlet (sufficiently significant to satisfy a full-blooded business or political ambition) in a great public life of individual enterprise: and, in the West, at the same time, through the agency of Science, all our standards of existence have been discredited. Many people protest against such an interpretation of what has happened to us in Europe and America: they do not see that it has happened, they say that at most 'there may be a danger of it' it: yet every detail of the life of any individual you choose to take, in almost any career, testifies to its correctness.

As to what is at the bottom of this immense and radical translation from a free public life, on the one hand, to a powerless, unsatisfying, circumscribed private life on the other, with that we are not here especially occupied. But the answer lies entirely, on the physical side, with the spectacular growth of Science, and its child, Industry. The East is in process of being revolutionized, however, in the same manner as the West. Let me quote Mr Russell:

> The kind of difference that Newton has made to the world is more easily appreciated where a Newtonian civilization is brought into sharp contrast with a pre-scientific culture, as for example in modern China.

> The ferment in that country is the inevitable outcome of the arrival of Newton upon its shores.... If Newton had never lived, the civilization of China would have remained undisturbed, and I suggest that we ourselves should be little different from what we were in the middle of the eighteenth century. (*Radio Times*, April 8th, 1928.)

If you substitute Science for Newton (for if Newton 'had never lived' somebody else would), that explains our condition. We have been thrown back wholesale from the external, the public world, by the successive waves of the 'Newtonian' innovation, and been driven down into our primitive private mental caves, of the unconscious and the primitive. We are the cave-men of the new mental wilderness. That is the description, and the history of our particular 'subjectivity'.

In the arts of formal expression, a 'dark night of the soul' is settling down. A kind of mental language is in process of invention, flouting and over-riding the larynx and the tongue. Yet an art that is 'subjective' and can look to no common factors of knowledge or feeling, and lean on no tradition, is exposed to the necessity, first of all, of instructing itself far more profoundly as to the origins of its impulses and the nature and history of the formulas with which it works; or else it is committed to becoming a zealous parrot of systems and judgements that reach it from the unknown. In the latter case in effect what it does is to bestow authority upon a hypothetic something or someone it has never seen, and would be at a loss to describe (since in the 'subjective' there is no common and visible nature), and progressively to surrender its faculty of observation, and so sever itself from the external field of immediate truth or belief – for the only meaning of 'nature' is a nature possessed in common. And that is what now has happened to many artists: they pretend to be their own authority, but they are not even that.

It would not be easy to exaggerate the naïveté with which the average artist or writer today, deprived of all central authority, body of knowledge, tradition, or commonly accepted system of nature, accepts what he receives in place of those things. He is usually as innocent of any saving scepticism, even of the most elementary sort, where his subjectively-possessed machinery is concerned, as the most secluded and dullest peasant abashed with metropolitan novelties; only unlike the peasant, he has no saving shrewdness even: and this is all the more peculiar (and therefore not generally noticed, or if recognized, not easily credited) because he is physically in the centre of things, and so, it would be supposed, 'knowing' and predisposed to doubt.

Listen attentively to any conversation at a café or a tea-table, or any place where students or artists collect and exchange ideas, or listen to one rising – or equally a risen – writer or artist talking to another – from this there are very few people that you will have to except: it is astonishing how, in all the heated dogmatical arguments, you will never find them calling in question the very basis upon which the 'movement' they are advocating rests. They are never so 'radical' as that. Not that the direction they are taking may not be the right one, but they have not the least consciousness, if so, why it is right, or of the many alternatives open to them. The authority of fashion is absolute in such cases: whatever has by some means introduced itself and gained a wide crowd-acceptance for say two years and a half, is, itself, unassailable. Its application, only, presents alternatives. The world of fashion for them is as solid and unquestionable as that large stone against which Johnson hit his foot, to confute the Bishop of Cloyne.[1] For them the time-world has become an absolute, as it has for the philosopher in the background, feeding them with a hollow assurance.

But this suggestionability, directed to other objects, is shown everywhere by the crowd. The confusion would be more intense than it is, even, if every small practitioner of art or letters started examining, in a dissatisfied and critical spirit, everything at all, you might at this point object. And, if that is the case, why attempt to sow distrust of the very ground on which they stand, among a herd of happy and ignorant technicians entranced, not with 'mind' but with 'subjectivity'? Was not the man-of-science of thirty years ago, in undisturbed possession of all his assumptions as regards the 'reality' he handled so effectively, happier and brighter, and so perhaps more useful than his more sceptical successor today?

This argument would carry more weight, if the opinions to which it referred were not so fanatically held. It is very difficult to generalize like that: sometimes it is a good thing to interfere with a somnambulist and of course sometimes not. You have to use your judgment. The kind of screen that is being built up between the reality and us, the 'dark night of the soul' into which each individual

[1] George Berkeley (1685–1753), the idealist philosopher.

is relapsing, the intellectual shoddiness of so much of the thought responsible for the artist's reality, or 'nature' today, all these things seem to point to the desirability of a new, and if necessary shattering criticism of 'modernity', as it stands at present. Having got so far, again, we must sustain our revolutionary impulse. It is an enterprising thought indeed that would accept *all* that the 'Newtonian' civilization of science has thrust upon our unhappy world, simply because it once had been different from something else, and promised 'progress', though no advantage so far has been seen to ensue from its propagation for any of us, except that the last vestiges of a few superb civilizations are being stamped out, and a million sheep's-heads, in London, can sit and listen to the distant bellowing of Mussolini; or in situations so widely separated as Wigan and Brighton, listen simultaneously to the bellowing of Dame Clara Butt. It is too much to ask us to accept these privileges as substitutes for the art of Sung or the philosophy of Greece. – It is as a result of such considerations as these that a new revolution is already on foot, making its appearance first under the aspect of a violent reaction, at last to bring a steady and growing mass of criticism to bear upon those innovations that Mr Russell would term 'Newtonian', and question their right to land upon the shores of China and do there what they are said to be doing.

In the arts of formal expression this new impulse has already made its appearance. But the deep eclipse of the extreme ignorance in which most technical giants repose, makes the pointing of the new day, in those places, very slow and uncertain. – Really the average of our artists and writers could be regarded under the figure of nymphs, who are all ravished periodically by a pantheon of unknown gods, who appear to them first in one form then in another. These are evidently deities who speak in a scientific canting and abstract dialect, mainly, in the moment of the supreme embrace, to these hot and bothered, rapt intelligences: and all the rather hybrid creations that ensue lisp in the accents of science as well. But is it *one* god, assuming many different forms, or is it a plurality of disconnected celestial adventurers? That is a disputed point: but I incline to the belief that one god only is responsible for these various escapades. That is immaterial, however, for if it is not one, then it is a colony of beings very much resembling one another.

So then before discussing at all the pros and cons of the 'subjective' fashion, it is necessary to realize that it is not to the concrete material of art that we must go for our argument: that is riddled with contradictory assumptions. Most dogmatically 'subjective', telling-from-the-inside, fashionable method – whatever else it may be and whether 'well-found' or not – is ultimately discovered to be bad philosophy – that is to say it takes its orders from second-rate philosophic dogma. Can art that is a reflection of bad philosophy be good art? I should say that you could make good art out of almost anything, whether good or bad from the standpoint of right reason. But under these circumstances there is, it follows, no objection to the source being a rational one: for reason never did any harm to art, even if it never did any good. And in other respects we are all highly interested in the success of reason.

But if, politically and socially, men are today fated to a 'subjective' rôle, and driven inside their private, mental caves, how can art be anything but 'subjective' too? Is externality of any sort possible, for us? Are not we of necessity confined to a mental world of the unconscious, in which we naturally sink back to a more primitive level; and hence our 'primitivism', too? *Our* lives cannot be described in terms of action – externally that is – because we never truly *act*. We have no common world into which we project ourselves and recognize what we see there as symbols of our fullest power. To those questions we now in due course would be led: but what here I have been trying to show is that first of all much more attention should be given to the intellectual principles that are behind the work of art: that to sustain the pretensions of a considerable innovation a work must be surer than it usually is today of its formal parentage: that nothing that is unsatisfactory in the result should be passed over, but should be asked to account for itself in the abstract terms that are behind its phenomenal face. And I have suggested that many subjective fashions, not plastically or formally very satisfactory, would become completely discredited if it were clearly explained upon what flimsy theories they are in fact built: what bad philosophy, in short, has almost everywhere been responsible for the bad art.

My main object in *Paleface* has been to place in the hands of the readers of imaginative literature, and also of that very considerable literature directed to popularizing scientific and philosophic notions, in language as clear and direct as possible, a sort of key; so that, with its aid, they may be able to read any work of art presented to them, and, resisting the skilful blandishments of the fictionist, reject this plausible 'life' that often is not life, and understand the ideologic or philosophical basis of these confusing entertainments, where so many false ideas change hands or change heads. As it is, the popularizer is generally approached with the eyes firmly shut and the mouth wide open. And the fiction in its very nature takes with it the authority of life – people live it, as it were, as they read: so it is able to pass off as *true* almost anything. The often very elaborate philosophy expressed in this sensational form very often not only misrepresents the empirical reality, but misstates the truth.

I dignify this critical work with the title of *system*, because as literature stands today, it in reality amounts to that. It is a system that will enable any fairly intelligent man, once he opens his mind to it, and seizes its main principles, to read under an entirely new light almost everything that is written at the present time. Works of sociology, fiction, history, philosophy, claiming to be on the one hand conceived 'objectively', according to the non-human methods of ideal Science, will be found on close inspection, in most instances, to be All-too-Human, and to be serving ends anything but scientific; and in another class, works of fiction claiming only to be ingenuous works of *art*, will be found to be saturated with political doctrine, or with attitudes of mind imposed upon the Many in the first place not by pure pleasure experts, anxious only to excite the palate of their clients, but by political experts, devising means of ruling people by working on their senses and emotions.

In order of course to employ this system effectively the reader must acquaint himself with many things of a sort that do not come his way in the ordinary course of life. He must accustom himself to regarding the means by which people are ruled today as very much more shrewd and elaborate than is generally believed. He must entirely discard all the notions of the essential brute stupidity of 'power' that formerly sometimes would have applied in Europe, but certainly does not at present. If he finds it difficult to believe that he is ruled with such a 'ruthless' cleverness, let him study for a moment the highly 'psychological' methods by which the Soviet rules its subjects. The Soviet do their ruling in public, indeed: they explain and explain, as did the german theoreticians of war: there is no excuse, therefore, for any one today not to be *au courant* with the way that he is likely to be ruled. For he can be sure that those open professors of intrigue and herd-hypnotism are not the only practitioners at work. Those who do *not* publish daily accounts of how they reach their ends are at least likely enough to be not less clever than those who do.[1]

CONCLUSION

The Conclusion to Paleface *discusses the future of the white race. Possibly its impact is greater today than at the time of its composition. There are some original insights: the tendency to represent a backward step as progressive, the fact that every age is a machine-age, the geometrical foundations of art, and the need for a new classicism. Next comes an allusion to Soviet imperialism made at the threshold of the decade in which Soviet power was so effectively sentimentalized by certain intellectuals. Finally, in the last part, Lewis makes a plea for a* European *melting-pot, a concept brought several steps nearer since his words were written.*

An appendix to Paleface, *not included here, discussed a book which caused a sensation on its appearance: Kathleen Mayo's* Mother India. *Published originally as a review in the second number of* The Enemy, *it forms an acute exposure of the distortions and exaggerations of that work.*

1. THE WHITE MACHINE AND ITS COMPLEXES

It was originally my intention, as an excursus to this preliminary essay, to provide a carefully sifted list of the great group of 'complexes' carried about by the average White Man today. (I use the word 'complexes' as that will convey to the general reader what is meant, and it also particularly recommends itself, since it is precisely Freud and his assistants, who, along with the idiotic word, have supplied the idiotic thing – have helped in short to build up the full Idiot, as he is emerging today.)

It would be necessary, of course, to overhaul this list every six months, as new material arrives by every post. But the main lines could now be definitely established.

I should have grouped these complexes under their specific

[1] The last four paragraphs are omitted.

headings. There would be, for instance, the 'husband' complex (virility-motif); age complex (A. young, B. old, variety); sex complex (shamanistic variety, sentimental frothing capitulation, etc. – the bastard-american negritic hysteria of 'I Want to Know Why'[1]); infantilism (the desire to remain in sheltered tutelage, refusal of responsibility), and so on. With each I should have provided a complete definition, and a set of concrete illustrations, of the foolproof sort. But as this would have greatly extended the length of my essay, it was necessary to abandon that part of the evidence.

As the White spirit shrinks, oppressed under its burden of war, business insecurity, blood-tax, domestic interference, domestic disunion, constant threat of revolutionary cataclysm, anti-cataclysm, and so forth, its very position of world-mastery, racial advantage and prestige, is inclined to become a mockery and burden to it. Everywhere today the White European (both as a European and also among the great White colonies and nations) is profoundly uneasy, and looks apprehensively behind him at all moments, conscious of a watchful presence at his back, or somewhere concealed in his neighbourhood, which he does not understand. *Dark Laughter* of the hidden watching negro servants is a typical concrete expression of this uneasiness: evidently, when masters become obsessed with their servants, they are then only masters in name. But this threatening something to whose presence I refer is, of course, in a different category of terror and menace from the fairly harmless concrete Negro. Meanwhile inside himself (there he never looks, though it is, of course, there that he should direct the most objective glance that he can muster), the ferment of the intellectualist disease goes on, and 'complex' after 'complex' is introduced, attacks some mortal centre of life and vitality, and a further portion of the White civilized soul is disintegrated: a further stagger, hop or shamble is given to the White machine.

2. 'INFERIORITY', AND WITHDRAWAL 'BACK TO NATURE'

So, in the books that we have been considering, where the White Man is confronted by the Black, the Red or the Brown, he now finds

[1] A story from Sherwood Anderson's *The Triumph of the Egg*, analysed in Part II, Section 22.

inside himself a novel sense of *inferiority*. He has, in short, an 'Inferiority complex' where every non-White, or simply alien personality or consciousness, is concerned. Especially is it in his capacity as *civilized* (as opposed to *primitive*, 'savage', 'animal') that he has been taught to feel *inferior*.

The trick of this inferiority could all be laid bare by any inquiring person who took the trouble to examine, not the purely curative doctrine of Dr Freud, but his philosophical, literary, sociological teaching, and its psychological ramifications throughout our society. There are many factors beside Freud: but Psychoanalysis is in itself quite adequate.

The trick of the *inferiority complex* that we have been approaching, via creative fiction, is to be sought in a certain belief that has been imposed gradually upon the White Consciousness, during forty or fifty years, namely, a belief (it reduces itself to that) that man *cannot* 'progress' beyond the savage or the animal: that when he tries to (as the White European has done, as the Hellene did), he becomes in the mass ineffective and ridiculous: therefore, that the sooner he turns about, and retraces his steps until he is once more like the Huns of Attila, or any community whose main business in life is to 'smite hip and thigh' some other rival community – or like the plain unvarnished man-eating tiger, or the wild boar, the better.

This direction of thought, and with the greatest definition this purpose is visible, has moulded all those schools of fiction, or fancy, specimens of which (from the pages of Mr Lawrence and Mr Anderson) I have given in evidence. The particular he-manism of Pound is cut from the same stuff (cf. *The Goodly Fere* of Pound, with the sentimental militant interpretation of Christ).

All through the range of his complexes the contemporary White Man can be observed at the same occupation, consisting everywhere in a *reversal* and a *return*. For instance, as *an adult* he looks back at *the child*, and he is taught to say in his heart that the child is a 'better man', so to speak, than he is. Therefore he seeks to become as infantile as possible, and to approximate, as far as may be, to the infantile condition. By the Bergson school of thought he has been taught to regard *intuition* (the 'intuition of the Woman', for example, contrasted with 'the mere logic of the Man') as superior to Intellect. So he looks *back* towards that feminine chaos, from which the masculine principles have differentiated themselves, as more perfect. As the Child is more perfect than, and the conditions of its life more desirable than those of the Man, so the mind of the Woman is more perfect than, and the lot of the Woman – in league with or immersed in Nature – more to be desired than the lot of the Man. So the contemporary man has grown to desire to be a woman, and has taken obvious steps to effect this transformation (cf. pages on shamanistic cult, *Art of Being Ruled*[1]). Then Power or Wealth has been represented as not only evil in itself, but not at all to be desired (cf. the 'higher type' of collective man of communism, according to René Fülöp-Miller). And so on through all the series of *backward*-cults, from primitivism, to fairyhood.

3. THE REVOLUTIONARY ROCK-DRILL AND THE LAWS OF TIME

As people stand and watch the rock-drill at work in the street, so they watch the engine of political destruction at work, asking themselves stupidly what it is all about. Why is all this going forward in our midst in this very strange and open manner? There is something here I don't understand! It is as though the authorities had sent the 'revolutionary' drill, under an armed escort, to break up the public thoroughfare. It's very odd! – I suppose my brain is not able to grasp these new ideas! whispers poor fuddled Mr Everyman to himself, apprehensively. He perhaps looks round guiltily, to see if his astonishment has been observed.

If one of these puzzled, staring members of the great Public consulted Spengler, that celebrated philosopher would reply, 'Well, according to the time-table of the best chronological philosophy (a time-table as absolute as that of solar eclipses – I have reduced it all to a very orderly and predictable scheme indeed), according to that time-table White Civilization is now virtually at an end. The various White Governments, realizing this, have directed various groups of "social workers" (as you see) to come and break up the White World with that up-to-date psychological equipment you perceive them handling with so much adroitness. Why they use that rather violent and noisy "cataclysmic" rock-drill is because, if they didn't do that, it would take a very long time to break up

[1] Part IX.

the firmly cemented White World (lots of money and energy was spent on cementing it, you see, and in making it solid and resistant *and then we should all be behind the Time-table*! The various governments, as it is, are exceedingly concerned at the length of time it takes to break up any specific bit of civilization. They had not realized how tough their civilization was.'

'But why do the Western governments want to smash up their own property, papa?' you can hear the puzzled Plain Man (making his little eyes and mouth three round O's) inquire of the portentous Professor.

'Because, my little man,' Herr Spengler would reply severely, 'because they *know* they're behindhand. They would never do anything that might result in my Time-table being contradicted or disproved. They will not risk – never fear! – offending *Time*! Not *Time*! You understand? When you little Plain Men say "Time is money", that is sacrilege. *Everything* – not only money – is Time.'

The Man in the Street would be no wiser than he was before, but he would be considerably impressed and frightened. A vast shadow across the sky, labelled *Zeitgeist*, would dimly emerge for him, the god of the rock-drill, a sort of scientific god. When next he saw the engines of upheaval and chaos at work, he would take care to ask no questions! He would hurry on, trying to look as much as possible like Brer Rabbit; or else like a little innocent Child, 'mindless' and irresponsible, slightly moronesque – as small and a hundred times as harmless as a fly.

4. THE 'JUMP' FROM NOA-NOA TO CLASS-WAR

What has 'primitivism' in art (taking Gauguin as a model of primitivist thought) got to do with the orthodox revolutionary doctrine of the Mass man, you may ask. That 'jump' is not a very long or difficult one, but it may be that some readers are not sufficiently trained, or have not sufficient political experience, to make it. So I will state very briefly how these things are connected.

All war is compelled to be anti-progressist in the first place; it has to deny not only the notion of 'progress', but also of humanity itself, as a privileged classification or principle of action. Every Western government has now accepted all that the new conditions of gas and aerial warfare entail. No future belligerent will be able to make use of a propaganda campaign about 'atrocities', as was the case in the last war: in advance every form of 'atrocity' is taken for granted. That is an entirely new situation in the civilized european world. It imposes a formidable change of attitude upon any civilized government taking up arms today. The first thing on the declaration of war that all the air-squadrons of those governments engaged would have to do would be to go and bomb and murder the sleeping citizens of the nation on whom war had been declared. The method of murder and poison, only upon a vast scale, which formerly was recognized as the peculiar province of Renaissance Italy and actually the monopoly of the Borgias, is imposed upon us by the development of our machinery of destruction.

But the marxian doctrine of 'class-war' is after all war: and it is impossible for revolutionary method not to keep pace with its militarist opponent. So you get most communists committed to the same anti-humane train of thought as the militarist. And further it is essential for people engaged in preparing for such events to instil into the Public a philosophy which must be 'ruthless', materialist and mechanical. And so a philosophy must ensue that is a contradiction of commonsense, and it will be quite unlike any other popular philosophy that has ever existed. For here with our rapidly-evolving machines of destruction at our sides we are in a different position to any former men.

The philosophy required will run generally as follows: The tiger is 'ruthless'; the Borneo head-hunter used to hunt a man's head as we go out with a butterfly net: *those* are the true models for you, Mr Citizen! To the 'Tiger burning bright' the political propagandist points enthusiastically: about that apocalyptic beast there is no nonsense, he is 'frankly an animal', without any sentimental squeamishness, he frankly enjoys the salts he finds in the human blood he taps; as he leaps upon his human prey, and squashes the entrails out of it, he 'thinks' of nothing, he is a machine that *acts*. That is what poor little Mr Citizen must do when the time comes. And the time is not far off, he is warned: and so with the class-war and the little communist.

No room at all is left for either (1) the chivalry of earlier nationalist war, nor for (2) the sort of humanitarian socialism of Fourier or Saint-Simon, or for that matter for the fabianism in which the very genial and benevolent Mr George Bernard Shaw was nourished.

But people do not believe in the alleged motives for wars any more today, and they are uncertain as to the benefits of revolutions. Henceforth then all those forms of organized violence must be gone into to some extent against human reason; they are henceforth motiveless, and hence mad. That is why the fever and delirium is essential, in those masses who are to participate in them. Organized mechanized violence must be made to assume the inscrutable face of a *necessity* – a necessity of *Nature*, not of man – man, indeed, must be carefully kept out of the picture.

But these same machines, which impose this type of war upon us, and hence also the philosophy that is required by it, in order to make it possible, also take us farther and farther away, in our everyday life, from 'savagery', or primitive conditions. The petrol engine and rapidly evolving transport facilities of all sorts, along with wireless and the cinema, make nationalism more unreal and unplausible every day. This is another desperate feature of the matter (from the point of view of the promoter of violence) that requires a desperate (philosophic) remedy. The ordered systematic, sensible atmosphere of our everyday life renders men recalcitrant to programmes of primitive violence. That is why violence today has to introduce itself *à la Borgia*. A propagandist religion of violence and 'action' that everywhere takes the form of a *return to Nature* cult, in one form or another, is born of these necessities.

5. HOW ALL BACKWARD STEPS HAVE TO BE REPRESENTED AS FORWARD STEPS

All this involves a *backward* step, then. From any standpoint at all that you care to adopt, except that of a mystical surrender of life altogether, such violence as is now involved in war must appear to the eye of reason as retrograde.

And here is the key to the form of a great deal of contemporary work in every field of activity. *The backward step has to be represented as a forward step.* 'Progress', it is true, as a notion, must be violently attacked and discredited: but at the same time it would be impossible to persuade people to do anything without some sort of idea of 'progress' or betterment. So, with an ill grace, 'progressist' imagery and inducements have got to be used. As a sister paradox to this, an extreme primitivism has to be preached, yet all the reality of what is truly *primitive*, chronologically, has to be removed from the pictures employed as baits and advertisements.

There is a very hasty sketch of *political primitivism*, as it could be called. It is not difficult to see how beautifully it agrees with the artistic primitivism of Mr D. H. Lawrence – with aztec blood-sacrifices, mystical and savage abandonments of the self, abstract sex-rage, etc., or Mr Sherwood Anderson's more muddled and less up-to-date primitivist bag of tricks. And, in a general way, how useful *art* is, in a philosophy that *must*, as its first condition, be *motiveless*.

As to the reason for my interest in these tolstoyan problems of War and Peace, it is not, of course, humanitarian. You need go no further than the very practical and unsentimental fact, or facts, of the most vital interests of an artist being ruined by orgies of violence and 'action', to understand my attitude, if you look for a personal motive in it. It takes a long time without interruption to do anything worth doing in an art or science, and for that (apart from the fact that it is a philosophy for brutes and the most complete 'morons', as they are called only) the accursed philosophy we are discussing denies us. You could not describe such opinions as 'selfish', seeing that the interests represented are identical with everybody else's in this respect, except those of such as make money or acquire power by means of wars of all sorts.

6. A WORKING DEFINITION OF THE 'SENTIMENTAL'

In my analysis of the primitivism of Messrs Lawrence and Anderson, especially with regard to their attitude to the Negro or Indian, I point out how in both cases they were careful to accuse all other people who had ever approached Blacks or Indians of being 'sentimental towards' or else full of hatred for *those coloured aliens*. It seems plain to me that this was a step, merely, to protect themselves against an accusation that they realize they have deserved.

It will be useful, however, to get some meaning into the tag 'sentimental' before we leave it.

Any idea should be regarded as 'sentimental' that is not taken to its ultimate conclusion. I propose that as a working definition of 'sentimentality'.

What is the 'ultimate conclusion' of anything? you could object.

But that evocation of the distant metaphysical limit has nothing to do with a working definition: we wish for a definition that will take us, not out of sight, but to the limits of our horizon only.

Why I regard the spirit of the works of Mr Anderson and of Mr Lawrence as sentimental, is because it indulges in a series of emotions that, if persevered in by the Public they are intended to influence, would cancel themselves. I regard Mr Anderson as more sentimental than Mr Lawrence, because I do not think that he suspects what the real issues are at all; whereas I daresay Mr Lawrence knows to some extent, though just as he was in the first instance a little vague as to where the ideas he used came from, he probably is not over clear as to whither they are bound, or what their affiliations are. Alternatively, if both Mr Anderson and Mr Lawrence see these conclusions with extreme clearness, then they are deliberately employing, at least, the machinery of sentimentality. But I think they both use it too naturally for it not to be native to them.

7. EVERY AGE HAS BEEN 'A MACHINE AGE'

The further investigation of those questions that have specifically to do with the machine, with an adumbration of what our attitude should be with regard to the machine, must be left to a later stage of this essay. In order to give some completeness to this first published part I will, however, make a few remarks before leaving the subject.

The hideous condition of our world is often attributed to 'dark' agencies, willing its overthrow. But there have always been such devils incarnate – it goes without saying that there are such evil agencies – 'dark' influences of every sort are certain at all moments to be at work. That alone would not account for the unique position of universal danger and disorganization in which we find ourselves all round the globe. It is obviously to its mechanical instrument, not to the human will itself, that we must look. Without White Science and the terrible power of its engines, such evil people as always abound would be relatively harmless.

How we might dispense with the Machine, or, rather, use it differently, can perhaps be suggested by a brief consideration of the mechanical, or geometric, as it appears in art.

Many attempts have been made to associate art with the triumph of the Machine Age. The question, 'Are machines beautiful in themselves?' has been asked for many years now. What people usually neglect to notice is that all the most splendid plastic and pictorial art is in a very strict sense geometric. *Every age has been a Machine Age.* At least you can say that as far as art is concerned, and as far as the machine is the application of geometric principles.

An alaskan totem-pole, a Solomon Island canoe, a siamese or indian temple, is *a machine,* inasmuch as it is, in its concatenated parts, composed of very mechanically definite units, and is built up according to a rigid geometric plan. The bunch of cylinders of a petrol engine has very much the same structural appeal as a totem-pole or the column of a mayan divinity. Engravings of such machinery have something even of the aesthetic appeal of the latter.

So, in the field of art, there is nothing novel in machinery. All primitive people have proved themselves a sort of aesthetic engineers. So, in a sense, a great suspension bridge, or a modern factory building – or a turbine engine – is only reintroducing into our life an element which the most ancient art supremely possessed, but which has been absent in european art, and which existed nowhere in european life to any great extent, until the industrial age.

Life itself, in all its forms, has always possessed this, however. The insect and plant worlds, much more than the animal world, have always carried their structure outside, as it were, and thrust it upon the eye. The insect world could be truly said to be a Machine World, much more than our age, as yet, is a Machine Age.

The idea that plastic and graphic art is a soft, indefinite, fluffy or vague sort of thing, is more than a victorian prejudice. It is almost a european prejudice. Plastic or graphic art is, in fact, nothing of the sort: it is essentially a geometric thing, a thing of structure. But with european art, *the structure*, the geometric basis of beauty, has always tended to be covered up, hidden away (and so lost very often), more than is the case with the great aesthetic systems of the East. The hellenic naturalism, the result of the greek scientific bias, had, as I see it, resulted in Europe in an art which, except in the case of a few individuals of very great genius, has been so inferior to the art of China, for instance, that it could almost be said that the European had never understood the secrets of the pure eye at all. It is for that reason that I have said elsewhere that I consider this century has to its credit more art of the best kind than all the other centuries of european art put together, except the age of the Renaissance. This is, no doubt, partly due to the jewish influence, partly to the fact that specimens of the art of the East and of the antiquity of the so-called Ancient East, have become available to the European. (The gothic naturalism, in its severer moments, produced a very great art: but the general effect of the gothic buildings, according to the standard I am advancing, is one of a cloudy, not truly plastic, naturalism, that makes it not a thing of the eye, but of the 'musical' soul – in Spengler's sense.)

8. WHAT IS 'THE WEST'?

There is a belief, or prejudice, that you cannot be a good plastic artist and at the same time 'a good European'. It would be an important step in the reform and rejuvenation of our beliefs if we could overcome such prejudices. The appreciation of the formal beauties of mexican pottery, for instance, does not in any way involve enthusiasm for mexican gods, though I daresay the Aztecs themselves would scarcely recognize Mr Lawrence's account of their beliefs. You could 'flash up' for Mr Sherwood Anderson the perspiring black back of a Negro without necessarily wishing to share Bildad's[1] lodging, marry his sister or daughter, or embrace his beliefs or habits. You could use the colours and forms of a half-dozen magnificent beetles without becoming an insect; you could use the shape of a grasshopper in an arabesque without taking to hopping, just as you could admire the shawl of a Hopi without wishing to be a Hopi; you could make use of the white expanse of an icepack for your picture without yearning to live the life of an Esquimau. These few illustrations will, I hope, be of assistance in bringing out this part of my argument, which is a matter of some importance for what we have been mainly discussing.

9. THE INTELLECT 'SOLIDIFIES'. (THE ARGUMENTS ADVANCED HERE IN THEIR RELATION TO THE THOMIST POSITION)

There is a similar confusion to the above which, since it has a good deal of bearing on what I everywhere have to say, I will attempt to

[1] A Negro in Anderson's story *I want to know why*.

dispel in passing, as well as using it to confirm the present phase of my argument.

Extreme concreteness and extreme definition is for me a necessity. Hence I find myself naturally aligned today, to some extent, with the philosophers of the catholic revival. Against the mysticism of the mathematician I find myself with Bishop Berkeley (though, of course, he is claimed by the enemies of the concrete, strangely enough): I am on the side of commonsense, as against abstraction, as was Berkeley, and as are today the thomist thinkers (though the militant neo-thomist would repudiate any association of their doctrine with that of the great irish idealist): and my position, inasmuch as it causes me to oppose on all issues 'the romantic', comes under the heading 'classical'.

To show you how this must come about I will quote a passage from a book which I have just obtained, *L'Intellectualisme de Saint Thomas*, by Père Pierre Rousselot, S.J. He is enumerating the charges usually brought against the thomist 'intellectualism'.

> 'On reproche à l'intellectualisme scolastique d'exténuer et d'abstraire; on lui reproche aussi de "solidifier". Ce nouveau grief, qui pourrait sembler, au premier abord, s'accorder mal avec le premier, n'en est, au contraire, qu'une expression plus adéquate. Abstraire, c'est mépriser le fluent et postuler la permanence, c'est donc cristalliser ce qui se répand, concentrer le diffus, glacer ce qui coule, c'est *solidifier*.'

Neglecting here the particular significance given to the term 'abstraction' by Father Rousselot, it will be evident that what is laid to the charge of scholasticism, in this account, could also be levelled at what I say: or rather I, precisely, would claim the possession of all these characteristics that are here catalogued as crimes. To *solidify, to make concrete, to give definition to* – that is my profession: to 'despise the fluid' (mépriser le fluent) and 'to postulate permanence' (postuler la permanence); to crystallize that which (otherwise) flows away, to concentrate the diffuse, to turn to ice that which is liquid and mercurial—that certainly describes my occupation, and the tendency of all that I think. That is why I range myself, in some sense, with the modern scholastic teachers.

This does not, however, at all mean that I share their historical prejudices, any more than it means that I share their dogmas. I do neither, in fact. 'Classical' is for me *anything* which is nobly defined and exact, as opposed to that which is fluid – of the Flux – without outline, romantically 'dark', vague, 'mysterious', stormy, uncertain. The hellenic age has no monopoly of those qualities generally catalogued as 'classical', so, according to me, the term 'classical' is used in much too restricted, historical, a sense; in a word, too historically.

10. THE NECESSITY FOR A NEW CONCEPTION OF 'THE WEST', AND OF 'THE CLASSICAL'

The opposition, as it is understood here, is not between the Roman Cult and Aristotle on the one hand, and the 'modernist' disorder of Nineteenth Century 'romantic', 'revolutionary', european thought, on the other. Rather it is a universal opposition; and the seeds of the naturalist mistakes are certainly to be found precisely in Greece: and I believe we should use the *Classical* Orient (using this distinction in the sense of Guénon)[1] to rescue us at length from that far-reaching tradition.

These are statements of principle only, and I am not able here to make them more than that. Bare as they are for the present, I hope they will have served to foreshadow the conclusions to which the whole foregoing analyses of my essay have been intended to lead. 'European' does not mean for me a fixed historical thing, for it is so little that, in any case. If you tried to make of gaelic chivalry and italian science, german music and norse practical enterprise, *one* thing, that would be a strange monster. Which is demonstrated by Mr Massis in his *Défense de l'Occident*, where his 'West' is confined to the latin soil. This is an evasion only of the problem. It is just against that separatism as between the different segments of the West that we have most to contend. We should have – should we not? – our local Melting-pot.

It is *a new West*, as it were, that we have to envisage: one that, we may hope, has learned something from its recent gigantic reverses. For it is only by a fresh effort that the Western World can save itself: it can only become 'the West' at all, in fact, in that way, by an act of further creation.

There are a great many common traditions and memories and a considerable consanguinity: that is the 'material', at least for one

[1] René Guénon, the French oriental scholar (1886–1951).

'West'. As it is, not only such people as Spengler, but also (but with better motives, and perhaps inevitably) the catholic thinkers and the best of the 'patriots', insist on regarding the problem historically, in terms of a rigid arrest. 'The West' is for almost all of these a *finished* thing, either over those whose decay they gloat, or whose corpse they frantically 'defend'. It never seems to occur to them that the exceedingly novel conditions of life today demand an entirely new conception: in that respect they are firmly on the side of the people who would thrust us back into the mediaeval chaos and barbarity; at whose hypnotic 'historical' suggestion we would fight all the old european wars over again, like a gigantic cast of Movie supers, and so fill the pockets of these political impresarios.

11. HOW THE BLACK AND THE WHITE MIGHT LIVE AND LET LIVE

Since I have been discouraging, to the best of my ability, those tendencies (found on all hands) of White capitulation and self-criticism, in the presence of the 'rising tide of Colour', and especially tendencies to invite the White Man to learn and to adopt the primitive communism (real or imaginary), nihilistic mysticism, and so on, of the primitive Indian or the Black, it is necessary to return to what I have said in the '*Moral Situation*',[1] and to insist once more upon the fact that it is not the Melting-pot I object to, but the depreciation and damage done to one of the ingredients. I should not welcome a race-war, or a holy war, either of an *ecclesia militans* or any other type, as a substitute for all the other obviously less real or fundamental class-wars that have been arranged for us. That is not my idea. Nothing will certainly ever convince me that a White Man is not more deeply separated from a Negro (race-separation) than a Poor White is separated from a Rich White, or a White Fish-porter from White Miner (class separation). But I have used a quotation from the *Vision of Judgement*, by Lord Byron, earlier in this essay to illustrate my attitude:

> His Darkness and his Brightness
> Exchanged a greeting of extreme politeness.

I believe that we cannot, in fact, be polite enough to all those other

[1] The discussion of T. H. Green at the beginning of Part I.

kinds of men with whom we are called upon to pass our time upon the face of this globe. We should grow more and more polite: but, if possible, see less and less of such other kinds of men between whom and ourselves there is no practical reason for physical merging, nor for spiritual merging, or even very many reasons against both – for there are such people, too. But why war? If the white world had kept more to itself and interfered less with other people, it would have remained politically intact, and no one would have molested it: the Negro would still be squatting outside a mud-hut on the banks of the Niger: the Delaware would still be chasing the buffalo. We could have been another China. Such aloofness today, as things have turned out, is an ideal merely, though to me it is not an ideal. I merely put the matter in that light because for the average unenlightened Paleface that would seem much better – he would like to be a powerful boss rather than a cosmopolitan wage-slave in the Melting-pot, and his ideas do not soar above some regional dream. It is always from an exaggeration, however, on one side or the other, that the actual comes into existence. Everything real that has ever happened has come out of a dream, or a Utopia. We are the Utopia of the amœba. Many of our lives would seem heaven to the apes.

Are the assumptions at the basis of this discussion as conducted by me entirely false or merely alarmist? Very many other people, better qualified, in important ways, than I am, to judge, share my views. Let me quote one or two.

> Several years ago I wrote an essay on 'The White man and his Rivals', in which I pointed out the menace to the domination of the European races from the awakening ambitions of Asia. Till about the beginning of the present century it was taken for granted by almost everybody that the permanent supremacy of the Whites was assured. ... We had forgotten ... how entirely that preponderance has been due to superiority in weapons and industrial inventions ... how formidable the Brown and Yellow races are by their intelligence, their vast numbers, and their untiring industry.
>
> Much has happened since then to confirm my forecast, and now we have an important very disquieting book by Mr Upton Close, an American (*The Revolt of Asia*). . . .
>
> He has formed the conviction that the suicidal war of 1914–1918 ushered in 'the end of the White Man's world'. . . . Russia as an asiatic nation entirely alters the balance of power between the two continents. . . . Russia has not ceased to be 'imperialist' and aggressive under Communism.

This is from an article by Dean Inge (*Evening Standard*, May 11th, 1927). In the *Criterion* (August, 1927), Mr T. S. Eliot, referring approvingly to a 'meditation on the decay of European civilization by Paul Valéry', writes: 'The Russian Revolution has made men conscious of the position of Western Europe as (in Valéry's words) a small and isolated cape on the western side of the Asiatic Continent.'

While I was writing the rough draft of this essay on the Atlantic the following news item appeared in the *Daily Mail*, Atlantic Edition, August 15th, 1927:

SERIOUS BOLIVIAN REVOLT
THOUSANDS OF REBELS AMOK
LA PAZ, BOLIVIA, SUNDAY

Five thousand Indians, under Communist influence, have destroyed the railway at Potosi and Sucre, and invaded the surrounding districts. They are murdering any who offer resistance.

The Bolivian Federal Army are fighting the savages, and heavy casualties are reported on both sides.

The revolt has assumed serious proportions and the Federal Army cavalry captured several chiefs and executed them, together with 100 of their followers. – *Central News*.

WHITES BEING KILLED
(*From our own correspondent*)
BUENOS AIRES, SUNDAY

Reports from La Paz, the Bolivian capital, declare that the Indian rising, under native and foreign Communist leaders, is most serious. Two hundred thousand well-armed insurgents are now holding the railway line.

Whites are being killed and houses burned. They appeal to the Government, which admits the situation is grave.

The sequel to this was reported (September 8th) in the *New York Herald*:

BOLIVIAN CHARGES
RED INTERVENTION
(Special to the 'Herald')
LA PAZ, BOLIVIA, WEDNESDAY

An alleged proof of Communistic activities in South America, directed and financed by the Third International of Moscow, was presented in Parliament today by the Bolivian Foreign Minister, who read letters signed by Bukharin and Zalkind, prominent Russian leaders of international Communism. The exposure was followed by a vote of confidence in the Government.

The documents included instructions to 'Comrade Martinez, member of the Latin-American section of the Communist International', to proceed to Paris to obtain funds. After this he was to return to Bolivia, open a business house to conceal revolutionary work, and foment Communist revolt among the workers.

One letter was addressed to 'Comrade Dastion, Paris'. It introduced Martinez and instructed Dastion to give 1,000,000 francs to the Bolivian agitator out of the propaganda fund.

I have quoted this to show how the regrettable imperialist and also humanitarian zeal of the Soviet probably is responsible for trouble, often, where Whites and the Coloured peoples are found together, as in South America or South Africa.

The 'open conspiracy', as Mr H. G. Wells describes it in *Clissold*,[1] rumbles and drags itself forward, spitting fire and brimstone, only very imperfectly subterranean: it is a pity that we should have to admit that the Communist is responsible for these Coloured aggressions, and that it should after all be a Paleface (a russian agitator) who requires our White attention. In any case we know that the Indian, like the Negro, is politically apathetic and would do little himself. But no *wars* are necessary to deal with this: only a strong movement of instructed opinion. The Indian, like the Chinese, is friendly and pacific. Even his *black laughter* is imported. The White teaches him that too. Really our White moral zeal is regrettable! for its *immediate* result can only be, when exercised so clumsily, to provide our bosses with labour cheaper than ours, rather like the feminist revolution. It seems to be playing into the White bosses' hands.

12. THE PART RACE HAS ALWAYS PLAYED IN CLASS

This section contains a long quotation from The Art of Being Ruled, *which is reproduced in the excerpt from that volume, pp. 110–111.*

13. BLACK LAUGHTER IN RUSSIA

In these last two sub-sections of my Conclusion I will return to the subject that occupied such a considerable space in my criticism

[1] *The World of William Clissold* (1926).

of Anderson and Lawrence.[1] The clumsy adulteries of the dull Whites haunted by the *black laughter* of their Negro servants was the contribution of Anderson. Much more thorough and fundamental, Mr D. H. Lawrence showed us all creatures whatever, in a position of servitude or defeat, 'taking it out' of their oppressors, successors, or masters, by malevolent laughter and mockery of some sort. Thus the parrots 'take it out of' the little dog, Corasmin, or out of his masters (Rosalino or Mr Lawrence), with their perpetual imitations. The 'high-pitched negro laughter', and the shrill voices of the parrots, come out of the same situation.[2]

All these are examples of revenge, in the form of mirth, directed against creatures who are evidently 'bourgeois' and recognized as Top-dogs. But Mr Fülöp-Miller has his story of Black Laughter of another sort. The Black Laughter no sooner has overthrown the overlord or master and stepped into his shoes, than up goes the Black Laughter against him. He is now the 'boss'. That is, at all events, the story. Here it is:

> For the new ruler of Russia, the Mass Man, who came to bring freedom to the earth, in a very short time learned how to use the resources and tricks of tyranny better than the cruellest tsars. . . . No one ventured on any protest, any resistance, however slight; there was not a single open word of censure. . . .
> But all at once it became evident that the subtly constricted apparatus of 'mechanized obedience' was not entirely reliable. . . . Something disconcerting happened, due to natural forces without any intervention on the part of the subjects: that unpleasant thing the 'soul' which in spite of all mechanization had never been completely eradicated, and was sleeping a sleep that looked like death, suddenly woke up in a smile that lurked on the lips of someone somewhere. With the first smile at the failure of the loudly trumpeted experiments of Bolshevism began the real, the dangerous, counter-revolution, for it worked in secret and gradually attained a sinister power. At first one person smiled, then others in increasing numbers. Soon the smilers united in a mystical organization and then mirth at last expanded into uncontrollable elemental laughter. This first revolt against Bolshevik oppression was the rebellion of the despairing; ever more frequently the hidden wrath became irony, ever loudly swelled an uncanny mirth, which threatened to shake the very foundations of the whole structure of State authority. . . .

---

[1] In Part II. § 3.
[2] The reference is to *Mornings in Mexico* and Anderson's *Dark Laughter*.

... in the provinces, among the peasants, laughter went in a triumphal march through the village streets, captured the market places, and began to press steadily forward towards the official headquarters. ...

... the dreaded masters of the Red Kremlin themselves trembled at this rising of laughers and jokers. In order to prevent an elemental outburst of all-dissolving universal mirth and to deprive this grave danger of all significance, the authorities hit on the clever idea of having recourse to an old institution, which has always been inseparably bound up with despotism, the office of the court fool. By this means the powers effectively took the initiative in this mockery of unpopular institutions and guided it into the right path. ...

... the old court fool was transformed into a circus clown and from the ring amused the people with his malicious jokes.

... 'Bim' and 'Bom' were the names of the two 'merry councillors' of the new tsar, the Mass man; they alone among the hundred millions of Russians were granted the right to express their opinions freely; they might mock, criticize, and deride the rulers at a time when the most rigorous persecution and terrorism prevailed throughout the whole country. Bim and Bom had received a special permit from the Soviets to express openly everything which was current among the people in a secret and threatening way, and thus to provide an outlet for latent rancour. Every evening, the thousand-headed Mass man, fawned upon by the whole court, sat in the circus and listened eagerly to the slanderous speeches of the two clowns Bim and Bom. In the midst of grotesque acrobatics and buffooneries, amid jokes and play, these two were allowed to utter bitter truths to which otherwise the ear of the ruler was angrily shut.

The circus in which Bim and Bom performed was crowded night after night to the farthest limits: people came from far and wide to hear Bim and Bom, who soon became star clowns. Their jokes were the daily talk of Moscow. One person told them to another, until finally the whole town knew the latest insults which these two fools had permitted themselves to make.

In the dark period of militant communism, people were particularly under the spell of the two clowns; at that time the loose jokes to which Bim and Bom treated them with untiring energy were the one respite from the continuous pressure of force and tyranny, the only possibility of hearing open criticism and mockery of the ruler, the Mass man. People abandoned themselves voluptuously to these precious moments of intellectual freedom.

In spite of their impudent criticisms, Bim and Bom were nevertheless one of the chief supports of the Bolshevik régime: the universal discontent would have burst all bounds if it had not been dissolved in harmless mirth by the two clowns. But, however biting might be the satire of Bim and Bom, the Government could rely on their never overstepping the limits of the permissible, for Bim and Bom were completely trustworthy members of the Communist Party, and at the bottom of their hearts loyal servants of their masters. They understood how to draw the fangs of the seemingly most malicious jest before they let it loose in the ring. Their attacks were never directed against the whole, but only against details, and thus they contrived to divert attention from essentials. Besides, every one of their jokes contained a hidden warning to the laughter lovers: 'Take care: Look out, we know you! We are aware of what you are thinking and feeling!'[1]

I do not suggest that there is any resemblance between the Black Laughter of Mr Anderson's negro servants and the official laughter of the Soviet clowns. The poor little provincial Whites of the american story have not the power of life and death over their negro servants. They do not go down into the kitchen beforehand and arrange what the Black clown shall laugh at and what he shall spare. The poor little White is at the mercy of his dark 'inferior', his traditional sense of 'superiority' dwindling every day: but of course, since he is not in reality superior, he should not have a Black servant, then he wouldn't be laughed at.

The Soviet clowns were apparently rather like members of Mr Henry Ford's propaganda department, which is supposed to have invented all the terms, such as 'Tin Lizzy', 'Flying Bedstead', and so on, that are thrown at the Ford car. Such an official, carefully regulated safety-valve is the greatest advertisement for the thing 'attacked'. It is like the jokes about the Scotsman's meanness which (I am glad to say) endear the Scot to all Britons.

The kind of *black laughter* I have been considering all along is of quite a different character from that. It, too, of course, describes itself as innocuous. The White is flatteringly assured that he is such a very secure Big White Chief that he can afford to become the laughing-stock of the rest of the world. But in practice that flattering picture is proved to be untrue. The account of the Black Laughter in Russia contains some apt instruction for us, if we can bring ourselves to be attentive to it.

14. WHITE LAUGHTER

There is nothing today for us to laugh about, it is true. Bernard Shaw and Company *laughed* all the time. A merry twinkle was

[1] From *The Mind and Face of Bolshevism.*

never out of their eye. Happy sunny White children of long ago! But their laughter was the opposite of what ours should be. They laughed ever so genially over things that, unfortunately, we can no longer *afford* to laugh at: today we are all, actually or potentially, *Poor Whites*. The prosperity even of America is a very precarious thing, as most Americans today realize.

Few people, as yet, even, understand that we can no longer afford to laugh in that sense. Nine people out of ten live in the past: they are aware that 'things have changed', but they do not realize very clearly in what specific way. They are creatures of habit: they go on laughing as formerly, at the same things, as though the same things were there, and as though the European were in the same place. This really tragic sloth, and unwillingness to admit anything unpleasant, of the Many, is our main difficulty in proposing a change of orientation for our satire, or indeed in proposing a realistic effort of any sort. *The Present can only be revealed to people when it has become Yesterday.* Another way of putting this is that people are historically-minded, and this, again and again, must be stressed. It is by taking advantage of this human peculiarity that the politician invariably operates, and brings off his most tragic *coups*. The *bovarysme* of man is as nothing compared to this trait (unless you take it as a department of *bovarysme*) – namely, that Man is an animal that believes he is living in a different time to what in fact he is. So it is that a firm and concrete, totally unromantic, realization of the main features of the Present, gives the man possessing it enormous advantages over others. It is, as it were, the hypothetic ground of the lever of Archimedes, when he said of his lever, 'Give me somewhere to rest it, and I will move the world.'

Bernard Shaw and his light-hearted fabian chums laughed at their own kind. In those remote days their kind was all-powerful. That kind is *us*. The White is still, in appearance, where he was: but he is not powerful: he has no triumphant world, all of his own kind behind him. We have all, less than a decade ago, issued from a war with each other – in which we *all* lost. We are surrounded by prophets announcing our doom. Our commerce, naturally, has languished and shrunk. It is a very different scene, in short, from that of merry, play-boy socialism, mischievously disporting itself in the midst of that power and plenty of the Victorian age.

But even that laughter, in its time, was foolish and ill-advised, as, earlier in the Nineteenth Century, were the romantic revolutionary tirades of Shelley and Byron. The Eminent Victorians, and their institutions, could not in their day afford to be laughed at as they permitted everybody to do. The proof of the weakness of the racial policy of the White Overlord (simply taking him as an overlord and assuming that it was his policy to remain that in some form or another, his lutheran conscience permitting) is to be read in the light of his present position.

Today we should not give up our laughter: for the White Man knows how to laugh, and the Anglo-Saxon has a kind of genius for it. But we should develop another form of laughter. We should make a more practical use of this great force, and not treat it as an irresponsible, mischievous luxury. Other peoples, their habits, their faces, their institutions, are just as ridiculous as ours. It is a little *over*-christian to be this perpetual, 'dignified' butt! But it is of no use at all for our laughter to be of that easy, 'kindly', schoolboy variety, that merely endears the people laughed at to the lookers-on. *We* are not laughed at in that manner. There is nothing of the advertisement-value of that kind of laughter in the Black Laughter or Red Laughter directed at us.

So let us get a point into our new laughter, if we are going to have it at all. Do not let us fear to hurt people's feelings by our laughter, since we may depend on it they will not spare ours. Nothing can help us so much as to develop this type of laughter.

Let the usual *Black Laughter*, or *Red Laughter*, directed at us, go on: but let it become a thing of the past for us to remain its amiable accommodating and self-abasing butts.

We can even dispense with the musical arpeggios of laughter itself: let us rather meet with the slightest smile all those things that so far we have received with delirious rapture – first, at all events, until we are sure of them. All this frantically advertised welter of ideas that pour over us from all sides, from nowhere, let us above all, at last meet *that* as it should be met. Do not let us spring up and prostrate ourselves every half minute, as the latest ambassador arrives with News from Nowhere, with an auctioneer's clatter. Let us remain seated, the feminine privilege, let us smile sceptically, also the feminine privilege: let us insist upon every feminine privilege: let us be faultlessly polite, or rather overpolite, crudely polite, let us show this political tout, dressed up as a wise man from the East, that we have expected him, that we should only have been surprised if he had not turned up: that we hope he soon will go. That is the only way to treat the Thousand and One Magi and Chaldeans who successively rattle our knocker.

A FINAL PROPOSAL: A 'MODEL MELTING-POT'

There are, in the specifically *moral* nature of the situation in which we find ourselves, factors that I do not propose to investigate. There is the contradictory spectacle, which we can all observe, of our institutions, as they dehumanize themselves, clothing themselves more and more, and with a hideous pomposity, with the stuff of morals — that stuff of which the pagan world was healthily ignorant, in its physical expansiveness and instinct for a concrete truth, and which, for the greatest peoples of the East, has never existed, except as a purely political systematization of something irretrievably inferior, a sentimental annexe of a metaphysical truth. It is natural that 'the Congo' should 'flood the Acropolis' (though I am not sure that I did not misunderstand the Princess[1]) when we see the attitudes of Renaissance culture, as illustrated by the great french stylists, being subtly combined with the militant emotional gloom of the Salvation Army: when the Salvation Army marches weeping, in jazz step, into the study of Montesquieu, then the crocodiles *are* on their way to Hellas.

What I shall especially neglect is to analyse the artificial character of this puritanic gloom, settling in a dense political smoke-screen about us, gushed from both official and unofficial reservoirs. I shall confine myself to remarking that the person who meets all these sham glooms with an anguished *De Profundis*, instead of a laugh (however unpleasant) is scarcely wise, though he may be good. To see a vineyard in the sun surrounded by armed federal officers of the law, who prevent anybody from taking the grapes and making them into wine, is absurd more than anything else. Foodstuffs rotting on the quays while people are starving, is a fact that should be met, if at all, not by stylistic theologic melancholy, that seems obvious. Or again, the abstruse principles of the manufacture of

---
[1] A reference to W. E. B. Du Bois' novel *Dame Princess*.

paper-money, like the arbitrary non-manufacture of a healthy and pleasant wine, and all that results from one as from the other – of gloom and of a sense of the *difficulty* of everything – this is not the material for profound heart-searching groans, although that is the correct unofficial response, it is true. But a reader of this book will be left with those sums or equations on his hands, to work out or not, as he may feel inclined. I have made it clear, I think, how the *ethical*, introduced into the physical problem of the Melting-pot, produces a gloomy and passionate infusion: that is all I set out to do. With a definite proposal, one that has been made often before by many people, I will bring this essay to a close.

In America the expression Melting-pot has been coined to describe the assimilation of european nationalities in the United States, and now of the negro population, ten million strong, which has begun in earnest. In Europe we have no such expression, for the excellent reason that there is no assimilation in progress. If the United States possessed fixed areas in which Danes, Spaniards, Germans, Negroes, Irish and so forth were segregated, as we are, each settled in certain states, with fortified frontiers, taught only their mother tongue and unable to converse with the inhabitants of the next state, then there would be no Melting-pot there either. America without its Melting-pot would simply be another Europe, plus a Black Belt and a few Chinatowns.

There is a radical contradiction between the european and american way of regarding this problem. Perhaps because it is so much taken for granted, this difference passes for the most part unnoticed by us. Whereas the rulers of America are committed to fusion (however dissimilar the racial stocks) in one form or another, in Europe the question does not even arise. Since the French live upon one side of the Rhine and the Germans upon the other, or the English and the French upon opposite sides of the English Channel, there is no 'problem' as to their mixing: indeed the great majority of Germans or Frenchmen or Englishmen never see a member of the neighbour-nation except during such times as their respective governments decide appropriate for a mass meeting, as it were, and they are despatched to kill one another with bomb and bayonet. Even then it is only the infantry who see members of the 'enemy' nation at all distinctly: and it is possible for an infantryman to pass many months in the Line without catching sight of more than a few of his european neighbours, and these mostly dead specimens, or even nothing more than their facetious skeletons.

Of these two attitudes – the melting and the non-melting – the American appears to me by far the better: I am heart and soul upon the side of the Melting-pot, *not* upon that of the Barbed Wire. That is why I have called this book 'The Ethics of the *Melting-pot*', and not 'The Ethics of the Barbed Wire'. But what a terribly sad thing it is to reflect that literally millions of Basques, Finns, Scotsmen, Danes, Normans, Prussians, Swiss, should be kept rigidly apart while in Europe, by the intensive perpetuation of purely historical frontiers (which the Versailles Treaty has made even more numerous and complicated than before), whereas if they emigrate to America they are liable suddenly to be hectored for an opposite reason – namely because they show some slight compunction in coupling with a jet-black Kaffir. Personally I consider they are quite wrong in looking down upon the transplanted Kaffir: but it is far more stupid of them (if, say, a Swede) to look down upon a lovely Basque, or (if a Bavarian) to look down upon an industrious Gasconesse. Yet have they not always been taught to do that, at least since the rise of the national idea in Europe or since the time of the great religious schisms?

My own view is that the Melting-pot should be set up in Europe, upon the spot. Instead of posters on our walls which say 'Join the Royal Air Force and See the World', there should be posters (and offices in every district to deal with applicants) saying, 'Marry a Swiss and See the World', or, more jocularly, 'Get spliced to a Finn, and Get About'.

What can there be against it, except that it would be impossible to have wars any more in Europe? If it is objected that there is no unifying principle in Europe to compare with *americanization*, it is necessary to recall that only five centuries ago the whole of Europe possessed one soul in a more fundamental way than America can be said to at this moment, and the actual appearance of its towns must have been at least as uniform as today (and that is very uniform), though in a more agreeable fashion. As to the individuals of the various races, there is no obstacle there. In the valleys of the Pyrenees, for instance, you meet with a great many people physically as like as two eggs to the inhabitant of Devonshire, Derby, Limerick or Caithness: a swiss peasant woman is in character and physical appearance often so identical with a swedish, english, german or french girl that they might be twin sisters. This everyone must have remarked who has ever travelled to those countries. It has always been fratricidal that these people should be taught to disembowel, blind and poison each other on the score of their quite imaginary 'differences' of blood or mind, but today there is less excuse for it than ever before. So why not a *Melting-pot?* – instead of more and more intensive discouragement of such a fusion. Europe is not so very large: why should it not have one speech like China and acquire one government?

But feeling about Europe in that manner, and all too familiar with that situation, the spectacle of the rather feverish opposition to that attitude, wherever these same Europeans leave their countries and live in the proximity of people so different from themselves as the Negroes or the Chinese, cannot but occur to one as a very sudden and from some points of view unsatisfactory reversal. On the one hand you have too absolute a segregation, on the other too absolute a freedom to mix. America is the child of Europe entirely, except for the Negroes and in Mexico and South of Panama the Indians, and the two problems should not be disassociated. What happens to Europe is of great importance to America, and vice versa, what happens to America, that other-Europe, must be of great moment to us.

This essay is much more to propose that we set up a Melting-pot in Europe – which would be as it were a Model Melting-pot, not at the boiling-point but cooking at a steady rate day in day out – than to venture any criticism of the principle underlying the american or african Melting-pot or, alternatively, Colour Line. Indeed a quite irrational attitude is often adopted by the American to miscegenation. Another factor of 'inferiority' feeling has its roots in a profound misunderstanding of the true situation. The american is apt to accept the false european attitude towards 'race', as it is called. It is a common experience in talking to Americans to hear some magnificent human specimen (who is obviously the issue of say a first-class Swede and a magnificent Swissess, with a little Irish and a touch of Basque) refer to himself as a 'mongrel'. It is inconceivable, yet indeed that is how such a 'mixed' product is apt to look upon this superb marriage of Scandinavian, Goth and Celt – all stocks as closely related in blood – if it is 'blood' that is the trouble – as the brahmanic caste of India. Merely physically this epithet is given the lie: for all you have to do is to look at this sterling type of 'mixed' American to admire the purity of line and fine adjustment achieved by the conjunction of these sister stocks. Far from being a 'mongrel', of course, he is a sort of super-European: the best of several closely allied stocks have met in him, in exactly the same way as was constantly happening in the noble european families − where the issue of a marriage between nobles, whether from England and Italy or Spain and Russia, do not constitute a 'halfbreed', but rather a more exalted feudal product, so subtly 'mixed'.

Some racial mixtures are not so fortunate as others, however, it is necessary to allow: the indian and spanish mixtures, in say Peru or Mexico, have not proved really very good. The Barber of Seville that peeps through the Inca removes him from Mozart, and yet does not make a good Indian of him, though there are exceptions. But practically all european intermarriage presents no problem at all, and it is politically much to be desired, as certain to abolish the fiction of our frontiers and the fiction of the 'necessity' of war. The asiatic elements in Southern Spain, Italy and Russia aside, the European is as much of one blood as are the inhabitants of the British Isles, and in many instances more so − for instance the Bavarian and the lowland Scotch are man for man as nearly one race (to look at them as well as in their character) as you could find anywhere at all. If they spoke a common Ido, the Austrian with his *Spielhahnfeder* and *Eichenlaub* stuck in his *Steierhut* would melt into the Crofter without noticing he had left his native village.

But (until they reach America, and all have to speak english, or in Latin-America, spanish) the great difficulty is language. In discussing such a question we always get back to the problem of Babel. It is in the interest of the Melting-pot that every European should wish to learn Volapuc as I do, or to have some language picked for him that it shall be agreed all shall speak and that he can easily learn and speak − woo his possibly distant bride in, and talk over all those subjects of common interest with his brother at the other extremity of Europe, which since the decay of Latin as a universal tongue no one has been able to do. I cannot imagine any person in Europe who, when the matter was presented to him in that light, would not plump for some Volapuc: but if there is anywhere a person who would not, how slender his reasons must be compared to those a Dutchman say in Africa could allege for refusing to match his daughter with a Cape-Black or a settler from the Dekkan! And yet even the Dutchman would not be right, would he? – how much more wrong then would not the man in Europe be who stood out, for in fifty per cent of the cases he would be vetoing a closer match than could be made even in the home-village at any given time – for I would guarantee to match a young man in a Devon village better in the Canton of Berne than would be possible probably, at any given moment, in his own english district.

On the other hand if the Dutchman in Africa had ten daughters and seized the other end of the stick (after a reading of Plomer) so fanatically as to pester them all to choose upon the spot a Black bridegroom, that would be a sentimental extreme that it would perhaps be allowable to deplore: if he should embellish his own persuasiveness with highly-coloured abuse of all owners of a pale skin, then he would definitely become irritating and perhaps even absurd, and if his ten girls took him and flogged him no one could find it in his heart to blame them, though if called to a Grand Jury it would be necessary to send the whole of the ten girls to jail of course, for they should not, strictly speaking, flog their father, either, however misguided, as potentially his whiteness would be the symbol of their consanguinity and the ultimate reason for their objecting to the break-up of their pigment. This last illustration touches upon a complexity which (in rare instances, so far) qualifies the absolute simplicity of this question – the problem of the *gaga* Paleface Papa who reads Plomer or Du Bois. But – as I have prophesied – he will be dealt with by his children or grandchildren, when he disinherits them and leaves all his money to the female Kaffir cook.

What in these concluding pages it has been my intention to stress is that the fiery ethics of the Melting-pot are conjunctly european and protestant in origin more than anything else (though the gallic invention of the 'great nation' plays its part as well). The fanatical ill-temper and the black intolerance that accompany the discussion and propaganda for 'race-fusion' can be traced to those sources, when they cannot be directly traced to the equally intemperate ethical zeal of the 'radicalist' righteousness.

At this time the Anglo-Saxon is no longer paramount in North America: but his language is still the general speech, and american civilization is in its main principles anglo-saxon. The alternation of emotional indulgence in liberalist programmes (and anglo-saxon 'radicalist' is a newer and more heated liberalism, merely) and unintelligent race-prejudice, with which distressing see-saw we are so familiar, is anglo-saxon, is it not? Neither the Spanish, Portuguese nor French as colonists have handled their respective Melting-pot in that manner. The latin tradition, more tolerant, catholic and mature, has not sentimentalized about the deeply-pigmented skin, nor fixed upon it, on the other hand, a stigma. You would not be likely to get adepts of jazz in a Black Belt in a latin land nor the ferocity of lynching neighboured by anti-White tracts, written by Whites, nor a universal thunder of psalms from Black and White throats mixed, and evangelist extremes of intolerance and hysterical expansion – it would be more likely you would find a firmer attitude, more satisfactory to both sides, far less superstitious, in the Latin.

Yet, although it is necessary to fix, for any such survey, the anglo-saxon responsibilities, they are not all anglo-saxon, and the nationalism of Europe as a whole is to blame, I think, both for the excesses of the 'Nordic Blondes' or what Mencken calls the 'Ofays', where they do occur, and for the excesses of their satirists and detractors. Must we not agree that it is the artificial principle of european *separatism* (of all the Irelands, Ulsters, Catalonias, Polands, Czecho-Slovakias and the rest) transplanted to America or Africa, that, there, is apt to issue in a quite new form in a hot bed of separatist, or of fusionist, passion – which in the near future may wreck those societies as it is wrecking ours?

If (to show my enthusiasm for fusion) I may allow myself a strikingly *mixed* metaphor, it is at the fountain-head that we should establish our Melting-pot – an example to all other Melting-pots. And it is here in Europe that we should start a movement at once for the miscenegation of Europeans – with *each other*, that is – Asia and Africa could be considered later, no doubt, for incorporation in our Model Melting-pot.

I have dealt with this subject before, but in another connection, in *The Lion and the Fox*:[1] I would refer the reader to pages 295–326 of that essay. There the problem of the Melting-pot as it applies – or rather as it does *not* apply – to England, was discussed at length,

[1] 1927.

particularly as it concerns the 'Saxon' and the 'Celt'. The 'Celt', I there demonstrated, was a complete myth: and I showed how, with a great deal of wit, Matthew Arnold, who was probably aware of the shadowy nature of his 'Celt', staged an ironical drama for the John Bulls and Fenian Paddies of his time. I will quote a few lines from Chapter VI, Part IX, in which I lay bare the full working of Arnold's ironical vision. I say –

> From the treacherous polished surface of Arnold's prose (its body clouded for its reception) I will now expiscate that laughing idea which we have been preparing to examine. It is the idea of two island neighbours and strongly hallucinated brethren, the Irishman and the Englishman, the Celt and the Teuton (both in the baleful grip of 'celtism', which stands between them and success in science, or any exact, unemotional study), involved in a curiously fratricidal strife and tangle of romantic misunderstandings. . . . Arnold is not himself (*I add*) at all the dupe of the 'celtic' notion: his whole essay is written to expose it. Yet he accepts the conventional nomenclature of 'Celt' for all that type of expression and sentiment that had been popularized under that name.

And then I quote him, where he says, apropos of this famous 'Celtism':

> 'Nay, perhaps, if we are doomed to perish (Heaven avert the omen!) we shall perish by our Celtism, by our self-will and want of patience with ideas, our inability to see the way the world is going, and yet those very Celts, by our affinity with whom we are perishing, will be hating and upbraiding us all the time.'

It is generally forgotten that Ireland was colonized, especially in the east, by the Norsemen, norwegian being spoken in Dublin, as it was in Bristol, until the fourteenth century. That famous 'celtic' literary buccaneer, Mr Bernard Shaw, is no doubt a typical Norseman, as to stock at least. And in the essay from which I have just quoted I illustrated (page 322) the upshot of all this in the following fashion, from an average experience of my own which I am sure many people could match. Here is what I wrote:

> During the martyrdom of the Mayor of Cork I had several opportunities of seeing considerable numbers of Irish people demonstrating among the London crowds. I was never able to discover which were Irish and which were English, however. They looked to me exactly the same. With the best will in the world to discriminate the orderly groups of demonstrators from the orderly groups of spectators, and to

satisfy the romantic proprieties on such an occasion, my eyes refused to effect the necessary separation, that the principle of 'celtism' demanded, into chalk and cheese. I should have supposed that they were a lot of romantic english-people pretending to be irish-people, and demonstrating with the assistance of a few priests and pipers, if it had not been that they all looked extremely depressed and english-people when they are giving romance the rein are always very elated.

It is singular that from the time of Arnold's *Celtic Literature*[1] to that of *The Lion and the Fox* there should have been nobody in England to detect this colossal anomaly – there where there have been so many people to foment, or (upon the other side) to take quite seriously the Irish Separatist passion. The fact is that it has always paid the Irish individually too well, to allow them to laugh at it (though now that it is all over they are beginning to do so, witness Mr Bernard Shaw in his article in *Time and Tide*, Dec. 1928): and the english politician in every case found Ireland such an uncomfortable problem that he was in no mood to relish the farce that might lie hidden under these disturbances.

That will terminate for the present what I have to say upon this difficult subject. A Volapuc for Europe and an internationally organized 'Melting-pot', a general interchange of workers and of women or men, an official Marriage Bureau, with photographs and pedigrees and all those certificates that are indispensable in such a case – arrangements with the republics of America to adopt our particular Volapuc – that is the idea, in its brutal outline. I will not work it out further until I hear what response the public makes to my suggestions, not only because that would be otiose, seeing the passionate atmosphere of jingo ideology that prevails at the moment, but because I am not so well qualified as many other people to draw up a practical scheme. But I shall be extremely happy to get in touch with any experts who are so qualified, and to offer them what merely theoretic assistance lies in my power.

[1] 1866.

The Art of Being Ruled 1926

Although this remarkable work was published some years before Paleface, *it is inserted here, in drastically abbreviated form, for reasons partly logical and partly politic. Of the two books,* Paleface *is the more immediately readable. To have plunged into the present* magnum opus (*the other being* Time and Western Man) *without due softening up or propaedeutic of any kind, would have been unwise. Consequently, it occupies this central position in order to lend weight and equilibrium to a compendium necessarily miscellaneous.*

Even so, to drag into place so formidable a block of concentrated prose involved the use of strong grappling-irons, and of machinery for sinking deep shafts into rich strata. On account of the difficulty of the operation, and the need to consider how best to omit without destroying the sense of continuity, the editor was obliged to exercise repeated restraint. Yet it was felt that the presence of so much wealth, weight and sheer originality of thought, would alone justify the publication of the present volume.

Realizing how few people had read The Art of Being Ruled *in its entirety, Lewis was accustomed to quote freely from it in his later works. Meanwhile, he believed that, like some other books which evade the conventional categories, it would slowly create its own public.*

In his book Nobody Talks Politics, *published in 1933, Geoffrey Gorer confessed to finding Lewis a wholly negative writer. This was a period of ideological skirmishing and exclusive political labels. But the genius of Lewis was that of prognosis, which had as its precondition the perception of things as they were. A perusal of the following pages will convince most people that on point after point Lewis hit the nail on the head. For one thing, he analysed the collectivist-welfare-state and its ethos in advance. His opponents, who were many, fell into two classes: those who did not face what was coming, and those who, realizing what lay ahead, pretended that its inevitability was in itself sufficient guarantee that it would work to the advantage of mankind. Whereas Wells and Shaw were always 'prophesying', Lewis was always 'presenting'; and presentation is a bleaker, less self-indulgent, more honest exercise than prophecy, because it eschews all apocalytic emotions. 'I am not occupied with prophecy, but with things as they present themselves.' The humanism of Shaw and Wells ended in despair, the last condition of the ageing Utopian. Lewis, never having indulged in their dreams, was spared their rude awakening. He excelled in the brilliant aside, which always served to buttress the central argument. Consider the following:*

> It is the life of the human average whose destiny we are attempting to trace. The man or woman would have two lives, then as now. There would be the serious life of work — and *professionalism, in that section of his or her life, would be as prevalent as ever, and specialization manifest itself as jealously as now. And then, work done, there would be* the life of play. But *the first thing to notice is that, although it would still be called play, this part of life which all the cultural activities would be pressed would now be the* serious *part.*

The reader who pursues this passage will see his own world bathed suddenly in that searching fluorescent light whereby Lewis, dispensing with the romantic 'dome of many coloured glass', revealed the cold face of temporality.

Lewis examines the revolutionary mind — 'the dullest thing in the world'; science, which is 'in league with the feminine'; youth and age; the exploitation of sexuality — 'everywhere the non-sexual tends to become the sexual'; rich and poor and their increasing 'spiritual identity'; the burden of freedom — in short, the conditions of being subject to government, *whether of an enlarging bureaucratic machine, or of fabricated popular opinion whereby men live increasingly at second-hand. Despite the surgical skill with which he undertook his dissection, Lewis was no latter-day Machiavelli, as some have suggested. Neither was he a nihilist. In the Introduction, we have credited him with a religious cast of mind, which is in the true sense disillusioned; and he even argued that the religious intelligence alone might serve to promote genuine scientific advance.* He did not ignore the good in the world: what he contended was that 'whenever we get a good thing, its shadow comes with it, its ape or familiar'. And it was that 'affable familiar ghost'[1] which Lewis here attempted to lay.

PART I. REVOLUTION AND PROGRESS[2]

I. REVOLUTION

Social reform is today a very fluid, mercurial science. That is only to say, however, that it is a science: for what is there more fluid and constantly changing than science? And all varieties of political belief, the more outwardly they seem violently to differ, inwardly grow alike. They agree to differ in order to resemble each other, so that the more they ostensibly change, the more they are the same thing. And all serious politics today are revolutionary, as all science is revolutionary. If you stop to consider it, this must be so; for since politics and science are today commutative, it would be impossible for one of them to have this revolutionary character and not the other.

Every one today, in everything, is committed to revolution. But when unanimity on the subject of revolution – of one type or the other – has become complete, then there will be no more revolution! When everyone agrees to be, or is forced to be, a revolutionary, then a new equilibrium will have been reached. At present there are, however, very many people exerting great personal authority, who refuse so to regard politics and science as one and refuse to be revolutionary. And the mass of the people are, of course, as non-political as they are unscientific. They are essentially conservative and not revolutionary. That man is 'a political animal' is of course completely false; it is as false as Hobbes' remark that he is 'a fighting animal'. He is neither. It is only the wealthy, intelligent, or educated who are revolutionary or combative. The political battle of today is between those political leaders who are 'political animals',

[1] Sonnet 86.
[2] Chapters I–VI.

and those who are not (as prominent and successful men they are of course both 'fighting animals').

The revolutionary state of mind is then, today, instinctive: the *all that is is bad, and to be superseded by a better* attitude. In this attitude there is an inherent falsity: but it has the advantage of stereotyping a revolutionary state of mind. When we say 'science' we can either mean any manipulation of the inventive and organizing power of the human intellect: or we can mean such an extremely different thing as the *religion of science,* the vulgarized derivative from this pure activity manipulated by a sort of priestcraft into a great religious and political weapon. In which of these senses we are employing this word we must generally leave it to the reader to determine.

The word 'revolution', like 'civilization', is a big reverberating one. In most people's minds it is associated with the rolling of the tumbrils and the baying of the mob. It invariably also suggests the overthrow of the rich by the poor, or of a tyrant or oligarchy by the populace. It must of course have a much wider interpretation than this to include many things that are certainly revolutions, and often referred to as such.

'Revolution' can be used to describe even the superseding of one parliamentary party by another: it is commonly applied to any marked and important change, political, scientific and religious, involving to some extent a break with the past, as though something had been *skipped*. The Reformation was, for instance, a great revolution. In the Canisius Encyclical[1] it is described as a 'rebellion', which is popularly synonymous with 'revolution'. That, thanks to the energy of Luther, was a bloodless revolution as far as Germany went. The same religious disturbance in France was very bloody. Again Sorel quite justly describes the *affaire Dreyfus*[2] as a revolution. It was a great political event, marking a great change of ideas. People thought and felt after it quite differently from what they did before it. Therefore it was a revolution. The Great War was of course not a war, strictly speaking, in a nationalist or dynastic sense, but a revolution. It was a gigantic episode in the russian revolution. From one end of the world to the other there was nothing that was not changed by it.

Therefore, when the big reverberating word is used, armed

[1] After Peter Canisius (1521–1597).   [2] 1893–4.

proletarian revolt is not necessarily intended nor fascist violence. If the theory of the armed insurrection of the masses occupies our attention a good deal, that is because socialist theory deals so much with that: and any revolution today, just as it must be involved with science, must to some extent start from and be modelled on socialist practice. This applies as much to a fascist movement or putsch, as to anything else. Socialist theory is the school in which we all graduate. Mussolini was, to start with, a socialist agitator. And all *change* today is rooted in science: and in science and its imperative of change, all active political creeds meet and to some extent emerge.

Armed proletarian revolt is, then, the archetype of the dramatic and militant aspect that the change we term 'revolution' takes. Sorel defines so happily the true nature of 'revolution', that I cannot do better than quote him rather fully. The following passage is from *La révolution dreyfusienne*:

> In revolutions, two distinct periods should be distinguished. The first comprises the disturbances which have accompanied the overthrow of the old order – battles engaged without quarter and sometimes of a sanguinary nature, between the parties struggling for power, a legislation *de circonstance* and often ferociously partisan, designed to abolish completely the power of the vanquished. At this point an accumulation of episodes of a type familiar to professionals of political history are met with. These are far more exciting than those met with in ordinary times. Consequently, men adroit in the art of extracting from documents stories calculated to interest a wide public, in such a time find golden opportunities for exercising their address. It is quite natural that so many authors should be attracted by events enabling them to employ their talents in a profitable manner.
>
> Next comes the period of calm, of repression, of dictatorship. This appears so colourless, contrasted with the preceding phase, that often it has been asked whether the national genius had not exhausted itself in the superhuman effort required of it to suppress the old order. These times when political life seems so flat, do not interest the chroniclers of great feats. Even they find it difficult to believe that these times can belong to the same *ensemble* as the times of violent disturbance. It is consequently to these latter that commonly the name of 'revolution' is affected, because they alone seem to bear the imprint of the genius of innovation....
>
> So one must not expect to find necessarily bloody adventures analogous to those of 1793. In 1848, everything might have passed off peacefully enough, if, in June, the parisian proletariat had not believed itself strong enough to put into practice the theory of *the right to work* – which, the publicists of the time say, was to be the basis of

the new order. The workmen succumbed in the ensuing struggle; and the republicans thought it politic to treat them like the *grands ancêtres* had treated the nobility.

Historians attach an exaggerated importance to the acts of violence by which, often, a time of popular upheaval closes. The description of these events relieves them of the necessity for seeking out the true causes of the change that has occurred. The vanquished denounce, with fury, the *méchanceté* of the greedy, ambitious, unscrupulous people who have broken the laws to satisfy their passion for domination. The victors contend that they have saved the country from the most terrible disasters, and appropriate the title of *pères de la patrie*. In this way it happens that the true meaning of these events becomes obscured.

What is really essential is the transformation occurring in *the ideas* of the community. . . .

There always arrives a time when the people no longer are moved by the absurd hopes that had filled the hearts of the first makers of the revolution. These hopes, even, in the end, are denounced by all sensible people as 'dangerous illusions, likely to mislead'. So from hopes directed to the regeneration of mankind, one passes to a consideration of the practical methods required to realize some quite limited social amelioration. The day on which a considerable number of the principal actors in the revolutionary drama consider that their interests, their passions, their prejudices have received a reasonable satisfaction, any statesman who has a taste for wielding power can try his luck, with the best prospects of success.

That is a very good description of the phases of a violent political revolution: and there Sorel emphasizes the fact that an *exaggerated importance* is attached to *the acts of violence*. He shows throughout this curious essay how the revolution is always a revolution of ideas. So what Fouillée (*Humanitaires et libertaires*) says of the '*hommes à la cocarde*' or '*les violents*' does not in every sense apply to the author of *Réflexions sur la violence*. At all events, in the essay from which I have just quoted, it is for him *a change of ideas* that constitutes a revolution.

But an 'idea' is a very great force, or an *idée force*, as Fouillée would call it. And one idea cannot overcome another without violence, though it may not be the stupid violence of physical force. Where the society is very materialized or brutalized, and ideas have to plough their way too much, it is no doubt difficult not to resort to surgical means. Besides, a very brutalized society is not amenable to ideas at all, in the way that the French, for instance, as a nation have shown themselves to be. Personality takes the place of thought, and physical things of spiritual.

> Every idea (Fouillée says) is the conscious form taken by our feelings and impulses, every idea covers not only an intellectual act, but also a certain direction of the sensibility and of the will. As a consequence of this, in a society, as in an individual, every idea is a force, tending more and more to realize its individual end. Thus with the idea of race ... (1) a certain conscience of itself which a race develops and which gives it a sort of specific self in each of its members: (2) and a tendency to affirm more and more this (general, racial) *self*, at the expense of other races and in dominating them. *The idea of race* envelops, in other words, a conscience of race. Undoubtedly, for instance, a white man has the *idea* of the white race.

This is a summary by Fouillée of his well-known theory of the *idées forces*. Each white man has a 'white' ideological seed, so to speak, as part of his make-up. Those seeds can on occasion expand till they fill the whole creature, the white man becomes nothing but 'white'. It is then that he is a *walking idea*, and his force is the force of his *idea*. But classes of every sort, as well as races, produce these *idées forces*. And it is such an *idée force* that Marx recommended the world to exploit in order to emancipate itself. Or he recommended the development almost of a class 'complex'. What he said was that people should fill themselves from head to foot with the idea of class, of the under-class, swell with the idea of its numbers, its power, and its wrongs. And he believed that this mighty ideologic engine, once primed and ready, would necessarily explode in an immense gesture of violence. That is the marxian theory of the 'catastrophe'.

But this 'catastrophic' conclusion to the 'revolutionary' process is not only inessential; it distorts, and I think degrades as well, the notion of revolution. To say that people cannot change their souls (or a good part of them) without destroying their bodies, is a very material doctrine indeed. If people are only 'walking ideas', you can make them parade one as well as the other. 'Dying for an idea' again sounds well enough, but why not let the idea die instead of you? As people insist on dying with their ideas (as people have been known to insist on succumbing with their pets) in the hope, of course, of surviving in some mysterious way through them, they cannot be prevented from doing it; and it is difficult to advance any very good reason why they should be restrained, except that it must probably lead to an undesirable confusion of the mind and the body, which has already gone so much farther than is comfortable.

II. REVOLUTION ROOTED IN THE TECHNIQUE OF INDUSTRY

'That it (science) grows fast is indeed its commonest boast,' Prof. Santayana says. It changes too quickly for the normal mind to keep abreast of it and retain its independence. But any creative mind – and science is one of its products – is devilish in that sense.

Kautsky, in a passage I will quote at length, gives expression to the normal feeling of the danger and damage there is for the human mind in this obsession of a mechanical *betterment* – especially where it is misapplied:

> The economic revolution prepared by the epoch of discovery was perpetuated by the introduction of the machine into industry. From that moment our economic situation has been submitted to a continual changing. Everything ancient is rapidly disappearing, novelties succeed one another at short intervals. The old, the traditional, is ceasing to pass for guaranteed, respectable, intangible. It is becoming a synonym for the imperfect, the insufficient, the superannuated. This way of looking at things extends beyond economic life, to art, to science, to politics. If formerly we held to the ancient without examination, today we are willing to reject it without examination, simply because it is ancient; and the time required to age and put out of fashion a machine, an institution, a theory, a tendency in art, becomes ever shorter and shorter. And where formerly we worked with the consciousness of working for eternity, with all the devotion which this consciousness gives, today we work for the fugitive effect of a moment. We know this, and the work is lightly done. Also our products are not only quickly out of fashion, but they are in a short time effectively out of use.
>
> The new is what we notice first, what we study most thoroughly. The traditional ... seems quite natural. (*The Social Revolution.* K. Kautsky.)

'This way of looking at things,' Kautsky says, that is, the revolutionary way, that regards anything that *is* as provisional, for the day, and anything that belongs to the past as part of the *bilan* of error and failure that is human history, 'extends beyond economic life, to art, to science, to politics'. Of these four things that he mentions, it is only the first really that has any particular meaning. For it is purely science that is responsible for this revolutionary attitude, not it for that of science. In the case of art, on the other hand, far from this spirit extending to our way of regarding it, it is quite the contrary. It is only to contemporary movements in art that it could apply. They, it is true, are subjected to the mechanical betterment and the time valuation. It is really the fact that it is impossible to apply these mechanical betterment and time standards to pictures and architecture, that provokes a certain hostility and contempt where the arts are concerned, at least on the part of the small popularizing practitioners of science, and the superstitious public. And so politics today are revolution, quite simply.

Nevertheless, there remains some truth in the statement: for loosely, vaguely, and in the form of a habit, the mechanical betterment and the time valuation (in which the new and not the antique is the thing possessing prestige) is applied *à tort et à travers* indiscriminately, where it is logical to do so and where it is not.

In a book recently translated, of Edo Fimmen (*Labour's Alternative*), how revolution, in the widest sense, flows from modern technical progress is well brought out; he shows how the movement of unification is due to it. 'An important impulse towards the concentration of capital,' he says 'originates, nowadays, from the technical side. The methods of production are continually being improved, and, as a result of such improvements, extant machinery has to be scrapped and replaced by new.'

He then quotes from the first volume of *Das Kapital* to support his description of the 'revolutionizing influence exerted by technical advance'. I will reproduce this excellent summary by Marx:

> Modern industry never looks upon and treats the existing form of a process as final. The technical basis of that industry is therefore revolutionary, while all earlier modes of production were essentially conservative. By means of machinery, chemical processes, and other methods, it is continually causing changes, not only in the technical basis of production, but also in the functions of the labourer, and in the social combinations of the labour process. At the same time it thereby also revolutionizes the division of labour within the society, and incessantly launches masses of capital and of workpeople from one branch of production to another.

Fimmen then proceeds, on this text from Marx, to show how the system of commodity production was made possible by the invention of machinery; how machines have made individual energy and capacity unnecessary: how the earliest machines were resisted by those workmen rendered superfluous by their invention: and how today the employing class is as much affected by the drawbacks from a general human point of view of the scientific technical *ramp* as the employed. The methods of sabotage, the suppression of some new invention temporarily to slow down this 'killing pace' and so forth, he examines. Finally, he points out how nothing but an absolute elimination of competition, and gathering of the control into the hands of one vast concern can appease this force, and remove its inconveniences.

What he does not say is that, once this were effected, the pace would certainly slacken. Sabotage and slow-down would be the rule, the happy rule, not the anomaly. The senseless and outstripping speed of the merely mechanical and ingenious side of science would terminate, once its commercial utility had vanished with the disappearance of competition, either in a vast capitalist system or a vast socialist system.

The foregoing examples will suffice to show how *revolution*, as we understand, it today, is in origin a purely technical process. It is because our lives are so attached to and involved with the evolution of our machines that we have grown to see and feel everything in revolutionary terms, just as once the natural mood was conservative. We instinctively repose on the future rather than the past, though this may not yet be generally realized. Instead of the static circle of the rotation of the crops, or the infinite slow progress of handiwork, we are in the midst of the frenzied evolutionary war of the machines. This affects our view of everything; our life, its objects and uses, love, health, friendship, politics: even art to a certain extent, but with much less conviction.

That so much restlessness and dissatisfaction can be a matter of congratulation, as we began by saying, does not seem at first so obvious. The average man feels that he was not designed, as far as he can understand the purposes of his 'noble machine', to live in the midst of a fever of innovation. He may even momentarily entertain a doubt as to the perfectly beneficent character of science. It is conceivable that he may mutter to himself, on rare but ominous occasions, that *plus ça change, plus c'est la même chose*; that it 'all leads nowhere': that to live in a world where nothing matures, but everything is technically nipped in the bud, as it were, where everything shines like polished nickel and pretends to superhuman *pep*, is an outrage on his 'noble machine'. The complaint of Lord Tennyson's Lotus-Eater about 'for ever climbing up the climbing wave', 'Why should I toil alone, who am the roof and crown of things', etc., would seem to him to exactly hit off the disgust at length resulting from his industrial experiences. As he felt the dead weight, not of the atmosphere but of the capitalist system pressing on his soul in the proportion of six tons to the square inch, resolutely forcing down his wages for the hundredth time, such a frame of mind might shyly peep forth. Short of abandoning the dogma that he is the 'roof and crown of things', he must have lapses in which such misgivings see the light.

These misgivings are without foundation. Without this *technical* dissolvent that has come to the assistance of philosophy and religion, men would have ceased to criticize life, perhaps, and a sad stagnation would have been the result. To be able at last to have a technique that enables men to regard life itself as something *imperfect*, like a machine to be superseded, should far outweigh any temporary inconveniences, or even murderous absentmindedness, of science.

Science, in making us regard our life as a machine, has also forced us to be dissatisfied at its sloth, untidiness, and lack of definition, and gives us in our capacity of mechanics or scientists the itch to improve it.

Our life and personality, viewed as science obliges us to, is not *humanly* true or *personally* useful, any more than is the scarified, repellent picture of our skin under the microscope. Science makes us *strangers* to ourselves. Science destroys our personally useful self-love. It instals a principle of impersonality in the heart of our life that is anti-vital. In its present vulgarized condition science represents simply the principle of destruction: it is more deadly than a thousand plagues, and every day we *perfect* it or our popular industrially applied version of it.

If a new and presumably better machine should not put in its appearance to take the place of the old, then the work of science would be purely destructive. And again, unless life possesses what the author of *If Winter Comes* calls *One Increasing Purpose*,[1] then

[1] A. S. M. Hutchinson. These best-sellers of distinction were published in 1920 and 1925 respectively.

science is a supreme misfortune. It is only a religious intelligence, in short, that would be disposed to favour science.

Above, science was said to have made us regard our life as scientific or mechanistic, and to have *given us the itch to improve it*. The question is evidently how far it can be *improved* without radical transformation.

But radical transformation is what the most typical modern scientific thought envisages. 'Philosophy can only be an effort to transcend the human condition,' Bergson has said: and Nietzsche proposed some sort of biologic transformation no doubt with his super-man. Do you want to be a super-man? Do you want to be a god? That is the question! Does 'conscience' make cowards of us *all*, as Hamlet asserted?

III. CREATIVE REVOLUTION AND DESTRUCTIVE REVOLUTION

The difficulty attendant on such a task as the one here undertaken is, that to treat of anything permanent in a society with a sort of religion of impermanence imposed on it, is not easy. But there is no intention to counter (even if such a thing were possible, which it manifestly is not) that condition. To treat of permanent values and metaphysical truths is the natural useful task of a small number of men, and one chaos is much like another to them. If they take illustrations from chaos and destruction for the things they believe never are destroyed, that is natural enough, for that is all the landscape provides. Then there are two kinds of revolution: there is *permanent revolution*, and there is an impermanent, spurious, utilitarian variety. Much 'revolutionary' matter today is a mushroom sort, not at all edible or meant for sustenance. There is *creative revolution*, to parody Bergson's term, and *destructive revolution*. A sorting out or analysis is necessary to protect as many people as have the sense to heed these nuances. A great deal of the experimental material of art and science, for instance, is independent of any destructive function. Reactionary malice or stupidity generally confuses it with the useful but not very savoury chemistry of the Apocalypse.

The present is of course a particularly 'transitional' society: but the transit must take some time, as it must go all round the earth.

Animal conditions, practically, must prevail while this progress is occurring. We begin already to regard ourselves as animals. The machinery of the transit is the 'revolutionary' dogma daily manufactured in tons by the swarming staffs specially trained for that work.

The virtues that we are apt to confuse in our excessive officially promoted pragmatism are the *disruptive* and the *creative* ones: or rather, katabolism comes too much to be described as *life*. If I kill you, that is a different thing from giving birth to you.

In our society two virtues are badly contrasted, that of the *fighter* and *killer* (given such immense prestige by nineteenth-century darwinian science and philosophy) and that of the *civilizer* and *maker*. But the ancient and valuable iranian principle of duality is threatened. We confuse these two characters that we violently contrast. The effort in this essay is to separate them a little. It is hoped that certain things that have flown a grey and neutral flag will be forced to declare themselves as Ozman or Ahriman, the dark or the light.

Many 'reforms' that are daily launched are deliberately suited for the weak and staggering body for which they are destined. Like a sort of intellectual sabotage imitating the industrial, a great deal of scientific thought is deliberately slowed down, distorted, or even it may arrive that stones are offered in place of bread. Under the present system this cannot be avoided any more than other forms of sabotage.

It is desired, with reason, that ambitious building operations should not be undertaken. So it is that social reform is a very fluid, 'futuristic' science. You can be sure that every social innovation you are witnessing will be scrapped, probably loaded with contempt, and forgotten, tomorrow; or, if not, the next day. It is not there because it is pleasant, beneficent, or abstractly desirable, but solely because it is at the moment *useful*. It is almost always a weapon of war. Almost all our arts of peace are today disguised weapons, for the good reason that there is nowhere anything that could be described as peace.

The popular prestige of the clinic and the laboratory is lent to the revolutionary experiments in progress. So the habits of the laboratory, as well as the life history of machines, substitute themselves for the rhetoric and play of animal instinct. The functional conservatism of the animal is exchanged for the revolutionary experimentalism of research.

The decretals of the scientist are received with great popular reverence. This is surprising, seeing how fugitive and fashionable merely the fiats of the laboratories are now proved by experience to be. This in the long run must effect a new mentality in the person submitted to these constant deceptions – a kind of fashionable attitude to his own beliefs. This alone would either turn into intelligence, or, what is more likely, a disposition to regard his personality as discontinuous – the attitude of mind that a dog who had a new master every day might get. Each spasm of faithfulness would produce a new dog.

In such a fluid world we should by all rights be building boats rather than houses. But this essay is a sort of ark; or dwelling of the mind, designed to float and navigate; and we should all be wise, with or without covenants, to provide ourselves with some such shell in everything, rather than rely on any conservative structures. For a very complete and profound inundation is at hand. After *us* comes the deluge: more probably than not, however, before that, and out of it its epigrammatic sequence.

Meantime, we have a duty where the *officials of the Flood*, as they might be called, are concerned. We have to serve them out with gas-masks, light navigable craft of a seaworthy and inconspicuous type, and furnish them with instructions as to currents, winds, head-swells, maritime effluvia, Saragossa seas, doldrums, sharks, water-spouts, and sea-serpents. The complete equipment of an inspector of the Flood would be of such a technical description that it is impossible, however, to more than hint at it.

When Heine's english engineer had made his automaton, it 'gnashed and growled' in his ear, 'Give me a soul!' Naturally, being an english engineer, he had never thought of that, nor was he able to invent it. Someday we shall probably be confronted with some such harsh request. And we shall probably be as ill provided as was the english engineer. We should remember what we owe to our machines, which are our creatures. 'Remember the machines!' would be a good watchword or catchword. We are imbuing them with our own soullessness. We only have ourselves to thank if things turn out badly as a result. We brutalize them as the Senegalese and other native troops are brutalized by contact with our ruthless and too barbarous methods of warfare. But, as I have suggested above, in all likelihood the evolution of the machine will eventually be guided into more humane channels, when the destruction phase is past.

The modern 'soul' began, of course, in the Reformation. The most beautiful illustration of that birth (where you could almost observe it being born out of the bowels of the Venus de Milo) would be found within the anxious brain of Olympia Morata, the saintly blue-stocking of Ferrara.[1] There the classical learning and beauty of the ancient world bred, body to body with the Reformation, this strange child.

When Luther appealed for the individual soul direct to God, and the power of all mediating authority was definitely broken, God must have foreseen that he would soon follow His viceregents. The individual soul would later on, had he been God, have known very well that when he abandoned God, he would before long himself be abandoned. The mediator should have known that too. In any case this necessary triad has vanished. The trinity of God, Subject and Object, is at an end. The collapse of this trinity is the history also of the evolution of the subject into the object or of the child back into the womb from which it came. And the section entitled *Sub Persona Infantis*, later in this essay,[2] is a description of the raid back into the ideology of childhood of the mature 'bourgeois' world of today.

IV. THE 'PHANTOM MAN' OF DEMOCRATIC ENLIGHTENMENT

Intimately associated with the notion of *revolution* is the notion of *progress*. The origin of this latter notion is traced by George Sorel to the rise of monarchy in Europe. In his very interesting book on this subject (*Les illusions du progrès*) Sorel starts by indicating the generally accepted theory which places the origin of the idea of progress in the quarrel of the moderns and the classicists occurring in the last years of the seventeenth century. He justly remarks how strange or paradoxical it must seem to anyone today that a literary quarrel could have engendered such an idea. For no one today would be disposed to admit the existence of 'progress' where art is con-

[1] 1526–1555.   [2] Part VI.

cerned. In the one activity that in the most ways is excepted from the system of mechanical betterment applied to everything else, this very idea is said to have had its origin!

'Nothing seems to us more strange,' he says, 'than the bad taste of Perrault[1] systematically claiming for his contemporaries a higher place than that accorded to the great men of the Renaissance or of antiquity – preferring, for example, Lebrun to Raphael.'

Brunetière (whom Sorel largely follows) believed that the idea of 'progress' originated in two cartesian theses relative to science: one, that science is never separated from *practice*; and two, that science goes on indefinitely *growing*. Indeed, from an acceptance of these two theses Sorel admits it would be natural to proceed (in applying them to the political or social world) to the belief in an *indefinite progress* for society too. But he prefers to reverse this explanation in a sense. When the notion of 'progress' first took shape, the political world was of such very great importance, and the idea of the monarchy enjoyed such great prestige, that it is more likely, he thinks, that the idea of 'progress' came from a contemplation of the kingly power, rather than from the notions of the stability of natural laws popularized by Fontenelle.[2]

The governments of the new monarchical model, even in the time of Descartes, with their centralized power and regular administration, could give effect, with great exactitude, to all their wishes. They could realize the stipulated physical union, in fact, of theory and practice. The grandiose dreams of the political primitives of Italy of the machiavellian type had become astonishing realities. The kingly power, in its culmination in such a figure as that of *le roi soleil*, dazzled everybody so much, its success seemed so stable and assured, and it seemed automatically increasing with the predictable acceleration of a law of nature, that it must have been from that, rather than from the new triumphs of natural science, that men got their idea of 'progress'. Sorel even suggests that Galileo perhaps derived his interest in the laws of gravitational acceleration from the type of constant force presented by the monarchy, with its power swelling under his eyes every day.

Instead of the gay, 'enlightened' notion of 'progress' coming to

[1] 1628–1703, instigator of the quarrel between the Ancients and the Moderns, but better known for his Fairy tales.
[2] 1657–1757.

birth in the eighteenth-century aristocratic world, such people as George Sorel or Lenin would have a gravity and pessimism much nearer to the religious mind than of the light-hearted, secular, pagan European. Their way of envisaging the problems that the idea of 'progress' was invented to meet would imply a static conception of the world, or of the world's mind, rather than a 'scientific' and evolutionary one. Their 'progress' would be a discipline and adjustment. Nor would it admit the whole, unregenerate human family on equal terms, as a jolly party of friends, with the humbug ensuing from such a notion.

In the contemplation of a partly latent political power (beside which the power of a Louis XIV would seem indeed a pigmy) rather than in science, a Galileo today could find support, no doubt, for even more formidable physical laws.

Bound up with the idea of progress is the democratic conception of social unification. It is this idea of *unification* inseparable from 'democracy' that Sorel, the syndicalist, is principally concerned to attack and if possible destroy.

Democracy has for its principal object (both according to the revolutionary school to which Sorel belonged, and equally according to leninism) the disappearance of the class feeling. The idea is to *mix* all the citizens of a given society into one whole, in which the most intelligent would automatically 'better themselves' and rise, by their talents, into the higher ranks. Such *social climbing* would be of the essence of this democratic society. The real social classes are, for the syndicalist, occupational classes or syndics, of course. 'Class' in the bourgeois sense is an abstract abomination. In following for a little the main line of the syndicalist we shall be arriving at one of the most interesting critical points where class is concerned in recent socialism. At the bottom of the syndicalist idea is the wish for a caste system. This is not explicit in the syndicalist doctrine: nor is, I had better add, much of the interpretation I am about to provide.

Europe has had 'classes', Asia 'castes'. The 'free' European has always been a *gentleman* for himself, through all his intermittent slavery. His power of self-deception has been very remarkable; all the realities of hard labour and subordination were replaced by a rosy abstraction of 'freedom'. 'Nosotros somos todos caballeros aqui!',[1] mixing his chivalry with his democracy, he would exclaim. Syn-

[1] 'We are all gentlemen here.'

dicalism is non-European in that sense. It would aim at breaking up this *abstract* dream, and abstract classification based on the unreality of 'freedom'.

Against the finished product of scientific popularization syndicalism also raised itself. The neat, simplified, *abstracted* truth, prepared for the democracy, it regarded as pernicious. It is that abstract machinery that manufactures the *abstract man* of democracy, the great european make-believe.

The *bourgeoisie* who seized the power at the Revolution concocts this abstraction now (before, it was the aristocratic *salon* who concocted it, or had it concocted). And by means of it the bourgeoisie imposes its galb[1] on the mind of the worker, so that he becomes a little bourgeois. But democratic ideals hold up to the workman images of a life that is not his, and to which he can never belong. He remains an eternal spectator – other people, the bourgeoisie, act his life for him, out of reach. He has no imaginative life of his own.

For this *up* and *down*, this *higher* and *lower*, this *betterment* of 'progress' and democratic snobbery, with its necessary unification into a whole, suppressing of *differences* and substituting for them an arbitrary scale of values, with the *salon* at the top, the syndicalist would substitute an equally dogmatic egalitarian *this* and *that*, a horizontal diversity.

If you are a pro-specialist to the extent that the syndicalist is, you will naturally not regard the phenomenon of vulgarization with favour. This *abstract* of truth or knowledge, this thin miniature pretended cosmos, over-simplified till it becomes meaningless, is a self-indulgent pretence not worth having. It makes a society of little sham gods, or know-alls (*Je sais tout* is the name of one of their organs). Everyone in this sense becomes a phantom man, namely *l'homme éclairé*.

This *homme éclairé* is nothing at all – he is not a bootmaker, an engineer, a carpenter, or a doctor. He is a man-of-fashion really, if he is anything – a man of conversation. And his habitat is the *salon* or fashionable, and at the same time intellectual, dinner-table. What has the hard-working country doctor, the busy engineer or bootmaker, to do with this strange figure of aristocratic leisure, senseless 'curiosity' and loquacity? Nothing at all. Then why be 'vulgarized' in that way, as though you and he were not yourself?

[1] blarney or humbug.

The cultural, 'all-round' personage (the ideal of the vulgarizer and of democracy) is the opposite of the narrow class-man, or, better, caste-man, the narrow *occupational* mannequin, the narrow integral self-effaced unit of the syndic. The bootmaker (for the theorist of syndicalism) must have only bootmaking thoughts. No godlike, *éclairé*, gentlemanly thoughts must interfere with his pure, sutorial one-sidedness – thoughts that in any case he would get all upside down, never have any time to properly enjoy, and which only make him absurd and diminish his utility; whereas, sticking to his last, he could be as 'noble' as any noble (the 'nobility of toil'), a figure like a sistine prophet, at his best. Contrasted with him, the courtier 'skipping nimbly in a lady's chamber to the lascivious pleasing of a lute' is far less grand, infinitely less to be respected or admired.

The majority of men should, and indeed must, be screwed down and locked up in their functions. They must be functional specialists – the doctor smelling of drugs, the professor blue-spectacled, bent and powdered with snuff, the miner covered with coal-dust, the soldier stiff and martial, etc. etc. The only person who can be an 'all-round' man, *éclairé*, full of scepticism, wide general knowledge, and 'lights', is the ruler: and he must be that – that is *his* specialization. This is naturally not the way that the syndicalist puts it. But it is what is implied in the political system of Sorel and the other syndicalists.

Now, if we were dealing in dreams, in impossible people instead of people as they are found in their daily life, we could argue with success, perhaps, against the syndicalist that people are *happier* when they are (although nailed down to their technical occupation) *imagining themselves something they are not*. It is perhaps in the Madame Bovary in everybody that is to be found the true source of human happiness. People like to have a dream or hope: to think they can 'rise in the world', become a 'Bourgeois Gentilhomme', or even perhaps, with very great luck indeed, a little noble. If you told them that this was very absurd and snobbish, they would perhaps reply that it is no more absurd than anything else in life, than remaining boxed down, for instance, in the specializations of some trade. Most men, again, do not really love their 'shop' so much that they *never* want to get out of it.

In this way you could represent this abstract region of useless but enlightened, sceptical, romance (to which democratic vulgarization admitted *everybody*) as the organization of a happiness that is a permanent invariable factor in the human make-up. The 'gentleman', the superb, unreal invention of the European, might seem worth preserving. It might even seem that the European must sink politically when he gave it up.

If people needed discipline less than they do, not more; if they were not so disposed to take advantage of these godlike conditions offered, even, only vicariously, and all wanted to be gods more than the resources of human life, and the patience or jealousy of men, will support (and so on with the tale of the reality of life and human nature): then, perhaps, these arguments would be true. But unfortunately they cannot meet these hostile requirements, forced on every one by experience.

V. THE OPPRESSIVE RESPECTABILITY OF 'REVOLUTION'

If ours is an 'already revolutionized society', it is very imperfectly so. We are in the position of impatient heirs, waiting for a long-expected demise, torn between pious concern for the poor sufferer, and anxiety, since now nothing can avert the catastrophe (which we hope will be a 'peaceful end'), to get on with our business.

This situation accounts for the fact of a certain anomaly where the 'revolutionary' tendencies in this 'revolutionized' but still formally traditional society are concerned. 'Revolution' is accepted everywhere, the battle is everywhere won, and yet nothing happens. When it does happen, as in Russia or Italy, no one can pretend that things are changed enough to meet our expectations.

'Revolution' today is taken for granted, and in consequence becomes rather dull. The Heir of all the Ages (as everyone is quite ready to admit that he is, and indeed it would be quite impossible to deny that he is an *heir*) stands by the death-bed – penniless. The immensely wealthy society, at its last gasp, lies gazing listlessly across the counterpane, staring at a Pom, which stares back at him. The evening comes, the day has been spent in idleness. The Heir of all the Ages retires to his garret at the neighbouring inn. The bulletin is issued, *No change*.

Revolutionary politics, revolutionary art, and oh, the revolutionary mind, is the dullest thing on earth. When we open a 'revolutionary' review, or read a 'revolutionary' speech, we yawn our heads off. It is true, there is nothing else. Everything is correctly, monotonously, dishearteningly 'revolutionary'. What a stupid word! What a stale fuss!

A really good, out-and-out 'reactionary' journal is, at first, like a breath of fresh air in the midst of all this turbulent, pretentious, childish optimism. A *royalist* publication is worth its weight in gold. Catholicism, we feel, is essential to our health. We fly to the past – anywhere out of this suspended animation of the so smugly 'revolutionary' present. Out of the detestable crowd of quacks – *illuminés*, couéists, and psychologists – that the wealthy death-bed has attracted, and who throng these ante-chambers of defeat; from all the funeral-furnishers, catafalque-makers, house-agents, lawyers, moneylenders, with their eye on the Heir of all the Ages, we fly in despair.

But the 'Reactionary' (a sort of highly respectable, genteel quack, as well, with military moustaches and an aristocratic bearing) is even more stupid – if that were possible – than the 'Revolutionary'. We listen to him for a moment, and he unfolds his barren, childish scheme with the muddle-headed emphasis of a very ferocious sheep. He lodges in the garret next to us at the inn, and is in arrears with the rent. The servants (who are all the reddest of revolutionists, of course) hate him. The Reactionary, in the long run, does not add to the cheerfulness of the scene.

This aspect of 'revolution', its increasing respectability, is well brought out by Kautsky in *Social Revolution*. He contrasts the difficult position of a 'revolutionary' formerly, in the *salons* of the *bourgeois*, and the very different position today. The 'revolutionary' of yesterday would at present find himself in the tamest situation, surrounded by a benevolent welcome everywhere he went, Kautsky shows. Indeed, he would find nothing but 'revolutionaries' everywhere. At the millionaire's table, in the millionaire's press, as in the cabman's shelter or the labour journal, he would find nothing but the most respectable and discouraging conformity to his eager beliefs. If he were incorrigibly desirous of experiencing the 'revolutionary' thrill and of tasting the rude delights of the outcast, it would be – oh, strangest of paradoxes! – in being *unradical* alone that he could hope to find it.

Formerly, it is true, when, even with the majority of cultivated people, socialism was regarded as a crime, as a madness, a *bourgeois* could only embrace socialism by breaking with the whole of his world. The man who under these circumstances abandoned the ranks of the bourgeoisie to join the ranks of the socialists had to be possessed of an energy, a passion, and a revolutionary conviction much more intense than that required by a workman engaging in the same revolutionary path.

It is a very different thing today: socialism is accepted in the *salons*, there is no longer any need of any particular energy, it is no longer necessary to break with *bourgeois* society, in order to bear the name of 'socialist'.

That is 'official' revolution, as it could be called. It is today everywhere obligatory, just as evening dress has become more or less obligatory, at the same time, in our society. Everyone who has money enough is today a 'revolutionary'; that and the dress suit are the first requisites of a gentleman. There are also a great many unemployed who naturally also are revolutionaries, sharing to the letter their revolutionary opinions with their prosperous brother iconoclasts. It is this that it would be well perhaps to break with a little, unless we are going to die of *ennui*. Things have gone so far with 'Revolution', it is becoming so palpably, dogmatically, wearisomely, and insolently 'top dog', that it may some day even have to be rescued from poor old 'Reaction'.

VI. THE NON-IMPERSONALITY OF SCIENCE

In Chapter IV we saw how vulgarization is not the indiscriminate scattering of *truth*, but the organizing and adapting of certain chosen *truths*, or discoveries, of philosophy or science, to an ultimately political end. The ideology of a time (ideology is Napoleon's word for the metaphysics of government) is that of the contemporary ruling class. So the finished product of scientific vulgarization is not an inhuman, objective bundle of pure scientific truth, but a personally edited bouquet or bundle, with a carefully blended odour to suit the destined palate.

But here we arrive at one of the most significant delusions of the present time, to which in passing we must devote some attention. The popular notion that science is 'impersonal' is one of the first errors we are called on to dispel. The *non-impersonality* of science should at all cost be substituted for the idea of its impersonality.

Science in itself, to start with, when it first began its revolution, was a force of nature sure enough: a thing and not a person. But this impersonal thing men have now got hold of and harnessed, to a great extent. So pure science is one thing; its application another; and its vulgarization a third.

One of the most ridiculous effects of the vulgarization of science and the application of its methods, *à tort et à travers*, to human life, is what could be defined as *the belief in anonymity*. From this many absurdities result. First of all the man of science himself begins to believe in it. He believes that he *is not a person*, that he is *not human*, that he is some way a part of nature. Then, through admiring this 'scientific detachment' and 'impersonality' so much, Tom, Dick and Harry begin to believe that *they*, too, are not *persons*, not *human*. A man (a quite ordinary man, not a man of science) will stand in front of another man (who knows him quite well and all about him) and pretend that he is not himself, that he is 'impersonal', that he is incapable of any emotions, appetites, or prejudices: that he cannot be angry, partial, offended, jealous, or afraid. And the strangest thing is that he *is believed*.

This delusion of impersonality could be best defined as that mistake by virtue of which persons are enabled to masquerade as *things*.

A simple belief in the 'detachment' and 'objectivity' of science, the anxiety of a disillusioned person to escape from his self and merge his personality in *things*; verging often on the worship of *things* – of the non-human, feelingless, and thoughtless – of such experiences and tendencies is this delusion composed. Its godlike advantages from the point of view of a hundred different classes of people are obvious.[1]

PART IV. VULGARIZATION AND POLITICAL DECAY[2]

I. THE COMPETITION OF THE 'SMALL MAN'

Giant Trusts and Cartels everywhere, at the present time, as they coalesce, approach the economic pattern of the soviet state. Whether

---

[1] The last three paragraphs of the chapter are omitted.
[2] Chapters I–VI.

the trust-king is a highly salaried servant (as Lenin said he should be, if proved to be the most efficient organizer), or a capitalist magnate (when these chiefs become fewer and fewer, as they do every day), does not particularly matter. The enemy of unification today is everywhere the 'small man'. The irrepressible village *kulak* is the typical russian 'small man'; in the West the small retailer and middle-man. This small representative of the remnant of 'free' barter and 'open competition' in our society is the real obstacle to a radical reform of human conditions. It is he who is rightly the *bourgeois* of the revolutionary tract.

The little shopkeeper has never been anybody's darling until today. In the past he has always been an object of contempt and usually of derision: the little, 'moneygrubbing', mean, smooth, soft-living, over-practical product, today he represents 'the old order'. The 'big business' celebrated in fiction by Zola in *Au Bonheur des Dames* – crushing out of existence the small rival in its neighbourhood – did not, in fact, do anything of the sort. Vandervelde's statistics point quite the other way. There are every day more, not less, small businesses. Their tenure is a precarious one, certainly. But they continue to spring up impassibly. They live a harassed, uncomfortable life; but that does not seem to discourage them from irrepressibly springing up everywhere. As soon as one has gone bankrupt, two more take its place.

It is difficult to regard the small grocer as a very sympathetic figure, nevertheless. He is 'human', it is true, where the salaried slave of the big 'business', or the bureaucrat, is a 'machine'. Whether he is 'too human', or not quite 'human' enough, is a dispute into which we need not enter. At all events, his humanity is of the sort that could be spared. But if that is true of him concretely, it is very much more the case when you consider the system that he represents. It is not even accurate to compare him with the master craftsman, or the small creative worker who was his own master, of the Middle Ages. He is *toto cœlo* different to that admirable figure.

What the small tradesman really represents, where his own personal occupation is concerned, is a more recent principle than that, or in the spiritual context of our lives a much older one. He is the emblem of the 'small man', with his small lawless, egotistic competition, throughout the ages. What he competes with is not his own kind, but a power superior to his own and an intelligence to his own. It is the upper crust of *nature* and chaos, as it were, *organized*. He is protected in his lawless war by the very 'civilization' against which he struggles, and which he himself would have been powerless to invent.

What is it that always brought to nothing the work of the creative mind, and made history an interminable obstacle race for the mind which would otherwise be free? Precisely the competitive jealousy of this famous 'small man', with his famous 'independence' – snobbish, 'ambitious', very grasping, considering himself better than the plain workman; making an unreal, small *middle-world*, or no-man's land, from which his vanity and uselessness can bite at and checkmate those above him, and exploit those beneath him. He is not only the enemy of a unification of the intelligent forces of the world; he is the symbol of what has always held back our race, held up all that challenged his self-sufficiency and small conservatism. It is his small superiority, egotistic 'independence', smugness, assertiveness, and uselessness, preying (above and below him) on anything that was creative, that has been the cause of human society losing, not gaining, by its efforts. His 'little touch of nature' does not compensate for that record!

We do not any longer want the competition of the 'small man'. The human race, anxious to be free to create, has had enough of this precious 'small man' and his small ways for ever! His clamour for 'freedom' is for *his* freedom, not ours: freedom to live on the creative work around him, to interfere with his betters with the power he gets from cheating his betters underneath: for he has 'betters' underneath him, and 'betters' above him. To be fair to him, this may not precisely be his situation today, very luckily for everyone concerned. But he and his 'freedom', and his small competitive instincts, symbolize an entire and very widely distributed human type, which (whatever else it does, or does not, do) the great unified machine will get rid of for us. It is rather as a unit of spiritual life, than as a unit of economic life, that I have been considering the 'small man'. But the one is not independent of the other. In every phase of life, social, economic, or political, there is the 'small man', with his small hard 'independence' that nothing about him justifies, with his small competitive push, entrenched in the forms and conventions of polite life, calling himself 'civilization', and defying the elements on the one hand, and the human mind (that has created him for its sins) on the other.

II. THE DEMOCRATIC *EDUCATIONIST STATE*

In the democratic western countries so-called capitalism leads a saturnalia of 'freedom', like a bastard brother of reform. With its *What the Public Wants* doctrine it enervates the populations. It is now, when crushed with debt and threatened with every form of danger, without and within, that the western countries are led in the great cities into a paroxysm of display and luxury. And the papers that call them to it with their massed advertisements admonish them on another page, which is quite safe because they know it will be unheeded.

It is not that, however, that need occupy us, for this contrast between our present growing beggardom and rapidly declining assets and our increasing splendour of appointment and personal display is a commonplace of our time. It is rather where the great system of *What the Public Wants* apes the system that is destined to supersede it, in all that wide, scientized field of 'progressive' vulgarization, social debate, social change arriving in half measures and strangely arbitrary compromises, that it is necessary to scrutinize it. And, to start with, the whole principle of vulgarization, on which we have already touched, must be briefly related to the ground we have already covered.

Education consists, of course, of a decade of soaking in certain beliefs and conventions. The jesuits considered that the first six years of life sufficed. However this may be, it is of course a soul, and not knowledge, that education signifies. It is character-stimulus, and actually the reverse of mind-stimulus, that popular education sets out to provide.

All education begins with reading and writing; and it is principally by means of reading that the 'education' gradually comes. At a certain age the work is done, not where the jesuit fixed it, for character only, but somewhere in the first years of adult life. It is rarely afterwards that the hard-working clerk, engineer, doctor, or mechanic has leisure or opportunity to supplement this basis of teaching. But even if he has, he seldom has the energy on his own account, to modify what has been imposed on him. The contemporary European or American is a part of a broadcasting set, a necessary part of its machinery. Or he is gradually made into a newspaper-reader, it could be said, rather than a citizen.

The working of the 'democratic' electoral system is of course as follows. A person is trained up stringently to certain opinions; then he is given a vote, and called a 'free' and fully enfranchised person; then he votes (subject, of course, to new and stringent orders from the press, where occasionally his mentor commands him to vote contrary to what he has been taught) strictly in accordance with his training. His support for everything that he has been taught to support can be practically guaranteed. Hence, of course, the vote of the free citizen is a farce: education and suggestion, the imposition of the will of the ruler through the press and other publicity channels, cancelling it. So 'democratic' government is far more effective than subjugation by physical conquest.

In a very small percentage of cases better brains and good social opportunities enable a person to extricate himself from this ideologic machine. Like a mammal growing wings, he exists thenceforth in another and freer element. But this free region is not conterminous with the arts and sciences; and free spirits do not, as is popularly supposed, inhabit the bodies of men of science or artists. For art and science are the very material out of which the law is made. They are the suggestion; out of them are cut the beliefs by which men are governed. And the teacher is usually as much a dupe as the learner.

So what we call conventionally the *capitalist state* is as truly an *educationalist state*.

The sporting training of the Englishman and the American makes him into a fighting machine. Even his military training is disguised as sport. This Robot is manipulated by the press. By his education he has been made into an ingeniously free-loving, easy-moving, 'civilized', gentlemanly Robot. At a word (or when sufficiently heated by a week's newspaper-suggestion), at the pressing of a button, all these hallucinated automata, with their technician-trained minds and bodies, can be released against each other. And if a war only lasts four or five years, it is something to be thankful for; since it could easily be prolonged to a hundred years, and these machines, and new ones constantly turned out on the same pattern, would never go back on the lessons they had learned so well, until the last man fell, gallantly resisting 'the enemy'.

Within ten years England would be at war with Scotland, mad as that may sound at first sight, if the propaganda and educational channels received orders to that end. If you believe that it would be impossible to stir up on either side of the scottish border 'race' feeling, through ten years, by acrimonious chatter in the press, frictions, small acts of violence and reprisals, appeals to history and its old feuds, patriotism and clanism, so that in the end it culminated in war, you are certainly mistaken. The organization of suggestion and the power of education are so perfect today that nothing, given a little time, is impossible. When the vast populations of Asia have been similarly organized, athleticized, introduced to 'sport', trained as boy-scouts and asiatic 'guides', the same will apply to them: the Japanese being for Asia what I have said Russia and Italy are for us.

All this great power in the hands of people whose intentions were charitable, not wicked, and they would instantly make, with all the resources of modern science, a paradise of the earth! The Utopia of the philosophers would then come true. When the present many-sided revolution is complete and world-wide, and competition no longer exists between rival groups of exploiters, that state of affairs should be a reality. But between then and now much water will flow under the bridges of the Thames, Seine, Spree, Danube, Manzanares, Liffey, Clyde, Tiber, and Hooghly. And unless mankind hastens to its unification under one unique control, far too much blood will flow with it.

III. CAUSES OF EUROPEAN DECAY

We have given as a capital reason for the political weakness of Europe the notion of individual freedom, as opposed to the greater solidarity of a community 'working together' under a centralized consciousness and despotic, or at all events very powerful, control. Yet in the last chapter we have shown how illusory this 'independence' must in practice be. But the confusion is not so real as it would seem. It is rather the *notion* of freedom than the fact of freedom that is, of course, in question; and it is just that idle pretence that is so wasteful and disorganizing. It is, in short, the aristocratic temper of the achaian Greeks extended and caricatured by vast numbers of people. The aristocratic liberties of the dominant race in a small city state applied to the whole white population of Europe has led to the *impasse* of white 'democracy'. And white, european democracy is, of course, an aristocratic notion at bottom, for it is a *race* notion: all caste, of course, of that sort originating in the fact of race.

Why Europe has never had a religion of its own (and that is naturally another great source of weakness, as weakness in 'mystery' in the long run spells political weakness) is because of the ascendance and persistency of this secular, aristocratic, græco-roman tradition that has fixed the European in a pagan, personal, non-religious mould. Let us exaggerate the circumstances of this so as to lay bare a sort of subterranean ideologic stream whose presence is usually only revealed by a sort of misty snobbishness. The nineteenth-century John Bull, we then can say, was the proud, aristocratically minded person he was because the migratory Achaian or Dorian was of divine race, or imposed himself as such on the subject population. The heroic demi-god of the homeric saga was the distant exemplar of the 'beer-drinking Briton' who could 'never be beat'.

It may be as well to go for a moment into the relation between class and race in the formation of the former. The *classes* that have been parasitic on other classes have always in the past been *races*. The class-privilege has been a race-privilege. Every white man until recently has been in possession of a race-privilege where other races of other colours were concerned, which constituted the white man as a *class*. The privilege was never developed to the extent that the achaian race-privilege of the athenian citizen, for example, was. But in a general way it formed part of the consciousness of the white man. Cleanliness was next to godliness, and whiteness was the indispensable condition of cleanliness. So to be a chosen people was to be a white people.

This class element in *race* expressed itself in the application of the term 'lady', for instance, to the most modest citizens of the anglo-saxon race. The *lady* in *char-lady* is a race-courtesy title. It is a class title that it was possible for her to exact on the score of race. This rudimentary fact very few poor whites have understood. They have been inclined to take these small but precious advantages for granted, as indicative of a *real* superiority, not one resulting, as in fact it did, from the success of the organized society to which they belonged. They have confused class with race – somewhat to their undoing.

Today race and colour are as distinctive features as ever: and it is unlikely in the future that *race* will cease to play its part in the formation of class – as again, many simple white people will discover to their great chagrin. But the character of our civilization, as defined by the great discoveries of modern science, with their unifying effect, must tend very rapidly not only to world-wide standardization, but to racial fusion. Or rather, this must be the consequence of the new conditions, unless this process is artifically held up, and national idiosyncracies and differences artificially preserved and fostered, as with the jesuits in the territories they controlled in South America, each tribe locked up in its tribal district or reduction, and friendly intercourse of any sort between the various tribes prohibited.

That most fundamental of all questions for us, namely, War and Peace, is dependent on these questions of class and race. If there were not today communities with an exclusive race-consciousness (with or without sacred books, and the theologic paraphernalia of race), the future of *class*, too, would be much more precarious than it in fact is. The people of the United States are or have been the nearest to an egalitarian ideal because they are the most racially mixed: this in spite of all the simple jokes to the contrary.

But even if race were abolished by intermixture, it would still be possible, of course, to get your class-factor, and with it your organized war, by way of sex, age, occupational and other categories. 'The intensity of organization is increased', as Mr Russell points out, 'when a man belongs to more organizations.' The more classes (of which, in their various functions, he is representative) that you can make him become regularly conscious of, the more you can control him, the more of an automaton he becomes. Thus, if a man can be made to feel himself acutely (a) an American; (b) a young American; (c) a middle west young American; (d) a 'radical and enlightened' middle-west young American; (e) a 'college-educated', etc. etc.; (f) a 'college-educated' dentist who is an etc. etc.; (g) a 'college-educated' dentist of such-and-such a school of dentistry, etc. etc. the more inflexible each of these links is, the more powerful, naturally, is the chain. Or he can be locked into any of these compartments as though by magic by any one understanding the wires, in the way the jesuit studied those things.

To return to the question of the race origin of caste-feeling, the notion of the 'gentleman' as we call it today is a race notion, originating in such things as roman citizenship and its universal aristocratic privileges. The most absurd as well as degrading spectacle that this notion has ever provided was when the roman citizen, in fact, was in question in the time of the Empire. All the wealth and power of the roman state passed more and more into the hands of the alien freedmen. The Roman began rapidly to die out (the custom of child-exposure contributed largely to this), and grew daily more impoverished. But the client-system kept those that remained just alive. The procedure of the allotment of food for the *sportula*[1] of the client, and all the rest of the humiliating life of charity of the latest Romans, was carefully organized. So it came about that living as a numerous class of decayed gentility in the midst of the luxury and wealth of imperial Rome were most of the true Romans. One emperor shipped a hundred thousand or so of them off to some colony. But there were still a good number of these proud, ragged remnants of republican Rome (or of cultivators of the surrounding land of original italian stock driven to the city by the introduction of foreign slave-labour on the *latifundia*[2]) remaining.

Class always takes with it the idea of race, then, and of some distant or recent conquest. How the notion of political personal freedom has spelt *weakness* in the end for Europe (so that it is not at all too much to say that that is the principal cause of its present decline) is that it is by way of this notion, through this gate, that all the disintegrating tendencies have entered.

IV. THE MISUSE OF THE INTELLECT

The great men of science of China, Babylon, or Egypt thought their thoughts and proceeded with their researches in spite of an entire absence of such conditions as makes Einstein's name, ten days after an astronomical success, broadcast all over the world, and his relativity theory painfully popularized for the toiling, tired, unleisured millions. What's in a name, if a workman is allowed to work? All

[1] Dole. [2] Large agricultural estates.

any true scientist or true artist asks is to be given the opportunity, without interference, indifferent to glory, to *work*. And it is just the popularization and vulgarizing of art that is responsible for the inumerable swarms of dilettante competitors who make of every art a trifling pastime, so that it is impossible for the rest of the world to regard that occupation as a serious one, seeing into what sort of hands it has fallen. So it would certainly be the redemption of art, and it would no doubt have the effect of protecting, and actually of encouraging, science, if they were both removed from the wide, superficial, 'democratic' (that is, aristocratic) playground, and reinstated as a mystery or a craft.

You could not get a better example than this of how much of the intelligent organization of the soviet authorities, because of its novelty and challenge to the old playful 'democratic' notions of the European, is misrepresented. They have taken in this respect the wisest and sanest step where both art and science are concerned, in curtailing the impossible freedom of art, and discouraging the people from gaping incessantly for new and disturbing novelties of science. For this they are blamed – by the playboy of the western world, not by the true man of science or the artist.

The 'freedom' of the last century or so has from any point of view been of a very remarkable nature. There was something about it that should have aroused misgivings in those, sometimes with too little measure or reticence, naively benefiting by it. For it was surely, from their point of view, 'too good to be true.' It certainly contrasted very strongly with the conditions under which people lived at the time of the religious struggles of the Renaissance and the Reformation.

The opinions and discoveries of the most 'advanced' of mankind, of the learned and splendid few, were thus made available for a mass of people (whom these opinions and discoveries reached in a garbled, sensational, and often highly misleading form) who were themselves, as they still are today in mental equipment and outlook, savages – only, savages degenerating rapidly under the influence of their own 'civilization'. They very naturally made of this mass of (for them, unequipped and unprepared) highly exciting, dangerous, and difficult matter what they had formerly made of the teaching of Christ. These theoretic, purely scientific, and aloof researches they transformed into some sort of weapon or tool at once, to get at food with, or sanctimoniously rip up their neighbour: the most disinterested idea became, in their hands, a pawn in the practical system of their life. As a doctor's scalpel might make an excellent dagger, or the axle of a car a good enough club, so most of these discoveries suggested some violent and destructive action to them, just as in Christ's teaching they found nothing but a sanction to kill and oppress.

How was it, under these circumstances, that any government in its senses allowed this orgy of revolutionary heresy to be published and broadcast? Evidently because they were either too weak, too ill instructed, or too heretical themselves to stop it.

It is a safe prediction, and one that is by no means to the discredit of the russian rulers to make, that the time will soon come when a copy of Tolstoy's *War and Peace* will be read by the person possessing it, if at all, *en cachette*; in the same way that a pornographic book is read today. It was a book written to rouse the consciousness of the oppressed: and from that point of view, when all that can be done for the moment has been done for that oppressed humanity, there is no further point in mechanically exciting it. The great beauty and truth of the book in other respects make it natural to preserve it, for the interest of those whose minds are not ignorantly inflammable, and whom it would not pervert to lawless actions. It should only be placed in the hands of those who are in a position to understand it. The people who read such books, after all, should be the rulers.

V. NIETZSCHE AS A VULGARIZER

When we are considering nineteenth-century vulgarization, Frederick Nietzsche at once comes to the mind as the archetype of the vulgarizer. His particular vulgarization was the most flagrant of all, and certainly the strangest. For what he set out to vulgarize, the notion of aristocracy and power, was surely the most absurd, illogical, and meaningless thing that he could have chosen for that purpose.

Nietzsche's lifetime saw the beginning of the heyday of the literary vulgarizer. By what elliptical and peculiar roads this vociferous showman arrived at his ends would be in itself a very interesting study. And the society in the midst of which such a proceeding was encouraged would certainly lend itself to a first-class farce. However that may be, in a frenzy of poetic zeal he alternately browbeat and implored the whole world to be *aristocrats*. They were naturally enchanted. Such flattery was unique in their experience of such popular events. Nietzsche, got up to represent a Polish nobleman, with a *berserker* wildness in his eye, advertised the secrets of the world, and sold little vials containing blue ink, which he represented as drops of authentic blue blood to the delighted populace. They went away, swallowed his prescriptions, and felt very noble almost at once.

If we consider for a few moments some of the characteristic phrases of this great vulgarizer's thought, we shall get in touch with the working of the most paradoxical nineteenth-century system.

The intellectual opportunism of Nietzsche associated him with the 'pragmatism' of the psychologists and philosophers who immediately succeeded him. The hollow, 'stagey', mephistophelean laughter of his *Joyful Wisdom* was directed principally against 'truth'. He would say, for instance:

> We now know something too well, we men of knowledge: oh, how well we are learning to forget and *not* know as artists! And as to our future we are not likely to be found again in the tracks of those Egyptian youths who at night make the temples unsafe, embrace statues, and would fain unveil, uncover, and put in clear light everything which for good reasons is kept concealed. No, we have got disgusted with this bad taste, this will to truth, to 'truth at all costs', this youthful madness in the love of truth; we are now too experienced, too serious, too joyful, too singed, too profound for that. . . . We no longer believe that truth remains truth when the veil is withdrawn from it: we have lived long enough not to believe this. At present we regard it as a matter of propriety not to be anxious either to see everything naked, or to be present at everything, or to understand and 'know' everything. 'Is it true that the good God is everywhere present?' asked a little child of her mother: 'I think that is indecent' – a hint to philosophers! (*Joyful Wisdom*.)

(Nietzsche's reproof could be addressed with some point to Freud, that more recent vulgarizer: for he located *le bon Dieu* in that very spot, and there only, which aroused the outburst of modesty that Nietzsche records.)

There you see Nietzsche not only unveiling Truth, but attempting to drug and rape her, after having, 'futurist' fashion, made her live.

For if his words mean anything, they mean that we should seek truth by avoiding it, or flying from it. Court the lie, and we shall find the Truth. But that is only another, and more or less (as presented in *Joyful Wisdom*) Bergson's way, as it happens. It is all extremely reminiscent of Christ's strategy of salvation and power: 'he who humbleth himself shall be exalted' – 'the last shall be first', and all those precepts that could be described as the *strategy of humility*.

So Nietzsche's 'Fly Truth and you shall find it' is a stratagem only, taken literally. But the passage I have quoted above is a very dramatic incitement to a certain attitude; although it is advice, needless to say, for others, and not for the philosopher himself. He had delved far enough, and anatomized, or otherwise in any case his words would have had no meaning.

Nietzsche was in fact himself, where philosophy is concerned, a sort of Christ. Under the pretence of a doctrine of *aristocracism* (with that attractive and snobbish label ARISTOCRACY) he went out into the highways and byways and collected together all the half-educated, anything but aristocratic student and art-student population of Europe. There was no small attorney's son, or small farmer's daughter who had been to a school where their parents had to pay, or had studied painting and music, who did not imagine themselves barons and baronesses, at least, on the spot. A few years after his dramatic exit from the stage he became the greatest popular success of any philosopher of modern times.

The character of his action as a philosopher, then, was not unlike that of Christ with regard to the religious heritage of the Jews. Both threw wide open the gates – Christ those of salvation, and Nietzsche those of Truth – to the 'publicans and sinners', the 'barbarian' strangers. And the doctrine of aristocracy arranged by Dr Nietzsche, for Tom, Dick and Harry, was a snobbish pill very violent in its action.

Had Nietzsche cared, in the passage quoted above, to be candid, he would perhaps have added: 'You poor little beast (how unlike my big blonde one!), whoever you are, who are not fit to touch the hem of the garment of *my* goddess, Truth. So go away and amuse yourself in your characteristic way. You *couldn't* stand the truth, in any case. It's not for the likes of you. So there's no use in your gaping around this exclusive pavilion. I can hardly support her embraces. Just look what she's done to me! So what do you suppose is likely to happen to you! Better make yourself scarce. No? Very well. It doesn't matter. Here's a permit for the holy mountain. Say the great Nietzsche gave it to you – they'll let you pass. But they don't much care who you are, as a matter of fact, any more than I do. Don't forget to look off the top – the view is splendid. Be careful not to slip. It's very *dangerous*. It's terribly *high*! Try and understand the privilege of such a glimpse: and remember *who* it was procured you that privilege. (*Sotto voce*) I hope the stairs are well greased! Tra-la-la!'

What he said instead was:

> Oh, those Greeks! They knew how to *live*; for that purpose it is necessary to keep bravely to the surface, the fold and the skin, to worship appearance, to believe in forms, tones and words, in the whole Olympus of Appearance! And are we not coming back precisely to this point, we dare-devils of the spirit, who have scaled the highest and most dangerous peak of contemporary thought and have looked around us from it, have *looked down* from it!

Had Nietzsche from the first followed these instructions himself, should we ever have heard of him? Yet his advice was not wholly perfidious. For it was not unlike a miner arriving at the surface from a very deep and uncomfortable pit, and saying, 'Ah! how pleasant the sun is! Give me the good old surface of this rotten earth. Never you *go down there*!' Or, if you like, it was Descartes' advice to people 'never to read a book'.

The influence of Nietzsche was similar to that of Bergson, James, Croce, etc. He provided a sanction and licence, as the others did, for LIFE – the very life that he never ceased himself to objurgate against; the life of the second rate and shoddily emotional, for the person, very unfortunately, smart and rich enough to be able to regard himself as an 'aristocrat', a man 'beyond good and evil', a destroying angel and cultivated Mephistopheles. If you read the following passage carefully it will be at once apparent how that, with his particular method, came to pass:

> Oh, how repugnant to us now is pleasure, coarse, dull, drab pleasure, as the pleasure-seekers, our 'cultured' classes, our rich and ruling classes, usually understand it! How malignantly we now listen to the great holiday-hubbub with which 'cultured people' and city-men at

present allow themselves to be forced to 'spiritual enjoyment' by art, books, and music, with the help of spirituous liquors! How the theatrical cry of passion now pains our ear, how strange to our taste has all the romantic riot and sensuous bustle which the cultured populace love become (together with their aspirations after the exalted, the elevated, and the intricate)! No, if we convalescents need an art at all, it is *another* art – a mocking, light, divinely serene, divinely ingenious art, which blazes up like a clear flame, into a cloudless heaven! Above all, an art for artists, only for artists!

Many great writers (and Nietzsche was of course a very great one) address audiences who do not exist. Nietzsche was always addressing people who did not exist. To address passionately and sometimes with very great wisdom *people who do not exist* has this disadvantage (especially when the imaginary audience is a very large one, as was the case with Nietzsche) that there will always be a group of people who, seeing a man shouting apparently at somebody or other, and seeing nobody else in sight, will think that it is they who are being addressed. Nietzsche was sufficiently all-there to realize that this must happen. And most that is unsatisfactory in his teaching was a result of that consciousness. Nietzsche imagined a new type of human being – the Superman; and to 'supermen' he poured out sometimes his secret thoughts, and sometimes what he thought they ought to know of his secret thoughts. But he lived in a Utopia, and wrote in and for a Utopia, hoping to make Europe that Utopia by pretending that it was. He had a very great effect on Europe: but an opposite one to what you would have anticipated from his creed, as was only to be expected. For a message getting into the hands of the many, or of people opposite to those for whom it is destined, has usually an opposite effect to that it is intended to have by its sender. Nietzsche was much too astute not to know that this is what would probably happen to his message: and as I have said, you are constantly aware of this consciousness.

Imagine, for a moment, the average 'pleasure-seeker' of our 'cultured classes', as he excellently describes a numerous class, reading the above passage. They would be very annoyed while reading about the 'pleasure-seekers of the cultured classes' and their 'coarse, drab, and dull pleasures'. But they would have read above that after an illness you were apt to be of a much 'merrier disposition', 'more wicked', and 'more childish', 'a hundred times more refined than ever before'.

They clap their hands ecstatically and 'childishly'. A HUNDRED TIMES MORE REFINED THAN EVER BEFORE! Just think of it (though was there so much room for improvement?)!

In the first place, every word written would be *applied to themselves*, inevitably and at once. It would be *they* who had had the illness: they who were now convalescent, and feeling so naughty and devilish. For had they not just been in a nursing home with a nervous breakdown, for a cosmetic operation, or haemorrhoids, for a fortnight? Yes, it was extraordinary how well you felt after being ill! It was almost worth it, to feel so well.

Having, with some pain, got through the part about the 'rich and ruling classes' and their 'coarse, drab pleasures' (and having with a gulp passed over 'spirituous liquors'), they would arrive at WE CONVALESCENTS (by this time they would have completely forgotten, or absorbed, the 'coarse and drab'): WE 'need another art!' (How true! how divinely true! that's just how I feel! they will think.) Then they come to MOCKING, LIGHT, VOLATILE, DIVINELY SERENE, etc. *Could* a better description have been found of what *they* liked, of what *they* were? It was all so true! Were not *they* artists? Was not Nero an artist? Were not all people of the best stamp (except Lady This or Mrs That, of course) artists?

So it is easy to imagine them (interrupted at this point by the visit of a friend) going off and being more *mocking, light, volatile,* and *divinely serene,* all at once, than ever before! With little wistful looks, a little 'sad and faraway', thrown in from time to time (to show that it was in reality a *mask* – the *latest* mask, or only a crust above plutonic fires!).

But it is in Nietzsche's Will to Power conception, the central feature of his thought, that we get to see most fully what it means to be a vulgarizer in such a world as his. If we wish to understand the penalty of such a function, it is there that we shall discover it.

Nietzsche, like his contemporary Von Hartmann, belongs to the Will-School, as it might be called, of which Schopenhauer was the founder. As such he was of course opposed to the evolution of Darwin, though very much influenced by the latter's notion of a hopeless and meaningless struggle.

Nietzsche repudiated the world of positivist knowledge which is essentially a world of disillusion and pessimism: and substituted for it a world of affirmation (his *Yea!*) and of ACTION. What he really proposed was that people should turn their backs on the *procès* made against illusion by the examining and cataloguing of the senses, and plunge back again into ignorance – or the world of will and illusion. Schopenhauer's pessimism was the pessimism of thought and knowledge. Action – and the will to action – was necessarily paralysed by that. So up against thought and intellect Nietzsche wished to raise *action*, with all its innocent light-heartedness, ignorance and superficiality. He was as much a believer in crude, undifferentiated action as the behaviourists of today. Only, his was emotional action, where the behaviourists' is *unemotional*, i.e. 'behaviour'.

Again, really, his *will to power* was not so fundamental a doctrine with him as what could be called his *will to action*. And his will to illusion was based on the theory (advanced by Lange[1] and many near and remote philosophic predecessors) of 'falsification'.

The difference between the lyrical strategy of Nietzsche – despairing as it was – and the strategy of defeat of the *mondain* type, was that Nietzsche saw the surplus – because, of course, he *felt* it in his own organism – left over from the Darwinian 'struggle for existence'. He thought that Darwin's struggle for existence, his mechanical brand of evolution, was too drab, utilitarian, and spiritless a picture. There was, for him, a *margin* in this struggle (like Peirce's[2] 'chance') which caused it to assume more the character of a struggle for something *marginal and over and above* too – a super-something. And this he described as the Will to Power.

In this idea of a superfluity of energy, enabling the warring organism to aim beyond mere destruction – higher than equilibrium or 'balance of power' – there was a beneficent effectiveness which was spoilt by one thing, but that a very fundamental one. Before coming to this heroical decision, he had become so used to the idea of a fierce utilitarian struggle, that what he did (or suggested that other men should do) with their superfluous, creative energy, was *to go on fighting and struggling*: just as though, in short, they had not been provided with a margin for play or a superfluity of energy at all.

[1] German philosopher (1828–75), author of a celebrated *History of Materialism*.   [2] 1839–1914, cf. p. 208.

Any criticism of Nietzsche must rest on that point: that of his suggested employment and utilization of this superfluous energy *to go on doing the same things that we should be doing without it*. And his will requires to see this precious *something over* put to the same uses that many of the lowest of his helots would have put it to. He was so impregnated with the pessimism of Schopenhauer, and his health was so broken by his experiences in the Franco-Prussian War, that he could not imagine, really, the mind doing anything else with itself than what it did in post-darwinian or schopenhauerian pessimism: to just go on contemplating the horrors of existence. And in reality the will to enjoy was dead in Nietzsche, much as he clamoured for latin light-heartedness. He had plenty of Will left: only, it was Will to struggle merely, not Will to live. Fine artist as he was, he passed his life in a nightmare, and was, I think, unable to benefit by his own falsification theory. Schopenhauer probably was a wiser man, and came to better terms with life than Nietzsche did.[1]

The average, worldly man does not, on the other hand, get beyond the conception of 'the struggle for existence'. He has no creative surplus at all. His strategy is as much a state of war as was Nietzsche's *will to power*. But with him it is a defensive war; and he is only aggressively cunning, not in the heroic 'dangerous' fashion suggested by Nietzsche. He disposes his forces very prudently and strategically. He is by nature what is called 'pessimistic'; he sees nothing but *defeat* in the sense of horror and struggle. This bloody struggle he is determined to subsist in the middle of, and yet keep it at a distance. He outwardly, like Nietzsche, has a powerfully developed 'falsification' theory and 'will to illusion'. Only (naturally) he is much more successful in the use of it than Nietzsche could be. He is, in short, that person disliked by Nietzsche to such a great extent – the 'cynic' against whom he directed such eloquent invective.

Of his 'power' complex, as the Freudian would call it, and his bellicose dogma, I shall leave the discussion until at a later stage I return to these questions.

[1] Cf. Lewis's later comment on Nietzsche (Part XII, Chapter VII): 'Nietzsche was a death-snob (as Whitman was a life-snob): and he was also a madness-snob. (This is a very ancient form of snob: but formerly the madness-snob never dreamt of going mad himself in his enthusiasm . . .)'

VI. GEORGE SOREL

George Sorel is an even stronger vulgarizer in some ways than Nietzsche, of whom he was a follower of sorts: he vulgarized aristocracy (as seen through the eyes of Nietzsche) for the labourer and mechanic.

George Sorel is the key to all contemporary political thought. Sorel is, or was, a highly unstable and equivocal figure. He seems composed of a crowd of warring personalities, sometimes one being in the ascendant, sometimes another, and which in any case he has not been able, or has not cared, to control. He is the arch exponent of extreme action, and revolutionary violence *à l'outrance*; but he expounds this sanguinary doctrine in manuals that often, by the changing of a few words, would equally serve the forces of traditional authority, and provide them with a twin evangel of demented and intolerant class-war.

If he must be given conventionally a 'class', he has that chilliness that you must associate more with the official class than with that of the artisan or servant. In this he is the opposite of Péguy. Yet in his criticism of the class he attacks, he displays sometimes so much fierceness and acuity that it is difficult to doubt his sincerity on such occasions. But 'sincerity' hardly enters into the question.

George Sorel is a mercenary who is devoted to his profession – that of arms – and is willing to fight without pay, since in easy circumstances. The 'cause' matters very little to him – the 'battle' is everything. And yet in the midst of this detachment you have to allow for some deep, and indeed rather mysterious, sectarian, passion. And intellectually he is a sensitive plate for the confused ideology of his time. He is a semitaur who sees red both ways, the bull-nature injects the human eyes with blood. He is, in brief, a symptomatic figure that it would be difficult to match.

As to his standing in the world of letters and politics (and in that as in everything else he is a fabulous hybrid, attacking himself, biting his own tail, kicking his own heroical chest, contunding his own unsynthetic flesh, and showing his wounds with pride – self-inflicted, *self* in everything) he has an enviable position. 'Sorel', says his English translator, Hulme, 'is one of the most remarkable writers of his time, certainly the most remarkable socialist since Marx.' (Introduction, Eng. translation of *Réflexions sur la violence*. T. E. Hulme.)

So this strangest of 'socialists' is described; no one would dispute such a claim: '... quintessence, extrémisme, individualité, différenciation élite, c'est du sorelisme intégral. Par l'héroisme, et par l'hétérogénité, M. Sorel est le grand excitateur du monde moderne.' (*Itinéraire d'intellectuels*. R. Johannet.)

That is the man, as he appears to many of his contemporaries, with whose ideas we are dealing. M. Johannet, the writer I have just quoted, believes that his ideas are ultimately of more use to reaction than to social revolution. I do not share that view, but I think his *practical* work of incitement to revolt must be considered apart from his more speculative work – though it enters into that, of course, and often causes some confusion.

M. Johannet prefers to leave Sorel as 'an enigma', an insoluble problem. 'Always enigmatic and reserved,' he writes of him, 'a master of obsessional ideas, and generator of the maximum of tension, always fleeting and unstable – so he appears to us – even in the depths of his confidences. Why! are we dreaming after all? The Sorel *individualist*, then the Sorel *socialist and traditionalist*, are they after all only attitudes of a curious student? Insoluble problem! ...'

'The faith in socialism,' says Le Bon (*Psychologie politique*, quoted approvingly by Sorel), 'gives back to the simple-hearted the hopes that the gods no longer provide, and the illusions that science has taken away from them.' Sorel has certainly the attitude of a lonely traveller who has gone into the comfortable atmosphere of a rustic inn, for whose appointments he has a superior townsman's contempt, just to be out of the *néant* for the brief period of his life. Once there, he seems to have been moved to entertain and excite his simple hearers with accounts of blood-curdling and quixotic adventures. He thought he would supply them with the epic and heroic material they had lost at the same time as they lost the comforts of religion and their 'simple faith'. That is the Sorel of the *Réflexions sur la violence*.

Fourier, with his *papillone*,[1] started revolutionary thought on a course of psychological exploitation. The child's 'love of dirt' (*les immondices*) was to be utilized to get the scavenging work of the phalanstery done with the efficiency of gusto. Sorel would supply the *papillone* system to humanity's noble instinct for blood and

---

[1] *Papillone:* love of change, one of the basic human instincts, according to Fourier (1772–1837).

carnage; very different, he is at pains to point out, to the rather despicable notion of Jaurés, by which their envy and *hatred* should be exploited (*la haine créatrice*, as he called it).

Genuinely *violent* – about that there is little doubt – he applies the nietzschean 'warlike' idea to the crowd, with a great deal of jugglery which it is not difficult to penetrate. He steals the philosophy of 'war', in short, and passes it quickly to the 'slave' *against* whom the romantic Nietzsche had designed that it should be used. But he does not at the same time fail to abuse the 'slave' with a few aristocratic airs that he has stolen, along with the 'war' – especially if the 'slave' does not snatch at his beautiful present eagerly enough. It is not surprising that at times it is difficult to tell where the stolen packet has got to, and in whose hands, at the moment, it is supposed to be.

His taunts with regard to the 'mediocrity' of his curious protégés never slacken. This crowd-master and this crowd are the most strangely assorted pair, in fact. He takes his revolutionary blessings to them 'whip in hand' with a girding pedagogic intolerance. Coriolanus could not be more contemptuous asking for their 'voices'. (Only, he has no wounds to show, although very martial and possessing a fine patriotic vein.) He approaches his 'proletariat' with the airs of a missionary among 'natives', with an armed colonizing government behind him. His colleagues also feel the weight of his lash. For example:

> The transformations that marxism has undergone illustrate very well the theory of *mediocrity*. The social-democratic writers, who have pretended to interpret, apply, and extend the doctrine of their so-called master, were men of a surprising vulgarity. . . . The great mistake of Marx was to under-value the enormous power of mediocrity as displayed throughout history. He did not understand that the feeling for socialism (as he conceived it) was extremely artificial.

The production of the *hero*, and of the *heroic*, was his constant preoccupation. It is that, as M. Johannet says, that took him to catholicism. He interrogated in turn Proudhon, Marx and Isaiah, Pelloutier, in search of this illusive phantom of a past world. Only in social revolution did he see possibilities of the old grandeur and vigour. His 'proletariat' is really the people of the 'Germania' of Tacitus:

> Greek christianity (he says) is very inferior to Latin christianity, everyone is agreed, because it had not at its service men spiritually

trained, rushing to the conquest of the profane world. The exceptional value of catholicism comes from its monastic institutions continually providing the conditions for the formation of such heroes. . . . What we know of the hebrew prophets enables us to say that the judaism of the Old Testament owes its glory to religious experience. The modern Jews only see in their religion rites analogous to those of the ancient magical superstitious cults. (*La ruine du monde antique.*)

To the Bible Sorel constantly points – but of course to the Old Testament, not the New. He tells the world of the universities and the *bourgeoisie* that if they would turn to that admirably savage and moral book they would once more become sublime by dipping into that fiery source. Like Cromwell (*His Highness' speech* to the Parliament in the Painted Chamber, at their dissolution upon Monday, Jan. 22, 1654–5), he might have pointed to such passages of an invigorating description as are to be found in the Bible:

1. Who is this that cometh from Edom, with dyed garments from Bozrah? this that is glorious in his apparel, travelling in the greatness of his strength? I that speak in righteousness, mighty to save.
2. Wherefore art thou red in thy apparel, and thy garments like him that treadeth in the wine-fat?
3. I have trodden the wine-press alone; and of the people there was none with me; for I will tread them in mine anger, and trample them in my fury; and their blood shall be sprinkled upon my garments, and I will stain all my raiment.
4. For the day of vengeance is in my heart, and the year of my redeemed is come.
5. And I will tread down the people in mine anger, and make them drunk in my fury. (*Isaiah lxiii.*)

It will be seen that the gaudy red figure is not without its sublimity: that action is his passion if not his element (perhaps his exoticism, as it is a woman's): and that such a man would not be likely to have great sympathy with Kautsky and his views. The tearing of men's hearts out of their bodies, and the stewing of their eyeballs in the gravy of their bowels, or the stamping on the pulp of their entrails and making a Burgundy of their blood, or making a hole in their abdomen and winding their entrails round a tree, as Brian Boru did to celebrate his triumph, is not the type of action that appeals to me most, for reasons already set forth. I found myself in the blood-bath of the Great War, and in that situation reflected on the vanity of violence. So that side of Sorel seems to me too literary. But all the emotional and 'heroic' section of Sorel is deeply romantic, and by that I understand untrue. A truer part of him, as I see it, you get in his analysis of progress and ideas about 'class'.

PART V. 'NATURES' AND 'PUPPETS'[1]

I. WHAT THE PUPPETS WANT

Our problem is, no doubt, 'to perfect a larva', but not, as that statement suggests, the larva 'Mankind', the whole of that dense abstraction. The system of 'breeding horses for speed' is a far better one. That is no doubt the solution. But the slowness, sloth and commonness of the stock of *Homo stultus* would still be there when the sub-species, or the super-species, had been bred. . . .[2] There would be two species, there would be two worlds. There would not be the lively competition, I believe, for entrance to the *upper* world, and its rigours, as you might suppose. On the contrary, the under world, the relaxed and animal one of *l'homme sensuel*, would be the favourite, probably.

Today there are, in fact, two species and two worlds, which incessantly interfere with each other, checkmate each other, are eternally at cross purposes. They *speak the same language* . . .[3] but they do not understand each other.

Goethe had a jargon of his own for referring to these two species whose existence he perfectly recognized. He divided people into *Puppets* and *Natures*. He said the majority of people were machines, playing a part. When he wished to express admiration for a man, he would say about him, 'He is a *nature.*' This division into *natural* men and *mechanical* men (which Goethe's idiom amounts to) answers to the solution advocated in this essay. And today there is an absurd war between the 'puppets' and the 'natures', the machines and the men. And owing to the development of machinery, the pressure on the 'natures' increases. We are *all* slipping back into machinery, because we *all* tried to be free. And what is absurd about this situation is that so few people even desire to be free in reality.

The ideal of obedience conceived by the jesuits, so that, in their words, 'a member of their order should regard himself as a corpse

[1] Chapters I–VII. [2] One sentence omitted. [3] Parentheses omitted.

to be moved here or there' at the absolute discretion of the superior, has often been described as an 'inhuman' one. But is it 'inhuman'? For is it not what most people desire, to be dolls of that sort; to be looked after, disciplined into insensitiveness, spared from suffering by insensibility and blind dependence on a will superior to their own?

'The more accentuated the complexity of forms or functions becomes, the more startling the inequality,' Professor Richet remarks in his chapter on inequality.[1] 'If two pebbles are always dissimilar, how much more two leaves and, with still more cause, two ants.' How will it be in the case of two men? To accept and to organize these differences is the solution of ills of which Professor Richet speaks. And Professor Richet's classification would no doubt serve: 'A moment's reflection will convince us that men can only be classified according to their merits. On the one hand, those who are industrious, upright, brave and intelligent; on the other those who are lazy, dishonest, cowardly, and stupid.' That would of course not be the way to put it, for the lazy, stupid and dishonest cowards would show themselves both industrious and brave, perhaps, in opposing this settlement.

A popular book of gossipy predictions that has recently appeared, called *The Future*, will provide us with few further pictures of 'Mankind' from the point of view of science. Its author, Professor Low, has the necessary scholastic quarterings, F.C.S., F.R.C.S., etc., and is a member of the Council of Patentees. His heart is in a different place to Professor Richet's. In the future, he says, 'boxers, footballers, and others who rely mainly upon their strength for a living will be regarded as "throw-outs" of low mental capacity'. ('Money can today be guaranteed for a concourse of athletes, but not for the maintenance of a hospital.' In the future men will be more sensible.)

The optimism of this writer about the future is at times a little oppressive (he goes into so much detail). But his scorn of the present 'Mankind' leaves nothing to be desired:

> Imagine a really intelligent thoughtful man – and future education will make men thoughtful – kicking a ball about in a field for a living! At present one of the most popular alleged amusements is dancing. When considering this it can only be agreed that it is fortunate that

---

[1] From his book *L'Homme Stupide* (1919), to which Lewis first referred in Part III, Chapter IV.

the planet to which people are confined by ignorance does not contain any beings of high mentality. Imagine a really intelligent person – one who had solved the electrical problems of life, who really understood planetary movement and the actual appearance of babies into the world – suddenly entering a hot, smelly room where a nigger band shrieked and groaned the latest jazz tunes to a crowd of dancers of all ages, and in all stages of intoxication, the soulless gaiety perhaps being enhanced by paper carnival hats! They would be regarded as interesting specimens, like performing mice, and efforts would be made to explain the phenomenon. Hysteria – result of peculiar breeding – local anæsthesia – very sad!

Thus this young professor: as Descartes strolled among the inhabitants of Amsterdam as though they had been the trees of a wood, so this contemporary representative of advanced thought regards his kind, surprised at one of their characteristic occupations as performing mice. 'Human life appears to depend to a large extent on some superimposed rhythm. People are like leaves agitated by the breeze; when the wind stops the leaf falls into rest, but does not appear to alter. The heart, lungs, eyes, and feeding intervals are all periodic happenings or modulations of some function of time.' So dancing can be a 'great relief', a 'dope'. But this popular scientific view of the moment could be extended to everything: indeed, science is extending it, in the sense that many psychologists of the *tester* type recommend orchestras in factories.

It is certain, I think, that by far the greater part of people ask nothing better than to be 'performing mice'. And (as has already been said) they do not mind having their tails cut off by a Dr Weismann,[1] as Mr Shaw thinks they do. Plato, ridiculing the mystery poets in the *Phaedrus*, says: 'What better recompense can they give to virtue than an eternity of intoxication?' But an eternity of intoxication is what 'the performing mice', or, if you prefer Goethe's word, 'the puppets', want.

When Plutarch's wife is mourning the death of her daughter, he recommends her to go and get consolation from the Dionysia. That was the advice of a kind and excellent husband. The philosopher who does not require this rhythm, recommending his own diet, the ecstasy obtained in 'the recollection of that which he has seen in a former existence with God', is unreasonable enough. Is that sensible advice to give to a performing mouse?

[1] German biologist (1834–1914).

The tone of studied contempt on the one hand, or despairing abuse on the other, for Homo sapiens, is unmerited probably. It is a mistake arising from the democratic standards from which the subject is approached. There is nothing contemptible about an intoxicated man (if it is nothing more than a bookful of words or a roomful of notes that he has got drunk on). A dancing-mouse, the little favourite of Mr Yerkes,[1] performs its function and keeps Mr Yerkes amused. A corpse is even not a *contemptible* thing. ('There's a good deal to be said for being dead,' etc.) It is the tone of indignation or of pedagogic displeasure that is the fault with the attitude of science towards man. Either rage, disgust, misanthropy, or the scorn of a public examiner is displayed. The attitude should surely be more truly scientific than that to give promise of effectiveness. There should be no unkindness or disgust. But all these tones are adopted by a certain class of men who from no point of view have very much right to them.

The differentiation of mankind into two rigorously separated worlds would not be on the old 'class' lines at all, to begin with. It would be like a deep racial difference, not a superficial 'class' difference. This would entirely remove the sting of 'inferiority' and the usual causes for complaint. A beaver does not compare itself with a walrus or antelope. There is no 'upper' and 'lower' between a cat and a dog. So it would be with the new species of men.

Under the aristocratic or feudal regime there were two worlds of thought, with amusements and so on adapted to the training and habits of these two communities living side by side. The arrangements were at no time perfect; they were always on a social rather than an intellectual basis, the small world of the european 'upper class' being merely a better washed, and scented, powdered, and laced replica of the animal standard from which it had merely snobbishly removed itself. There still were certain banalities from which this segregation protected the fortunate few.

This *aristocratic* separation of classes on the old bad model was wounding to the susceptibilities of those who were not fortunate enough, as they thought, to be born into this select and brilliant world. This was because the separation was artificial, in the sense that it reposed on the heredity principle and accident, that it was conducted and upheld (naturally) in an insolent and unintelligent

[1] Psycho-biologist and zoologist, authority on the great apes (1876–1956).

spirit, and perhaps because it too plainly reproduced (in a sumptuous form) the less fortunate state – the 'third estate' – with which it was contrasted. This 'top-dog' did all the things, with an ostentatious relish, that the poor, envious under-dog, squinting jealously at him from his kennel, would like to do. The aristocrat pretended to be 'of another clay' to the proletarian: but the proletarian knew better. He knew that he was exactly of the same clay as himself. There was no spiritual or intellectual chasm – only a rather dirty little social ditch.

Now, instead of a separation in which a small group of people gets the upper hand, the 'power' separates itself, builds a fence round itself, and proceeds to do with an extreme monotony, and usually without much taste or intelligence, all the animally pleasant things that all those left out in the cold, down in the basement or out in the slums, would like to do, let us imagine a separation not the result of a skin-deep 'power', or of social advantage, but something like a *biological* separating-out of the chaff from the grain. Or to put it in another way: if, of two men, one wishes to go and play cricket, and the other wishes to go to a shed in his garden, where he has fitted up a small laboratory, and spend the day in research, neither one envies the other: they both recognize that nature has turned them out so differently that what amuses the one does not amuse the other. 'It takes all sorts to make a world,' they would no doubt both remark, if discussing it. All would be well, and harmony would reign between them.

If, on the other hand, there were two men, both of whom were passionately fond of cricket. If one, by cheating the other in business, or by arming himself and robbing the other, became extremely wealthy, and then proceeded to lay out a beautiful cricket ground, to have golden stumps manufactured, a lovely bat with a big diamond on the top, and laced pads, and left a hole in the fence so that the poor man, at whose expense all this luxury was built up, could peer at him playing the favourite game of both (not especially well, perhaps): then we can at once understand that a great deal of animosity would result.

Such a separation as would be obtained by an examination system instead of heredity, perhaps; or such a separation as the instinctive growth and differentiation of another type of man, heredity serving a biologic and not a social end: that is one solution of the present difficulty. There would be no stigma attached to a devotional adherence to the routine of the animal life. *L'homme moyen sensuel* would cheerfully, or 'cheerily', confess that all 'highbrow' matters he had from the cradle disliked, and would disappear round the corner to the local bridge-club with cheery words on his honest lips, ejaculating contentedly, 'It takes all sorts to make a world.' And angry professors would not be allowed to call him *Homo stultus*. He, as much as the more creative type of person, would be *Homo sapiens*. It would be the Professor who would be convicted of *stupidity* then, if he called *stultus* after this well-satisfied, 'good-natured, unambitious' man.

It is not by any means as an aspirant for the highest biologic honours that I am writing. But the scorn of the man of science and the rage of the philosopher have to be met. They cannot much longer be neglected, or resisted, rather – for they are now an integral part of the great system of *What the Public Wants*. As they originally appear in the speculative brain or superbly trained eye, they must be allowed some foundation in the common observation of all of us. Although personally unambitious, I am not indifferent to the interests I serve. It is in that spirit that I set out to consider how *What the Puppets Want* might differ from *What the Public Wants*, and to see if the growing hatred and contempt could not be lifted a little from these very ticklish relations. The threatening attitude of Mr Shaw and Mr Russell to the Yahoo tallies too much, I thought, with the suave malignity of the publicist.

Another way of regarding it would be this. The ferocious misanthropy of the adepts of *What the Public Wants* is a very compromising thing for the intelligence to be associated with. The puppets Ozymandias and Semiramis, as conceived by Mr Shaw, have to be destroyed. But those puppets are a libel on the Public – or they would be if it were intended to identify them, and that seems Mr Shaw's intention. In reality they are another genus of puppets, a genus of homicidal puppets, sure enough. And they bear a strange resemblance to the misanthropic masters of the doctrine of *What the Public Wants*.

II. 'LIBERTY' IS DEAD

It is a belief that has never been formulated, but it is at the root of a great deal of behaviour today, that *freedom and irresponsibility are invariably commutative terms.* The first object of a person with an ambition to be free, and yet possessing none of the means exterior to himself or herself (such as money, conspicuous ability, or power) to obtain freedom, is to avoid responsibility.

Absence of responsibility, an automatic and stereotyped rhythm, is what men most desire for themselves. All struggle has for its end relief or repose. A rhythmic movement is restful: but consciousness and possession of the self is not compatible with a set rhythm. All the libertarian cries of a century ago were based on unreal premises, and impulses that are not natural to, and cannot be sustained by, the majority of men. Luxury and repose are what most men undeniably desire. They would like to be as much at rest as if they were dead, and as active and 'alive' as passivity will allow. When action is required of them they prefer that it should be 'exciting' and sensational, or else that it should have a strongly defined, easily grasped, mechanical rhythm. The essential fatigues and poorness of most organisms, and the minds that serve them, is displayed in nothing so much as in this *sensationalism*. Every low-grade animal is to some extent born sadic, for that is the only way he can *feel*. Sensationalism and sadism are twins. The only effort that is acceptable to many people is violent, excessive and spasmodic action. 'Simple' delights, as we call them, appear to be the privileged possession of the chosen ones of nature.

All the old libertarian claim was for a liberty involving the opposite of this. Consciousness and responsibility are *prose* contrasted with the *poetry* of passive, more or less ecstatic, rhythmic, mechanical life. There is, therefore, the intoxicated dance of puppets, and besides that the few *natures*, as they were called by Goethe; moving unrhythmically, or according to a rhythm of their own, which is the same thing. The conventional libertarianism of a century ago envisaged this latter form of personal freedom, this *prose of the individual*, as it could be called. The libertarianism of today rejects with horror the idea of that 'independence'. In place of this *prose of the individual* it desires the *poetry of the mass*; in place of the *rhythm of the person*, the *rhythm of the crowd*.

The extreme expression of this desire is the jesuit ideal of self-annihilating obedience so that the adept becomes a disinterested machine, ecstatically obedient, delighted to find himself entirely in the power of another person, his superior in will and vitality. The very principle of authority is his bride. That is the release of ecstasy, absolute repose of the *will* (which, with the generality of men, require a great deal of rest): also complete abandon of the principle of self, which is the principle of effort too, and the cause of all suffering. The 'apathy' of the Stoics was also intended to secure this rest.

If the traditional idea of Liberty, or what is *to be free*, is no longer satisfactory, but if really 'freedom' is perhaps the opposite of what the *grands ancêtres* were persuaded it was, then 'revolution' will tomorrow have a different meaning, though by no means a less 'revolutionary' one. If that notion of 'freedom' were indeed imposed on people by philosophers, or by ambitious rulers – just as a restless, active man's idea of an enjoyable afternoon's entertainment (incapable, as such active men usually are, of putting himself in other people's shoes) might be imposed on a sluggish party; or a very 'intellectual' person's notion of a jolly evening's relaxation imposed on a gathering of friends, snobbishly adapting themselves to his vigorous 'highbrow' appetites – then the sooner this mistake is corrected the better: or (since this is under correction, for these 'betters' are not naturally the object of my interest) perhaps at least that may be so.

But there is another consideration here: that is, that people have found this out for themselves – who can doubt it? for they certainly do not behave any longer as though they were under the old delusion. Far from behaving in that way, they seem to have embraced the new, and much more true, idea of freedom, if anything too indiscriminatingly. It is easy to see that before long people may have actually to be warned off this more recently appreciated form of 'freedom', which formerly they would, under the influence of early libertarian, saturnalian excitement, have described as 'slavery'. It is possible yet that masses of people, many of them big strong men, will have to be warned off and driven away from the fleshpots of feminine submission; they may have to be prodded by lictors to prevent them from sinking into a lascivious coma, and told not to be such naughty little slaves! That is at least a situation that the responsible authorities may have on their hands, unless the ruler is to be surfeited with submissiveness, and find his occupation, that of ruling, gone, or grown very unexciting.

What a peculiar fanatic of energy ('professor of energy', as Stendhal called himself) the liberty-obsessed personage seems today!

The more indignantly humanitarian he is, the more sturdily he swells his chest and points to ancient 'liberties', and the more he whips himself into a rage at the thought of the monstrous, disgraceful *enslavement* of mankind, the more he almost seems like an agent and emissary of the despot – as of course in the first instance he was – putting a little spirit into the cattle to be ruled. In the times when the herd was wilder and more unruly, he had to pretend to lead them to the attack, misleading them (back to their pens and corrals) instead. He is without any function today, but he often looks as if it were his function to stimulate the jaded performers.

Like wildfire, since the termination of the War, the truth about 'freedom' seems to have flown from mind to mind (it has not been formulated or appeared in words). It is a *secret*. It is even in the nature of a rather dirty secret, none the less, I am afraid, appreciated for all that. With an immense sigh of relief it has been learned that all personal effort, after all, is vain; that the notion of 'liberty' was, by those who wished to impose it on men, a programme of monstrous heroism, a labour of Hercules, a colossal burden, to no purpose. Not the word, but the thought, has gone round, of immense *acceptance*, of the end of *struggle*.

'Liberty' was a nightmare like death. That at length has been perceived. It is a weight off every mind today that it is *dead*; for *death once dead, there is no more dying then.* The enemy of the race, 'liberty', is dead – and men are free once more! But at once, naturally, they begin to abuse this freedom: especially men – for women have always to some extent possessed it.

So the great revolutionary afflatus, the plough of science that has gone across the necropolis of the past, the sudden opening up of the whole earth to its children, has turned out to be something of a more prodigious nature than was at first supposed, or is yet much understood; more truly new and revolutionary, for Europe at least, than anyone would have thought, watching the first, aggressive, libertarian mobs, with their phrygian caps and cockades. Let us, now that we are acquainted with this *secret* of our contemporaries, examine it, still warm from the bosoms from which we have wrenched or otherwise secured it. We shall see that it is the first genuine philosophy of slaves that has ever been formulated. Christianity, with its aggressiveness towards authority, and its insistence on 'a new law' as opposed to the 'old law', was misrepresented by

Nietzsche. It was, if a philosophy of slaves, a philosophy of slaves who desired to rule some day, and to discredit power. The present is very different: it consists in an exploitation of the joys of slavery and submission. 'How enjoyable to be a slave!' the really sensible woman must often have said, lazily awaiting her lord and master. 'How divine to have *a master*! How delightful to have everything done *for* one, and everything done *to* one, and have to do nothing oneself! *Dolce far niente!* How happy I am!' That (sometimes minus the sensuality, and sometimes with it) is what the new discoverers of freedom have said. It has led, of course, to inversely libertarian excesses. But the mind of the world is easier today than it has been for a long while – I am speaking of the european world.

So far so good, we must all agree. Many difficulties, however, occur in the way of the realization of this new dream. It is not certain that it is any more practicable than the other. Perhaps the world has sighed with relief too soon. Also the abandon displayed by many people in enrolling themselves in this new, as it were, secret host is open to objection. Let us at all events examine this esoteric theory of life without fear and without favour.

III. SUPER-FREEDOM OF THE REVOLUTIONARY RICH

The instinct for the supreme condition of freedom which is at the bottom of every great revolutionary movement today could be explained, then, by some axiom as *Emancipation and irresponsibility are commutative terms.*

But behind that are arrayed two schools of thought, or theories of happiness. One is practicable, the other is not. One will no doubt establish itself in the future into which the world is moving. The other is merely a phenomenon of transition.

When these popular movements of thought, expressing themselves as highly infectious fashions, are described as *theories*, it is not meant that they are a body of formulated social doctrine, of course, but rather an instinctive and unconscious process, which is only a theory, properly speaking, for the observer. But from the lucretian watchtower we are possessing for the moment we are able to formulate for ourselves this pattern of instinctive behaviour observed, into an intelligible system of life.

The theory that has, of the two, been described as an ephemeral one is far too good to be true, to start with. Also it is a corruption of the old, rather than an entire convert to the new, libertarianism. This is the distinction that we have constantly to make in dealing with western society today. We are in a mixed society, destined eventually to separate itself out. Of this mixture many corruptions and mongrel forms spring up. Almost every variety of mixture is to be found.

In the heart of this new doctrine of freedom, then, there is a cleavage, rather like that other cleavage that produces the doctrine of *What the Public Wants* on the one hand, and revolutionary idealism on the other. One is a corruption or caricature of the other, an accommodation between the old and the new. Both types of 'freedom' are to be found in the West, side by side and often confused, and one rather compromised by the other. The disciplined *fascist* party in Italy can be taken as representing the new and healthy type of 'freedom'. Perhaps it is simpler to discriminate between them by saying that one is *political* and the other is *social*. Where the political one does not yet properly exist, a social *precursor*, cheap advance copy, social caricature of it exists.

What is happening in reality in the West is that a small privileged class is *playing* at revolution, and aping a 'proletarian' freedom that the proletariat has not yet reached the conception of. The rich are always the first 'revolutionaries'. They also mix up together the instincts, opportunities, and desires of the ruler and the ruled. They have *the apple and eat it* plan in full operation in their behaviour. It is they who have evolved the secondary, heterodox, quite impracticable notion of 'liberty' which it will be our especial task to analyse.

This type of freedom, synonymous with irresponsibility, and yet impregnated with privilege as well, is a very strange growth indeed. It will be found on examination to be the most utopian type of all.

It is only achieved sometimes by one category of creature, the human child; in a lesser degree by the young of animals. But any one *not* a child attempting by some ruse or other to secure it, seldom can succeed; for the simplest and most inexorable law of nature is there to frustrate such a plan. But it can be successful under special and very artificial conditions, in consequence of the protection and assistance of some other factor that is the equal in power of the natural principle that is challenged by it. As an instance of this, we can take the case of an old, rich, and pampered invalid lady who succeeds in attracting to herself, by means of her riches, all the advantages of childhood. She in this way may arrive at being carried about, waited on, fed, bathed, flattered, put to bed, and in the morning, washed and dressed, and so steeped continuously in an atmosphere of self-importance. But this is the effect of her wealth, which brings in the element of power and authority – which though not hers, she is able to use and enjoy. So you must also add to the wealth the advantages of the 'weaker sex'. But the child is the only creature that in its own right, and under favourable conditions, can enjoy unchallenged, and without forfeiting something else that cancels the advantage, this divine irresponsibility, which is the most ideal and utopian type of *freedom*.

The other sort of freedom – or that that it is most natural to contrast with this irresponsible variety – is the responsible freedom of the individual in authority, possessing power (position, or wealth, or both). This is a precarious, imperfect, anxious, laborious freedom: but it is the only freedom within the grasp of the average man, except the great patent of ecstatic submission, the feminine type of freedom or self-expression.

The type of freedom of which the child is the perpetual emblem, irresponsible freedom, and that other of which the king or millionaire is the emblem, that reposing on authority and power, are both rigidly dependent on other people, and the servitude of others is their condition. The third type of freedom, the feminine type, is a parasite of power, and the first requisite for it is a master.

There is another sort of very rare freedom, that possessed by the intellect alone. It is contingent on no physical circumstance, is not obtained or held at the expense of others – indeed, is altogether independent of people; and although it is a source of power, is an unrecognized and unofficial source, and takes with it, under favourable circumstances, some of the advantages of irresponsibility: and at the worst, and deprived of all power, still as freedom, remains unaffected by fortune. But it is not a type with which we need concern ourselves here.

It is not as a routed army, but as a triumphant one, that the luxurious, hand-to-mouth, capitalo-revolutionary society of the interregnum has installed itself in the nursery. There is a cult being evolved by all these highly sophisticated elders, living for sensation, around the figure of a mechanical doll. But as we have been attempting to show for many chapters now, this mechanical doll, or puppet, is the idol, or at least the symbol, of the great majority of men. It is from them that those privileged groups have stolen it. Their wild nursery devotions are conducted in its expensive shadow. There they eat bread and jam round it, dressed in short print frocks and bibs; sit in demure and silent rows, while one dressed as a martinet scolds them, and then administers shuddering *fessées*. With costly toys, pranks, and strictly juvenile games, they conform to the object of their devotion, and do nothing inappropriate in its presence.

By this particular luxurious Western society the *artist* and the *child* are the two figures most heavily imitated and exploited today. So of course both true art and true infancy are in imminent danger of extinction or, 'worse than death, dishonour'. To these two figures should perhaps be added, as a doubtful third, *woman*.

It would be presumptuous, and indeed mad, to suppose that anything could be done, by even the most eloquent disquisition, to change this situation. If, however, *one* artist, and a *single* child, are preserved intact and unpolluted owing to my words, I should consider my pains richly rewarded. To a call to protect the children, and in a lesser degree the women – though the women and children must always go together – the English-speaking public would never fail to respond. It is less certain that they would take action if it were merely a question of saving artists and art. It is encouraging for the artist, however, to reflect that the destiny of the artist, in this instance, is bound up with that of the child. Both the Nursery and the Studio and Study are equally and simultaneously threatened, and by the same people. Both are being pillaged and over-run by a vast crowd of 'grown-ups' who covet the irresponsibilities and unreality of those two up till now sacred retreats.

To state in its awful simplicity the true inner nature of what is happening, *every one wants to be a child*, and *every one wants to be an artist*; which is of course impossible. All the privileges of lisping innocent and petted childhood, and all the privileges of art, are coveted by the masses of the mature and the rich. The mature have developed this particular covetousness because *their* privileges, the privileges and ambitions of mature life, have been ravished from them. The rich have developed it because, as it is impossible to enjoy openly the privileges of riches in the present period of transition, to exercise power openly, and openly surround themselves with its emblems and satisfactions; as it is necessary to pretend to be merely private citizens when in reality they are the rulers of the world, – so they covet the privileges of the artist to which, and to the privileges similarly of the child, they with some reason consider that their irresponsibility affects them. Both the grown-up and the rich man find the natural outlet for their ambition and vitality blocked. Neither can expand upwards and forwards, so they are forced back into these roads that terminate respectively in the Nursery and in the Studio and Study of the artist.

That is, put very briefly, but as fully as at this stage of our argument we need, the nature of the threat to art and to infancy. Already a degrading effect can be registered on all hands. It is possible to generalize in the following way as well: that whenever men are prevented from satisfying their ambitions in a full, active and competitive life, they will loiter on, or, if expelled from, return by the back door or the back window to the Nursery.

And the rich and powerful, if prevented from indulging their natural taste for pomp and display (which in a socialist epoch is impossible) – if prevented from being artists in action (all actions containing naturally a great aesthetic element) – will invariably seek to be 'artists' in some other way.

'*Action*' *today is starved of art*. That is why there are so many 'artists' and so little good art at all.

IV. MILLIONAIRE SOCIETY

We shall often have occasion to use the term 'millionaire society', and to avoid misunderstanding some definition had better be given of what is to be meant by it. We are busy tracing the revolutionary impulse back to the head of Zeus, as it were, from which it leaps, then taking this form and that. God cannot help *thinking* of change, at all events when He thinks of us. We are all infected by His thinking, and we all interpret His thought differently. The revolutionary rich interpret it differently from the revolutionary poor. For the former it becomes *variety* or fashion, a more or less immobile thing; or when it takes the form of movement it affects them on the

Mademoiselle Julie pattern – they have an instinct to cast themselves down. That is the truly *aristocratic* impulse, of the satiety of power and life. But as today there is no aristocracy left, a different and more complex impulse manifests itself. That, in the course of this essay, I hope to throw some light on. There is at least no *humility* about the great ones of our day. There is no tendency to precipitate themselves from their fortunate eminence. And there is none of that dangerous tolerance of a true aristocracy that makes them eager to *look on themselves* – to be their own spectators.

Marx deprecated all *valuation* of the great mass of new things dumped upon the world everyday, 'until the revolution'. Till that happened it did not matter very much how things stood, so long as the radical change was effected. To that we adhere: what values are popularly attached to things is of the slenderest importance, no doubt, in such a time.

We accept the marxian formula of the usefulness of capitalism as it exists today, as a machine building up an immense irrefragable power that eventually can be used by rather pleasanter people than at present have the handling of it. We match our optimism against Marx's. We are quite sure that the most glorious people will shortly appear and use all this unparalleled power, made possible by science and capitalism, more like gods than men. We admit also that it does not sound likely.

In spite of this resolve to regard giant industrialism as a great power willing night and day the evil, and destined to produce nothing but the good – and therefore forestalling somewhat this happy event, which we take on trust, treating it already as a notorious public good, – that does not enable us to live with our eyes shut. There is really nothing very lovely about millionaire life, millionaire art, or millionaire thought. That is why we hope that it will soon show *the good* we have been led to expect from it – that is to say, disappear or transform itself.

When, then, we use the term 'millionaire society' we refer to the capitalist world of great wealth that has been given this mandate by Marx, and which has come into its own since the War. However few actual millionaires there may be in it, we mean all new-rich society that has the millionaire touch. In this unavoidable poor-rich classification it is not meant that all the rich are wicked and dishonest, and all the poor honest and good, but merely that the rich are rich, with all that entails: and that the poor *are* poor, with what ensues from that as well. The great millionaire in person usually has few of the faults of millionaire society. It would be an insensitive man indeed who did not feel drawn towards such a man as Henry Ford, with his splendid energy and unsocial character. He is what Goethe would call *a nature*. So with most millionaires proper. But the sub-millionaire population of the world of Ritzes and Rivieras is often very ugly.

This millionaire society is replete with a barbarous optimism now. It is no wonder that, as Benda[1] notes (and to which observation we will return later on), there is no artist or philosopher to be found to say anything disagreeable about it – so creating a record of slavishness in literary history! Or there may be some other reason. The artist or philosopher who refuses to identify himself with the aristocratic world may feel better able to accommodate himself to the millionaire world! It is so democratic – that may be it: or there may be other reasons.

This optimism is not to be wondered at, for it is a *new* world; nor, for the same reason, can its barbarity cause any surprise. It is naturally, for itself, the best that has ever been – it is for it that the earth has laboured for so long: the least of its sons and daughters exists in a swoon of luxury besides which the appointments of a medicean prince or princess would appear rustic and coarse. It is as pleased with itself as Punch, and very naturally (with all this wealth and power and comfort) not criticism, but paeans of exultant praise – similar to those you meet with in the advertisement columns of its newspapers, advertising its superlative goods – is what it expects of the writer, philosopher or artist, the traditional appanages of moneyed life. And that is what 'these charming people' get. For itself it appears emphatically to possess every imaginable advantage over former ages that money can buy: for is it not more *democratic*, to start with, than any other society comparable to it in power has ever been? Is it not more exquisitely 'artistic', and above all (and that is the thing about which there can be least question of all) more intelligent, more on the spot, more knowing; so that it is almost – or is it not quite? – intellectually 'self-supporting', as it were?

Finally, under these circumstances, it is able to do what no former society has been able to do. It is able to dispense with the disguises

[1] Julien Benda (1867–1956), author of *Le Trahison des Clercs, Belphégor,* etc.

and graces of art and the painful tasks of culture, its traditional shell. That remoteness that art can throw over even the most scarified, pitted, oozing, and shining close-up of the insolently bared human soul is denied us.

When this society has some invention parodied or watered down for its purposes, and a corrupt reflection of the thought of the true revolutionary results, you will be expected to exclaim, 'How daring! How admirable! How expressive of the New Age!' But you may know better than that, and so find it pointless to exclaim for ever in that way.

So it is if you are truly irreconcilable, truly revolutionary, you will find many curious paradoxes in your relation both with the fashionable life of the wealthy amateur of the millionaire world, and with the revolutionary popularizer. A prophecy of a civilization that will emerge from the present ruin will be present to you in the work of a few inventive men of letters, science and art. A propagandist of the vulgarest capitalism, such as Marinetti[1] was or is, will in consequence not please you much. All that absurd and violent propaganda of *actuality*, stinking of the optimism of the hoardings and the smugness of the motoring millionaire, disguising the squalor of the capitalist factory beneath an epileptic rhetoric of *action*, will not stir you to sympathetic barbaric yawps. You will recognize that the Regent Street which has just disappeared had (although not much to boast of) a certain pleasant meaning that is absent from the present pretentious, solid structures. But a deadweight of organized optimism will press on your chest. Everything will conspire to bully you into a *best of all possible worlds* attitude. You will have to be a very irreconcilable individual not to find yourself on this much too-obviously 'sinning-side'.

V. THE PUBLIC AND THE PRIVATE LIFE

What would be the principal difference between a rigidly organized bureaucratic socialist state and a 'democratic' state of 'get rich quick', open competition, parliamentary government, etc.? The difference, where the average male citizen was concerned, would be that the same opportunities would no longer be found for his individual 'climbing' instincts, or commercial 'push'. Fixed in the

[1] 1876–1944, apostle of futurism.

midst of a carefully regulated hierarchy, his future would be as much earmarked and evident as his past, in the sense that with the automatic graduated salary, rising a few pounds every few years, he would be able to regulate his private life on his life of work, without any likelihood either of interference or, on the other hand, of any accidental and 'lucky' element modifying his destiny spectacularly from one day to the next.

In the democratic competitive system a certain type of energy of a not very valuable sort (except to its possessor) constantly carries men up into the ruling class. That has been happening ever since the establishment of the industrial system. The ruling class becomes more and more a collection of personalities with no traditions, no intellectual training except such as is involved in speculation in stocks and shares or business deals, no religious beliefs usually or any attachments at all in a wider system than that of the stock market or commerce. In a bureaucratic system, inevitably before long a different type of man to this chance jettison of the most brutal sort of success would be evolved. The *static* nature of the system would not be against it, but on the contrary for it, where the production of a valuable administrative *type* was concerned. The breezy elasticity of competitive commerce would not be there. Life would not be a 'lottery' any more. There would be no golden accidents, in which success was usually secured by the least desirable type of being. *Sheltered* from the coarsening rough-and-tumble of commercial life, developing freely a religious consciousness of the destinies of their caste, intellectually equipped in a way that no former european rulers have ever been, you would get (to place against the certain disadvantages of a too static system) an inbred and highly organized body of rulers. Access to this caste would be by way of examination, perhaps; at all events, by some other route than the brutal and unsatisfactory one of commercial success. They would form that necessary versatile and universal man above the specialist. That is of course at present in the nature of a myth of the future, but it is just as good a recommendation to say that the gods will trace their descent from us, as that we trace our descent from gods.

To return to what is happening under our eyes – and which is the first phase of a long process, differentiated from what it supersedes. The spirit of undisciplined enterprise, along freebooting commercial lines, is being crushed out of people by the great concentrations of capital which make it more impossible every day for the 'small man' to advance. Within a few years this process must put a term to individual commercial enterprises. Already the great majority of people are salaried servants of some big trust. Their futures are as cut-and-dried and predictable as the career of a post-office clerk.

Let us imagine this system somewhat more consolidated and developed than it is today. It would probably result in a caste system of family trades, on the pattern of India or Egypt, for instance. There would no doubt, in addition to a bureaucracy, be a priesthood: for the present irreligion of the Soviet, for instance, must not be taken as anything but a transitional and destructive phase. Eventually it is not difficult to predict that revolutionary idealism will slip more and more into some religious mould: though it is not likely that the revolutionary handbooks of christianity, with their greek idealism, will survive the opening of the millennium.

But it is the life of the human average whose destiny we are attempting to trace. The man or woman would have two lives, then as now. There would be *the serious life of work* – and professionalism, in that section of his or her life, would be as prevalent as ever, and specialization manifest itself as jealously as now. And then, work done, there would be *the life of play*.

But the first thing to notice is that, although it would still be called play, this part of life into which all the cultural activities would be pressed would now be the *serious* part – just as the dressing and dances are the serious part of a woman's life: the dressing the preparation of the goods for the market, and conveyed on foot, by taxi, or bus to the dance-hall, the market place. Whereas now in the recreative life the majority of people are quite content to find their pleasure in the convenient role of spectator, then they would insist on a competitive activity. Whereas today (although that today is fast approximating itself to the not very distant future we are describing) the workaday business and money-making life (in which a man is proud of being 'good at his job', and sets his vanity on that) is the *serious* one, then the arena would be what is now the 'private' life of recreation and amusement. Whereas now competition, at least for a man, is confined, in a serious form, to his working business life, then the competitive instincts would find their full expression outside in the world of play.

An *æsthetic* ideal would be substituted, in short, for a masculine abstract one; a personal for an impersonal. If you go into a smoking compartment today in an Underground train you find yourself surrounded by *men*, a very different humanity (as you gaze round at their serious, free, unselfconscious faces, ignorant of the grace that they have never sought beneath their raw hides) to what you would find in a compartment of women. This will very rapidly change. These *men* that you can examine today on their way home in the evening have left their best life, their life of work, behind them. In the future they will under such circumstances have just left a mechanical dream-life of duty, and be expanding and becoming themselves as they approach the seat of their private and personal life. At least this description will apply to the most active and ambitious.

But today the development of colossal industries has already driven off the field most of the crowd of small, ambitious men, the energetic minority of climbers and get-rich-quicks. All outlet to their competitive and ambitious instincts is already occluded. In the human machinery of a large establishment, as in the government services, zeal is not encouraged. An ambitious individual, with a devouring energy and fond of work, will hardly find an outlet for that energy in future in business. For any display made of that energy among his fellow-workers in a large anonymous industry would cause him to be regarded with disfavour, and he would gain nothing by it at all.

There is one way open to each individual today – the sort who in the days before the ascendancy of the cartels and trusts would unscrupulously fight his way up to the top of the tree. This career of the business climber, where as a sort of legitimate criminal he could plunder his way up, is closed for all and sundry, or is rapidly closing. Only lawless and criminal activity, blackmail, poison, and the revolver will soon be left to him. Already today the difficulties put in the way of a man who yesterday, as a small business crook (of small but distinct predatory energy), would make money in 'business', are so vexatious that he is forced to become openly a criminal. In this way, of course, many a small-scale bird of prey is brought to light, smoked out of his business labyrinth by the advance of the anonymous power of the trust and syndicate.

The blocking up of the avenues by which the competitive instinct vented itself, and the crushing uniformity of fortune in which, in the salaried industrial armies of today, it has no play, is one of the circumstances that force these energies back into the non-working life; with many of the more energetic competitive people, into crime; and with others – less energetic – into sport and 'life' *tout court*, the social life.

Meantime press suggestion hammers at this discomforted little man. 'Don't worry, Mr Everyman: never worry! Life – so the scientists tell us – is a small mechanical affair, pleasure is the only reality. Competition and the cares of state and success are all very well. But for simple people like you and me a quiet secure life is what we want, isn't it? If your insurances are paid up, your "home" bought, an aerial installed (the hire-purchase payments kept up), a week arranged for at Worthing or Southend, or if you are near a nice city park, with sand-pits for the kids, if you have a motor-bike, etc., etc., – well life is not so dusty! Pleasure, or the home-life, is the thing!'

Of course, 'art' and 'culture' are introduced as further baits usually into these exordiums. A *Keep off the grass* notice where the wielding of ambitions is concerned, or the great prizes of this world, that whole enclosed realm of 'power' and government, warns Mr Everyman of changed times. But he is recommended to approximate as nearly as possible to a 'gentleman of leisure' and cultured tastes – reduced to earning his living from nine to six every day. Never mind! He can be cultivated' (and Mrs Everyman can be 'refined') for the rest of the time!

Round these abstract flames – one cold and repellent beyond description, the other gay with promises, the William Morris world, the happy valley, the eternal spring, of an electioneering poster – the multitudes of moths press and strain.

This is of course the democratic humbug of the *What the Public Wants* system. A sort of sugar-sweet misinterpretation of the period of mediæval rebirth, when everything was happy and the workshops were full of songs, and craftsmen jostled with amateur masons, is sketched. *The World's great age begins anew, the golden years return*, is in lyrical language, the message of this political afflatus.

It is true that *action* would still be the catchword of this new paradise. Only, the mechanical dogma of *action*, or the vitalistic dogma of 'life', would be turned back on the world of play and the private life of the individual. It would be discouraged thereby – or led gently away – from any designs it might have in the world of *business*, or what has so far been regarded as *real* activity.

Men and women would in this way both be thrown back into what is today still the conventional 'woman's world'. It is true that men, as well as women, dress, go to dances, and so forth. And it is true that these occupations already take on a seriousness, an *art for art's sake air*, which is novel, and very pleasantly novel. Where it is unpleasant it is owing to the inevitable cheapness injected into everything by *What the Public Wants*. Still, the world in which love is manufactured, and young 'homes' built, the race perpetuated, is still conventionally regarded as the woman's province; and the 'day's work' as the man's.

When you are dealing with 'the world' in the sense of the social world, it was said above, you are dealing strictly with a *woman's world*. And so in the humbler world of the great crowds, all that is not ambitious and competitive money-making and 'bread-winning' has been generally regarded as a feminine province. The wholesale invasion of that province, and the fusion of the rôles of the two regions, is what the War and its sequel has resulted in. Already the bridges are built by which the psychology of the masses (with the weakening of the deep sex distinction and sex barriers) will pass back to the conventional female pole, or transfer their energies in that direction.

The old 'man's world' of the abstract (non-personal, non-feminine) life of the earlier European is, then, today, rapidly becoming extinct. The power of money and the vast interlocked organization of 'big business' has gradually withdrawn all initiative from individual males. *Bourgeois* or parliamentary politics is today such a thin camouflage – so harassed, pointless and discredited – the puppets have so little executive power (Lord Curzon is reported to have said shortly before he died, for example, that he had not enough 'power' to send a messenger across Whitehall), that politics no longer afford an outlet for energy comparable for a moment with the opportunities of a game of tennis or a flirtation. Hence every one, ambitious in other ways or not, is sent indiscriminately to the *salon* or the playing-field or dance-hall, and that is the only real battlefield left for masculine or feminine ambition. 'Private' life, in short, has taken the place of 'public' life.

That this is a very sad thing for many people is certain. For such a man as the Marquess Curzon to find himself starved of what he so hungered for, 'power' (over other people, to send them not only across Whitehall, but to the galleys, or anywhere else in or out of this world), is a sad disappointment. But the people who want this sort of power are not very interesting – often by no means so worthy of notice as the people over whom they exercise it. Again, it is a very sad thing that no office-boy today can be very sanguine about ending his life as a magnate. It is no longer so easy, in fact it becomes more difficult every day, to 'get on' in this sensational way in commerce. That is very pathetic: but *qua* office boy and *qua* magnate people are not necessarily worthy of notice, nor as the latter does a man recommend himself more to us than as the former; unless he showers his wealth on us, which is very unusual.

So that politics and business should have closed down on aspirants to honours and great wealth is not such a very great tragedy. But of course that is not the end of it: and all this energy bursts up in other directions. But it does not follow, because as political or commercial specialists these men were not necessarily very interesting, that as social specialists they are more so. Probably they are even better at their masculine tasks than at their feminine ones.

What has been gained is this. In the former 'democratic', parliamentary régime, and régime of open competition, all the machinery worked in public. The ambitious 'public' specialist was watched by millions, his speeches quoted with great care, his bold financial undertakings eagerly noted. Now all this will go underground. We shall never be bothered with real live politics or commerce again. At least, we shall suffer them, but have no part in them. The accounts of them in the newspapers will become more and more unreal and meaningless and difficult to follow; and then eventually they will disappear altogether. The *results* will appear, however, in social life. Enormous pearls will collect on the necks of ladies, reaching their necks *from nowhere* – for it is unlikely that wealth will be explicit. All the ponderable forces of the world will be occult, and only flower mysteriously in social phenomena such as pearls and motor-cars. As though waited on by genii, favoured persons will flourish in social life, and their 'power' (instead of revealing its larva stages to the world, and parading its vermiform 'public' shape in politics and industry) will appear in its final butterfly transformation as a social phenomenon.

For those who (like great artists and others) love shapes of masculine splendour and power, belles Héaulmières, prophets, visions of Infernos and so forth, and on whom the finished social article, the eternal butterfly, is likely to pall – for them also, beyond this phrase, there will be others, no doubt, in which eventually, like a tremendous serpent, 'power' once more issues from its subterranean retreat, and asserts itself again in massive magnificence. But that of course is very distant. The joys of the Leviathan are not for us. What at least will be gained for the moment is that all the decaying and unsightly publicity of *imperfect* power will disappear. And when the social world organizes itself as the only serious world, it will be very different to the place it is at present – and will remain, until the occult political machinery is consolidated.

VI. THE CONTEMPORARY MAN 'EXPRESSES HIS PERSONALITY'

The 'class war' is of course a notion that extends to every possible class. And sex is of course a very important 'class' indeed, and 'sex war' a very important war.

A great deal of abuse has been levelled at Marx by the opponents of Marxism, as the author of this diabolical invention, the 'class struggle'. That is quite natural; it is a tribute to Marx's sagacity, and to the effectiveness of the engine. And it is not to be disputed that Mr Russell is right when he says that 'the intensity of organization is increased not only when a man belongs to more organizations, but also when the organizations to which he already belongs play a larger part in his life – as, for example, the State plays a larger part in war than in peace'. The higher the state of organization, the less individual play, initiative, and ultimately power possessed by the individual so 'classified'. But although Mr Russell regards such organization as extremely sad, I find it difficult to do so, for the reasons I have just advanced. What is of more importance, of course, is that the people concerned, as I have already pointed out, do not. Men and woman like nothing so much as being 'classified' – not, it is true, for a 'war' (though they do not object to that so much as is supposed: they are drugged into a state of anæsthesia by the rhythm of their 'class'), but for anything else there is no surer way to their hearts than to invent a new 'class' for them. And sex is of course the most popular 'class' of all.

Men have to found a class for the reception of any newly recognized idea of importance. Before it possesses this human repository it is not a fact. To be *good, a deceived husband, an artist, a one-legged man*, at once lands an individual in some aggregation or class, and adversity or good fortune both drop him in the midst of the strangest bedfellows. But, of course, first of all he has to be recognized as possessing the quality – the goodness, credulity, artisticness, or one-leggedness, or whatever it may be: and sometimes luckily, it takes people a long time to arrive at the truth, except in the simplest and most conventional cases. Saints often have been known to spend their entire lives in the class of devils, and so on.

Instead, then, of the idea being left free to pass from place to place and man to man at will (which would be the dispensation most favourable to elasticity and life), it has to be penned at once – or a man representing it has to be penned – with a large collection of people, where it, or the man representing it, very likely will languish. To the herding of men nature attends: some of course can elude her rough herding, but a few sports only.

The *idées forces*, it will be recollected, result in a walking 'idea' – which is the dynamo. And it matters very little what the 'idea' is: though we have an arbitrary class of ideas the adoption of which has very serious results for a man; for example, should a man have for his motive idea a 'potato' – should be believe himself a potato, or a piece of potato-peel, as it were – we clap him into a madhouse. But outside of this there is a wide choice.

Generally speaking, it can be said that people wish to escape from themselves (this by no means excluding the crudest selfishness). When people are encouraged, as happens in a democratic society, to believe that they wish 'to express their personality', the question at once arises as to what their personality is. For the most part, if investigated, it would be rapidly found that they had none. So what would it be that they would eventually 'express'? And why have they been asked to express it?

If they were subsequently watched in the act of 'expressing' their personality, it would be found that it was somebody else's personality they were expressing. If a hundred of them were observed 'expressing their personality' all together and at the same time, it would be found that they all 'expressed' this inalienable, mysterious 'personality' in the same way. In short, it would be patent at once that they had only *one* personality between them to 'express' — some 'expressing' it with a little more virtuosity, some a little less. It would be a *group personality* that they were 'expressing' — a pattern imposed on them by means of education and the hypnotism of cinema, wireless and press. Each one would, however, be firmly persuaded that it was 'his own' personality that he was 'expressing': just as when he voted he would be persuaded that it was the vote of a free man that was being cast, replete with the independence and free-will which was the birthright of a member of a truly democratic community.

Here, in this case, you get an individual convinced that he is 'expressing his personality': that he has a thing called a 'personality', and that it is desirable to express it. He has been supplied with this formula, 'expressing the personality', as a libertarian sugar-plum. He has been taught that he is 'free', and that it is the privilege of the free man to 'express his personality'. Now, if you said to this man that he *had* no personality, that he had never been given the chance to have one, in any case, in the standardized life into which he fitted with such religious conformity: and secondly, that he did not *want* to have a personality at all, really, and was quite happy as he was, — he would reply that you might be very clever, and might think that you were funny, but that *he* was the best judge of whether he possessed a personality or not: that as he 'expressed' it every Saturday afternoon and evening and on Sundays, he probably knew more about it than you did; and that in consequence your gratuitous assumption that he did not want one was absurd, as well as offensive. If he were a savage Robot, he might confirm this statement by directing a blow at your head.

The truth is that such an individual is induced to 'express his personality' because it is desired absolutely to standardize him and get him to rub off (in the process of the 'expression') any rough edges that may remain from his untaught, spontaneous days. Where the avenues of 'expression' suggested to him are more 'original' and sensational (as in Germany, where the *Rhythm-army of naked male life,* the *Joy Group,* or *Naked Men's Club of Sun Pals* would perhaps attract him), the case is no different, but he is of course then far more convinced, even, that his personality is being 'expressed'. But, drawn into one orbit or another, he must in the contemporary world submit himself to one of several mechanical socially organized rhythms. There is really less choice every day: the number of group-personalities available, of course, diminishes just as the number of newspapers decreases. And it seems impossible to dispute that, as regards this side of life, and leaving aside the threat of unemployment and fresh wars, people have never been so happy. The Not-Self (and *not* the self at all) is the goal of human ambition. And not 'freedom', or the eccentric play of the 'personality', but submission to a group-rhythm, is what men desire.

But even if they did not desire it, it is the condition of all successful practical life, into which neither metaphysics nor personality can really enter. George Sorel's account of his manner of work emphasizes this:

> You remember what Bergson wrote [he says] about the impersonal, the socialized, the *ready-made*, which contains a piece of advice addressed to students to whom the acquiring of knowledge that would be of use in practical life was essential. The pupil has all the more confidence in the formulas offered to him, and he retains them, in consequence, all the more easily, if he imagines that they are accepted by the majority of people. Thus his mind is relieved of any metaphysical preoccupation, and he is accustomed not to desire any personal attitude to anything. Often in the end he comes to regard as a superiority the absence of any *inventiveness*. My manner of working is the opposite of that. I submit to my readers the effort of a mind which seeks to escape from the constraint of past formulas, invented for the general use; a mind which wishes for the personal. (*Réflexions sur la violence*.)

It is a combination of these two happy things that promises the best result for human happiness. Sorel's desire for 'the personal' is everybody's desire, *verbally*. That is the 'ready-made' formula, which is known to be 'accepted by the majority of people'. And the delights and proud assertions of seeking for 'the personal' can be undertaken on one big, crowded track, laid down in any of a hundred text-books, with the certainty that every one else will be seeking it at the same time and in the same place and in identically the same manner.

VII. PEOPLE'S HAPPINESS FOUND IN TYPE-LIFE

As in another essay I have examined very thoroughly the idea of class, I will not go into it here. I need only in conclusion make a few remarks with regard to it. If from the standpoint of philosophy the sorelian science of class is negligible, and even rather childish, from a practical standpoint it is of great importance, and of the utmost potentiality. An *esprit de corps* can be worked up about anything: the *regiment* is the unit of discipline and romance, rather than the region from which it comes. And a 'proletarian' class obsession is essential to bind together the 'proletariat', whatever that may be. Without some such fictitious ('artificial', as Sorel says) bond it would fall to pieces. And even the parade of objective science and historical paraphernalia is justified if it is understood by the director of the movement which it is seeking to save.

Actually, again, the more you specialize people, the more power you can obtain over them, the more helpless and in consequence the more obedient they are. To shut people up in a water-tight, syndicalized, occupational unit is like shutting them up on an island. Further, occupation, in a world of mixed races and traditions, is the most natural classification (though it could be said from another point of view, of course, to be the most unnatural).

The ideally 'free man' would be the man *least* specialized, the *least* stereotyped, the man approximating to the *fewest* classes, the *least* clamped into a system – in a word, the most individual. But a society of 'free men', if such a thing could ever come about, which it certainly could not, would immediately collapse.

The chief thing to remember in such a discussion is that no one wants to be 'free' in that sense. People ask nothing better than to be *types* – occupational types, social types, functional types of any sort. If you force them not to be, they are miserable, just as the savage grew miserable when the white man came and prevented him living a life devoted to the forms and rituals he had made. And if so forced (by some interfering philanthropist or unintelligent reformer) to abandon some *cliché*, all men, whether white, yellow, or black, take the first opportunity to get their cliché back, or to find another one. For in the mass people wish to be automata: they wish to be conventional: they hate you teaching them or forcing them into 'freedom': they wish to be obedient, hard-working machines, as near dead as possible – as near dead (feelingless and thoughtless) as they can get, without actually dying.

PART VII. THE FAMILY AND FEMINISM[1]

I. WHY 'SOCIALISM WISHES TO ABOLISH THE FAMILY'

It is round the question of *the family* that all the other questions of politics and social life are gathered. The break-up of the family unit today is the central fact of our life: it is from its central disintegration both in fact and in our minds – the consequent readjustments of our psychology – that all the other revolutionary phases of our new society radiate. The relations of men to women, of the child to the parent, of friendship and citizenship to the new ideals of the state, are all controlled by it.

This can easily be seen by taking a few examples from the things we have just been discussing. The *child* obsession, the flight from responsibility, would naturally result from the decay of *the parent*, in the old sense of a symbol of authority. In a communist state, where children were taken from the parents at birth to a public *crèche*, the state becoming the 'breadwinner' and the effective centre of authority or All-father, as it were, the parents would never be 'parents' at all.

The economic incentive of the upkeep of a family circle, a wife and children, again, must affect a man's attitude to his dignity and duty in a great many ways. Relieved of that, he would care far less about his position in the world, 'getting on', whether he remained in an irresponsible subaltern position or became a master. It would affect very deeply his attitude to women if marriage were entirely eliminated from his transactions with them. The bachelor's or the 'old maid's' interests are very different – where interests exist – to the 'family man's' or the 'mother of a family's'. And lastly, sex inversion is evidently not disconnected with the existence and coercive influence of the idea of the family in a man or woman's life. And to the end of their days Fortune is like a cherishing parental figure to the man or woman of fashion and fortune: however many children they have by accident, they must remain eternally the spoilt child themselves, and the family is seldom a reality for them. In that they resemble the most emancipated worker in the most complete of communist societies.

. . . .

[1] Chapters I–XI.

In this part the feminine, generally, is to be discussed, then, and the problems arising from family life, sex specialization, and the relations of men and women. My entrance into it is effected without the accompaniment of set teeth and battle in the eye; a few elementary precautions are observed, but none of a slighting nature. I am able to observe very little difference between men and women, and my liking and interest are equally distributed. If anything, women represent, I believe, a higher spiritual average. Even the instinct of primitive races that accorded women mystical and creative attributes denied to men seems to me very worth attention. So there where I certainly wear a uniform, it does not dispose me to militancy in a quarrel that I understand too well to become violently partisan. Great feminists like Ibsen, for instance, have usually been followed by a great reactionary and anti-feminist like Strindberg. The headlong liberal partisanship of the first, with all it entails of stupid bitterness, raises an opposite champion, who, with excesses on the other side, soon organizes male zeal, and the sexes are on a war footing. The fit of hatred he throws himself into shows he is nearer to the feminist than he thinks – probably too near to the feminine, in the secondary sense, altogether. Feminism is a movement directed to the destruction of the family, which is a good thing. But needless to say, the true motive is never avowed: and a quantity of fantastic doctrine is manufactured which is as seriously disputed as though some valuable discovery depended on it.

P.-J. Proudhon was not a feminist. Edouard Berth remarks on that fact as follows: 'If one wishes to estimate the depth of the *détraquement* of the contemporary world, there is no better witness of it than feminism. And that Proudhon was not a feminist is one more proof that he incarnated, in the heart of the socialist movement, the reaction of good sense and of classical reason.' (*Les méfaits des intellectuels.*) He then proceeds to quote Proudhon (from *Contradictions*): I give a part of his quotation:

> Love and marriage, work and the family circle, property and *domesticity* . . . all these terms are equivalent. On that point all mankind is unanimous – all except the socialists, who alone, in their ideologic void, protest against this unanimity of the rest of mankind. *Socialism wishes to abolish family life, because it costs too much.* It wishes to abolish property, because it is prejudicial to the state. Socialism wishes

to change the rôle of the woman: from queen, as society has established her, it wants to make her a priestess of Cotytto. . . .[1]

Proudhon, the great French revolutionary of the nineteenth century, was, however, violently assailed by the feminists for his reactionary attitude as regards feminism. This attitude was dictated, certainly, as Berth says, from sheer French 'classicist' good sense. He was accused of wishing to keep the woman as a family drudge, because he wished to maintain family life. He upheld the necessity of this against all the shallow and fashionable insistence of his socialist friends, who, for the most part, wanted to destroy it. *Socialism wishes to abolish family life, because it costs too much,* he said, far too bluntly! He wanted economics to accommodate itself to the family instead of *vice versa*. In this he showed himself an imperfect realist.

He saw the threat of a new slave-state, worse than any former slavery. He realized that as 'free' creatures, in the utopian, the european sense, the man and the woman must remain united. United they would stand, he considered, but forced apart by economic exigence or political intrigue they would fall – that is, no longer be free. So according to his lights, he fought very hard for the freedom that he prized so much. What that freedom really was, and whether it was anybody's freedom, I have already discussed. Later, in connection with the general theories of Proudhon, I shall again briefly consider it.

Proudhon was nothing if not a moralist: but in this matter it was really not as a moralist that he was speaking, but from the deepest sense of what he saw to be the interests of european free institutions. He says, for instance, in *La pornocratie* (the book he wrote in reply to his feminist opponents):

> I have blamed, with all the energy of which I am capable, incest, abortion, rape, prostitution, all the crimes and offences against marriage and the family – I could equally say *against woman*. I have denounced them as the signs and instruments of despotism.

But the elderly harpy of Byron's *Don Juan* putting her head out of the window in the town that is being sacked, and inquiring impatiently, 'When is the raping going to begin?', suggests by its truth to life that Proudhon was talking of *crimes against women*

---

[1] A Thracian divinity, worshipped with licentious rites.

too much from the man's standpoint. Contraceptives may be inventions inimical to women in their functional capacity of mothers. But a great brood of children is not every woman's affair. There is a personality in every woman that is independent of function that has to be taken into account at least. These things that Proudhon capitulates are against the family, and against marriage certainly. But they are not for that reason *against women,* as they are represented to be by him. That is the weakness of his position. *Woman* was his Achilles' heel as a revolutionary. The Utopianism of which Marx accused him is most visible in that. And he was a utopian despot.

Marriage is often against a woman (or a man). And the family is 'a despotism'. In many senses it could be said that the things enumerated above – as abortion or prostitution, at all events – were signs and instruments of freedom rather than despotism, exactly indeed as the conventional feminist would assert.

II. MR CHESTERTON'S CONCERN FOR THE FAMILY UNIT

Before proceeding with our analysis of Proudhon's notions relative to the family and to woman, I will consider a contemporary view of the same subject, also dogmatically in favour of the family unit. It appeared in an October (1925) issue of a liberal weekly, for the direction of which Mr G. K. Chesterton is responsible. It has the additional advantage of introducing into our debate this liberal colleague of Mr Shaw's, who is a sort of caricature of 'a Liberal' as seen by Rowlandson.

The liberalism of Mr Chesterton, complicated with a romantic conversion to roman catholicism, and installed in an obsessing cartoon-like John Bull physique, is very different to that of Mr Shaw. The well-fed high spirits of the old liberal England, the strange association of humaneness with religious intolerance, a sanguine grin fiercely painted on the whole make-up, compose a sinister figure such as you would find, perhaps – exploiting its fatness, its shrewdness, its animal violence, its blustering patriotism all at once – in the centre of some nightmare Bank Holiday fair. He is all for the freedom of old England, whose 'beer-drinking Britons can never be beat', all for 'infallible artillery' to support the infallibility of that potentate he has heavily embraced, and to support anything else that can afford artillery to advance its peculiar claims. He cannot understand why a jolly old war (with all the usual accompaniments of poison gas and bombs, you know) cannot be arranged between Ireland and Scotland on the score of the heresy of the latter; and while this was going on he would urge the English to invade Wales, and finish off the job so half-heartedly dropped a thousand odd years ago by the ingaevonic tribes.[1] The cackling and grimacing humorousness, punctuated with flabby puns, of this strange individual, would increase immeasurably if he were able to observe the british catholics preparing to attack the british anglicans in the rear, while the latter were finishing off the last of the chapel-going Cymri.

The article is named 'The Fear of the Family', and saw the light in consequence of a pronouncement of another liberal, of rather more mixed opinions. The writer describes the thesis of his opponent as follows. He says that, owing to 'the exhaustive and profound studies in economics' of this erring gentleman, he had reached the 'sensational' conclusion that 'the present industrial system, founded on coal, petrol, steam, iron, railways, factories and laboratories cannot by any conceivable means any longer support the institution known as the family, not at least in the form in which it has come down to us since the days when the first christian priests insisted that the privilege of marriage should be extended even to slaves. The continuance of marriage and the family as an institution universal throughout society is bound to land industry not merely in trade depressions, strikes, lockouts, and extensive unemployment, but in complete stoppage and disaster'.

Under these circumstances the good economist's conclusion is that the *family must go*, of course. In this he resembles Proudhon's 'socialist'.

The writer of this article, having stated the position of his renegade, too 'economical', opponent, explains the situation from his own pure-liberal point of view. 'The real difficulty with industry today is that the man who works in the mine, in the factory, or on the railway is by tradition a free man; and he is a free man in virtue of the fact that christian civilization has made him the actual

[1] Ingaevones: a branch of the Teutons living along the north sea, as well as the Weser and Ems.

or potential head of a family, morally, socially and legally responsible for the maintenance of that family. It is this that makes the working man of today so intractable. Take away from him that responsibility and that freedom, and you will make him more tractable. . . . If a man has a wife and family to support, he can always make some show at the bar of public opinion in every strike and every lock-out. If the state supports his wife and family for him, he can make no show at all. He can be told to get to work at once. And the *Daily Mail* and the people in trains and motor cars would not be slow to tell him so.'

What this says is that the workman has always been able to hide behind his wife and children; and the more children he had, the more sandbags he had. But has this responsibility been pleasant either for him or for them? They, the rampart for his more and more fictitious 'independence', have received the brunt of the economic attack. As to the responsibility and the freedom with the loss of which he is threatened, he would be far happier without them. He never asked for them, and has never enjoyed them. For these two expensive words he has suffered enough hardships. It is the greatest cruelty to him to urge him to hang on to them today. If gives a fine sensation of heroism, no doubt, to the theorist so advising him. But for the head of a family on a low wage it is less romantic.

The romance of the *family as a unit* is a prosperous nineteenth-century english middle-class romance. To tell the impoverished english labourer today to keep at all costs his home-and-castle-in-one, and continue to cling to this phantom of authority, is to urge the continuance of a stupid torture.

The women and children, on their side, would be very much relieved if the state would take over their maintenance. As to the 'home-life', the well-to-do have seldom any conception of what a mockery it is to speak in sugary or heroic terms of that to people who, like the majority, have to live in a half savage condition of poverty.

Socrates proposed that, in his ideal state, the children should be removed from the parents. The problem of the woman, owing to the peculiarities of his greek training, he neglected. The German idea of *Gemütlichkeit* and 'home' was the last thing that would have occurred to a Greek, of course. It was rather the thing to escape from than the thing to cling to. Then his idea of 'freedom', as well, would be different to the german, which latter would be based really on the notion of *physical* freedom, as Goethe defined it to his friend. The patriarchal is the *physical* ideal. But to be anything that can remotely be described as 'free' in industrial conditions is not to be patriarchal, or burdened with a family.

III. 'THE WOMAN', PROUDHON'S ONLY REVOLUTIONARY DISCOVERY

Proudhon vaunted the latin, the roman heritage. He was very fond of returning to the law-giving and law-loving *fond* of the french nature, the roman in his inheritance. No roman father could have devised more despotic conditions than he did for the woman. He even (cf. *La pornocratie*), in the true fashion of roman antiquity, would have given the husband power of life and death over the wife. But with a slave system, and the terrible *patria potestas*, the Roman was very successful politically. It is not christian principles, which is the same as socialist principles, that make a state 'great'. And Proudhon (in the condition of complete mental confusion in which the European has remained ever since his turbulent egotism and western and northern 'push' tied itself up to its opposite, christianity) was all for a great and even warlike 'city', on the antique, pagan, pattern.

Let us say that women are *men with a handicap*. It is a natural handicap. Proudhon was a fine example of the natural man. Nothing would have convinced him of the reasonableness of removing the handicap socially, surgically. For, being the natural man, he hated uniformity. Everything would seem for him, as for Sorel, to gain in force and power by *differentiation*. And everything about him was highly reasonable – all but his socialism, which was a madness he never completely overcame. That was the christian overlay, beneath which the pagan and roman limbs could be seen perpetually moving, evidently with iron discipline, to the most warlike and primitive airs.

So, as Proudhon regarded himself as eminently of the party of revolt (the only way in which he was not a revolutionary, he might have supposed, was in his anti-feminism), the woman was the only 'revolutionary' that he challenged. But on the principle which impelled him to challenge her, he could have challenged equally *every* item of the revolutionary programme that he so ardently supported, and so become a unique revolutionary.

The idea of government, he says, is modelled on the experience of the family; its tenacity is owing to the fact that men have always had under their eyes the small model of the state in their own family circle. The family is the embryo of the state. The father is *the king*, the mother is *the minister of state*, the child is *the subject*. Thus the fundamental age and sex categories have regulated, immemorially, the notion of government. 'That is the reason why,' he says (*Idée générale de la révolution au xix ème siècle*), 'the fraternalist-socialists, who take the family as the model of society, all arrived at the idea of dictatorship, the most exaggerated form of government.' He finishes by asking, 'How long will it take us to understand this affiliation of ideas?'

It is, however, an attempt to trace the affiliation, the *family* relationship, as it were, of all these revolutionary ideas, that has occupied us throughout this essay. Proudhon never understood, apparently, any affiliation except that of the man and woman. 'The woman' was his sole *philosophic* discovery. She shook him, apparently, out of his conventional Utopia: for some reason he saw her very clearly indeed. And his attitude to *her* was in direct contradiction to all his anarchist teaching; although very much in agreement with all his highly non-revolutionary instincts.

Above we have seen him setting out to show (in his chapter on 'The Principle of Authority') that men have always gone wrong in their revolutionary activities because they have insisted on modelling their idea of the state on the obviously family paradigm. From the obsessing image of *the family* they have not been able to escape. So it is that, no sooner is one despotism (modelled on the traditional family) cast down, than another equally despotic is set up in its place.

Of all the great revolutionaries of the last century Proudhon dogmatized the most about the family, in the opposite sense to most of his revolutionary contemporaries. The family must at all cost be retained: that was one of the corner-stones of his system. Alone the family was able to guarantee freedom, and stood between despotism and mankind. And yet above we see him indicating it as the model of all governmental despotism.

IV. THE FAMILY AS AN OBSESSING MODEL

If you have followed my argument and understood my meaning you will know that this essay *On the Art of Being Ruled* could be described, if such a description were required, *as against the family*. On the other hand, it is not *against women*. Eventually, I believe, a considerable segregation of women and men must occur, just as segregation of those who decide for the active, the intelligent life, and those who decide (without any stigma attaching to the choice) for the 'lower' or animal life, is likely to happen, and is very much to be desired. This, in its turn, no doubt, in the end, would lead to people being born into these respective planes of existence. Different species cut off from each other, and no longer free to choose, would be found. Interplanetary communication might settle this problem in the future. If this idea of segregation seems a disgusting one, all that can be said is that it is often suggested to us that more intelligent beings than ourselves may exist in other worlds, and may even be able to influence or control us. But we live our life just the same. It is not much to boast of; it is a little brief thing, but we call it, at least, 'our own'.

Returning to the paradigm of the Family (at the basis, Proudhon affirms, of all ideas of government up to the present): a gerontocracy – that the old should rule the young – would be an excellent mechanical arrangement if years brought wisdom to people; or if the majority of people ever had, to start with, any intellectual power. But we know that that is not the case. There is very little difference between the old and the young, just as there is extremely little difference between men and women. People pretend or really believe that there is a mysterious difference; but if you go in search of it, it is hard to find. An 'old boy' is very much like a boy: in anglo-saxon countries, with the insistence on athletic sports, the whole education tending to confirm this uniformity. Its tendency is to take the spiritual quality away from youth, and to bestow a sort of degraded athletic 'youthfulness' on age. It deliberately stunts the spiritual growth, so that a man remains of adolescent stature, as far as the mind is concerned, to the end. 'Most men die at thirty-five,' a french writer suggests. Thirty would probably be nearer the mark: but the demise is a small matter and is scarcely noticeable.

The family, however, perpetuates this idea of authority. No

doubt in more primitive societies, where people have sometimes been allowed to develop more freely, here and there, their faculties, there may have been more reality in this contrast: and hence the stability of such forms as the indonesian, polynesian, or australian gerontocracies. But today, in contemporary Europe, there is no such contrast. An english cabinet minister or a great business magnate reads the detective-story fiction of Phillips Oppenheim; and his son and grandson read Phillips Oppenheim, one in book form and the other in serial form in the shilling magazine. The footmen and valets of these various gentlemen also read Phillips Oppenheim, when their masters have done with him; they all equally live in a Phillips Oppenheim world of 'deep diplomats', 'keen-eyed' men, iron-willed, hard-headed business giants, 'sporty, knowledgeable girls', 'matey' and 'clean-limbed'. The scullery-maid reads *Peg's Paper*, and that is the same thing, only it costs her less: and the boots reads *Sexton Blake* or *The Magnet*, which is also the same thing. These people are most truly *equals* – and they all equally hate the 'highbrow' with a mighty hatred – that 'highbrow' who is another of the myths of their backstairs world.

These people cannot be divided into age classes, or into social classes, into classes of the educated and uneducated, or into any class that has any reality except the class of those who have a lot of money and those who have none. Péguy insisted that there is a greater chasm between the Rich and the Poor today than ever before. They lie *horizontally* side by side, with the economic chasm separating them in between; there is no vertical identity of race or religion: as, for instance, in the case of the lowest feudal serf and greatest feudal chatelain there would be the mystical unity of the catholic christian world. I think Péguy, in that description, is neglecting the fact of the community that an absence of anything spiritual gives to those merely mechanically separated worlds of Wealth and Poverty. There is greater brotherhood today between Dives and Lazarus than has existed probably for a long time. For both are equally *poor in spirit*, and consequently to some extent equally *blessed*. That is a great freemasonry. That could almost be called the great secret of the political world today: all inequality in wealth and comfort is forgiven the greatest millionaire, on account of his vulgarity, in which he is apt to far outdo his chauffeur or employee. That *little touch of nature* (or of ill-nature, as Butler would correct it), that spiritual identity, that cunning invitation to the basest form of *humility*, and the commonest form of a common humanity, is the millionaire's political secret.

But with all the resources of his fabulous wealth, the democratic magnate is apt to drag the poor into depths of spiritual poverty undreamed of by any former proletariat of former ruling class. The rich have achieved this awful brotherhood with the poor by bleeding them of all character, spirituality, and mental independence. That accomplished, they join them spiritually or unspiritually in the servants' hall. All the privileges conferred by wealth are, however, still theirs. Frederick the Great, living with his *heiduques*[1] and grooms, was better off, in the sense of enjoying greater freedom and power, than he would have been as a more conventional ruler among his courtiers. But the latter he also reduced to the level of grooms as far as possible when he went into society. If all the nobles and officials of Prussia at that time are imagined as living similarly on familiar patriarchal terms with their servants, some idea will be obtained of what the millionaire society of today is becoming. It is part of that wise and excellent programme of socially and politically *having the apple and eating it too*. The advantages of the poor man's child – the freedom from restraint of the animality of the life of the gutter, emancipated from *noblesse oblige* (the infantile love of dirt and garbage made such a curious use of by Fourier) are astutely combined with all the advantages of the rich man's child – the expensive toys, servants and so forth. A travesty of revolution is wedded to the least severe and onerous advantages of aristocracy.

A kind of gigantically luxurious patriarchate is what democracy and monster industry together have invented. The analogy between a great industrial city and the desert – the emptiness and abstractedness of industrial life – is patent enough. So patriarchal conditions in contemporary urban life are not so unnatural as would appear at first sight. There is no king; but there are many mercantile despots, more or less benevolently patriarchal, indistinguishable in taste, culture, or appearance from their servants, or subjects, or 'clients'. This is how it comes that the family once more occupies the foreground of our lives. With a new *familiarity* and a flesh-creeping 'homeliness' entirely of this unreal, materialist world, where all 'sentiment' is coarsely manufactured and advertised in

[1] Hungarian soldiers.

colossal sickly captions, disguised for the sweet tooth of a monstrous baby called 'the Public', the family as it is, broken up on all hands by the agency of feminist and economic propaganda, reconstitutes itself in the image of the state. The government becomes an emperor disguised as Father Christmas, an All-Father, a paterfamilias with his pocket full of crystal sets, gramophones, russian boots, and flesh-coloured stockings, which he proceeds to *sell* to his 'children'.

V. FOURIER'S THEORY OF GROUPS

We have seen – in a chapter named 'The Public and the Private Life' – how the other great factor of the barring of the roads of open competition and individual enterprise, and the consequent death of ambition, has contributed to this. In his *Theory of Groups* (ch. ii.) Fourier considers the best method by which one can establish 'le lien sociétaire'. The groups or elementary modes of social relationship, he says, are to be counted to the number of four – like the four elements, earth, air, fire, and water.

The analogical chart he draws up as follows:

Groupes	*Eléments*
Majeurs	
d'Amitié, affection unisexuelle.	*Terre*
d'Ambition, affection corporative.	*Air*
Mineurs	
d'Amour, affection bissexuelle.	*Arome*
de Famille, affection consanguine.	*Feu*
Pivotal	
d'Unitéisme ou fusion de liens.	*Feu*

In examining this curious table it will be seen, if our account of the tendencies of society is correct, that (1) the *unisexuelle* (friendship) affective category is being merged in the *bissexuelle* or sexual; that is to say, that friendship between man and woman, or between woman and man, tends to take with it sexual and physical implications, and the spiritual, abstract nature of this relationship becomes less clearly defined. That is to say, everywhere the non-sexual tends to become the sexual, as the family (and the normal or sexual with it) tends to disappear. This of course affects the revolutionary top layer of society first, the conservative and lower classes not yet being deeply influenced.

It will be seen that (2) the category of Ambition will shortly be obsolete, and ambition itself be extinct, for the mass of salaried slaves. In this way earth and the atmosphere disappear. Only *sexual love* and *the family* are left. We all are in the category of Minors. But *the family* today is also disappearing, only (in its essence) it is disappearing into government and into social life; that is to say, that social life is being modelled more and more on a vast family pattern, with the nursery (but a universal nursery, equipped with a complete universe of toys) as its conventicle, and a state of childlike tutelage as its supreme paradigm.

But in the above chart Fourier appends a fifth category, a *pivotal* category, as he calls it, of 'unityism' or unification. In that all the social ties are fused. Such is perhaps the position of our society: but in its case the 'unification' is all impregnated with the neighbouring family metaphysics. It is further reinforced and furnished with the bankrupt stocks of the other categories.

In social life, as in the government, the family image obsesses people. Even in an ectogenetically produced society,[1] where the family would have ceased to exist, it is quite possible that the family paradigm, the phantom of the superseded family organization, would still exist, in its full conventionality. So I agree with Proudhon that the obsession of the family should be overcome except for the purposes of the narrow family circle – so long as that exists: that its reflection, in the life of government or in the life of society, should be abolished. But I do not agree with Proudhon that the family itself should at all costs be retained. For, if you object to its shadow so much, and call that shadow 'despotic', why should you be so eager to embrace and cherish its substance?

VI. THE WAR OF 'ONE HALF AGAINST THE OTHER'

Wealth is the only thing today that confers power or 'class' on an individual. Wealth is an abstract thing independent of social organization, or of national organization, or of a secular 'stake in the country'. When it pretends to delegate power to other categories

[1] i.e., that in which children would be produced artificially, without gestation.

of things or of people, the democracy or what not, it is merely acting through them, they are its helpless and hypnotized instruments. And naturally it chooses for its instruments the most helpless and ill-equipped classes of the community. It is thus that a hundred things are done today in the divine name of Youth, that if they showed their true colours would be seen by rights to belong rather to old age. Things are done, likewise, in the name of Liberty, that are, in truth, the promptings of oppression. As Proudhon truly says, 'Grâce au prestige de ce mot *liberté*, si étrangement prostitué, on a rendu les travailleurs eux-mêmes complices de leur propre infortune.' ('Thanks to the prestige of this word *liberty*, so strangely prostituted, the workers have been made the accomplices of their own misfortune'.) (*La capacité politique, etc.*) All the rashness, ignorance, and weakness of women are similarly exploited. Things are undertaken in their name, or in that of their supposed cause, *feminism*, that have nothing at all to do with them. The following speech from Renan's remarkable continuation of the *Tempest* of Shakespeare puts the matter in its true light, for every epoch, for ever and ever without end – unless the capitalistic unification of the world works the miracle that it may, and the cannon-fodder is turned into a more productive, humane article:

> ORLANDO . . . A clear, reflecting, self-loving, consciousness would say to itself that the essential thing in a battle is not to be killed. It is, therefore, necessary to maintain a vast reserve of ignorance and stupidity, a mass of people so simple that they can be taught to believe that if they are killed they will either go to heaven or that their lot is to be envied by the living. They make their armies of such creatures as those and not out of the intelligent classes; for if all were people of sense, nobody would be sacrificed, as each would say, 'My life is worth more to me than anything else.' As a rule, all heroism is due to a lack of reflection, and thus it is necessary to maintain a mass of imbeciles. If they once understand themselves the ruling men will be lost. A man rules by employing one half of these animals to conquer the other half. In the same way the art of politics lies in dividing the people and controlling each section by means of the other. To do that one of these halves must be brutalized, so that the rest may be more easily separated from them; for if the armed and unarmed once realize their position, the very structure of society will be wrecked. RUGIERO. That is truly spoken. There is one thing which always fills me with uncontrollable laughter, and that is when Turks and Christians go to war. Each fights without nourishment or pay, and each buoys up his

heart with the assurance that if the fortune of battle decrees his death he will go forthwith to paradise. Now, either the Turk or the Christian must be deceived, for if the Christian's heaven exists it must preclude that of the Turk, on the ground of total unlikeness. . . . It is impossible that both of the enraged combatants can be right at the same time . . . etc. (*Caliban, Act II. Scene i.* Renan.)

If you do not regard feminism with an uplifting sense of the gloriousness of woman's industrial destiny, or in the way, in short, that it is prescribed, by the rules of the political publicist, that you should, that will be interpreted by your opponents as an attack on *woman*. But it is not necessarily that, of course. It might even be a chivalrous *defence* instead of an attack. I lay no claim here to any chivalrous intention; but it is certainly not as an anti-feminist that I am writing.

Traditionally women and children are the most helpless and ill-equipped categories of mankind. Up to the present, equality of opportunity has not been achieved, and they are still the most credulous and influenceable of us. It is natural, therefore, that a great political power, interested only in domination and in nothing else, would seize on them as its most readily manipulated tools. By flattery and coercion it would discipline their ignorance and weakness into an organized instrument of social and political domination. As an alternative to the system suggested in the speech quoted above, by which one half of the mass of 'those animals' or 'imbeciles' is used against the other half, there is that by which the mass of the ill-equipped, easily influenced, and credulous can be used to destroy the minority that knows a little more than it is proper that it should know, that it is not easy to fool, therefore, and is not so helpless. The 'war' of the lowbrow against the highbrow is a conflict fomented on the same principle.

We live beset with civil wars, in the envenomed and bitterly organized world. Almost any generalization must range against you the legions of this or that zealous social host, daily subjected to press discipline, breathing defiance, whether really affected by your statement or not. I am about to examine very briefly a prediction of Mr Haldane's. In doing so I shall occasionally refer to 'woman'. Before permitting myself that dangerous licence I must define what I mean. A very great superficial difference still exists between women and men. As you see women walking about the streets they are (as far as possible) luxuriously and exquisitely dressed, very neat, as far as possible 'chaque cheveu à sa place'; their clothes are chosen as far as possible of flimsy and seductive material, they are still, in short, more ornamental, silken, frail, treated with cosmetics, and sedulously trimmed than are men. The sex specialization is with them in the nature of an obsession, therefore, to that extent, in the sense that they still think of themselves more as 'women' than men think first and foremost of themselves as 'men'. They get themselves up so that they shall be graceful and seductive. But the mind of the woman, stripped of this secondary equipment of grace and feminineness, is not, almost everyone will admit, very different to that of the man.

When speaking of 'women', then, as we must sometimes do, it is naturally of this artificial, secondary creature – not of a platonic androgyne, of a naked soul, or of the violent or gentle, charming or offensive creature that you know Rose or Mary to be at the heart of her specialization. Every specialization or 'shop', when earnestly attended to for a long time, is apt to take on an obsessional tinge. The woman's 'shop' no doubt is no exception to this rule. The 'woman' – the delicately perfumed, carefully arranged, stilted, painted, and coloured feminine shell is a thing that a training as a painter can only help you to appreciate. I do not believe that any painter would be inconsolable at the thought that he lived in this backward world of sex differentiation. In the present essay the 'manly' male is written about with sufficient boldness for us to be permitted perhaps a brief though penetrating glance at the complementary figure of the woman: though if attacked in consequence of this latter licence, I am well aware that it would be a more serious affair than would be the resentment of the poor, bloated cave-man.

VII. SCIENCE AND THE FEMININE

In *Daedalus*, recently published, Mr Haldane has briefly prophesied the triumph of ectogenesis, placing its experimental realization in the year 1951. In spite of the fact that he asserts that opposition to these innovations will come from the feeling of the conservative majority that such innovations have an air 'of presumption and indecency' (p. 53), it is not really the majority that is in question;

and of course, what is intended in any case, is to stress the essential 'indecency' of the present arrangement, and the great decency of the proposed ectogenetic realization of life. All of which confirms us in the conviction of the essential puritanism and squeamishness of the scientific outlook – the outlook, that is, of the average man of science. The 'substitution of the doctor for the priest' is not really, as it would seem to be, in the interest of carnal joys. Science, as a *religion*, would be a very austere affair indeed, outdoing all, it is most likely, in its cheerless intolerance. Let us consider, for instance, with Mr Haldane, the simple act of milking a cow:

> Consider so simple and time-honoured a process as the milking of a cow. The milk, which should have been an intimate and almost sacramental bond between mother and child, is elicited by the deft fingers of a milkmaid, and drunk, cooked, or even allowed to rot into cheese. We have only to imagine ourselves as drinking any of its other secretions, in order to realize the radical indecency of our relation to the cow.

This is in order to show how, if it were proposed to milk a cow electrically, and we protested that that was 'indecent', we could be convicted of an agelong indecency in milking it with our hands. But biological inventions are abhorrent to humanity, and they call them 'indecent', Mr Haldane thinks. Yet such inventions, beginning as a perversion and monstrosity, end as a ritual. 'Even now surgical cleanliness is developing its rites and its dogmas, which, it may be remarked, are accepted most religiously by women.' (p. 50.)

It is precisely the clinical rites of cleanliness and the growth of a whole network of ordinances, whose administration might be at first in the hands of women, that will probably produce the most intensive ceremonial that has ever been elaborated. When the clinic becomes the temple, and the white-coated surgeon the officiating priest, men will surpass themselves in cleanliness, spending the day in lustrations.

The puritanical potentialities of science have never been forecast. If it evolves a body of organized rites, and is established as a religion, hierarchically organized, things more than anything else will be done in the name of 'decency'. The coarse fumes of tobacco and liquors, the consequent tainting of the breath and staining of white fingers and teeth, which is so offensive to many women, will be the first things attended to. A scantling[1] of the immaculate,

---
[1] sample.

non-carnal world of the future can be examined on all sides today.

Two ideas of freedom are involved in these opposite principles of the mechanical disposal of the detritus of life and the natural disposal of the same. *A philosophy of dirt* (which is a tract which should be added to Messrs Kegan Paul's series) would oppose nature to art, the ancient or animal world to the non-animal world of science. What we still call 'art' is the science of the ancient world — that of nature. Michelangelo, aside from his primitive titanism, would be a suitable hero for such a philosophy, which would dwell on the admirable picture of this ancient master engaging in his yearly change of boots and nether garments, which never quitted his body except to make way for a new outfit. We are told that when he pulled them off, the skin used to come away with them. His colossal prophetic images, and scenes of the first creation, and his rough personal habits, would provide the requisite background for that thought that gave its preference to the natural. It would be contrasted with the world of the microscope, and the minutiae and tidiness that have been a preserve conventionally of the feminine. That squeamishness (suggesting, physiologically, a bad conscience) of the woman, always heading to some ascetic ritual of orderly automatism, would be there opposing the animal *sans-gêne* of the workman of the early world.

'Surgical cleanliness . . . developing its rites' is 'most religiously accepted by women.' The liaison between the woman and applied science is as evident as the ascetic tendencies of science, and the puritanic standards that must ensue as its organization grows. It is science that will lay by the heels the last descendants of the 'colossal, impetuous, adventurous wanderer' of the early world, as well as the *animally-working* pre-industrial man, substituting the machine, of far greater power than any animal or 'titan', controlled by some creature, ectogenetically produced, with a small beardless shaven head, very fussy about specks of dust and dirt, very partial to 'cosmic' studies, bitterly resenting anything indecorous, with most of the beliefs and innocence of the nursery, a highly organized, shrewd, androgynous Peter Pan. That is the logical forecast from the tendency of the moment. But of course, so many things may interfere with this that there is as much chance of its not reaching its goal as of its doing so. Indeed, what is suggested here, with every possible apology for its flagrant optimism, is that it will probably not happen. That is not the sort of world that will necessarily ensue. It is the nightmare, nothing more, that the present tendencies would predict if literally worked out. Their realization would imply, however, that people have ceased to be conscious personalities. The world would in that case have melted into inanity.

It is only a question of being pessimistic enough, or irreconcilable and thorough enough in your revolutionary zeal, and you find yourself quite naturally emerging into the region of healthy optimism prescribed here as a change from the unwholesome reality of the moment.

VIII. POSSIBILITIES OF BIOLOGIC TRANSFORMATION: AND LOCKE'S HUMANISM

What is responsible for that nightmare is the dogma of *Science for Science' sake*, which, like *Art for Art's sake*, or, as Proudhon said, Liberty for the sake of Liberty, or any of the other *closed* formulas, is an absurdity. The mephistophelean picture with which Mr Haldane ends his book – 'Black is his robe from top to toe,' etc. – is not only a ridiculous and sentimental, an unscientific, one, but one that human beings of any sort at all, highbrow or lowbrow, do not want. The humanization of science could only strengthen it, just as it must strengthen art. The war on 'the human' – which is simply a war on all life, 'human' being not merely anything particular, feeble, and peculiar to us, but something common to all forms of life, a mountain even being 'human' in so far as it is *alive* – that war will cause men soon to revolt against not science, but Science-for-Science'-sake. That is a sort of *revolutionary* for whom our time cries out.

As to the possibilities of biologic transformation, the following remarks may prevent misunderstandings. The human body appears very ridiculous, feeble, and even grotesque, no doubt. The impression loses all solid support when the mind has its proper ascendancy. Regarded as an entelechy (this term not involving here any especial theory of substance, but only standing for any non-mechanical animating principle), space and dimension become insignificant. For him a cabbage the size of three universes would still be a cabbage. Explanations of the mystery of life by the tape measure become meaningless.

It is found by creative artists that all the resources of the palette – the accumulation of every possible colour and technical device – or the most elaborate orchestra, containing every imaginable instrument, is not at all a guarantee of successful expression. *One* instrument, *one* colour, and the discipline imposed by the simplest and most restricted means, is often the most satisfactory. So the conservatism imposed on us by the peculiar and not very striking vessel through which we exist is not necessarily a misfortune. Pineal eyes, great stature, a formidable carapace, would not necessarily help us. The greater our spiritual power and development, the less such considerations would occupy us: transformation, if it came, would come necessarily in the incandescence of some endeavour.

That question – of biologic transformation – is significant in some ways, for the essence of the futurist form of thought is an accumulation on the *individual* of all the instruments and physiological extensions or 'interpenetrations' of which life is susceptible. But if we *control* a thing, it is *us*. And the physical joining-up, as it were, of the futurist (which is also the bergsonian) sensibility, seems beside the point. It produces a monster, a hydra, a leviathan, and is a megalomaniac creation. The latter tendency seems to be the expression of the 'scientific' in the vulgar and shallow sense – the last stage of the mechanical, material fancy, the bankruptcy of the imagination.

A few of the questions that scientific advances present have been dealt with in the course of this essay. That the era of vulgarization and popular discussion of *everything* is drawing to a close, I signalled as something to be thankful for. Locke, a long time before the spectacular development of natural science, stated this problem very well. Here is his estimate of what human life (always from the point of view of the human conservative average which is the object of all orthodox revolutionary solicitude) can hope to benefit from natural science:

> Could we discover the minute particles of bodies, and the constitution on which their sensible qualities depend, they would produce very different ideas in us. Microscopes discover to us, that what to our naked eye produces a certain colour, is quite a different thing. So sand or pounded glass, which is white to the naked eye, is pellucid in a microscope. Blood to the naked eye is red, but a microscope shows only some few globules of red swimming in a pellucid liquor.

> Our wise Creator has fitted our senses and faculties for the convenience of life, and the business we have to do here: we are able to examine and distinguish things so as to apply them to our use; but God, it appears, intended not that we should have a perfect and adequate knowledge of them ... were our senses made much more acute, things would have quite another face to us, and it would be inconsistent with our wellbeing. If our sense of hearing were but 1000 times quicker, a perpetual noise would distract us; were the sense of seeing in any man 100 or 100,000 times more acute than it now is by the best microscope he would come nearer to the discovery of the texture and motion of the animate parts of corporeal things, but he would be in a quite different world from other people. Such a quickness and tenderness of sight would not ensure open daylight. He that was sharp-sighted enough to see the configuration of the minute particles of the spring of a clock, and observe on what its elasticity depends, would discover something very admirable; but if eyes so framed could not at a distance see what o'clock it was, their owner would not be benefited by their acuteness. (Locke, *Essay on Human Understanding* II. xxiii.)

The vulgarization of science accounts for many of the most threatening aspects of modern life. The selling of science to the rich – that sort of rich man, that is to say, who is at about the neanderthal stage of existence – is perhaps the greatest crime of any. If what Le Bon calls the *élite* could only combine against this outrageous sub-man, instead of selling him deadly gases and weapons and inventing things for him to destroy everybody with – if, IF! – what a syndic that would be! But it is unfair even to mention such an absurd dream. It is much better to say: Since you *must*, arm him to the teeth. He may destroy *himself*.

IX. THE MEANING OF THE 'SEX WAR'

The sex war, which we will now study a little more closely, is destined to free not only women, but men. But it led off, naturally, as a war to free the woman. The woman was the chattel or slave of this terrible little despot, the father of the family. There were millions of such despicable little despots. Their power must be broken. The 'despot' smiled indulgently; he knew he was not much of a despot, he didn't know what all the fuss was about, but concluded that 'those women' had become possessed of some obstinate piece of illogic that they had better be allowed to 'get on with'.

'Socialism wishes to abolish family life, because it costs too much,' was Proudhon's explanation of feminism. And that in one sense must be accepted as the true one, on the economic side. Feminism in that sense was simply the conscription, under a revolutionary egalitarian banner, of an army of women, for the purpose of the attack on and destruction of the home and family. There is much more in the war in the family than the economic factor that persuades capitalism to favour the feminist movement and urge the conventional socialist to this form of 'war'.

Men as a 'class', the masculine class, have recently had to support a great number of wars all at the same time: the 'Great War', which was of a traditional type, and yet very novel in its barbarity; the 'class war', of course; and then a war that was regarded originally as a joke, the 'sex war'. All these wars are wars of freedom: but their ultimate objects are generally misunderstood.

When *feminism* first assumed the proportions of a universal movement it was popularly regarded as a movement directed to the righting of a little series of political wrongs. Woman had been unjustly treated, had been a chattel to be bought and sold and disposed of, men were *free*, women in chains – chained to the hearthstone in the home, which was also referred to as the *castle* of the male gaoler. A thousand chivalrous gentlemen leapt to arms and rushed to the assistance of this matron in distress. With great gestures of christian magnanimity they divested themselves of all traditional masculine authority or masculine advantage of any sort. Tearfully they laid them all at the feet of the dishonoured matron, who dried her burning tears, and with a dark glance of withering indignation picked them up and hurried away. The general herd of men smiled with indulgent superiority. So that was all settled; it was a bloodless revolution.

Feminism was recognized by the average man as a conflict in which it was impossible for a man, as a chivalrous *gentleman*, as a respecter of the rights of little nations (like little Belgium), as a highly evolved citizen of a highly civilized community, to refuse the claim of this better half to self-determination. There were spectacular wrongs that had, 'in all decency', to be righted. The issue was put to him, of course, in a one-sided way. He accepted it as a one-sided thing. Ever since it has continued one-sided, in the sense that, although the 'wrong' has been 'righted', the man is still in the ashamed position of the brutal usurper and tyrant. He finds his rôle in the 'sex war' something in the nature of the immense conventional figure of the 'boss' in the neighbouring 'class war': although there in the 'class war' his own rôle is probably a very humble and far less imposing one. How the sex war links up with the class war, the age war, and the war of the high and lowbrow, is as follows. 'The prevalent dominance of men' is a phrase used commonly. Man in himself is a symbol of authority. *Masculinity* (in a state describable as above) is in itself authoritative and hence arbitrary. The most miserable and feeble specimen of the male 'class' is in that paradoxical position of representing the most devilish despotism and symbolizing brute force. He suffers from the accident that he symbolizes 'authority' in an era of change and military revolutionary revaluation.

So, in the sex department (conterminous with that of administrative political power, or of the master-man relationship in industry or in domestic life, and with the family relation of parent and child), the revolutionary attack would, in its most generalized form, have the character of an attack on *man* and on masculinity. For apart from *man as father*, or *man as husband*, or *man as leader* (in tribe or state), there is an even more irreducible way in which a man is a symbol of power and domination. *Man as man tout court* is an anachronism, is 'unscientific'. When Christ said to the Rich Man, 'Give all to the poor and come along with me, barefoot, and I will show you the road to heaven,' the Rich Man usually laughed and went his way. Man, or his political representatives, when recommended to give up all his privileges enjoyed at the expense of 'woman', did not show this cynical front at all, except a few contumacious figures here and there. He immediately disgorged *everything*, in a true christian and chivalrous spirit. He considered himself most amply rewarded with the nice kiss that his generous action earned him. Had someone asked the same man to give all he had to the poor, or to hand over a thousand pounds of his capital to a distressed friend, he would, like the Rich Man in the Gospels, have laughed. Yet effectively he was doing the same thing in his sentimental capitulation to the feminist propaganda. This is merely noted as a matter of historical interest. Had men resisted, the struggle would have been more bitter, but would have had the same result. It was very lucky in this particular case that the usual veil of stupidity let down over their eyes obscured the issue: and anyone looking back on these events when the movement is complete, at some future day, will agree that the feminine combatant was even blinder. In the long run both will be the gainers, in being relieved of too much of each other's company, and all the domestic burdens and responsibilities imposed by the family. The nightmare, 'sex', will not force people into each other's society for life, when a half an hour would answer the purpose. But from the conventional point of view of the moment, certainly the women were the least wise: for according to those standards, they had most to lose.

So man gave up his privileges 'like a lamb', but, needless to say, it is not the Rich Man, either of the Bible Story, or of any other story, who is the loser in these or any similar transactions. He gives nothing up – quite as in the days of Christ. But man also in this will in the end be a little better off. Prohibition is another case of the same sort. The Rich Man wishes it, of course, in order to get more work out of the Poor Man: he does not propose, himself, to knock off drink for the moment – only to make it so expensive that the workman cannot get it. But also, whatever you may think of this one-sided law, the workman will be better without drink. It is true that the Rich Man immediately sells his workman a crystal set and a cheap motor-car, and (so the Tester assures us) gets forty per cent more work out of him. But the workman enjoys using the crystal set as much as the Rich Man enjoys selling it to him.

The object of the capitalo-socialist promoters of the sex war was dual. One object was the quite temporary one of discrediting authority, and reducing this smallest and feeblest of kings, the little father of the family squatting rather miserably in his shabby uncomfortable little castle, like a 'king' of *Alice in Wonderland*. But the break-up of this expensive and useless unit, the family, and the releasing of the hordes of idle women, waiting on little 'kings' for industrial purposes, was the principal object. Ten housewives daily performed in the way of washing, cooking and so forth, what two could perform under a communal system of the Fourier type, or that being introduced in communist Russia. The remaining eight would then be available for other forms of work. That is the economic object of the destruction of the idea of the family and the home. Incidentally it will break up and root out all those little congeries of often ill-assorted beings; and terminate that terrible, agelong *tête-à-tête* of the husband and wife, chained to each other for life for the practical purposes of perpetuating the species, which could now be effected more successfully *without* this often unhappy union.

In the mind of the most villainous and black-hearted of 'capitalists', no doubt, it presented itself solely as a problem to get hold of cheap female labour. The hordes of unmarried women would be formed into a *third sex* like the sterile female workers of the beehive. This could not be done without the displacement of an equal quantity of men. So a 'sex war' would be a good thing. Funds were forthcoming for feminist equipment. Such an attitude did no doubt exist, and does, among a certain type of men. But that does not affect the ultimate utility of the movement; nor is it any reflection on the motives of such a man as Fourier, who recommended a social reorganization on these lines a century ago in his phalansterian system.[1]

If, every time a great man of science, like Faraday, was about to engage on some research, he reflected what terrible uses it might be put to: if, every time an inventive artist was about to engage in some kind of experiment in literature, painting, or music, he grew disgusted at the thought of all the travesties and vulgarizations that must ensue, degrading and caricaturing his invention: or if the social reformer like Fourier were overcome with the thought of what quantities of evil people would exploit and corrupt his dreams of human regeneration: then perhaps all these men would never create. So we should not benefit by that. Whenever we get a good thing, its shadow comes with it, its *ape* and familiar. It is in order to disentangle these things, principally, that this essay has been written. The extreme complexity and intermixture of the good and the bad, in the sense of what is good for people in general and what is bad for them, makes this task a difficult one. It is the supreme task for the sociologist or philosopher today. But almost anything that can be praised or advocated has been put to some disgusting use. There is no principle, however immaculate, that has not had its compromising manipulator. All that must be borne in mind, and the shadow and the reality, the 'real thing' and the imitation, brought forward to some extent together.

At all times there have been a host of men who performed a simple work which a woman, or a child for that matter, could under-

[1] A phalanstery or phalange was a unit of 400 families or 1,600 persons, covering all human capacities.

take equally well. On account of the sex prerogative, and sex privilege, they claimed a wage superior to what a woman would claim for a similar employment. It was for this reason that *male privilege* had to be broken. 'Woman's rights' was, from the point of view of many of the most influential of its supporters, simply an expedient to reverse this position. The pretentious claims of the white male had to be broken.

Now the sequel of the 'sex war' is in many ways very unpleasant. It must be remembered, however, that the change round is only very partial as yet, and the period of conflict and friction has not ended. Also it must be remembered that in western society the destinies of this war are still in the hands of people likely to exploit it for the most evil motives. Let us consider it from this point of view for a moment, as a struggle carried on in the midst of a system bound to exploit it and turn it to its own detestable uses.

We observe today that technically women 'have won their war'. Yet so far, the 'peace' after the 'sex war' is of the same dubious character as the peace after the Great War. Even the 'victors' are a little laughed at by the less delicate of the agents of the great system on which their success reposes. The soldiers, in the same way, were laughed at when, their Great War over, they came and showed their mutilated limbs, lost jobs, and broken health to their masters. This cannot be better illustrated than by an article entitled 'Is there really a Sex-war?' in a great Sunday newspaper, which devotes a good deal of space to chattily instructing its readers (the soft *drilling* of the great and docile public which is the great function of publicity) as to how they should go, and what attitude they should take on great domestic and international questions.

The writer of this particular article starts by mocking the 'feminist' and the partisan of the sex war as an 'unsexed', rawboned, unattractive tribe of 'female' cranks. No wonder, he says, there is a 'sex war' for them! But does any pretty girl think there is such a thing as a sex war?

> The result [of the fact that 'the female constitution is of sterner stuff' than the male] is the well-known surplus of women, roughly 2,000,000 in this country.
> There is nothing more curious than the way life adjusts itself to local conditions. Since a large number of women are plainly condemned to sterility by the fact of the surplus, a percentage of the female population

automatically and instinctively makes a type that can be seen in large numbers at any university, and with all the plausibility it can command it preaches a career and celibacy for women, and hatred of man.

... The 'sex war' of the feminists is a thing of which no woman of average good looks and pleasant temper is ever conscious. No pretty woman ever complained of the hostility of men as a sex. No normal man ever complained of the 'sex war' waged against him by woman.

Never was a war so peculiarly carried on as that alleged by the feminists to be incessant between man and woman. These mortal antagonists apparently cannot exist apart. Take any thoroughfare at random. The immensely preponderant proportion of the passers-by are two-and-two in the smiling company of a person of the other sex. The unhappy ones are those who are without the company of members of the opposite sex.

There the poor disappointed 'feminist' type, claiming her 'rights', which she had secured in her 'war', gets it 'straight and strong'. The industrial boss – in the person of his journalistic employee – laughs at her, of course. 'You poor, hard-featured, unsexed drone, that no man would have – who goes *alone* down the street, envying all the pretty girls hanging smiling on the arms of their beaux – or, if in company, in the company of another female much like yourself – *so you want more money*, do you? Well you won't get it. You have slightly misunderstood the significance of your "famous victoree". It was a victory for *me*, not for you!'

Woman frequently gets the job because, not having another woman and several children to support, she can afford to accept a lower salary than a man. And then, resenting this lower salary, she sometimes talks bitterly about *sex discrimination* and the *sex war*. The agitation of the female school teachers for salaries on the male scale, though not quite on the same plane, is a cognate case.

The 'feminists', having obtained practically all they had ever clamoured for, now unanimously chorus the slogan, *Equal pay for equal work* – whether performed by man or woman. They are pathetically unconscious of the fact that, apart from the teaching profession, were this principle to be enforced, a great percentage of employed women would immediately lose their jobs to men.

Since the principle of equal pay is not in force, they raise the old cry of the 'sex war' and point once again to the brutal domination of the unscrupulous male.

The harsh fact, however, is that the 'sex war' as between man and woman is a myth. It does not exist. There is, indeed, a 'sex war' always in full swing – a war in which no quarter is given on either side – and that is the 'sex war' between woman and woman.

One 'war', you notice, is guffawed away, and another little one started, or an old one restarted.

'There *is* a war,' he says in effect, 'but it is a war between woman and woman.' And he recommends them more or less to go and pull each other's hair out, and to forget the 'sex war'. *That* is over, that has served its purpose.

The readers of such an article grin: and insinuating itself beneath the veil of 'kindly humour' and gossip, the sense slips into their minds and installs itself there. They notice that the writer is 'a man' – if he is impolite about the other sex, they giggle and express the opinion that he has probably been 'jilted'. In any case they regard him as a harmless gossiping personality, supposing him to have the same prejudices and preoccupations as themselves, since it takes a good deal to show to people that others are not invariably just like themselves. A little 'sex war' talk springs up, perhaps between Mummy and Daddy; to which the children (part of quite another category or 'class') disdainfully listen, or else attend to something else.

X. THE MATRIARCHATE AND FEMININE ASCENDANCY

All orthodox opinion – that is, today, 'revolutionary' opinion either of the pure or the impure variety – is anti-man. Its terms are those of a war or insurrection still, although theoretically the war is over and the position gained. But subtly and in the nature of things, it is no longer a question of adjusting an inequality, but of advancing (as of a *superior* nature) the qualities of the 'down-trodden', of the 'weaker' sex. On the scientific, or the pseudo-scientific, front of the world-movement of sex reversal, it issues in the form of a great deal of insistence on the phenomenon of the Matriarchate. The Matriarchate tends to be represented as a more absolute thing than it ever was, and as in a sense the *natural*, the *primitive* social organization. Such a war as the 'sex war', as was to be expected, does not end in a stabilization in which the man and the woman exist on *equal* terms. It necessarily ends in a situation in which feminine values are predominant.

That the 'sex war' is not at the finish (whatever it may have been at the start) an egalitarian movement is certain. It is not an insurrection with an egalitarian watchword any longer, but a 'war' for domination, not 'equal rights'. The nietzschean notions that converted in the vague general mind the darwinian formula of a *struggle for existence* into that of a *struggle for power* operates here as elsewhere. In innumerable books and articles on the subject this tendency can be traced. A highly characteristic one is *The Dominant Sex*, by Mathilda and Mathias Vaerting. (Whether the order in which their names are printed is a survival of the days of chivalry, or is a token of the surrender of Mathias, we are not told.)

Abusing and over-using the slender evidence of the Matriarchate, these writers' theory is that sometimes men have ruled the world and sometimes women: that the pendulum swings backwards and forwards: but that *equal rights*, or a rule shared equally by both, is only a transitional state, and is not the characteristic one. That one or other should be the top dog is the natural condition.

> There is, indeed, a tendency towards fixity in the relationship of power between the sexes, whatever that relationship may be. But there is a still stronger countervailing tendency towards change, towards progressive modification. The relationship of power is subject to the laws of motion. The present authors' researches seem to justify the contention that the movement of the relationship of power between the sexes is undulatory, or that it resembles the swing of a pendulum. Automatically, masculine dominance is replaced by feminine, and feminine by masculine. In the swing from the prevalence of one form of sexual dominance to the other, the pendulum necessarily traverses the stage in which there is a balance of power between the sexes: this is the phase of equal rights.
>
> This movement, however, does not seem to be a simple oscillation. We do not find that the power of one of the sexes continuously diminishes, while that of the other continuously increases. The subordinate sex experiences from time to time reverses in its march to power, these reverses being followed by fresh advances. . . . The dominant sex, on the other hand, the one whose power is declining, will win occasional victories even during that decline. . . . The highest point of the movement of the pendulum is that at which the reversal of the movement begins. After the dominance of one of the sexes has been pushed to the pitch of absolutism, and when the power has reached a climax, the descent into the valley of equal rights begins.

These writers excuse themselves presumably for the unsatisfactory nature of the evidence on which they have to rely for this mechanical and well-ordered picture by inventing something like Freud's *Censor*. They imagine a despotic and marvellously thorough sex soul, carefully erasing all traces of the rule of the sex recently dispossessed.

It will be seen that the Vaertings deal in a type of historic psychology like the fatalism of the *decline and fall* of all empires; although for the foundations of their statements they have to get into the vague, 'vast', convenient region of proto-history and unlimited pre-history. But as to any movement on the part of these two minds to question the desirability of 'empire' and *domination* at all, you would look in vain for it.

If this mechanical oscillatory movement were, for the history of which we have any reliable record, correct, then would it not be strange to find these 'rebel minds', because a certain mechanical movement has always taken place, accepting it for all time? Should not the 'progressive' ticket oblige its holder to something different to that? Is not, in fact, the historic attitude the very negation of 'progress' – if 'progress' is to break the spell (for is it not that?) of mechanical necessity? So the historic conservatism of such mechanistic writers throws them into the sort of strange opposition with their 'revolutionary' label that we have noticed occurring elsewhere. Their evidence is collected on the same principle as that directing the inquisitorial procedure in which the functions of judge, attorney, jury, etc., were vested in one person: their evidence of the order and value of that extracted by torture and hypnotic suggestion.

To wish back the patriarchal family (with the *patria potestas* of the roman domestic despot at the end of the reactionary road, or the slave-wife) because feminism seems to be rapidly becoming affected to a vast scheme of political exploitation; or because men, not yet free of women, have not the necessary initiative to institute a secondary war, to hasten the dissolution that has begun, and which, as things stand at present, falls most heavily on them, – is the natural reactionary gesture. Men do not do anything, but they are dissatisfied. They feel too guilty in their capacity of hereditary 'tyrant' or 'sultan' to say much openly. And 'chivalry' is a great obstacle to declaring war.

The recommendation of Christ to the Rich Man has already been mentioned in connection with the Man as an emblem of sex-authority. The surrender of the Plain Man to the feminizing woman was a piece of chivalrous nonsense, if it was not coercion. So christianity is responsible for it, since chivalry dictated it, unless force covers the whole transaction. But if the Rich Man, when he had given up his possessions, should howl like Timon because he was not then of so much importance, he would be a poor christian. It is against christianity that man should turn, the source of all his sexual woes. These two actions – that of surrendering any wealth you may have accumulated or inherited by the caste or sex to which you belong – are highly to be commended, in my opinion. But what is not usually recognized is that they are of exactly the same order: just as a magnanimous christian self-sacrifice in sex is the same as it would be in race. According to any worldly standard they are both excessively stupid.

The 'right' of the child to freedom from family control is of a piece with the 'right' of the woman to an 'independent' existence. They and the rest of the sex innovations and theories of the family are in the nature of factory regulations, nothing more. The multitudinous mollusc in the body of which these changes occur has to be found a soft or a sentimental reason for everything that happens in such a tender or respectable place. But the real reason, although matter-of-fact enough, is not from the public point of view threatening or alarming. The truth *always* has to be hidden, whether it is good or bad. In itself it causes alarm: *any* truth is impossible to utter.

Sorel writes: 'Marx, as is known, proposed this law, that "every class which, successively, has seized power has sought to safeguard its newly acquired position of mastery by imposing on society conditions calculated to ensure it (the conquering class) its own revenue". Several times the same principle is employed by him in attempting to predict what would happen to the world as a result of a proletarian revolution. It is in this way that he comes to announce the disappearance of the bourgeois family, because the proletarians will not find themselves in conditions likely to permit them to practise this type of sexual union.'

Since the great masses of the people are not likely to be in a position to prolong the family arrangement based on an individual 'home' (marriage and the family circle to which the European is accustomed), it will be abolished. That is the economic fact at the bottom of 'feminism'. Given industrial conditions, the Plain Man and the Plain Woman will be better off if the unit of the family is abandoned. But that consideration would perhaps not have been sufficient to bring this revolution about. It is an economic adjustment primarily: after that a great deal of relief from responsibility, and from a too constant tête-à-tête, is to be laid to its credit.

XI. THE PIECEMEALING OF THE PERSONALITY

Race is the queen of the 'classes': but in Europe today its power is very slight – for one reason, because it lacks all organization or even reality. But there are less fundamental ones, but usually far more present to our consciousness in everyday life, needing the greatest attention, and involving a variety of ritual. The other 'classes', it is true, have never been recognized as of the same standing as *race*. As a *casus belli* they have been inferior to it. None of these other differences, or the membership of any of the other classes, was recognized as a pretext for taking life. Race or nationality, on the other hand, has, in the modern world, been recognized as a sanction for murder by every State. But this sanction usually had only 'nationality' to repose on, which was a very different thing to race. Marx, with his 'class war', indirectly demonstrated the absurdity of these privileges of race – especially when it was not *race* at all. The success of his system has shown how easy it is to substitute, in a disorganized, non-racially founded society, any 'class' for the classical 'racial' unit of the State.

Once 'war' between classes started spreading, from the teaching of Marx, it did not stop at social 'class', naturally. Schopenhauer, for instance, early in the last century, called women 'the short-legged race'. So women were thenceforth one *race* and men another *race*. The idea of race substituted itself for that of sex. But where there are *races* there are *wars*. The 'sex war' was soon in full swing. Schopenhauer himself, it is interesting to recall, was one of the first in the field. He early in life flung himself on a strange woman whom he found conversing on the staircase of the house where he lived, and threw her downstairs. For this pioneer engagement, however, he was forced for the rest of his life to pay a crushing pension to this crippled member of the enemy 'race'.

Women are notoriously unamenable to strictly *racial* mysteries. The classical example of this is that of the Sabine women deciding, as it is supposed, to remain the property of the Sabine ravishers rather than return to the defeated men of their own race.

The *child* is the 'class' that is most nearly associated with the sex-classification: or rather, the age-difference it represents. 'The child is father to the man': and the child is, as primitive societies saw, actually a different being, in spite of physiological continuity to the grown man into which he develops. It is the case of the worm and the butterfly – only in inverse order, the butterfly coming first. So Master Smith and Miss Smith are as different almost (when they are the same person at different ages of Smith's career) as though they were offspring and parent.

But the difference diminishes when you are dealing with *Isaac Newton*, or even with Clara Vere de Vere, in place of poor 'Smith'. The more highly developed an individual is, or the more civilized a race, this *discontinuity* tends to disappear. The 'personality' is born. Continuity, in the individual as in the race, is the diagnostic of a civilized condition. If you can break this personal continuity in an individual, you can break *him*. For *he* is that continuity. It is against these *joints* and sutures of the personality that an able attack will always be directed. You can divide a person against himself, unless he is very well organized: as the two halves of a severed earwig become estranged and fight with each other when they meet.

A good demonstration of the rationale of this piecemealing of the personality for attack was given the other day by a caricaturist. He divided his celebrated victims into their Young and Old Selves: in this way he had them in half, like hydras, and made the angry tail discourse with the fiery head. But you can effect far more than this. You can with luck cut men up so thoroughly that they become almost 'six-months men', as they might be called, rather than men of one continuous personal life – than 'life men'. It is only necessary to mention the central subject of the very effective and fashionable plays of Pirandello, to show how, systematically presented in a dramatic form, this segregation of the 'selves' of which the personality is composed can affect the public mind.

But there is no way in which people differ, however minutely, that does not supply material for a 'war'. And the general contention throughout this essay is that they cannot have too much of 'class': that people's passion for 'class' and for reposing their personality in a network of conventional 'classification', is not often realized. Where war is concerned you must, of course, disregard entirely the humanitarian standpoint. *Passively* men may even enjoy war, as the bird enjoys being drawn irresistibly to the fang of the snake. The blowing off of heads and arms is a very secondary matter with the majority of people. But that does not justify you as a responsible ruler in abusing this insensitiveness.

When really mixed into a good, strong group, men are so many automata: they hardly notice any disturbance, like a war. But that the conscious self (in so far as it remains) of the average human being is terribly bloodthirsty and combative, much as I should like to, I find it difficult to credit. *By themselves* people are, everyone admits, averse to fighting: it demands too much energy. Perhaps a really *perfect* group, or class, to prevent itself dying of inanition, would favour war, as a stimulant. But I think the more the question is examined, the more certain it is that people *for themselves* (not for others – they enjoy seeing other people fighting, and dying, naturally), and *in the mass*, prefer eating, sleeping, fornicating, and playing games of skill to killing each other. But even if *the happiness of the greatest number* is not so individual a matter as Bentham supposed – even if the happiness of dying, let alone living, with a huge crowd of people must have a serious claim upon our attention – nevertheless the individual, betrayed momentarily by some collapse or etiolation of the communist medium, does object very strongly to dying. As *an individual* he is all for not dying or being crippled – that is the law of nature. And the ruler who bases his action on the stability of this Artificial Man of communism constantly risks sinning against God.

PART VIII. THE 'VICIOUS' CIRCLE[1]

I. THE PHYSIOLOGICAL NORM AND THE 'VICIOUS'

Of all the tokens of the flight of the contemporary european personality from the old arduous and responsible position in whose rigours it delighted, now made too hot for it, there is none so significant as the sex-transformation that is such a feature of post-war life. A few years ago this topic would have been exceedingly difficult to deal with in a book destined for public sale. Even today it is not an easy one, but for rather different reasons.

On what tone are we to address ourselves to the consideration of

[1] Chapters I–IX.

this inverted fashion, abstracting ourselves, of necessity, from any prejudices we may feel for the purpose? Dr Matignon (*Archives d'anthropologie criminelle*), the greatest authority on China, said that he had never heard a Chinese express any disapproval of sexual inversion except that it was universally agreed to be bad for the eyes. Until quite recently european society took a very severe view of it; which dislike was apparently a sort of tradition in any case among the germanic peoples. Genuine, fully developed physical inversion in men is probably quite rare: in a time unfavourable to its practice it makes a sort of martyr of the individual born with it – a martyr to his glands, like 'the painter called Sandys' in the limerick, or in the sense that we say 'a martyr to the gout'. People regard it askance as a sort of possession; and in many rough communities every misfortune would befall these delinquents of natural processes, whose quite simple and harmless topsy-turvydom was associated with witchcraft and treated on that basis. Even so late as the famous 'nineties the english courts made a martyr of that description of Oscar Wilde. He became almost a political martyr, other countries using his well-advertised agony to point to the philistinism of England. A very amiable and charming person, he awakened the chivalrous instincts everywhere, like a very attractive maiden in distress. And as he possessed to the full the proselytizing zeal that usually goes with sex inversion (as with any other intensification of sex), he prepared the ground with his martyrdom, ecstatic recantations, eloquent and tearful confessions, and the great prestige of his wit, for the complete reversal of the erotic machinery that has ensued or is ensuing.

An admission of complete *moral* blindness and indifference, although it might be damaging under certain circumstances, will not be misplaced in handling this subject. But there is another aspect of the matter that also claims attention. There are many people, perhaps, who would be lacking, as I am, in *moral* sensitiveness, and who would yet be in some way physically offended by practices 'against nature'. This would be extremely unreasonable, as I have already suggested; for to an impartial taste, divinely exempt from participation in either normal or 'abnormal' joys, as we call them, their 'normality' would be just as offensive. They might very well offend the most fastidious god more than the object of *their* disgust; for their 'norm' would be merely the dislike or revolt of the senses against something *different*, not part of their personal norm or system. It would, in short, be the animal self-complacency, and self-love that thinks itself 'natural' and engaging, and everything else 'unnatural' and disengaging.

The physical is the only aspect that interests the majority of people, however: which makes the non-physical impracticable as a basis of discussion, or at least very difficult. That there is any other side to a fundamental thing of common experience – about *themselves*, in short – they require much persuading. Nevertheless, the attempt has to be made, since the subject is important.

There is still, of course, one thing, but that a physical and exterior one, that plays an important part with many people in such questions as this. A drunkard soon develops a red nose and generally inflamed, bloated and dissipated appearance. Red noses are for some reason universally disliked by both men and women. So in the case of the drunkard, although no one would be likely to raise any objection to or to experience any disgust at the physical act of pouring into the mouth a probably attractively coloured liquid, the result of this action in the long run is the red nose by which many people are generally repelled for some reason. The 'Nancyism' of the joy-boy or joy-man – the over-mannered personality, the queer insistence on 'delicate nurture', that air of assuring those met that he is a 'real lady', like the traditional music-hall 'tart' who is always a 'clergyman's daughter', the grating or falsetto lisp, or the rather cross hauteur of the democratic tea-shop waitress – are to some human norm almost as central as that which resents the red nose, or the big paunch, offensive.

But the drunkard is at peace with his red nose, probably, and left to himself can live on terms of mutual respect with his paunch, no doubt. Some human norm – the same one perhaps, that is outraged by the red nose – hates the rat and the beetle. But the idea of the rat is not at all that which the rat has of itself; it loves its swift clammy sausage of a body as much as the human being does his hairless, erect machine. That erect, conceited human norm may yet have to bend to the will of the rat or the serpent, and go about on its belly near the ground. And then it will be just as pleased with itself as at present: and indeed be happier relieved of the white man's burden *cum* the human burden *cum* its amazing moral rectitude.

I suggest that it is only the over-instinctive person, the slave of the human-all-too-human norm, who would be such a stickler for the 'natural' as the reactions sketched above imply. It is this unfortunate conservative human-all-too-human norm that we are incessantly combating. It is even that Old Adam in the 'Nancy' that makes him so satisfied with his humble eccentricity, and insignificant loudly-advertised change of gear – like the exultant cackling of a hen who had laid an egg of an, for it, unwonted calibre.

It is not, alas! by victories of such modest proportions over our too rigid physiologic norm that we can hope to break it down, if that is our intention. We merely flatter and preserve it by such indirect attentions.

But in order to advance a little farther into the physical problems involved in such a scrutiny, let us take the objections of the conventional bridegroom on his marriage night to evidences of unchastity in his bride. Marrying, the man of the approved masculine type is distressed and disillusioned if he finds that someone has forestalled him in the tasting of this fruit. The gilt is off the gingerbread. This painful situation we usually take at its *face* value. We think we know what we mean by the gingerbread, and where it is situated. It is on the *physical* plane, in short, that we believe this deception to have occurred. In this, I think we are wrong.

Suppose, for instance, that the disappointed bridegroom learns that instead of being deflowered in the course of a love intrigue, his bride has been deflowered against her will on a lonely road by a tramp. Then the situation changes for him at once. There is a flood of bitter tears on the part of the bride; he folds her in his arms and all is well. *For it is not the physical fact that has disturbed his repose of mind.* It is the person, *she*, gazing at him out of her lovely, *personal* eyes, that has caused him such a disagreeable shock to find he was not the first with. The act of deflowering, it is true, occurred, technically, on the physical plane. But that – were there no *person* attached to it – would be of no more importance than something happening to an automaton: no more than the daily dirtying of the hands, which are washed and then they are clean again: no more than the figure in the Bois, in Mallarmé's prose poem, observed embracing mother earth. For it is a person, a mind, that he has married; incarnated and expressed, it is true by a certain body. But that body is, in a sense (in the things that happen to it, if that is possible, independently of the mind), as unimportant by itself as the materials by which it is surrounded – its clothes, the tables and chairs, dust on the road, or bricks of the house. Disconnect it from the *person*, if that may be, and it is *dead*. In short the body outraged by the tramp would be a *corpse* only. The body enjoyed by an earlier lover would be *alive*. In the latter case it would be *she*, Daphne, Joan or Elizabeth. It is the personality he is in touch with when he looks into her eyes (and not a bit of flesh – that is, as flesh, of the same impersonal order as a bit of cloth, a lump of clay, a sponge, a vegetable) that all the trouble is about.

This illustration will, I hope, suffice to suggest to us that in all such things the physical event is of very little importance by itself. In the case of sex, more than anything else, the fuss is supposed to be about that, and localized to physical experience. In reality we are always dealing with something else. It is in this misunderstanding that morals thrive. The shallow disgust or indignation of the moralist is installed in an elementary materialism that appeals directly to the animal machinery of combat or rut. Its pompous censure is able to surround, as though with an aureole of intelligence and martyrdom, something that is – what? If we paused to think what it is we should no doubt laugh at the conjuring trick: the piece or sardonic illusionism to which we all surrender. But when that comic screen has been removed, at the heart of the tissue would be found the same entelechical reality which gives significance to all the material life we know.

But that physical delusion, with all its mocking symbolism, that has roused us to protest or repulsion – clasping to our hearts, with no repulsion, an almost identical object ourselves – ! is of the very essence also of the practice responsible for it. The moral indignation, or loudly expressed disgust, of the Plain Man or the Plain Woman is the twin and the complement of that self-satisfaction and sense of outrageous discovery that is the incentive on the other ('unnatural') side of this sexual pale.

The sex revolution of the invert is a *bourgeois* revolution, in other words. The *petit bourgeois* type predominates: a red tie, or its equivalent in the approved badges of sexual revolt, tells its theatrical tale. The puritan conscience, in anglo-saxon countries, provides the basis of the condiment, and gives sex inversion there its particular material physiognomy of *protest* and over-importance. How moral, essentially, the anti-moral stimulus must be is not difficult to grasp, when you are privileged to witness its operation in the English or American. And so the 'vicious' circle is described.

II. THE INTOLERANT TRADITION OF THE ANGLO-SAXON

These disparaging remarks (for in employing the epithet *petit bourgeois* I have gone as far as human vituperation will go) do not of course apply to those people whom a displacement of the sex psychology marks out for physical paradox. The most agreeable inverts to be met – and every one, in post-war society, meets a great number of every sort – are the true-blue inverts: those who, whatever the orthodoxy of the moment, would certainly be unaffected by it, and would be there busy with all the rather complicated arrangements incident to their favourite pursuit. This malepole type of invert is often entirely free from that feminine bias, resulting in caricature so often, of the female of the genus; or that of the convert to inversion, the most fanatical of all. What this male invert thinks of his female it is impossible to say without being one yourself. But certainly he gives the impression of being much more *male* in the traditional and doctrinaire sense than any other male. His pride is often enormous in his maleness. If perhaps a little overfine and even mad, he can meet on equal terms the male of any other species – either the lion, the male of the farmyard-fowl, the Samurai, the powdered male gallant of the Stuart stage. The frantic and monstrous cock, that notorious nobleman, Monsieur le comte de Six Fois, of the Casanova dispensation, he would easily put to flight.

Just as there are few born revolutionaries, but in great numbers people who are 'revolutionary' because other people are: so in the ranks of each respective legion of revolt today there is the small nucleus of 'pukka' material, the 'regulars', and the sheeplike indoctrinated majority. So it is that the neglected, despised, and rejected adept of Sodom, so well described in his formerly outlawed state by Proust, suddenly finds himself, owing to one of those freaks peculiar to political life, the leader of a highly disciplined host. It must be an Arabian Nights entertainment for some of the more hardened old perverts. All their life they have been chivvied from pillar to post, till very recently living in the shadow of the Oscar Wilde case, the British equivalent of the *affaire Dreyfus*. Then all at once, as though by magic, they find themselves Princes of Sodom: every university in Christendom is pouring out, as thick as herrings, shoals of their natural prey, duly indoctrinated and suitably polished. They must rub their old heavily painted eyes and pinch their corseted ribs to ascertain if they are dreaming or not.

If the physiology of abnormal love does not seem to you a matter of great importance; if you have not the puritan itch or the spur of an over-sharp vanity to make such things important and indirectly, mentally exciting; if 'righteousness' as Arnold would say, or sanctimoniousness as Butler corrected him, is not your strong point, – there, you would think, must be an end of the matter as far as you are concerned. But you would find very soon that you had reckoned without your host. First of all you would discover that other people were not so accommodating as yourself. Indeed a violent and jealous intolerance, you would begin to notice, accompanied most people's devotion to a sex fashion. You would find, if you began to examine the machinery of fashion, that all fashions today tend to be organized on religious lines; and that, where sex especially is concerned, the same puritan spirit, in the anglo-saxon countries, that made people in the anglo-saxon past such intolerant maniacs where 'immorality' and all sexual 'enormities' were concerned, makes them also, when they are recruited to an *opposite* fashion, just as snobbishly intolerant on behalf of the 'immorality' to which they have gleefully, and with a sense of diabolical naughtiness, surrendered. You will perhaps recall the traditional *laissez vivre* of the French, and the wide measure of liberty left to personal taste – so that in the streets of Paris (the home of fashion) it has always seemed impossible to astonish or attract the attention of the passerby, by even the most revolutionary costume: whereas any departure from fashionable convention has been met, always, with fierce resentment or fierce ridicule in England. Oscar Wilde invariably referred, I have been told, to 'Get your hair cut!' as the english national anthem.

Far more important you would find that this prairie-fire of sex revolution (of feminism and then of inversion) altered fundamentally the status of ideas socially. As the psychic element existing in even the simplest sexual operation escapes people, so the percurrent nature of a great sex fashion is either not understood or not admitted. Certain people, highly educated, and belonging to millionaire circles, indulge in an ancient, universally prevalent 'vice' or pleasure, of a privileged and exceptional kind, which, because it seems to contradict nature's arrangements, we call 'unnatural'. And there, for most people, is the end of it. It is on the pleasure or distraction basis alone that discussion of it is relevant.

That attitude resembles another obtuseness that sees in the newspaper, cinema, or wireless only one of the innocent, non-political distractions of mankind: or that attributes 'serious' political significance solely to the Parliament and Crown. 'Mr Gossip' in the newspaper is a harmless, idle, 'gossipy' fellow. The novel, again, is as little of a 'political force' as little Jackie's new rag doll or scooter. Those weighty columns that occupy the centre of the *Times*, dealing with matters of patent consequence; or (to contrast with the mere novel) a political history of England, for instance – they are the only things worthy to rank as 'politics'. . . .[1]

The social value of ideas, you would find altered, then, by this revolution in a novel sense. Not only was it a case of one set of ideas being exchanged for another set, as usually happens. But in place of anything in the shape of an *idea*, a *sensation* had been installed, you would discover. The very organ responsible for the making of an idea would be looked at askance. The sex revolution started as sex, but had ended as something else, rather in the way that religious ecstasy may begin as religion and end as sex. The various forms it has taken since the war did not, as they became more 'social' and less 'political', become less militant. So this revolution had often little to do with sex ultimately. And then, of course – at last – it might enter your head that *in the first place*, too – not only in its result, but in its first motive – it was not sexual either. 'The socialists wish to abolish the family, *because it costs too much!*' we have heard Proudhon saying. (It is strange that the 'socialists' so early in the day should have been preoccupied to that extent with ways and means and displayed such an anxious foresight!) May it not be, too, that all the phases of the sex revolt – from the suffragette to the joy-boy – are equally *political* at the start – as they certainly become at the finish? Is it not the same old hag that in a 'morality' would be labelled Power, and for whom pleasure, in the simplest sense, means very little, who has pupped this batch of related fashions?

[1] One sentence omitted.

III. THE RÔLE OF INVERSION IN THE WAR ON THE INTELLECT

A sort of war of revenge on the intellect is what, for some reason, thrives in the contemporary social atmosphere. This has for effect a substitution of animal 'creation' for intellectual 'creation'. It is as though a war broke out between the picture or poem and the proud and jealous beauty that it represented: a war between the Vouzie and its waters. 'Creative' becomes a term of abuse in consequence: and elegant sterility, or cautious and critical eking out of a little jet of *naïveté* left over on purpose, is the idea, instead.

These readjustments are undertaken with a view to meeting the democratic requirements of 'the greatest vanity of the greatest number'. That vanity must be sheltered from painful comparisons and revenged for humiliations in the past. So a revolution in favour of standards unfriendly to the intellect, and friendly to all that had been formerly subordinated to it, is the first and most evident result of sex-transformation. The 'passions', 'intuitions', all the features of the emotive life – with which women were formerly exclusively accommodated – are enthroned on all hands, in any place reached by social life; which is increasingly (in the decay of visible, public life) everywhere.

In this admirably organized sensationalist philosophy resulting from the common objects of these movements, life would seem to end where the baby was produced. The creative act of producing the baby is the first and last 'creative' act understood or allowed by it. The human being is only legitimately creative on one occasion, namely, in the production of *another* human being. And not only is the baby the supreme 'creation', but babyhood, in one form or another, is the supreme condition of perfection.

We will follow for a moment the probable stages of this revolution as manifested in the life of 'society'.

First the *salon* (the home of the *précieuses ridicules*[1]) will be pitched next door to the nursery; then gradually the connecting door will become a large folding-door; and then at length all septum[2] of any sort will disappear. The *précieuses ridicules*, dressed in baby frocks, will be on the floor with their dolls, or riding rocking-horses in Greek draperies.

[1] Cf. Molière's play.   [2] Partition (employed usually in biology).

The next stage in this human dissolution will almost certainly be spared the future generations. For the house is to be rebuilt, without any doubt at all, on a more admirable pattern than ever before. But at the moment at which the last scrap of wall between the *salon* and the nursery disappears, you may find it difficult to summon your optimism to this prophetic reconstruction. These pages are written principally in order to enable you to grasp the method of that especial social *ritournelle*,[1] and to play your part without *gaucherie*. Once you have the key to the transaction, you may find it diverting up to a point.

The part that male inversion, the latest child of feminism, plays in these neighbouring battlefields of the high and the low-brow, or the specifically feminist battle of feminine ecstasy and 'intuition' against the male 'intellect', is of the highest utility. It, too, is in arms against the family, with all its 'natural' machinery – namely, of human affection and man-and-woman sexual love. With that insurgent and militant instinct of an oppressed brotherhood defined so accurately by Proust, it helps its brother or sister insurgents in their attack on science, the fine arts, established, and usually desiccated, culture.

It is the 'refaynment' that goes with male inversion (the *obligation* of culture, of a 'refayned' speech, and the unreality of millionaire luxury as a necessary background) – that is where it comes in touch and into conflict with the more generalized life. (The mannishness of the woman invert – so different from and so inferior to the manliness of the male of the masculine side of inversion – is the counterpart of this 'refaynment'. The deep throaty voice, the rather rough gestures, of the woman invert contrast again with that shrinking modesty – the 'shyness' of the transformed *shaman*, 'the well-behaved' child, in whose mouth butter would not melt, who will never, never, never speak-until-he-is-spoken-to – of the female of the species.)

IV. THE 'HOMO' THE CHILD OF THE 'SUFFRAGETTE'

To come, then, to the heart of the reason why it is worth while to spend so much time in analysing this fashion: it is because in the contemporary world it is a part of the feminist revolution. It is an

---
[1] repetition.

integral part of feminism proper that it should be considered, a gigantic phase of the sex war. The 'homo' is the legitimate child of the 'suffragette'.

The reason, again, why an analysis is so difficult is this. The majority of people live in the ordinary way, at any period, principally through *sensation*. The atmosphere of ideas or 'the intellect' is not congenial to them. Their reactions to their environment seldom rise into the region of 'clear ideas', or indeed of any detached definition at all of what happens to them. It would be a hypocrisy to pretend that it matters very much how, under such circumstances, they spend their time.

The difficulty today is that, owing to the high state of organization of the different democratic communities, and the insane requirements to which liberalist doctrine has led, sensation is drilled to masquerade as intelligence. Multitudes of people who under a more reasonable system would be living, without self-consciousness or 'the pale cast of thought' at all, animal lives of plain unvarnished *sensation*, are now compelled to adopt a hundred pretentious disguises. Each little sensation has to be decked out as though it were a 'big idea'. Again, simple sensation has become ashamed of itself. It is persuaded to complicate itself, to *invert* itself with a movement of mechanical paradox. So, in reality, sensation pure and simple is disappearing, and a sort of spurious idea is everywhere taking its place.

But side by side with this disintegration of sensation, a very learned, intricate, and ingenious *philosophy of sensation* is built up. The result is that the more sensation *borrows* from the intellect, the more it abuses it and points to *sensation* (which it no longer is in the purest sense) as the aim and end of life. Similarly, the more self-conscious it becomes, the more it repudiates consciousness and also (for another reason) 'self'. The more 'conscious' it grows, in a limited and ineffective way, the more it talks about the 'unconscious'. It is as though it were breaking into a dithyramb about what it *just* no longer was.

The difficulty lies, then, in (1) the propaganda *for* sensation; (2) the propaganda *against* the intellect; (3) the imitation of the intellect, and of the things of the intellect, by all that is most deeply committed to pure sensation; and (4) the movement to merge cleverly these opposites and pretend that they are one, forcing what has outstripped the human sensational average to return on its steps and put itself at the service of what it had laboured to transcend.

The strangest contradiction of all is that every movement *away* from the intelligence (and how can the term intelligence be disassociated from intellect?) is encouraged in the name of *intelligence*. That is the secret of the difficulties that most people experience in analysing this order of things.

The male-invert fashion is not by any means favourable to the woman, of course, although it is feminist. But, on the other hand, it is hostile to many things to which the average woman is hostile. Through it the stupider, more excitable and aggressive kind of woman will revenge herself on those things towards which she has always been in a position of veiled hostility; or on people she has come to regard as responsible for her misfortunes. It is often said that the male invert shelters himself behind – uses and acts through – women. But it would be equally true to put it the other way round.

There are two snobberies which exercise a very great leverage in all sex fashion. 'Intellectual snobbery' is very powerful, as has just been pointed out; it is on the score of 'intelligence' that extreme sex revolution is effected. Social snobbery also plays a great part. To boldly concentrate on a less humdrum practice where your pleasures are concerned has always been, you are reminded, the habit of the privileged few. Membership of the highest or richest organized society – reflecting the egalitarian revolutionary glare from the masses beneath, while floating like a sumptuous emanation at a safe distance above them – is essential.

To be 'revolutionary', yet a social snob: to be an 'intelligence' snob, and yet to run sensation against *intellect*, to sniff and curl the lip at the advantages of the intellect – such are the contradictory habits that go hand in hand.

'We speak sometimes in these pages', says Benda in his *Belphégor*, 'of the bad taste of our "democratic" society. We mean to say that society of which the tastes have become those of the people, at least those that one expects of the people (namely, indifference to intellectual values – religion of emotion). We do not intend either to abuse or flatter any especial political régime. Further, we would say willingly with an eighteenth-century woman: "I call 'people' all those who think vulgarly and basely: the court is full of them."'

Actually the vulgarest people of all, it has only recently been recognized, thanks to the fashionableness of revolutionary doctrines, have always been, necessarily, in the court or among the rich. For what has a so-called upper class been but a set of people furnished with the means to gratify the most ordinary tastes? Or what is the use of riches except to enable some unpleasant fool to be vulgarer than it would otherwise be possible for him or her to be?

A road to a new conception of *class*, in which the intelligence in reality, and not as a make-believe, took its place, would be via such analyses as these, with all their implications thoroughly apprehended.

V. GENIUS IN THE RÔLE OF CALIBAN

No one has explored the regions of post-war decay so brilliantly, if superficially, as Julien Benda. And the pages in his *Belphégor*, where he describes the organized hatred of the intellect existing everywhere today in our society, are so just that I cannot do better than quote from them:

> One of the most curious traits of this society (is) its hatred of the intelligence. Elsewhere we have specified the numerous forms by means of which it expresses this hatred: its wish to confuse intelligence with reasoning of a dry and uninventive sort, in order to thoroughly misrepresent it; to believe that the great discoveries are due to a function (the 'intuition') which 'transcends intelligence' . . . its delight at witnessing what it believes to be the set-backs, the 'failures', of science (instead of regarding them as misfortunes). . . . This violent dislike, conscious and organized, of the intelligence – 'intellectual' has become almost a term of contempt in our *salons* – constitutes something entirely new in French society. . . . This dislike will be the mark of our time in the history of French civilization.

Admirable as it is to be able to see that situation as Benda has (being almost alone in that, and with the surplus of courage to give expression to it), he does not go in search, very seriously, of the reasons for what he has described. People are – french people – for some reason, he says, the enemies of that culture of which they used to be the friends: french culture and european culture in general. And that state of affairs is apparently regarded by Benda as natural, although very unfortunate. What he means by *french society*, and how far what he so describes could in the nature of things be expected to carry on the traditions of feudal and monarchical France, he does not specify.

For him Taine, Renan, and Anatole France (I believe) are the last great representatives, in all probability, of french culture. There will be no more figures of that sort: of that stature, of that integrity, of that aloofness. But that does not mean the French State will not be wealthy and powerful. The Roman Empire got on very well as a state with a frantically materialized society in which the light of learning and the intelligence was extinct, as with us. Such conditions do not prevent people from making money. It rather enables them to do that better than ever before. Greek speculative intelligence is not good for war or commerce.

In spite of the fact that Benda describes this 'hatred of the intellect' as 'something entirely new', and in a sense peculiar to contemporary society, he does not wish to go into the reasons for it. He rests within conventional historical parallels. Having first said it is a novelty, he then says it is common to many societies. So he forgoes the merit of having grasped the relative novelty of this fact. For example, he says (and very well and very truly):

> At the bottom of this taste of our contemporaries for the writer without clear and distinct ideas, let us learn to recognize something profounder still, and common, it seems, to every fashionable gathering or circle: namely, the preference for the *feeble* intelligence, the aversion to the powerful one. Let the reader recall, going back a little way into history, the gallery of talents – poets, thinkers, journalists, talkers – especially favoured by society. How many minds described as 'fins', 'délicats',' aimable', 'plein de grace', he will find: how few minds to which 'vigoureux' would be applied! How many Meleagers, Pliny the Youngers, de la Fares, Abbé de Choisys, Jules Janius, de Caros, Bergsons, there are, how few de la Rochefoucaulds or Montesquieus! How many feminine natures: how few men!

That is of course a matter of common observation. It is evident that the hero of the intellect, no more than the hero of war or finance, is a suitable inmate for the world of the *salon*. The Bachs and Handels, David Humes and Schopenhauers of this life have always been somewhat uncouth. Such names evoke such familiar pictures as that of the Princess of Wales saying, 'Hush, hush: Handel is angry!' when the courtiers preferred talking to listening to the great abstract orator: or of David Hume, like a burly carving in red brick, in the front of the box at the Paris theatre, hung with a festoon of several ladies of the court. In such instances the intellect, or its possessor, is treated like some strange – it is true – but very sacred animal. The most spoilt of societies in the past have not repudiated their intellectual obligation – while making full use of it, as we do. Where we differ so much is in our repudiation of the debt. We compose ourselves into a militant league of hatred against the 'creative' monster, the inventive brute. Genius has become for us Caliban: what *we* have become, to make this possible, we do not care to consider.

VI. THE TABOO ON GENERIC TERMS, AND THE ABSTRACT CREATURE OF DEMOCRACY

As the result of the feminist revolution, 'feminine' becomes an abusive epithet. When you say that the *salon* world, society, is essentially a *feminine world*, you encounter that difficulty for which provision has already been made. The number of generic terms that you may not use increases daily. This is natural in a period of radical upheaval. Classifications which people wish to transcend are indicated by them: so when you say 'feminine' it is though you said 'women before the revolution'. Any term of differentiation is taboo. The recognition of the human standard of industrial standardization, the abstract 'man' without narrowing specifications, is *de rigueur* in forms of address. That is the ultimate stage of the democratic system. It is not, I need not point out, what we regard as the goal of revolutionary thought. For us, as for Sorel, it is the last decadence of that false-revolutionary movement that began with the great monarchies in Europe in the sixteenth century. It is of the essence of democracy, not of radical social revolution and non-democratic revaluation.

The central question, then, is still (and in this part of our discussion as much as elsewhere) that of differentiation or non-differentiation. Some things, which from every human standpoint we should regard as bad, feeble, corrupt, or even imbecile, we should nevertheless regard as *good* and profitable in their destructive capacity. But their essential degeneracy remains. They are, like the mercenaries, to be got rid of as soon as possible.

So, with these things in mind, we can go on with our questions.

Whether it would be better, as it appears to you, if the world were peopled by and society composed of persons differing from each other in certain well-marked ways (not necessarily the ways in which they have so far differed, perhaps very different ones or modifications of them)? or would it amuse you more if they were all on one pattern?

Sex is one of the capital respects in which people differ from each other. And as far as sex is concerned, one of four things can happen. People can either be divided (1) into men and women as we know them – into people, roughly, like President Roosevelt, Nurmi,[1] Dempsey or Bernard Shaw, to take at random some notorious *men*, on the one hand; and Signora Duse, Lady Diana Manners, Jane Austen and Mary Queen of Scots on the other, to take some celebrated *women*: or (2) they can resolve their secondary sex characteristics and become either all *feminine* or (3) *all masculine* (approximating to one or other of the poles illustrated above); or (4) evolve some other undifferentiated human type, at least as far as sex went, unlike either of the two that we know.

At present a fusion is taking place: carried to its logical conclusion, it would result in a standardization on the feminine side of the secondary sex-barrier. This appears to me a less promising adjustment than that which No. 4 of my table would produce. No animosity to women but rather a feeling of the psychic lopsidedness that would result accounts for this preference.

Perhaps the exact half and half would be a solution – not so good, I believe, however, as No. 4. The latter would involve a new creative element. It would not always be reminding people what a close shave it was that they had not divaricated to one side or the other.

As I am not occupied with prophecy, but with things as they present themselves today, it is with the second eventuality that we are confronted – that is, with an increasingly feminine world. This, under correction, would be more puritanic and fastidious, more excessive and emotional, than a masculine one. No make-weight of typical masculine phlegmatism would *deaden* it. More uniquely alive to the things of the moment: more docile and mercurial; more burdened with and swayed by the tidal movements of the unconscious – finally, more *unconscious*, less 'intellectual': that is what, for convenience, I call 'feminine'.

[1] The famous Finnish champion long-distance runner.

Once more, perhaps, it will be better to insist that it is not meant that (1) 'all women' are more 'emotional' than any man; (2) that some cannot be so indifferent to hamperingly polite rules as the standard man; (3) that women cannot be as 'phlegmatic' or as highly 'intellectual' as that same not very inspiring standard.

A miner or drayman gets from his occupation a certain body and habits, and the majority of women get certain well-defined characteristics from theirs; both inherit others. So we can forbear from argument as to whether the drayman could not be made into a picture-postcard beauty, or the woman made to support the heaviest drudgery. We know that the women of Dahomi are reported (or were by Burton) to be hardier and more masculine than the men, and to do the heavier field-work; and that if the drayman makes his fortune, his grandson, who goes to Eton, is not so big and rough and may become very small and smooth. We are obviously talking of realities as we find them, and not as some interested propagandist would arrange them.

The european ideal of force – even when it has the majesty that was given it in renaissance art – is not so much favoured in the scheme outlined here as forms slightly less monotonously martial and heroic. Especially I think the present moment is inappropriate for insisting on this masculinity. Its weakness we must, as Europeans, have found out recently, unless very blind indeed. So far from wishing to engage in propaganda for the physical standards of the policeman, I would rather see these monuments to the vanity of physical force abolished and have nothing but policewomen. Also, those battleships that today can keep no enemy that matters out of a country get up the nose of any patriot. The really powerful modern enemy contents himself with buying a rail and ship ticket, and is propelled or dragged comfortably into your fatherland, while the battleships, flashing their bull's-eyes over the waves, go rolling majestically round the coasts. When you behold these traditional symbols, therefore, can they appear anything but animated satires on the poor European's obsession of the efficacy of the physical? It is even astonishing that that bubble, which is a Beadle or a John Bull, was not pricked by some little Charlie Chaplin-like pin long ago. So alas for our helpless, childish, masculine idols of force, then!

VII. SAMUEL BUTLER'S 'LOVE', AND THE 'ROMANCE OF DESTRUCTION' OF THE MAN OF SCIENCE

Before closing this section of my argument I will make a few more general observations which may help to clarify it further. Samuel Butler, in his *Note-Books*, describes all human love as eating and swallowing. Here are his words ('Who would kiss an oyster?'):

> *Loving and Hating*
> I have often said there is no true love short of eating and consequent assimilation; the embryonic processes are but one long course of eating and assimilation – the sperm and germ cells, or the two elements that go to form the new animal, whatever they should be called, eat one another up, and then the mother assimilates them, more or less. . . . We think we dote upon our horses and dogs: but we do not really love them (because we do not eat them).
> What, on the other hand, can awaken less consciousness of warm affection than an oyster? Who would want to press an oyster to his heart, or pat it and want to kiss it? Yet nothing short of its complete absorption into our own being can in the least satisfy us. No merely superficial, temporary contact of exterior form to exterior form will serve us. The embrace must be consummate, not achieved by a mocking environment of draped and muffled arms that leaves no lasting trace on organization or consciousness, but by an enfolding within the bare and warm bosom of an open mouth – a grinding out of all differences of opinion by the sweet persuasion of the jaws, and the eloquence of a tongue that now convinces all the more powerfully because it is inarticulate and deals but with the one universal language of agglutination. Then we become made one with what we love – not heart to heart, but protoplasm to protoplasm, and this is far more to the purpose.

This is the darwinian nightmare of the struggle for existence, operating on a sensitive mind, converted into a spectacular paradox. 'I could *eat* you!' one lover says to the other at the paroxysm of their lubricity. And indeed, if one were considerably smaller than the other, as in the case of the male of the epira, that no doubt would happen very often. But if the supreme caress is to swallow the person you love, either at a mouthful or in pieces, then it seems reasonable to say that there is little difference between sexual love and swallowing a half-dozen oysters. 'All men kill the thing they love,' Oscar Wilde says (in his *Reading Gaol*). 'All men eat the thing they love,' Butler says in his *Note-Books*.

In the above quotation our affection for a dog is contrasted with our lack of affection for an oyster. Yet we do not love dogs, or we would *eat* them, it says. I believe a definition of beauty is to be found by following out the dog and oyster parallel. It is only when something is independent of us, a non-assimilable universe of its own that we 'love' it, as we call it. Most men dislike the look of an oyster, as they dislike the appearance of the underneath of their tongue ('love is the *pearl* of the oyster' in Sappho, not the oyster), but they find it 'lovely' to *eat*. Two creatures of opposite sex 'love' each other: they do not eat each other usually, or *come together* in that way. As Butler says, they 'pet' and kiss each other. There is a 'superficial temporary contact of exterior form' only. It is in the creation of a third, and again separate, being that they *mingle* completely.

This act of *creation*, of a something more, is an act of love. The eating of an oyster is an act of destruction, however it may, indirectly, make tissue.

The 'superficial contact of exterior form' which characterizes the 'love' of the more complex animals is essential to the existence of 'love' or 'affection'; that is an emotion for something different to the self, that cannot be absorbed into the self, in the sense of being eaten. That *detachment*, *distance*, and, as it were, chastity, and intense *personal* sensation on our side, is at the bottom of all our *spiritual* values, as we name what about us is independent of feeding and renewing our machine.

Butler's sentiments for the oyster would literally have to become *platonic* (on the principle of Gilbert's 'affection à la Plato, for a bashful young potato, or a not too *french* french bean') for him to be justified in giving the same name for it as to what he would feel for Mary or Kate.

The platonic condition (always in the gilbertian sense) is essential, then, also to the existence of *beauty*. The ideas of beauty, of a god, or of love, depend severally on separation and differentiation. The savage ate his god to procure divinity for himself, so showing his foolishness; for his act was like attempting to devour the *beauty* of a mountain or a river, or to convert his *love* for another person into the tissue of his own body, or like buying or selling a dream. Freud's obsession with incest is in the same order of things.

Bergson has a lot of one side of Butler in him (perhaps he consumed a good deal of him at one time of his life): his *creative evolution,* like Nietzsche's *will to power* and glorification of carnage and the sentiment aroused by acts of destruction, is of course (like Butler) under the shadow of Darwin. Mr Shaw's version of *creative evolution* (cf. *Methuselah,* preface) relates Bergson and Butler further.

I have devoted so much space to this definition of love because it has a great deal of bearing on what presently I shall have to say on the subject of bergsonism. Bergson's doctrinaire immersion in the waves of the vital flux is the same thing – only, in that case it would be the 'love' of the eater, as he englobed what was plunged into him, the love of the blood stream for the juices that reach it.

Returning again to Butler's amusing 'note', in the ordinary way we take these desperate statements with a grain of appropriate salt, as a philosopher's jest or a poet's madness. We know that all the married couples in a London suburb do not, in fact, eat each other, except figuratively. Nor do they make meals off their children, nor vice versa. At such extravagances we feel we can afford to smile with civilized superiority: yet we register the truth they symbolically contain.

As we have erected, developed, and organized ourselves in a variety of ways, become 'human', and deliberately and by a great effort of consciousness marked ourselves off from 'animals' (when we say we are 'humane' we mean precisely that we do not *destroy* and subsequently *eat* one another, or eat one another alive), then it is certain that biology or science generally is not helping us in our ambitious make-believe by referring us back gleefully to the oyster, the male of the epira, the ichneumon fly, etc. Science, or the man of science – of the Butler type, or like Mr Haldane – are romantically destructive. The *romance of destruction* is as natural to them, and they can resist it as little, as can a child. And it is both possible and useful to associate this *romance of destruction* of the man of science with the *romance of destruction* illustrated by the nihilist – by Herzen or Bakunin.

This *romance* can become a *rage.* Both with the man of science, drunken with the notion of the power he is handling, of the vastness of the forces he is tapping, of the smallness of the individual destiny, of the puniness of the human will, briefness of life, meanness of human knowledge, etc., and with the nihilist, from delight in frightening other children, the warm egotistic glow, this *romance of destruction* can easily pass over into sadism and homicide.

With what Dostoievsky described as the *possessed*, with people at all events *obsessed* by some such thing as this *romance of destruction*, as I have called it, the step from a beneficent activity to a malevolent one is imperceptible. *All* love, in that connection, could be said to turn into hate. The 'love' of the fanatic – like the brotherly 'love' of the primitive christian – always takes the form of destruction.

> Je t'ai aimé trop; voilà pourquoi
> Je t'ai dit: Sors de cette vie!

The christian notion of the destruction of the world, *other-worldliness* altogether, was an expression of the fanatical love – hate, *romance of destruction* – of the religious variety. Scientific thought (or rather the *feeling* produced in men of science by scientific thought) is full of such material as that. Mr Haldane ends his little book, *Daedalus*, on a note of that sort: he says:

> The scientific worker of the future will more and more resemble the lonely figure of Daedalus as he becomes conscious of his ghastly mission and be proud of it.
>
> Black is his robe from top to toe.
>
> All through his silent veins flow free
> Hunger and thirst and venery.

The verse ends in a description of the diabolical figure riding along 'singing a song of deicides'. So Mr Haldane's ideal man of science is a *god-killer* like Kant in Heine's romantic picture: that in which the author of the *Kritik* is compared to Robespierre, only more formidable than the latter, because the philosopher's natural prey is a god instead of a mere king. Mr Haldane's scientist is riding along on an apocalyptic charger (suspect), trampling with the plunging movement of a ship, in the waves of a thick blood-red cloud. It is very likely, indeed, that the *Three Horsemen of the Apocalypse*[1] suggested this pretty emotional ending to Mr Haldane. For it is a matter of common knowledge that most biologists and physicists spend their spare time in the cinema, especially favouring the apocalyptic or

[1] The novel by V. B. Ibañez (1867–1928).

sensationally historical type of film. After inventing a new poison-gas, for instance, Professor X will drop into the nearest super-house if a good war film is being shown there at the moment (to get people into the mood for the next war), and to the intoxicating thumping and throbbing of the large orchestra will, in fancy, launch his latest discovery on a choking mass of the less scientific of his kind.

I will quote from another man of science, certainly with more justification in useful works than Mr Haldane (from an essay appearing in another series produced by Messrs Kegan Paul):

> But, let the consequences of such a belief be as dire as they may, one thing is certain: that the state of the facts, whatever it may be, will surely get found out, and no human prudence can long arrest the triumphal car of truth – no, not if the discovery were such as to drive every individual of our race to suicide! (*Chance and Logic*. C. S. Peirce.)

I should not dwell at such length on this subject if it were not of such obvious importance to us, who are not men of science, to understand the personal and private dispositions of those who are. Science is often referred to as *the religion of the present day*, just as socialism is. Like the socialist, the man of science is apt to be of a religious and fanatical temper. (He may even be a socialist as well.) This involves a lack of 'human' feeling as a principle. No scotch pastor, genevan mystic, parson from the world of the 'Way of All Flesh', not St Augustine himself, could be more callous, intolerant, militant, and resolved to make 'existence' a very bitter 'struggle' indeed for the survival of the holiest, fittest, humblest, strongest, and best in the imperium of a bitter and jealous god, than the average man of science for whom Mr Haldane is the spokesman. We are told that 'there can be no truce between science and religion', that 'we must learn not to take traditional morals too seriously'. What painful verbiage that must sound to anyone not a sectary of science or its enemy religion! For, whoever 'we' are likely to be, shall we be able to dispense so gaily with traditional morals? The large lay audience of such a book as *Daedalus* is left with nothing more useful than the conviction that it will shortly be finished off in a most ingenious manner, and so all its trouble brought to a timely conclusion.

You cannot insist enough, it seems to me, on the human factor in the man of science. Scientific discovery or the teaching of science is one thing, and the man of science as private man, reflecting on his functions and applying his discoveries or selling them to other people, is another: the layman wants often reminding of this to counteract his romantic tendencies. An engineer may build a remarkably fine bridge to enable people to cross a wide and powerful river; but if he sits down to write a little book about his engineer's function, it may become apparent, after you have read a few pages, that he is really explaining to people what an excellent jumping-off board his bridge is for those tired of life and desiring to get right into the middle of the river without trouble. The *romance of destruction* could be regarded as a sort of vertigo that haunts the minds of those handling the forces of nature, in touch, at least, with almost magical powers.

VIII. WHAT THE ANONYMITY OF SCIENCE COVERS

And here it is perhaps apropos to point out once more how criminal the egalitarian position is in its logical results. We depend entirely, for our relatively enviable position above the animal flux and chaos, on a very few men. To reduce men to an abstract average of 'phantom men' of the type envisaged by the Enlightenment, is to repudiate our sense of those discrepancies the maintenance of which is so important to our welfare. To pretend (for some motive of egalitarian vanity) that most men are not like the mad and brutalized crowds, charged with a sadism that identifies love with murder, at a bullfight, is criminal for this reason: it delivers *us all* over into the hands of *anybody*. *The anonymity of science covers that howling, foaming mob.* Why should we expect the average man of science – a man of very average intelligence, trained as a physicist or a chemist by some chance, instead of as an accountant, an acrobat, or a solicitor – not to behave, if he gets the chance, like the average of the mob at the Plaza de Toros or in the roman amphitheatre? Why should we expect him to resist the thrilling spectacle of our agony and blood? Have we any reason to expect him not to make a 'penny shocker' *out of us* if he can: since we know that his natural mental food is *Sexton Blake, The Magnet,* Phillips Oppenheim, and the films?

With the artist alone we are safe in that respect. He has no need, we know of our *real and living blood* and *real* tears. But most men of science are not artists. They *do* need these realities to play with. From this it will be seen how we prepare our own destruction when we lose our sense for people, or deliberately destroy it, in the interests of an abstraction – the one and only, equal and undivided, human average. Why, as Peirce says, the very word *average* is a journalistic absurdity in its origin.

That these things *on the surface* are different to what they are in the depths or in the interior and that we are *surface creatures*, is the truth that Nietzsche insisted on so wisely. All the meaning of life is of a superficial sort, of course: there is no meaning except on the surface. It is physiologically the latest, the ectodermic, and the most *exterior* material of our body that is responsible for our intellectual life: it is on a faculty for exteriorization that our life depends.

Butler's *swallowing of the oyster*, to return to that, shows us very well the nature of our problem. It is the separation of one organization from another, this merely *exterior* cuddling of which he speaks with irony, that constitutes our human nature. Love, as we discursively understand it, can only exist on the surface. An inch beneath, and it is no longer love, but the abstract rage of hunger and reproduction of which the swallowing of the oyster, or the swallowing of the male by the female epira, is an illustration. And it is the spirit of the artist that maintains this superficiality, differentiation of existence, for us: our personal, our detached life, in short, in distinction to our crowd-life.

Where Julien Benda is discussing the *emotional* – and hence decadent, imperfect, romantic – character of most art today, he writes: 'Note, also, *a strong emotion*, caused at the sight of this innate conjunction procured between the soul of the artist and that of the object, such as the sight of two people intimately embracing would awaken. Let us learn to recognize, also, in their will *to instal themselves inside* things, a kind of thirst to sexually invade everything – to violate any intimity, and mix themselves in the most intimate recesses of the being of everything met.' (*Belphégor.*) That describes admirably the spirit in which Butler's *note* on love and the oyster was written.

Science (on its human, non-technical, philosophic side) tends to the reverse, then, of what is ideally the function of art – a function which, as Benda says, it has forgotten. Science is the Science of the *inside* of things: art is the science of their *outside*. Art is the differentiator: science is the identifier. Science would merge us into a mutually devouring mass. That is the ultimate tendency of religion too, with its Ends of the World and Apocalypses. The *pagan* and the *artist* sensibility is on the side of life, and is superficial in the sense indicated above. Religion and the philosophy (or religion) of science are on the side of death, and are impregnated with the *romance of destruction*. The primitive christian, the nihilist like Herzen, and the man of science of the type we have been discussing, are all *destructive* first and foremost. They recommend, or prophesy, each in his own way, the suicide of our race.

IX. THE PROS AND CONS OF DOMINY-ATION

Suppose that (*one*) you were a ruler: that (*two*) you lived in an educationalist era, that your rule, like the Jesuit rule in their paraguayan *reductions*, necessarily took the form of pedagogy, that you ruled by means of popular instruction and *suggestion*, rather than of armed force – as is the case in a modern democracy: what type of person would you favour? You would yourself be a typical dominy. And ideally the Infants' Class would be what you would choose to take.

The reason for your choosing the Infants' Class, or for your being a dominy at all, would be an innate desire to boss others, and be a little providence or all-knowing god to a little world lying in the palm of your hand. And these characteristics would be found in all of your kind. But also the drastic, top-to-bottom, changes that had to be effected in the generations you had come suddenly to control – in order to change them quickly from their agelong habits to other very different habits more in conformity with your own taste – would necessitate this. The 'Give us a child up to six, and do what you like with him afterwards' of the jesuits would also apply to your task. It took the jesuits in their *reductions* three generations to transform the Indians into civilized people. This meant a three-generation-long concentration on the child population. That too would be your task. Both from your pedagogic disposition and the political requirements of the case, the child would be your natural quarry. Or a race of Neuters would be preferred by you to anything galvanized into independent life by sex. (Fourier very justly called children before the age of puberty the *neuter sex* – rather on the principle of Schopenhauer's famous description of woman as 'the short-legged race'.)

When the children grow up a little, sex descends on them: at puberty this threatens to 'make men of them', or 'women', as the case may be. They are inclined to be no longer so tractable. They think for themselves, they begin to ask awkward questions. In short, they are no longer helpless, suggestionable, credulous children. Your interest in them is at an end.

Now *sex*, when it means marriage and for a man the responsibility of a family, destroys the 'child' at once. This descent of sex at the age of puberty, turning the child's thought to images of love and courtship, is a social, and so a political as much as a physiological event. *Sex* always has for the popular mind a physiological – *pleasure* – connotation. But this *simpliste* manner of regarding it obscures many things about it which have nothing to do with pleasure, as we have already attempted to show. The uniquely sensual interpretation of it enables many a three-card trick to be played in its shadow. The isolation, for political purposes, of the *pleasure* principle in sex is a tried and ancient expedient that seldom fails the person who has learned its use. In the result it leads to an attitude towards sex as false as, and very similar to, the popular and contemporary way of regarding the fine arts. In both cases *the isolation of the pleasure principle*, and the interpretation of their function only in terms of pleasure, result in a distorted and untrue idea of them.

That pleasure is the incentive to both – to both sex and art – is certain. But what pleasure enables you to reach is something different to itself, or, if you like, different sorts of pleasure: for all life must in some way be pleasure – even, as we discussed earlier, the horror of destruction or the 'narrow escape' from it – namely, the pleasures of the battlefield, or of any 'moving accidents', political or domestic.

In a society, the political and social machinery of which could be logically reduced, for the purposes of grasping it in its simplest, most radical workings, to such a figure as the above, what type of being would be pointed to as the ideal of human perfection? Obviously a child of some sort – of the same race of 'little children' as that of which Christ proposed to build his heaven. But Christ's charm would be absent. The grace and gentleness of his evangel would not come to mind on reading the harsh and fussy text-books of this political faith, prepared for the mechanization and fixing of the new child-type. It would inevitably be some sort of neuter and sexless creature that would be pointed out to us as a model for all citizens of that New Jerusalem. When the citizen was no longer physiologically a child or a neuter, he would be recommended to remain a child or a neuter or both, in every way except in age. Especially would the necessity of remaining in tutelage, in helplessness, in neutrality, in childishness, *mentally*, be insisted on. The image of the famous child of Kensington Gardens 'who never grew up' would be constantly held up before him as a cherished ideal.

As to sex and the family, the same line would be taken in suggestion and argument. Sex – the crude cutting up into 'men' and 'women' – destroys that divine neutrality of the tender, tractable first years. This would involve something else. It would be preferable that only the pleasure principle should remain in sex: and so far as possible it should be isolated in a neuter organism.

But what sort of person would be held up for the scorn and hatred of all, the great model of all that human beings should *avoid*? 'P.J.', or professional jealousy, on the part of the dominy would come into that. And sure enough what would be regarded as another potential dominy would be the target chosen. 'Intellectualness' would be the thing to which, above all others, no one must ever aspire. Intellectual matters must be the dominy's prerogative – but he would not put it that way to his little charges. He would say, 'An "intellectual" is a supercilious dog, mark you: have nothing ever to do – ever – with an "intellectual"! He is known to corrupt little children – he has been known to kidnap them. So beware of him! *Spit* – and make the *mano fica*, as I have taught you to – at the mere name of "intellect": for *that* is the disgusting thing that the wicked "intellectual" uses to corrupt little children with. Amen.'

In the contemporary world the intellectual will slowly get a position similar to that of a witch or practitioner of the black arts in the Middle Ages. Men will yet be burnt because they have been discovered reading a forbidden scientific treatise. But when that time comes it will certainly testify to a contumacious, evasive and dangerous disposition for a man to have done such a thing. We are talking of the present, of course.

So with this know-all, knowing dominy in charge, with a 'jealous' eye on the fruits of the tree of knowledge, anyone who knows anything will not be liked. So you must know as little as possible to be popular. But there is nothing very unusual in that: for we all know that an at all active or ambitious man or woman – such as might become a dominy or a master or mistress – is only interested naturally, being a *dominy*, in people he or she can *dominate*. People who desire power experience interest in, not to say love for, only those inferior to themselves in knowledge or capacity. *Their world is a world of inferiors*. It is for that reason that they desire and attempt to bring about *an inferior world*! Therefore, if you wish to recommend yourself to such a man or woman, it is only as an ignorant, helpless, eternally subaltern individual that you can do so. And this is always true of the sort of man or woman with a taste for domination.

There is one further thing to be added to this picture (which will relate it to the contemporary picture already drawn): that is, that all the behaviour to which the children are urged will invariably be in the name of *intelligence* and culture. It is more intelligent to model yourself on the fashionable social diagram of this highly political schoolroom, and to become what the dominy wishes you to become, etc. How this can be reconciled with the hymn of hate against the 'intellect', there is no necessity to go into, for everyone can discover that by means of a slight effort of observation.

When all this has been said – in order that a few of us should understand exactly what our position must be in the modern world, and the exact nature of the forces at work, and all the significance of the social fashions by means of which they operate – it is necessary to add at once that this is by no means a tragedy for the majority of people. The standardized type evolved will be well enough off for a short time. The reason for this I have given at considerable length in the discussions on the question of responsibility and irresponsibility in Part III.[1] It is not by any means the worst fate for a man or woman to be fooled, or led by the nose as asses are. Where ignorance is bliss is the proverb – but ignorance is bliss everywhere. Sex – all except the pleasure principle – is, like art, an almost intolerable burden. The family is a curse. And this, in some ways, unpleasant picture is merely an intellectual organization, on 'rigid scientific lines', of what has virtually been the struc-

[1] Entitled 'the "Small Man" ', with its principle 'You cannot aim too low'.

ture of society at all times. The attitude towards the 'intellectual' means only that the era of vulgarization, of 'free speech' is drawing to a close: not that the intellect is bankrupt or can be dispensed with. It can be dispensed with in its travestied form of absurd *enlightenment* on the popular plane, that is all. And that is the last thing to be regretted. It will only be the private and unauthorized study of science that will be black magic. Only, during the revolutionary violence of this change of standpoint, the intellect has to be shielded.

PART XIII. BEYOND ACTION AND REACTION[1]

I. IS 'EVERY ONE UNHAPPY IN THE MODERN WORLD'?

No logical future has taken pictorial shape in these pages. All that has been done is to lay down a certain number of roads joining the present with something different from itself; yet something necessitated, it would appear, by its tendency. Both what is desirable and what is not in it contribute contradictorily to this impression. It is this *double* movement (proceeding from the combined disgust and satisfaction) that must make the planning of these roads so difficult.

Like all engineers, we are of sanguine disposition. To build even a bridle path across No Man's Land with the Trump of Doom sounding in our ears is evidence of that. But as far as possible this enviable cheerfulness has been concealed from the reader. *Tout le monde est malheureux dans le monde moderne*, Péguy, on the preceding page, chants. He is, of course, so wrong that his error can be neglected. It would be impossible to find a world in which everyone was unhappy. First of all, a striking amount of unhappiness always meant exceptional fortune for the few lucky ones that are not. In that sense it is an evidence of happiness, rather. Then Péguy himself is a living contradiction of his own statement. He was happy, for the noblest reasons, at the spectacle of so much misery. And for the most ignoble reasons there would always be plenty of others to be found whose satisfaction could be observed to grow as universal misfortune increased.

But in spite of all the evidences of deliberate maleficence in the modern world, when you have reckoned all that is deliberate, there

[1] Chapters I–VI.

still remains a great amount of *automatic* evil. In spite, similarly, of the small evidence of effort to produce any good, *automatically* a surplus of good comes into the world every year. For all the organization designed to convert it into evil with great despatch, there is still left over a respectable amount, which has either escaped attention or been found intractable to present methods. This brief statement must serve the purpose of an apology. The high spirits implied by such a work as we have been engaged on does not signify the existence of a secret store of good, or as it were a secret still where high-spirits is manufactured. It is entirely the result of a prolonged contemplation of statistics.

The philosopher or the man of the type of Sir Thomas More is always accused of confusing the *possible* with the *desirable*. He is described as 'utopian' or as 'a dreamer'. But he might, with some reason, retaliate that the emphatic 'practical' man is guilty of that confusion. For his prudent prejudices have the same result educed from contrary impulses. His preoccupation with what is possible is apt to make the 'practical man' describe that as desirable which usually is not.

Whether the Utopia I have been occupied in defining is possible, I do not know. You may consider it too much mixed up, in my exposition, with the real, to be a Utopia at all. Or you may think it entirely 'utopian' to hope to devise a means of paralysing the dangerous forces of human life without injuring them, or without 'catastrophe'. Annihilation is Mr Shaw's only solution (as it was Swift's) in his *Back to Methuselah*. Those Yahoos, Ozymandias, and Semiramis, after they have bitten and killed a promising sculptor, are destroyed. This appears to me too savage a doom. The destruction of any living thing involves the destruction of all, as is understood by the buddhist. It could, however, be castrated or otherwise treated, put to work and made innocuous, without involving one in vegetarian problems. Again, the spectacle of this retribution (overtaking the historic puppets brought on the stage, and blasted by the shavian sages) will not perhaps see so much to choose as Mr Shaw would have us believe between the bickering three-year-olds, conceived evidently by Mr Shaw on some pseudo-classic, New Art, or Chelsea, pattern, and the dolls they make. The mesmerists that are called Elders, always sententiously rapt in thought, are no better. They seem to have no right to kill the dolls.

II. BEYOND ACTION AND REACTION

This essay is a statement of a position that would be entirely irreconcilable, but irreconcilable outside of the cadres and clichés of any recognized federated opinion. Above all, it would seek to disassociate from the pure revolutionary impulse of creative thought all those corrupt imitations which confuse so much the issue, in their overnight utilitarian travesties. The agency it naturally envisages is that of spiritual ascendance or persuasion, with the avoidance of all violence as an article of faith. It is nothing but a rough working system of thought for the wild time we live in.

Committed to one theory or another of revolution, to something radical and deliberate, that is: in capitulating about your divorce, in consequence, from the world of sentiment and quiet animal growth, it is well to remember that everyone is 'a rebel' today, to some extent. So your natural opponents will all be 'revolutionaries', all 'modern'. A flag, a badge, or a uniform is, under these circumstances, no indication of friend or foe.

The statement of a position *beyond action and reaction* is our aim. That would be something as irreconcilable as primitive christianity, as radical as the truest speculative thought: which type of things are, as I have tried to show, the very source of revolution. I believe what I have outlined must in this sense be the attitude of the European of the future. He must be neither a 'good European' nor a 'bad European' – but in short, a 'beyond-the-good-and-bad European', if anything at all. To parody another famous saying by a great phrasemaker, it could be said that you must *drive your plough over the bones of the unborn*. Use your revolutionary impulse as a magic carpet to transport you constantly into the future: this will act healthily on your present. You will fly back to your present to see how it is progressing, and will find it very slowly sprouting with less impatience than if you were unable to imagine its ever becoming anything else but what it is.

The naïvely conventional 'revolutionary' is a stereotyped, routine protocol of a living activity, vulgarized for the purposes of mass use. It is really only put into the form of 'revolution' to make it comprehensible. But what is asserted here is, further, that this vulgarized version is apt, by the religious tenacity with which it is held, to affect its original authors. Such extremely highly organized vulgarization as exists today is productive of that.

But all creative activity at the best of times must have been influenced, if not controlled, by political necessity. Von Hartmann finds it 'amazing that Locke's sensationalism should have dominated the eighteenth century as it did'. The intellectual domination of certain schools of thought today would similarly seem 'amazing' to some Von Hartmann of the future. What happens is, however, that in every epoch thinkers of different, opposite types occur: there is always a Leibniz and always a Locke. It has been the political tendencies of the time that make one or the other prevail.

The phenomenon noticed by Benda – namely, that today, in the intellectual world, there is no Opposition, is caused by the infinitely higher organization of our time. *This enables politics to dominate speculation and invention in a way it has never done before.* There is virtually no intellectual opposition in Europe: Julien Benda, for instance, is a very marked exception. Similarly, there is no real *criticism* of existing society. Politics and the highly organized, deeply entrenched, dominant mercantile society has it all its own way. Proust, who may come to mind, is not a critic of the society he described. He is a partisan as much as he is the novelist writing for the millionaire Mayfair public: he likes every odour that has ever reached him from the millionaire society he depicts, while, of course, thoroughly competent to appreciate its weak spots. Whether this is a good thing or a bad in principle, where pictures of contemporary habits are concerned, it is certainly crippling for more abstract activities.

The proof of this political ascendancy over thought is not difficult to grasp. The history, geography, etc., that a child is taught are not conceived as science but as a political pabulum flavoured with this or that specialist truth, just so much truth as is politically safe. Useful and docile citizens, not learned ones or people trained to think for themselves, is what is desired.

But the press, which is an extension of the school on its political and informative side, is controlled by the same interests, naturally, as control the school curriculum. Science and philosophy, beyond this, invent and speculate somewhat to order. Neither the Lockes nor the Leibnizes can ever be said in their public teaching to be free. They are in a sense freest when most controlled.

I have already given you my reasons for not regarding an honest Inquisition as a bad thing. If it entirely abolished the *vulgarization of the best thought* – confining popular teaching to a routine in the hands of the small educational bureaucracy – it would have an excellent effect on the higher activities of the human mind, which should not be asked to turn teacher, but be left free to create.

The Zeitgeist has nothing to do with the workshop or laboratory, but is a phenomenon of the social world. Moving in millionaire circles, he hears today much talk of the *Méfaits des Intellectuels* (the Misdemeanours of the Intellectuals), naturally. At all times he is a *salon*-spirit, the spirit of fashion. And that sort of fashion has nothing to do with the creative intelligence, is a stranger to its habits, and lives in a different universe. If you are known to be of a 'revolutionary' or of a 'pioneer' complexion, a 'rebel', as it is called, you will be expected to call the Zeitgeist by his christian name when you meet. But in fact you will hardly speak the same language.

Sorel encountered all these difficulties in the course of his revolutionary career. For instance, when he began (when he became a social revolutionary, that is), if there was one thing that was blindly accepted as part of the equipment of every revolutionary no matter of what shade of opinion, it was anticlericalism. But Sorel, the most extreme of the french social revolutionaries of his time, was a very militant catholic, as was Péguy. Again he was in all his tastes a doctrinaire classicist, with roman antiquity as his political anchor, in this resembling Machiavelli. But to the deceptions of the conventional (of those with minds composed of comfortable clichés) there is no end. The 'revolutionary' will not even be 'revolutionary' in the way you want him to be; and he is often revolutionary about things that no one ever dreamt a person could be 'revolutionary' about!

III. THE GREAT DEVELOPMENT OF ASSOCIATIONAL LIFE

Everything assumes an increasingly associational form. A vast system of interlocking syndics – pleasure syndics, work syndics, sex and age syndics, vice and race syndics, health syndics, and valetudinarian syndics – is imposed. In *Sodome et Gomorrhe* Proust shows the working of this very well in his analysis of the powerful instinctive freemasonry of the pederast. But the Philatelist, the Anti-Semite, the Rollsite, or the Daimlerite, the Player of Chess or of Mah-Jong, can form equally well-cemented brotherhoods.

The association habit in its present development is the result of mass production. It is fostered in the interests of economy in our overcrowded world, and people are encouraged to get as quickly as possible into the category that offers the nearest approach to what they require or what they can hope for, and there remain. The mass mind is required to gravitate to a standard size to receive the standard idea. The alternative is to go naked: the days of made-to-order and made-to-measure are past. The standardization of women's dress, which is effected by the absolutist machinery of fashion, is the type of all the other compulsions tending to a greater and greater uniformity of standardization. There a colour – 'nigger-brown', for instance – is imposed. The great syndic of the manufacturers, dressmakers, etc., agree on 'nigger-brown' for a season, with perhaps a streak of mushroom-pink exuviae from the last season. In the interests of great-scale industry and mass production the smaller the margin of diversity the better. The nearer the fashion is to a uniform the bigger the returns, the fewer dresses unsold – for where there is little difference in cut, colour, and fancy, there is less temptation to be individually fussy. When there is so little essential difference between one costume and another, the difference is so slight it is not worth holding out about.

This closer and closer enregimentation of women, with the rhythmic seasonal changes of sex-uniform, is effected without difficulty by simple fiats of fashion. The overpowering instinct for conformity, and the horror of antiquation or of the eccentric, sees to the rest. In all this vast smooth-running process you see the image of a political state in which no legislation, police, or any physical compulsion would be required: in which everything would be effected by public opinion, snobbery, and the magic of *fashion*. We have, historically, in the hebrew state, a type of non-executive state such as might be arrived at on those lines. The legislature, of the greek city-state sort, did not exist; of all coercive administrative machinery, only the judiciary was required. God did the rest, or rather the teachings of *righteousness*, the anxious fanatical conscience of the citizen, and a great system of ritual. That is an example of moral rule, or rule by opinion, as opposed to rule by physical force:

of much more effective *interior*, mental, domination, in place of a less intelligent *exterior* form of government. Theocratic and theurgic forms of government are the highest form of democracy – a kind of super-democracy, in fact.

The ideas of a time are like the clothes of a season: they are as arbitrary, as much imposed by some superior will which is seldom explicit. They are utilitarian and political, the instruments of a smooth-running government. And to criticize them seriously, especially today, *for themselves*, would be as absurd as to criticize the fashion in loofahs, bath-mats, bath-salts, or geysers, in children's frocks or soft felt hats.

Those who actually like uniformity are naturally open to an unflattering suspicion. If, for instance, you protest too much that 'all men are much the same' – does it not mean perhaps that you wish all men to be much the same? You have no hope of benefiting by a general recognition of their being otherwise? You see your interest best in a *degradation* of men, rather than in a belief in their potentialities and in the excelling of some? If you reply that I or another are similarly arguing for privilege or discrimination because we have a personal interest in such an arrangement, that would have to be accepted by us. There would be no dishonour in such a conclusion to the argument. At all events, that is the danger run by the person too emphatic for the uniform. Again, the physical size of a living organism at any given moment of time is as the same value as the size of a stone. A man six foot high and a stone six foot high are both six foot. But since the man is living, goes on, and multiplies himself in space, there is no meaning in comparing them in that way. By saying that the stone is alive, only living slower, you do not alter the matter on our plane, which is alone the plane on which we are conscious, and about which we are talking. Outward uniformity is highly deceptive in any case.

The associational herd-instinct has one peculiarity that is very much to the point. The higher up in the scale of intelligence and vitality people are found, the less do they care, or are they able, to associate with each other and lend each other help. The inherent weakness of this natural isolation is the cause of all human misfortune, since the inventive individual is constantly exposed to destruction in a way that the uninventive, mechanical, associational man is not. Had the best intelligence at any time in the world been able to combine, the result would have been a prodigal of power, and the result for men at large of the happiest.

What makes the present time, then, so hopeful a one is that in the ever closer and more mechanical association of the great masses of people into an ever more and more rigid system of clans, societies, clubs, syndics, and classes, the original man is more and more forced out of these groupings, since there is no play for the inventive or independent mind within them. All these *odd men out* stand at present glaring at each other as usual, remarking perhaps to themselves that adversity brings them strange bedfellows. But the time must arrive when *they*, too, in spite of themselves form a sort of syndic. That will be the moment of the renascence of our race, or will be the signal for a new biological transformation. While the philosopher of the sort of Mr Russell, of the author of the *Anatomy of Melancholy*,[1] or of Professor Richet, would be swept down into the underworld of subconscious automatism, wringing their hands, in attitudes of apocalyptic despair.

Earlier in this essay it was remarked that: 'Left at the mercy of this vast average – its inertia, "creative hatred", and conspiratorial habits where the "new" is concerned – we shall always checkmate ourselves; and the more we "advance" the more we shall lose ground.' But if this inertia (1) is *satisfied* by a businesslike organization of its desire (its *What the Public wants* requirement), and if (2) this inflexible organization severs it entirely from all the free intelligences in the world, which it more and more isolates, then a new duality of human life (introducing perhaps a new species, and issuing in biological transformation) would result. That is why, far from molesting or subjecting to damaging criticism (of a vulgarizing description) the processes of *stultification* which are occurring, everything should be done (publicly, and at large, of course) to hasten it. So it can be truly said with fullest good sense that whenever you see a foolish play, read an especially idiotic article, full of that strident humbug to which we are so accustomed, you should rejoice. Mental food changes people in the same way as what they eat and the climate of their habitat. Those who like or can stomach what they are given in Western democracies today will change and separate themselves naturally from those who reject or vomit at that fare. A natural separation will then occur, and everybody will

[1] Robert Burton (1577–1640).

get what he wants. 'Nature's ethereal, human angel, Man', will become segmented, and the divorce will be to the good of both these sections which are being forced apart.

IV. HOW MUCH TRUTH DOES A MAN REQUIRE?

Sorel draws our attention to what he affirms is the importance of the *anticipatory* spirit by a quotation from von Hartmann:

> The melancholy which is spread like a *presentiment* over all the masterpieces of greek art, in spite of the life with which they seem to overflow, is witness that individuals of genius, even in that period, were in a condition to penetrate the illusions of life, to which the genius of their age abandoned itself without experiencing the need to control them.

And Sorel comments on this to the effect that 'there are few doctrines more important for the understanding of history' than that of *anticipation,* reminding us of Newman's use of it in his researches in the history of dogmas.

This melancholy presentiment of the truth, that the tragic drama possessed in Greece, enabling it to tear aside the veil of illusion, as Shakespeare did so terribly in our own time, was a possession (in both senses of that word) not shared by greek philosophy as a whole. Heraclitus, the 'dark', the 'weeping', philosopher, owned it. But the platonists were busy, as in their capacity of teachers and healers they were bound to be, with happier pictures. The artist's truth is in this way the deeper and more terrible. His classical tragic task of providing a *catharsis* – his diabolical rôle of getting as near to destruction and terror as that is possible without impairing the organism – requires of him a very different disposition to that of the philosopher.

When the tragic artist takes life in hand for representation, secondary characteristics disappear as he manipulates it. It is at life itself, rather than at our particular social life of the moment, that his terrible processes are directed. His 'truth', if it were not deadened by a rhythmical enchantment, would annihilate us. But the philosopher, who is responsible for the Utopias, although he may have his 'presentiments' as well, is typically engaged in bestowing life, not in pretending to take it away – however salutary that threat may be in the event. He heals the wounds inflicted by natural science, or tries to; dovetails his midwifery with the purges of the more terrible form of artist; investigates life's gentler and nobler possibilities with the serener sort of artist. So he defines his discursive functions: showing himself as indispensable as the dock leaf is for the nettle, and claiming to stand between man and the artist, as well as between man and the man of science. He is the *lover*, his wisdom or system his carefully collected nest.

That our contemporaries have an aversion, as Sorel says, to 'every pessimistic idea' is indisputable. But what people have not had? He means, however, that they refuse to take on even so much of the harsh truth as is necessary for life's bare preservation. But they get their truth all right, in spite of themselves. Mechanically it reaches them, without their knowing how, by way of the vulgarization of scientific thought. They actually get much too much, far more than what would be a suitable ration. It is plainly the popularization of science that is responsible for the fever and instability apparent on all sides. To withhold knowledge from people, or to place unassimilable knowledge in their hands, are both equally effective, if you wish to render them helpless. As Einstein is reported as saying in conversation, the characteristic danger to human society is that the outstripping intellect will destroy the backward mass of men by imposing a civilization on it for which it is not ready.

The question, of course, remains if it will ever be ready. That is the capital question where its destiny is concerned. It is on the answer to that that all political thought must repose. What has been suggested in the foregoing pages is that ample evidence has been accumulated by now that *men, as a whole, will never be ready*. Instead of sitting down and abusing them as the man of the type of Robert Burton does – or as Professor Richet has just done, and as have numbers of other philosophers, ecclesiastics, etc., in the past, – and instead of fixing an eye of hatred on them, and deciding that they must die, as Swift did, or coolly blasting them (with the gesture, oddly enough, of benediction), as Mr Shaw does with Ozymandias, a quite different course, luckily, today presents itself.

In 1849 Lange wrote: 'Should it not be clear to every reasonable man that civilized Europe must enter into one great political community?' Earlier Goethe was a constant advocate of a world-state, and of the suppression of nationality. In other words, he was an 'internationalist'. Today, in spite of very great efforts to artificially preserve 'national' frontiers, these frontiers being a more disreputable farce than at any former period, *automatically* – the automatic defeating conscious strategy most plainly in this instance – internationalism is becoming a fact. The standardizing of giant industry, and its international character will have it so, in spite of the international industrialists. When all the Russians wore beards and all Americans were clean-shaven, it was a much more easy way to make them believe, respectively, that they were of different clay. But 'nationality' is the one thing that cannot be manufactured. Once you have destroyed, or allowed to be destroyed, the ancient customs and arts of a country, you cannot reimpose them. The Maypole or Jack o' the Green in the Council-School festivity is too evident a lie: it is like a sphinx in St Paul's, or a Carthaginian galley on the Spree.

There is today a new reality; it is its first appearance in terrestrial life – the fact of political world control. Today this may be said to be in existence, and tomorrow it will be still more of a fact. Neither can it be hidden – short of destroying everybody's sense of reality altogether. People no doubt could be persuaded that they did not see the sun and moon: but the effort to assimilate this gigantic lie would destroy their brains altogether, and universal imbecility would ensue.

Thereby the whole problem of government is altered. New methods are suggested that formerly circumstances did not allow people even to imagine. With a world-state and a recognized central world-control, argument about the ethics of war would become absurd. More profitable occupations could then be found for everybody. In a society organized on a world-basis, 'revolution' would not be encouraged, either, any more than today it is encouraged in fascist Italy or soviet Russia.

The idea for which Professor Perry stands, that of the comparatively recent growth of war, and of the fundamentally pacific nature of man, when not trained or organized as a 'fighting machine' (for it is only as a machine, even, that he can fight – by himself he is not very pugnacious or brave), is supported by a great deal of very good evidence. And there seems no reason at present why this period of chaotic wastefulness should not be regarded as drawing to a close. In order to wind it up, further wars and revolutions may occur. But they are not any longer necessary. There is even no political excuse for them. There may soon therefore no longer be any reason for the despairing philosopher to inquire, 'Who made so soft and peaceable a creature, born to love mercy, meekness, so to rave, rage like wild beasts, and run on to their own destruction? How may nature expostulate with mankind, "I made thee a harmless, quiet, a divine creature!", etc.'

For we know quite well what makes such a soft and peaceable creature into a warrior – it is his rulers in the course of their competitive careers who effect this paradoxical transformation in their extremely soft subjects. If all competition were eliminated – both as between the small man and the big, and respectively between the several great ones of this earth – then this soft and peaceable, or 'mad, careless, and stupid', creature would be spared the gymnastics required to turn him into a man-eating tiger. It is also absurd, and even wicked, to attempt to turn him into a philosopher. He should be left alone and allowed to lead a peaceful, industrious, and pleasant life, for we all as men belong to each other.

The optimism of socratic thought might even be rehabilitated, and not seem so aggravating as Sorel found it. His serene picture, without coming true, might no longer enrage: the 'presentiments' of the prophets and artists could be taken or left – left by most people, who would hum and buzz as monotonously and peaceably through their life as even the most fortunate bee. Those who had a taste for other forms of life, or who were bred, by means of eugenics, to a different existence, would not rage against their soft and peaceable fellow-man as formerly. For every one would be perfectly satisfied.

V. DIFFERENT MAGICS

In the Mind and Body war, the war of Sensation against Intellect, the war of the high and the low-brow, the war of women and men, you are expected to be obediently, conventionally, militant. If you agree, and if in the first, for instance, your occupation thrusts you into the ranks of the Mind, then you have imposed on you an attitude of artificial hostility to the Body. This may be against your nature, which disposes you to be friendly to both. The same through the whole list. The intolerance, the militancy-to-order, the savage partisanship imposed on you on every possible subject, is a conscription that, intellectually, you must learn to evade.

'Qui terre a, guerre a' is a French proverb. But without 'terre' it is apparently the same thing. Everything is done to make people wish to be animals rather than men. A writer in the *New Leader* recently quoted what purported to be a letter from a perplexed correspondent. It expresses very well the widespread discouragement of the moderately ambitious man:

> 'What is the use of being told about books [he wrote] when I can't read them! I haven't the money to buy them, and nine times out of ten my local library hasn't got them; or if it has there is a list as long as your arm of people waiting for them.'
>
> Beginning on this personal note, his argument proceeded to wider considerations, raising the whole question of the value of civilization for the poor. A progress in culture, he said, meant a reduction in happiness; the more complicated a man's needs became, the more refined his tastes, the greater their liability to be outraged. The man who is used to good books is revolted by the sunday papers that satisfy his fellows; the man who likes good music is a martyr to noise and shudders every time a barrel organ comes down his street; the man who recognizes a lovely building when he sees it, turns in loathing from the squalid ugliness of our towns.
>
> If he is rich he can to some extent obtain compensation for the pain his cultivated tastes cause him, by spending time and money on their satisfaction. He can only shudder away from a world of savages and hooligans and shrink into himself in pride and disgust.
>
> 'Thus [my correspondent ended] if I had to choose today between being a pig happy or being Socrates unhappy – and wisdom seems to point to the necessity of being one or the other – I should plump for the pig-stye every time.'

To be 'happy' is the object of the person illustrated in the letter. If you want to be 'happy' you must not be a man but a pig. And that that is especially true today is indisputable. Well, the Circe of Capitalism is able to achieve this for our shipwrecked world. We can either decide among ourselves, or draw lots as to who shall be happy and who unhappy.

There is a story that in the early days of socialism a certain labour leader had organized a demonstration in Trafalgar Square. Thousands of strikers assembled, and large forces of police were reported as approaching from all directions. The organizer of the demonstration passed round the word that all the manifestants, at the first sign of the police, should *sit down*. In due course the police appeared: they rushed furiously into Trafalgar Square from Whitehall,

Cockspur Street and the Strand. But a non-resisting carpet was spread out at their feet: the entire crowd, as ordered, was *sitting down on the ground*.

Some of the revolutionary movements in full swing today are an unconscious adoption of this method of meeting the difficulties of the time. It was a particularly good way, and one that people cannot be blamed for adopting. The only magic that the ruled have at their command in face of the demands of the ruler is such as baulked the police in the above story. Complete industrial obedience would, no doubt, absolve you from constant doses of war and revolution. The corrective of civil disobedience since the world began has been military discipline, war and blood-letting.

Fourier refers to the magical effect of the capitalist transformation of his day in words already quoted:

> One is ready to believe in magic on seeing kings and empires thus circumvented by a few commercial sophisms, and the race of monopolists, stockjobbers, *agioteurs*[1] exalted to the skies ... who employ their influence in concentrating masses of capital, in producing fluctuations in the price of products – ruining alternately all branches of industry.

We have got used to the money magicians. The Good European (perhaps Nietzsche's 'good European' was after all a mockery), the *Brave* European (*brave*, as in german) is not very good at magic. He is very good at war, however. Of this he is very proud indeed: any time you ask him to fight and show how good he is at war, there is no holding him. What a pity he is not a better magician and, on the other hand, a less remarkable fighter! Oh, that 'fighting face' of the novelette!

Celui qui sera mon curé, je serai son paroissen (Whoever will look after me can call me his client) is a *good* proverb for a good man, or 'Good European'. 'Whoever will be my Circe, I will be his swine' would be the proverb for the writer of the letter quoted above. That argument turns on the desirability of 'happiness', which each man instinctively resolves for himself.

Happiness is the chief material also in the construction of Utopias. Christ's is the most famous and the nearest to socialism. And the Utopia of Christ can conveniently be compared with the Utopia of

---

[1] stockjobbers or gamblers.

the Ford industrial colonies or the ideal working-class community of Port Sunlight.

Christ's millennium was the old jewish dream of a land of promise. The hard cash of suffering and enslavement that the Jew was willing to pay down, in vicarious atonement, through his long genealogical sequences, passed on to the sombreness of the puritan: the 'dogged old jewish optimism' vanished: and the European must have a very imperfect notion of the dream of Jesus.

'However much, therefore, Christianity may have insisted on renouncing the world, the flesh, and the devil, it always kept in the background the perfectly jewish and pre-rational craving for a delectable promised land. The journey might be long and through a desert, but milk and honey were to flow in the oasis beyond.' Beyond the puritan's savage gloom there was no Valhalla, however, much less the delectable oasis indicated above by Santayana – the honey-pot of the hebrew faith.

However, whatever Christ's Kingdom of Heaven may have meant to his followers, there are certain elements in it that are accessible and generally understood. The difference between it and Port Sunlight, say, is this. Lord Leverhulme promised what he could perform, whereas Christ was in a very different position. The former was more honest, and, if allowed to, would, I think, in the fullness of time have been a greater *benefactor* (measured by material cleanliness and comfort) than Christ. Port Sunlight is (in more senses than one, as I have suggested) a certainty. There is no *last shall be first* about it; it is a dead level of sanitary life – sunlit, but not pretending to be Heaven. (It would be impossible for a man to say that he had Port Sunlight inside him, as he can say that he has Heaven within him.)

On the other hand, is Christ, promising what most likely can never come about, for that reason less of a benefactor than Lord Leverhulme or Henry Ford, promising what can and will (most likely) come about? Christ's perfection was full of impossibilities, on the mundane plane, and to stage them he had to take his audience *out of life* altogether. His doctrine was a drug: beneath its influence men saw their wrongs being righted, saw the 'oppressor's wrong, the proud man's contumely' punished and humble faith rewarded, the last first and the first last. Is it the action of an honourable man to give people these flattering visions? Is not the modern benefactor of big business (possibly sometimes of the type against which Christ inveighed) really the eternal *rich man* justifying himself, stealing a march on the magician and so-called Saviour? Even if this whitewashing of the whited sepulchre only resulted in a sanitary tiling such as we associate with lavatories and hospitals, is not perhaps this stone that the Builder rejected (namely, the *rich man*) becoming the head-stone of the corner?

But does he not also get much more out of it than Christ? it might be objected. Even there it is not certain that Ford or Lord Leverhulme could make good their claim for a bigger halo than Christ's. I have no means of knowing what exactly the author of Port Sunlight got out of life, or what Henry Ford is still enjoying; but I should think that probably, on the model of most millionaires, they both must have led a harassed, frugal, lonely existence, full of distrust and indigestion. The experience of Christ – like a lyrical poet dying young, under romantic conditions, worshipped by throngs of people attracted by his personal magnetism, living to some extent the rosy dream that he recited daily – this experience sounds on the face of it more enviable than that of the modern millionaire.

'Malheur à celui qui en rit, il ne comprend pas l'esprit humain, sa fière originalité, petits esprits qui n'apprécient pas ce qui dépasse la vulgarité d'un salon, les étroites limites d'un bon sens vulgaire.' So Renan writes of those who are apt to laugh at the holy passion of Sainte Thérèse, or other saints and madmen. 'Malheur' indeed, and we must not be too hasty in taking Port Sunlight into our hearts in the place of the full christian or other dream.

But is not Christ's too exceptional a phantasy for the average of human desires? The more discriminating arrangements of the hindu heaven – or system of heavens – respond probably more accurately to the reality of human wishes.

VI. THE POLITICS OF THE INTELLECT

That when I am speaking of the intellectual I evidently experience no shame (reflecting on the compromising nature of my own occupation), that I do not pretend to be 'a plain, blunt man', is true.

Far from that, it is my effrontery to claim that men owe everything they can ever hope to have to an 'intellectual' of one sort or another. And that is true both of the business magnate and his meanest employee. I claim further that the intellectual is the only person in the world who is not a potential 'capitalist', because his 'capital' is something that cannot be bartered. What he deals in, even when it gives him power, gives him no money.

For this splendid and oppressed class nothing is done in the social revolution. But that it is a refuge for the scum of every other defeated class – or any class temporarily lying low – is true. And it is no doubt the great mass of pseudo-artists, writers, and so forth who discredit it. Therefore, when the agitator hurls his abuse at the intellectual, if he would be more specific and pick out the sort of figures that abuse the shelter of the too hospitable intellect, he would be doing a service.

The intelligence suffers today automatically in consequence of the attack on all authority, advantage or privilege. These things are not done away with, it is needless to say, but numerous scapegoats are made of the less politically powerful, to satisfy the egalitarian rage awakened. The intellect, so exposed, so helpless in such a case, suffers most of any category, which is a danger to all of us. It is our own brain we are attacking – while the stomach looks on and laughs 'to see such sport'.

The possession and exercise of intellectual power in no way affects a person to a class enjoying political ascendancy. There is nothing 'aristocratic' about the intellect: its noticeable simplicity makes it unpromising to look for analogies to sit in a complex society at all. An early society would offer better parallels, and indeed, in many primitive communities the chief or leader is chosen as the man known to have the best head. But the word 'aristocratic', with its implication of a crowd within the bigger crowd, organized for the exploitation of the latter, is peculiarly inapt for the essentially individual character of the intellect.

The intellect is more removed from the crowd than is anything: but it is not a snobbish withdrawal, but a going aside for the purposes of work, of work not without its utility for the crowd. The artificial barriers that an aristocratic caste are forced to observe are upheld to enhance a *difference* that is not a reality. It is because they are of the same stuff as their servants that they require the disciplines of exclusiveness. In the case where an aristocratic régime represents a race ruling as the result of conquest, as has generally been the case, often the aristocrat is inferior in every respect to the subject population – that is, except in organization for war.

The primitive, 'democratic', picture of the intellectual leader living his life simply among the people, with admirable simplicity and without fuss, has too many ready illustrations in history to require specification. But this leader claims the authority of the function that he regards as superior to any mechanical dominion of physical force or wealth. Also it is not for his own sake that he claims it; in this he resembles the king. More than the prophet or religious teacher he represents at his best the great unworldly element in the world, and that is the guarantee of his usefulness. It is he and not the political ruler who supplies the contrast of this something remote and *different* that is the very stuff of which all living (not mechanical) power is composed, and without whose incessant functioning men would rapidly sink back to their mechanical origins. The objectionable *difference* that is such an offence, or can be made to look so, is the very sign by which he should be known and accepted.

The life of the intelligence is the very incarnation of freedom: where it is dogmatic and harsh it is impure; where it is too political it is impure: its disciplines are less arbitrary and less *political* than those of religion: and it is the most inveterate enemy of unjust despotic power. In its operation it is less violent and more beneficent than religion, with its customary intolerance of emotional extremes. It does not exercise power by terror or by romantic pictures of the vast machinery of Judgement and Destruction. It is more humane than are the programmes of the theological justiciary. And its servants are not a sect nor an organized caste, like the priest or the hereditary aristocrat, but individuals possessing no concerted and lawless power, coming indifferently from all classes, and living simply among other people. And their pride, if they have it, is because of something inside themselves which has been won at no one else's expense, and that no one can give them or remove from them.

But if you want to take him at his lowest, there is an intellectual who is the most valuable specialist in the service of capital. The capitalist would have neither machine-guns nor aeroplanes nor bombs without this intellectual: for he could not invent these things or anything else himself. The intellectual is thus a 'worker'. What the capitalist does occasionally is to stir up the other workers against this highly salaried, specialist worker.

For the intellectual workman in general it is necessary to claim isolation and freedom from interference: that is if the best intelligences of the race are to work for us and produce their best results. This greatest and most valuable of all 'producers' should be accommodated with conditions suitable to his maximum productivity. He should not, if that were to be realized, be regarded (and hated) as the 'great man', but regarded, more scientifically, as the chosen vessel of our human intelligence. He should be no more the object of envy and dislike than Dempsey is because an unmatched gladiator. And he should be relieved of the futile competition in all sorts of minor fields, so that his purest faculties could be free for the major tasks of intelligent creation.

It is easy to see how the passing of democracy and its accompanying vulgarities owing to which any valuable discovery has to fight its way in the market-place – and the better it is, the bitterer the opposition – must facilitate this putting of the intelligence on a new basis. The annihilation of industrial competition and the sweeping the board of the Small Man, commercially and socially, should have as its brilliant and beneficent corollary the freeing for its great and difficult tasks of intelligence of the first order.

Our minds are still haunted by that Abstract Man, that enlightened abstraction of a common humanity, which had its greatest advertisement in the eighteenth century. That No Man in a No Man's Land, that phantom of democratic 'enlightenment,' is what has to be disposed of for good in order to make way for higher human classifications, which, owing to scientific method, men could now attempt.

The Doom of Youth
1932

The Doom of Youth *came near to being a stillborn work. The circumstances of its withdrawal, involving an injunction which was later dismissed, may be passed over, though it is difficult to understand how so charitable a book could, by its supposed reflection upon Alec Waugh's novel* The Loom of Youth, *published many years earlier, have been considered libellous. As copies are difficult to obtain, a lengthier extract might have been recommended for inclusion, if only because of the terse, exuberant writing; but the bulk of the treatise, containing numerous extracts from the daily press, supports rather than extends the argument.*

Like much of Lewis's pamphleteering, The Doom of Youth *resembles excellent conversation, not least his own. In life as well as in art and literature Lewis enjoyed a rollick. Beneath the dancing surface, however, great erudition and moral concern are evident. Allusion after allusion springs surprise and usually commands assent. Lewis was not merely one of the most informed writers of his time, but he took great pains over his 'field work'. Some of Orwell's essays are the nearest approximation to Lewis's pioneer studies in this genre.*

Is the central thesis of The Doom of Youth *invalid or at least superannuated? The immediate reaction is yes: for youth, far from having vanished, is surely more to the fore, more worshipped and kowtowed to, than ever. But that is precisely what Lewis predicted. His contention was, however, that this systematic exploitation of youth was the means to its destruction, and of much else besides.*

If not merely youth but age too had to be young, then society would be reduced to a condition of juvenility all round, and the world, though grown up, would become 'a vast nursery' for which a special amusement industry would cater.

There is much in the following to stimulate reflection, particularly the remarks on 'promise' which never reaches fulfilment, and on the emergence of a new kind of matriarchy, a system 'promoted by men'. All this was written long before the television epoch, which some future field-worker in the Lewis tradition may regard as a decisive turning-point in social life.

If, on the other hand, there are certain remarks which tend to 'date' the book, it is because such topical commentary cannot be expected to unfold a view sub specie aeternitatis. *There is a prophecy of unemployment of up to six million people. Britain did not reach half that number; but another country, famous or infamous for its own special youth cult, attained it with dire results.*

A kind of appendix to The Doom of Youth *was the short essay,* The Old Gang and the New Gang (1933), *a 'simple-hearted little pamphlet', as Lewis called it. It was concerned appropriately with the exploitation of youth by Dictators, with the fallacy inherent in the idea of 'the great blank of the missing generation', and with the significance of the spate of war books. Like* The Doom of Youth *itself, it has some wildly funny moments, but its deliberately-assumed baby-jargon may on occasion conceal its serious intent.*

FOREWORD[1]

The traditional European Family is 'doomed' – about that I do not think there is any occasion for us to argue. But 'Youth' in the european sense, that also is 'doomed'. It is the same purely economic consideration 'dooming' the Family which dooms 'Youth'.

The subject of this essay is the doom of 'Youth': by this I mean that the European generally has had a certain fixed conception with regard to the leisurely growing-up of a human being, and certain hard and fast ideas of what 'Youth' should feel like, and do with itself – as a *separate* communion, of a different clay to the adult

[1] The opening paragraphs are omitted.

world. If affluent, 'Youth' would be different (in this way) for a period of anything up to twenty five years – or a quarter of a century. Then 'adult' life began. This segregation is at an end. At ten to-day the human being is a little 'adult'. 'Youth' in the old sense will tend more and more to disappear.

Meanwhile by means of 'Youth-politics' of the most highly organized, astringent, and mechanical (rock-drill) type, 'Youth' is being broken up. It will be superseded by another, a far less sentimental, conception. The old 'Youth' is beyond any question 'doomed', in that respect, it is going the same way as Sex – as the old over-emotional love-relationship.

All these ancient, fundamental, european concepts – 'Youth', 'Woman', 'Man', 'Sex', etc. – are being demolished. The idea 'Woman' (with all the chivalrous and sensuous colours with which it has always been bathed and distorted – for the Celt, the Anglo-saxon, the German, the Provençal), that has long ago ceased to be intact. (A much more masculine contour is already transforming it beneath our eyes.) And the 'Man' – of the war-like, military, european tradition – the conception is for all practical purposes so out-of-date today that all that was 'manly' in the old sense is scarcely better than a laughing-stock, as it survives among us (the foot-baller, 'strong-man', cave-man, or police constable). Its *specific* time-honoured attributes are now tokens of inferiority.

'Youth' then will go the same way as 'Woman' and as 'Man'. And this book clearly indicates the methods, and the causes, of its translation.

INTRODUCTION

II. THE AGE COMPLEX[1]

A dispute occurred between two Frenchmen in a café in Marseilles last summer: I was not able to gather how it started, but the climax, which I witnessed, divided itself into three well-defined phases. First one of the men called the other fool (an 'imbecile'). The man addressed in this way merely laughed pityingly. *Fool* had no effect whatever. Next the other called him 'an old' something or other.

[1] Passage beginning on p. xiv.

Result the same: he gave only a contemptuous sniff: the epithet 'old' was useless – that dart had no sting. Then the other man called him 'a dirty coward'. *'Coward' was the word required*! That had an instantaneous effect, and the 'coward' kicked the other man at once in the belly.

It is evident that a man's behaviour, in such a case, will depend upon his business interest, his vanity, his age, his sexual make-up, his profession, his class, his country, his race, his standing, and the qualities upon which it rests – a mass, in short, of very complex factors indeed. All of these three arrows – fool, old, coward – might be completely ineffective if directed against a member of a very sophisticated system, especially if the subject enjoyed a sheltered position near the top of it. But there are certain laws, I believe, that could be shown to control the major orders and classes of men at any given time.

There are three very simple persons known to me, their reactions I feel I could with some accuracy predict. With one of these I should bet on 'stupid' (or 'imbecile') as the word that would do the trick. With another I am sure that 'Old' would get nearest the bull's eye (although both are of the same age). In a behaviourist experiment the figure would work at the word 'old'. I know only one person (and he is very simple, he belongs to a very primitive race) who would mind being called 'a coward'. He is half Corsican.

But of these three terms of opprobrium, there is no question at all which of the three would register most hits in a very complex society, such as ours. Indeed there is only one of the three that would do any execution at all. That is the word 'old'.

Let us consider the potentialities of the three words in question, one by one. First, no Everyman today needs to be 'brave'. Indeed it would be extremely foolhardy, after the experiences of fourteen years ago, to allow the fact to leak out, if by any chance he did happen to be that. On the other hand, as to 'intelligence', it is a great handicap to be intelligent. It is far better to keep that to yourself too – unless you are in a sufficiently secure and privileged position to be able to afford to reveal it. But even the very rich today are compelled to give themselves out as being perfectly naïf and stupid.

The steam roller of Big Business having gone over the democratic mass pretty thoroughly and achieved a mechanical 'levelling' (a uniform flatness never dreamed of before), no *exceptional* qualities are any advertisement at all for Mr Everyman. No. The democratic average has nothing to gain by being 'clever': and the most conspicuous bravery, if not rewarded by death by shell-fire upon the field of battle, is apt to lead to a much-bemedalled beggar's tin-mug for coppers, and a fine view of the back-sides of the prosperous passers-by from a position in the gutter.

But *age* is for the average man about the only value (in workshop, office, or factory) that survives, in a world from which all personal ambition has been banished, and which there will soon be, in any fair-sized country, five or six million out of work. As a humble cog in the machinery of Big Business your *only* value is that you are fresh – and of course, as a consequence, *cheap*. So as cannon-fodder for the great Peace Offensive of competitive Big Business all exceptional qualities of brain or character are taboo: the major asset is a fresh bodily machine – for machine-minding and mechanical tasks involving no responsibility there can, logically, be no other value.

But if this is true, then it is not surprising if, in a general way, 'old', much more than 'fool' or 'coward', would be the word of the three – if indiscriminately discharged – which must do most execution, say, in among a Post Office or Banking Staff, or among a Railway personnel – on the Permanent Way, or in the Offices and Workshops.

'Old', of course, as an epithet of denigration, could only be effective with a person already on the borderline of Youth and Not-Youth. But this conventional limit is today not much past the Thirty mark – the year when Villon began his *Testament*. And given circumstances of intense sexual, or homosexual competition, even twenty-five may have a very nasty sound – in the course of my field work I have encountered great age-sensitiveness (mainly, it is true, in homosexual quarters) around twenty-two and twenty-three. (In *Destins*, the well-known novel by Mauriac, which I shall quote later on, such a case of precocious age-complex plays a prominent part.)

In the *Evening Standard* (March 4, 1931) appeared a piece of gossip about undergraduate life. I will quote it and then make my comment.

UNDERGRADUATE DEBTS

Once every two or three years or so an agitation is engineered against the monstrous methods of the University tradesmen. These shrewd but amiable merchants are accused of soliciting the young to buy their wares without regard to the parents of the said young nor yet to the fact that the credit system breeds debts. . . .

FLATTERY

I remember that five and twenty years ago a certain Oxford wine and cigar merchant had a habit of praising the taste of undergraduates in their first year in order to sell them expensive vintages and brands.

A youth of nineteen knows nothing, or next to nothing, about such matters, yet often I have heard an eloquent salesman come out with some such rigmarole as 'Of course, sir, we *have* a port at 48 shillings, but it would not suit a connoisseur like yourself. Now this at 150 shillings we should like your opinion on.'

And so forth. The silly young man was flattered (as most young men would be), settlement of the bill was not pressed for another two years, and then, when it was one of three figures, father paid.

That is no doubt a true account of how the deal would have been effected five and twenty years ago. But today I think the really 'shrewd' wine-merchant would administer the flattery upon quite different lines — indeed his strategy would be diametrically opposed to that of his predecessor (or of himself) in 1905.

Today he would address the 'youth of nineteen' as follows: 'A bottle of port?' (He would be careful not to say 'sir' lest it might wake the reflex responding to *seniority* rather than that of social eminence: also, one cannot say 'sir' to a kid.) 'A bottle of *port*? What next — a bottle of *milk* is what an infant like you should be requiring — it is the *dairy* you want, not the *wineshop*, my little lad!' Having paused to allow the pleased giggle of the 'youth of nineteen' to escape and spend itself upon the academic air, he would return to the charge. He would exclaim: 'What would your father say if he could see you asking for port, I should like to know! Still, I daresay it is for somebody a little *older* than you are, my little suckling. A bit of hospitality, what! In that case, I have a reputation to keep up in this University, and I shouldn't like anyone to say that I had taken advantage of a baby-in-arms and sold the poor kid an indifferent wine. So it's up to me, I suppose! I couldn't sell *an old hardened connoisseur like yourself*' (heaviest sarcasm and great sneers of infinite seniority) 'anything but this wine — and when I say it is 150 shillings a bottle, it is only that *for you* — I shall make nothing out of it at that price, I don't mind telling you! — but the price has to be tempered to the shorn lamb — even if you have been born with a silver spoon betwixt your ikkle tossie-pegs! One hundred and forty shillings – and if you tell any one what you paid for it I shall give you the best spanking you ever received, do you hear, my little fellow-me-lad!'

That (a little exaggerated, but not a great deal) is much nearer the mark, I think. Certainly with fifty per cent of his first-year undergraduate clientèle the 'old connoisseur' approach would be not only out-of-date but disastrous. On the other hand, the method indicated above by me would ensure success. Any manual of up-to-date salesmanship, having careful regard to the psychology of the young customer of the 'better classes', would contain the most emphatic warnings on this head. Reverse all your technique of flattery, or something to that effect, an important section would be headed. And what would apply to the youngest boy, would (with certain obvious modifications) apply to the *oldest boy* in Britain. The *white-bearded alone* may be safely credited with 'experience', or the palate that comes only with experience and years, and even they will not thank you so much as all that.

If as a social historian I am unequalled, that isn't what I am here for in the present instance, and I must leave it to the reader to multiply the illustrations which – begging his pardon – his experience may suggest to him. I am sure that, reviewed in the light of these novel remarks, his memory will disgorge a great variety of scenes and incidents calculated to bear me out in all that I have just asserted.

As a summary of this, I would suggest that it is in fact no obstacle to the ravages of the *age-complex* that a person should be extremely young. It is, of course, quite true that many people are quite untouched by this malady; but on the other hand, it is surprising how many you may discover that are down with it. And it is one of the oldest symptoms of the suffering Zeitgeist that the truly 'young' should be infected with this obsession, one proper only to age; and, more curious still, at first sight, that the *male* should be infected by it even more than the female, though *age-complex* is traditionally a complaint of women, like the victorian 'vapours', or cowardice in the face of mice.

PART II

XIII. 'PROMISE' AS AN INSTITUTION[1]

In our jargon there are two things – there is 'greatness', as we call it, and there is 'promise'. 'Promise' obviously means that *some day* So-and-So will be 'very great' or just 'great'. But how long can 'promise' last? How long is it possible – in politics, literature, or whatever the field happens to be – to *do* nothing, but just go on 'promising', and promoting the belief that if one were not so 'young' one would be very 'great'? *That it is certain* that, the moment that one ceases to be 'very young', one will become upon the spot 'very great'?

The answer to that question will depend upon a variety of things. But there is one thing that is quite certain, and that is that a great number of people, long after they have ceased to be in any significant sense 'young', go on calling themselves young and inducing other people to do so – either through cajolery, fellow-feeling, or sheer hypnotism – without being in the least discomforted by the fact that 'greatness' has not supervened with the passage of years. In fact, they often seem disposed to argue that, as they are clearly not yet 'great', then they must obviously still be 'young', since one or other of these things they *must* be, in order to *be* at all!

But, it may be objected, the habit of *encouragement* involved in the epithet 'promising', although it may cause many people to pass themselves off for a while as something they are not, may nevertheless result in that rare bird, authentic 'genius', getting the encouragement that it needs in those early critical years. In practice, however, that advantage is cancelled by the fact that (1) a swarming of pseudo-young-geniuses obscures the real young-genius; and (2) the universal *lowering of standards all round* involved in the adjusting of this starry and superlative term to fit a thousand and one aspirants is so destructive of all those values upon which, in the nature of things, all 'genius' depends, that the harm done far outweighs the good.

The art of advertisement, after the american manner, has introduced into all our life such a lavish use of superlatives, that no standard of value whatever is intact. And the word 'genius' of our

[1] Chapter XIII.

popular jargon has now become as cheap as dirt, of course, commandeered for the productions of not even a respectable second-rateness, but in the service of the dullest extremity of vulgar nothingness, in order to cause that great gull, the Public, to *buy, buy, buy*! Hence there is no difficulty whatever in appropriating this term, and any other that confers distinction upon everybody – just as *everybody*, in a truly democratic state, might be presented with the Legion of Honour, or the Order of Merit, upon attaining the age of ten. And, of course, sometimes the distinction may be merited. But to suppose that those superlative qualities for which such superlative distinctions were invented can possibly benefit by this wholesale bestowal of accolades, would, I am afraid, be naïf and groundless.

But there is something that is more important still. When a bluff is pushed too far, even the very simple cease to be taken in. And in the present case that point has been reached. No one any longer, *in fact*, believes that the world is swarming with embryo-'geniuses'. They accept the formula. They do lip-service to the 'promise'. But they have come to recognize that there is usually nothing beyond the 'promise'.

The whole idea of 'fulfilment', however, is alien to our time. The Time-god of Professor Alexander, or of Bergson, 'a god-in-the-making', does, upon the philosophic plane, represent what people have in the mass come to feel about all achievement.

Hence, gradually, everyone is accommodating themselves to the view – or, better, to the *feeling* – that there is *only* 'promise'. There is only immaturity. There is *only* a desire, but, in fact, no consummation. They still speak of 'promise', in consequence, in a state of half-belief: they respond to the word automatically; but it is at bottom *as if* there were beyond something perfect and unassailable – no more than that.

One reason for this attitude is the obsessing model of natural science. With the spectacle of the physicist, advancing hypothesis after hypothesis, which one after the other he tears up and begins again, it is natural to get into the way of regarding personal values, too, as impermanent, and to look upon the artist's work, or the religious or political belief, as fluid in the extreme. Yet of course we know that, in fact, the human values possess a permanence for us that the hypothetical machinery of the technique of the physicist does not possess. Homer and Shakespeare remain a human limit, and such persons are few and far between.

How 'Youth-politics' operate upon, and are responsible for, this 'in-the-making' state of mind – which erects 'promise' into a sort of God – I have shown. The 'Youth-politics' assert that to be young is to 'promise'; and the Time-philosopher, who converts into philosophical theory the politics of the masters of the material situation, he asserts that 'to promise' is in fact 'to be'. If there were also a religionist who was at the beck of this same political Zeitgeist (Zeitgeist being the term we employ to indicate whoever it may be possessing the political power and wealth necessary to compel us to believe and do what he wants, and so make of our 'Time' whatever he desires it to be), then that religionist would set up the Great God Flux in some form or another. And we should bow the knee – however, murmuring (just one or two), 'Still it does *not* move!'

PART IV

II. A VAST COMMUNAL NURSERY[1]

Now a 'motherable' nursery-world, of 'motherable men' – feminine values everywhere in the ascendant, universities as forcing-houses for the nucleus of the great Neuter Sex of the future, in politics a toy-bazaar and puppet-show in place of the 'panoply of war' and the majesty of effective ministers of state; a cringing vulgarity upon the part of Princes, and *Child* Cult even among them – that is not exactly a good world for 'genius' – and I write, it will be remembered, *from the standpoint of genius*. The 'feminine' values are all the lowest poorest-blooded – the most featureless, boneless, softest, the most emotional. And, of course, if it is a Matriarchy in fact that we are in, then it is a *male-matriarchy* – not in fact a world ruled by an enormous Super-Mother, but by a ruling class of very *motherly-men*. For if 'feminine values predominate', and if a Matriarchy is more than half on the way (as we are often told), it is feminine values promoted by men, and a pseudo-matriarchy (of a puppet-matriarch – a pantomime figure in the 'modernist' carnival) which conceals a figure (or a congeries of figures) in trousers.

[1] pp. 210–211.

But since 'feminine' in the only sensible way that one can use that term (and in this any intelligent feminist would be with me) is low-grade, second-rate, child-minded, mesmerically-receptive, dependent, etc., etc., etc. – then of course how this should come about is evident. For when you get government by Press, Radio, Film, and Fiction, which, in order to capture *every* Mrs Everyman, has to be uniformly stupid stuff, you get also the glorification of every value that is feminine. You get (automatically) hatred for every value that is truly masculine.

The Family Circle – a small closed system full of the interference and despotism of brothers and sisters and unintelligent Authority, in the person of a dual-governorship of Father and Mother – is not an institution, *from the standpoint of genius*, that is very deeply to be regretted, should it be completely abolished. But *from the standpoint of genius* there might be no gain at all, but the reverse, if the world became one vast Nursery, reproducing, on a large scale, all the most oppressive and stuffy features of the traditional Family Circle. The old dispensation did at least leave open a hundred exits into the Public world *outside*. But if there were no *outside*, why then 'genius' would have nowhere to go at all, except out of the world altogether, if the domestic oppression and jealous interference became more than it could bear.

Such are the problems of Family Life and post-Family state-domestication, *from the standpoint of genius*.

PART V
II. THE *SCHEINWELT* OF THE TRANSITION

Turning to what is more particularly the subject of this book – the technique of the 'Politics of Youth' – the effect of those politics upon the popular plane is often productive of the most barbarous anomalies and patterns of fantastic vulgarity. In a general way, the 'Politics-of-Youth' is not designed to affect the upper social layers, as at present constituted. Obviously the supreme leaders of the world (still less the powers behind the throne) will not ever be blushing schoolboys, or coy maidens, at any time. The Popular Press is strictly reading matter for wage-slaves; it is the bulletin for the slaves. And the 'Politics-of-Youth' is hypnotic instruction for cannon-fodder, the servile masses – that is clear.

But in Western Democracy, since the submerging and disappearance of the privileged families – the old 'ruling class' – the slave-consciousness, and slave-manners, has invaded every circle of the plutocracy. There, in Mayfair or Long Island, the manners, the vernacular, and the attitude of mind, on the surface, is very little different to that of Broadway or Commercial Road. Under these circumstances (with an exceedingly important difference) the 'Politics-of-Youth', intended for the servile-circles (for Workshop and Factory), also gives its colour to the lives of the gilded, super-tax circles as well. The *important difference* mentioned above is, of course, that whereas for the workman these effects are a matter of grim earnest, for the more fortunate plutocratic minority they are not. The latter patronize the fashions of the Underworld. They sing the slave-songs of the industrial serfs of the metropolis (their sobbing factory-folk-music). But all that is borrowed, in this way, from the arts and manners prevalent in the Heartbreak House of the Underdog, is taken up in a spirit of light-hearted cabotinage.

Although nothing vital is really at stake, however, the *passage-of-the-years* (grey hair, pot-bellies, and wrinkles) *is* a humanly stimulating topic (it is a best-selling topic for a book, I hope – the Old Adam apart from Youth-Politics has a tremor at the thought of baldness, deafness and gout). So the *Age-war* raging in the jungle down below – a matter of life and death for the small employee – is, up above, among the plutocratic Olympians, often a very venomous sham-fight.

We now are all *class-warriors*, are we not, more or less, just as in the old Christendom the Royal Courts maintained at least the outward show of devoutness? Every *class-war* is dutifully reflected from beneath upon the gilded surfaces up above. But homosexuality has also been a master-fashion for some time: and homosexuality more than anything breeds age-consciousness (cf. Chapter 2, Part IV). The pathic and old homosexual beau (or 'Aunt Mary') takes to age-class-war as a duck to water.

The age-values imposed upon the popular mind thus obtaining, in a playful form, in fashionable-bohemian circles (the World of Ritzes and Rivieras), the 'Youth' up there does not of course *get the sack* at the end of his Ten Years, but something mildly analogous happens to him. The eclipse of the 'Youth' – and his violent transformation, resembling in its abruptness the transformation of insects, into an 'Ex-Youth' – is often very sudden. It is not with such a sickening bang as the *sack* – as with a deadly dismissal in the slave-world; but there is a *smothered report*, as it were. (In Mauriac's *Destins* we saw 'Bobby' being practically executed at twenty-three by his gilded patrons – as the first specks and frecklings of *age* appeared upon the fruit, as it were.)

No rules can be laid down – pronounced homosexual habits, for instance, will make a great difference; but in the ordinary way an individual, who thinks himself somewhat of a great guy and has money, may announce to his friends 'I will give myself another two years' – or he may say 'eighteen months'. That means that after that period has elapsed he will no longer be 'young'. It will be in the nature of a promise to put up the shutters and retire from active life. He may subsequently – if he has a great deal of hair (and if his efforts to remain 'young' have not sprinkled it with unpigmented strands of a disgusting silver) and if his stomach is in place and does not out of reason protrude, and if he is rich – give himself another twelve-month. It will depend what his friends say. But at least he will take himself for a ride (go a long sea-trip), or put himself, so to speak, 'on the spot'. Publicly he will pass over into the Elder Half of the World.

There (if he is rich, again) he will proceed to make himself comfortable. (With a woman this is all managed differently; I am confining myself here to the description of the male dying – or burying his 'youth' rather, with an unhappy pomp.)

In artistic circles, of rich amateur, or bourgeois-bohemian life, in order not to lay himself open to ridicule, this 'deceased' person must go the whole-hog at once – there must be no half-measures. If a wealthy bachelor, at once an enormous pair of slippers (such as belong to the 'lean and slippered pantaloon') must make their appearance. He must never move too quickly up or down stairs, in however great a hurry (although in point of fact he is by this time – if he has 'carried on' till nearly forty, say – usually quite unable to) lest his friends should whisper that he is affecting 'youth'. He must rise slowly from a gigantic sofa of a chair, and for preference carry his hand to the lumbar region, to suggest lumbago. If he has a bold bald patch, he must make the most of that. Then with a painful ostentation he must for preference converse of events that occurred twenty or thirty years before. This last point is exceedingly important: it must be clearly understood that he is in fact dead – that openly (and loyally) he lives with the Past (with Death in the form of Chronos).

III. GOVERNMENT BY INFERIORITY-COMPLEXES

An 'Atmosphere' – a *stimmung* – is created by means of the 'Youth-politician', and a very oppressive atmosphere it must be, from thirty upwards, in workshop, office, and factory. What inevitably must be produced is an *inferiority-complex* on the part of all those people unable to call themselves Flaming 'Youths' – and how exceedingly useful this must be to the Big Business directorate has already been pointed out. A man with an acute *inferiority-complex* because five years has passed over his head since his last rise in salary, is scarcely likely to be a very difficult customer to deal with when it comes to discussing perhaps a *reduction*, rather than a rise – with the black spectre of Unemployment in the background.

A girl clerk starts, I suppose, at fifteen, at 7s. 6d. a week. Being under age that is all she gets. But to-day she is apt, in time's revolutions, *to come back to that 7s. 6d.* if she stops on the job long enough. Large businesses are at present using quantities of cheap *old labour* – just as they have always used cheap *child labour – paid at the lowest rates:* the child of fifteen and the crone of fifty are in the same minimum category. One hears of squadrons of superannuated typists, between forty-five and sixty years old, working in invoice departments at 10s. or less a week.

Inferiority-complex is a term that has not been current for longer than twenty years or so. *But all government has been conducted since the world began upon a solid basis of 'inferiority-complexes', as much as upon a basis of armed force.* Make a person feel *small* – that is, give him an *'inferiority-complex'* – and he is in your power. Even though you yourself are unarmed, he will not dare to touch you. In the heyday of kingship it took a very original and independent fellow to pluck up his courage to lay a finger upon 'a king' – even if he and the king were alone, and the king unarmed, old, and feeble.

A *History of Inferiority-complexes* would make a most interesting book. Until very recently there was in Europe a standing example of this *spell*, as it were, of 'inferiority', namely in the spell that had been put upon the Jew. Fifty years ago to have been 'a

Jew', that would have been a very strange sensation, I should imagine. This terrific superstition has been extirpated from mankind – within, as a matter of fact, a very few years, almost as if by magic. And in England the superstition of 'birth' – of the 'upper classes' being of a different clay – that was a tremendously powerful superstition as well. The 'inferiority-complex' of a 'common' man or woman, under Victoria, that must have been a very intense sensation – though of a different and less absolute order – than all that was suggested by the word 'Jew'.

No sooner than one superstition is overcome, however, than another takes its place. For mankind is inveterately snobbish and superstitious. It *must* have these spell-binding superstitions – the mystical-values. And I do not think that the intensity of the old 'class' superstition (now long dead) of the 'gentleman' or 'lady', and the men and women who were distinctly *not* – even that would not outdo, I think, the superstitious value of the *age-snobbery* now in process of crystallization.

It is by Snobbery, in fact, that a community is ruled: for if you say that it is by means of carefully-fostered 'inferiority' and 'superiority' complexes, that means the same thing. If you wish to get the better of a man in any field whatever, in whatever matter you may be competing with him, *get him feeling 'inferior'* and you cannot fail to overcome him.

That, then, is the principle at the back of all 'Youth-politics' – both upon the economic and upon the political side – in our Western Democracies at present. Once you have seized firmly this key to an at first sight complex situation – or once you have entered into possession of *the whole bunch of skeleton keys* with which, in fact, I have provided you in this book – why, then, you will really have (mentally at all events) the freedom of this 'transitional' dream-city – this paper *Scheinwelt* of ours – and go where you will. There is only one door I do not recommend you to use your skeleton keys on. But there are some things, after all, you must find out for yourself.

IV. THE ABOLITION OF YOUTH

It is not in the least to reverse what we have just been saying to assert that there has probably never been a period less superstitious than the present (whether as regards rank, race, age, or any other superstition) among those people really possessing political and social power. The *superstitions* are all for the underdogs – those in very fact *inferior*; such as are unable to see through, or to shake themselves free of, superstitions. The conspiracy of power to-day is – as Mr H. G. Wells has called it – an open conspiracy. It is all fair, square, and above-board. There is no excuse for any one at present not to be politically enlightened. Yet there have never been so many people entirely ignorant of everything that is happening to them. Which only shows that 'openness' is the best policy. If Guy Fawkes had explained publicly to all the citizens of London exactly what he intended to do, then probably the Gunpowder Plot would have been a signal success. (For is it not only 'madmen' who carry out their destructive designs openly?)

As to the *Age-complex* again (manufactured, for commercial and political reasons, expressly for use against the emotional herd, for *class-war* purposes – to take the starch out of the european adult – by discriminating against him in favour of Women and Children – to soften him at the core with a novel 'inferiority-complex', and so on): it would be true to say probably that among an enlightened minority *less* meaning is attached to mere physiological age than at any other time. But that only applies to a small percentage. Feminism having in large measure destroyed 'sex', in the old, romantic, overheated sense the *age-bogey* with woman (which was a sex-bogey, of course) has disappeared: as a consequence the small minority of intelligent and active women take as little notice as did formerly men of the age-classification. But those women are still the exceptions.

To bring home the great advance in civilized standards that the last twenty years has witnessed (always at the top in the civilized and leading classes, not throughout the masses), let me cite the attitude to 'beauty', as that applies to the faces of women. At this moment there are great numbers of women going about with great reputation for 'beauty', who would have been compelled under Victoria to hide their heads and creep away into a corner and die, shamed by their repulsive 'ugliness'. They would have had to resign themselves never to marry, for they would have been labelled – with that deadly victorian label – PLAIN. No side-whiskered Victorian (however 'homely' himself) would have dared to 'take them to the altar'. He would have been eternally shamed had he done so. Their faces failing to conform to any recognized chocolate-box canon, thousands of women far better fitted to continue the race than the indolent characterless chocolate-box-faced monsters of 'prettiness' in vogue at the time must have been practically sentenced to death, or at all events (for it was the race more than them who would suffer) condemned to barrenness.

This does testify to an enormous advance *somewhere* in the taste and intelligence of the community. A woman with an exquisite parchment-coloured face, or one of an attractive mildewy wax, is not damned with the silly word *sallow* – because she does not sport a complexion of monotonous roses, or one of crushed strawberries and cream. What is more lovely than *sallowness*? That to-day is fully recognized in those quarters where such recognition is most important, namely the richest and most powerful. 'Chinese eyes', again, do not cause a woman to be an outcast: thick lips relate her to the much-honoured types of Africa: and a large boxer's hand and iron jaw bring every pathic to her feet.

The tables have been turned in a most thorough manner, everywhere, upon the 'chocolate-box': and if this catholicity brings in with it a certain number of abortions – who under the Prince Consort would have been strangled out of hand at birth – the gain is very great. With the opening up of the meaning of the word 'beauty' a very foul superstition has been exploded. *At the top*, at all events, we can all breathe freely again, if we are women, whatever our faces (with their features and organs and skin-covering) may be.

Now 'Youth' was – or it came to be – a superstition as pronounced as any. And in most respects the doom of 'Youth' – its suppression, at the hands of the 'Youth-politican' – is (or will be) a notable achievement. That, too, will find its way to the Waxworks, the historical museum, where in the future all these classes of superstitions will be classified and exposed to the gaze of the sightseer.

To abolish the prolonged period of ignorance and primitiveness artificially maintained at great expense, for twenty years or more, at the beginning of life, is surely an excellent policy – something like 'daylight saving', and the adjusting of the clock to suit the seasons. It is not only unobjectionable, but a welcome innovation, to eliminate the 'childish' child – either lisping dreamy-eyes, or pulling legs off frogs and behaving like a miniature savage.

And if the 'doom of Youth' ('Youth' according to the old sentimental conception) also means *the doom of Sex* (and all its old superstitious romantic attributes) rather upon the lines occurring to-day in Russia ('The Land of Love Locked Out') – well, would not that be a very good thing too?

But I have now enumerated all the problems involved in this proposed readjustment, I think. Really what the 'doom of Youth' means is the erecting of 'Youth' into a *unique* value, and by so doing abolishing Youth altogether. For something that is *everything* in human life cannot be anything so limited as 'Youth' as understood upon the merely emotional plane.

A 'Youth' (Peter Pan) that *never can grow up* – that is the *all-youth* of the super-sentimentalist. For him there is nothing whatever in the world of any value but 'Youth' in the traditionally romantic, the sugar-and-spice sense. 'Youth-politician' – that is diametrically the opposite to Sir James Barrie's sickly variety, or the bogus and lisping species that is peculiar to the Invert's paradise.

For the 'Youth-politician' there is, strictly speaking, *no youth.* There are only different degrees and powers of an abstract energy. There is one long *adult life*, if you like. No life is worth considering, for the 'Youth-politician', except adult life. And adult life is not worth while, of course, once the person is no longer active and capable of creative or at least of useful work.

This appears to me to be not at all a bad ideal. On the other hand, the use of the term 'Youth' – as a result of the technique of 'Youth-politics' – for this *inclusive* valuation, is confusing. But as interpreted by a stupid person, anything at all becomes stupid.

It is quite clear what is intended, and what is destined to come about. 'Youth' is to be abolished altogether (just as the old 'sex' conception was wiped out by Feminism). And it is also quite certain that it is the very reverse of that to the mind of Everyman, that is on foot: nothing but endless, irresponsible, something-for-nothing 'Youth' is their *simplest* of 'Youth-politics'. And, of course, for the *Everymans* it *will* be the reverse. I have said that I was a prophet. And I prophesy that two centuries hence a long and sweeping snow-white beard will be an emblem of aristocratic privilege (no 'Everyman' will live beyond twenty-nine and a half) – just as long skirts returned to us, but as a token of social distinction, on the principle of long finger-nails in China. Obviously *long* skirts suggest that the wearer *does not work*: long finger-nails the same. The long white beard will be the supreme token that the person possessing it belongs to the ruling-class – that he is a member of that super-class who do not die, like dogs, after ten years of active life.

The Enemy of the Stars 1914-1932

The first version of this play appeared in 1914 in Blast, No. 1. *It was republished with some alterations in 1932, together with a postlude entitled 'The Physics of the Not-Self'. This essay, of which only a section is here reproduced, forms a kind of metaphysical commentary upon the action of the drama.*

An anthology of Lewis's prose fiction would no doubt include some of the prose passages of the play itself. These have the same remarkable visionary quality of Childermass.

Complete in itself, the passage on 'Greek "goodness"' shows Lewis's mastery of philosophical argument and ease of dialectical exposition. Just as he had studied oriental art, so he was well read in oriental thought. The comparison between the two great metaphysical traditions, Platonic and Hindu, is an important one. Lewis's stress upon the primacy of intellect — which he described as 'the traditional enemy of human life', meaning by life the empirical or phenomenal flux of Maya — *placed him among the Western interpreters of the orient who eschewed the sentimental, 'mystical' approach. In this, he anticipated writers such as René Guénon.*

GREEK 'GOODNESS'

At the end of the *Symposium,* Socrates is described as persuading the last of the revellers that 'the same person is able to compose both tragedy and comedy, and that the foundations of the tragic and the comic arts are essentially the same'.

Since there is a unique point of common emotion from which these two activities arise, to which both can be traced back (and on account of which common source the same poet is enabled to excel at both), so no doubt the different categories of forms, and their archetypes, would be fused, for such a mind, somewhere or other, into one composite body. No doubt beauty, pity, justice and the rest of the socratic predicates would melt into each other in some more general perfection. But ἀρετή which we translate as goodness, seems less specialized than most of them: and 'goodness' in its modern sense is, as a translation, misleading.

John Burnet tells us that 'goodness', for a Greek, had no ethical significance. 'We are left in no doubt as to what "goodness" (ἀρετή) meant in the language of the time . . . it was, in fact, what we call efficiency. To the Greeks goodness was always something positive': and so on. Liddell and Scott have for ἀρετή 'goodness, excellence of any kind, especially of manly qualities, valour', etc. Also 'excellence in any art'. They cite Plato as the authority for its ethical use. But Burnet, as we see above, does not agree to this. Like 'virtue' in English, it may have traversed several meanings – the utilitarian, the martial, and something like the christian. *Excellence* in anything is, however, what Burnet sticks to. And Burnet is a great authority: he even says it meant for the sophists 'little more than skill in the arts of party intrigue'.

But Socrates has several 'goodnesses': his highest philosophical goodness (φιλοσοφική ἀρετή), is the one identified with knowledge, and which can be taught, like a trade: and there is a popular 'goodness' of the lower order.

In the *Phaedo* (81–82), Socrates shows what happens at the close of this life to the bad man: and whatever ἀρετή may have meant to a fifth century Athenian, it is quite evident what is meant by it in this socratic dialogue. The soul of the philosopher goes to dwell with 'that which resembles it, the invisible divine, immortal and wise'; in a place 'excellent, pure and invisible'. The unjust, and the only popularly 'good', are in Socrates' ethical Zoo, allotted their respective shapes. Asses, wolves, hawks and kites are inhabited by souls that have shown their aptitude for such destinies as these lives imply. The 'good' citizen, however, may hope to become a bee, a wasp or an ant. For, like all the ancients, Socrates idealized these small industrious machines.

This goodness which is essentially an excellence, like excellence in craft, and which merges into the wisdom and piety of the philosopher, is like the upanishadic Karma; and the returns to the animal world, or the annihilation and peace in the bosom of the Absolute, or Brahman, are similarly parallel to the Indian conception.

The 'knowledge' that is identified with 'goodness' is, like goodness, of two kinds in Plato, the less empirical knowledge being called δόξα (belief) and only the eternal lending itself to such knowledge as can deserve the name of ἐπιστήμη. This epistemological absolute is much the same as Brahman; and the inferior knowledge of the world of temporal experience is much the same as the upanishadic *avidya*. The quality of the known and the object of knowledge, and the impossibility of anything but a wisdom of metaphors, glimpses and trances, in terrestrial life, you get in Socrates and in Plato as with the Indian (cf. the subject of Yã jñaval Kya: 'Thou canst not see the seer of seeing, thou canst not hear the hearer of hearing, thou canst not comprehend the comprehender of comprehending, thou canst not know the knower of knowing').

Socrates (in the ecstatic language of physical life, it is true) taught abstention from bodily desire. Philosophy gives freedom from the obscenities of existence. 'Imprisoned' in the body, using it and its senses only *just as much as is necessary* (otherwise 'the soul reels like an intoxicated man', inflamed and disordered by contact with the objects of sense), you should abstract yourself, and, as far as possible, withdraw your mind till it passes momentarily into the cathartic peace of the Eternal. 'Philosophy . . . endeavours to free the soul by showing that the view of things by means of the eyes is full of depression as also is that through the ears and the other senses, persuading an abandonment of these so far as it is not absolutely necessary to use them, and to believe nothing else he hears . . . for that a thing of this kind (one which differs under different aspects) is sensible and visible, but what she herself perceives is intelligible and invisible.' (*Phaedo* 83.)

This is an invitation to plunge into the 'soul', the opposite of the plunge into Life suggested by Bergson. Instead of outside, inside. It is an invitation that has often been repeated. Perhaps 'the soul' is sometimes *at home*, and sometimes *not*. There may be some ages when you are likely to find it rushing about outside: others when the inside-plunge is the likeliest to be rewarded with success. People as far as their own egos are concerned possess an instinct where this erratic psyche is; and, in fact, in most ages, the great majority have plunged *outwards*.

The empirical world, the εἴδωλα of Plato, then, could yield nothing but a spurious knowledge. And the conception of knowledge as the highest goal – identified with goodness – was the same as the supreme upanishadic conception. To *know* the atman, to *know* yourself, appeared the supreme efficiency in both systems. The fusion of the idea of goodness with that of knowledge we see in the teaching of Mani, for that matter; with his Persian ontology, the principles of Dark and Light, he taught that as the mind of a person contains increasingly more light, so it contains correspondingly more goodness. Socrates held that it was impossible for a man to *understand* and be evil. This is usually regarded as the supreme example of socratic unwisdom: the most 'irritating' of all his many challenges to commonsense. 'The question involved in the argument with Polemarchus is really the same. Is it possible to regard goodness as a purely neutral accomplishment of this kind, or is it something that belongs to the very nature of this soul that possesses it so that it is really impossible for the good man to do evil or to injure anyone?' (J. Burnet.)

If it is in the introduction of ethical and aesthetic forms upon a footing of equality with the mathematical that the originality of Socrates, as the successor of the Pythagoreans, reposes, then in a sense ethics is only introduced to be disposed of; for the *skill-cum-knowledge-goodness* of Socrates, or the approximation to perfect knowledge, are very mathematical conceptions, when compared with those of more emotional ethics. The idea, in its simplest development, seems to amount to this:

1. It is the philosopher's business to dispose of all desire.
2. If you know or understand *fully* you no longer desire.
3. It is the philosopher's business to *know* as fully as possible.
4. In this way the socratic 'goodness' is seen to be the same as Nirvana.
5. And with regard to this statement: You can only be just,

moderate and beneficent if you are not involved in what you are called to act upon – if you are withdrawn from it and 'not interested in it'.
6. Therefore the ruler should be a philosopher – in order that he may dispose of what he rules over, as though he were an indifferent god.

There is, in short, no emotional value attached to 'goodness' – and its implementation in justice, truth and generosity – whatever. It is your duty to yourself, or the wisest thing to do, to drug yourself, so that you shall not feel fear or disappointment. And no emotional idea of 'power', even, must be attached to the highest knowledge. For would not that be erecting knowledge into a possession – a thing you would fear to lose? Love, too, is in this category. If 'goodness' were an emotional thing at all (as is, for instance, evangelical christian 'goodness') it would necessarily entail *suffering*. And the object of the philosopher is to avoid suffering, or the turbulent 'intoxication' of action or feeling, in every sense. It is in these doctrines of Socrates that you find most readily the ascent to him claimed by the Stoics: and you see in its first state their celebrated ἀπάθεια or the 'cynicism' of Antisthenes.

You cannot logically 'love' or admire, either, if you *fully* understand. The conclusions to which the intellect and nature of Socrates were directed must have been, I think, a complete nirvana.

But the promiscuous, sceptical, feverish atmosphere of postpericlean Athens affected the mode and development of his teaching. Discrimination into a *prakrita* and its opposite could not, for instance, in those social conditions, be entertained; and the underground cults, such as the orphic, were not the same thing as a widely accepted religion, with its machinery of emotional compulsion. Plato's reasons for the dislike he professed for the writing-down of philosophic dogma indicated that popular uncontrolled instruction must have been a *pis aller*. And in any case, the main proof of this is, that, in the case of Socrates, a popular teaching culminated in political execution.

It is a fundamental example of socratic 'irony' which has escaped most people, that he should appear in history as essentially a *popular* teacher. Mr Bernard Shaw has put him forward and held him up to admiration as 'the ideal journalist of his age'. Whether Mr Shaw would have claimed or not that this was a super-irony of his own, the fact remains that Socrates, 'always talking about great market-asses, and brass-founders, and leather-cutters, and skin-dressers' (the raw material of his famous 'induction'), as Alcibiades shows him, lends himself to this interpretation.

Yet of 'the real Socrates' we have the exactest description put into the mouth of Alcibiades in the *Symposium*: 'Know that there is not one of you who is aware of the real nature of Socrates; but since I have begun, I will make him plain to you. You observe how passionately Socrates affects the intimacy of those who are beautiful, and how ignorant he professes himself to be; appearances in themselves excessively silenic. This, my friends, is the external form with which, like one of the sculptured Sileni, he has clothed himself, for if you open him you will find within admirable temperance and wisdom. For he cares not for mere beauty, he despises more than anyone can imagine all external possessions, whether it be beauty or wealth, or glory, or any other thing for which the multitude felicitates the possessor. He esteems these things, and us who honour them, as nothing, and lives among men making all the objects of their admiration the playthings of his irony.' (*The Symposium*, 216D.)

If this is intended to enlighten us, and it seems that such is the case, what it says is as follows. Not only were 'the great market-asses' and 'the brass-founders' merely the rumbling stock-in-trade of this supreme market-place performer (properties ironically chosen, ironically handled and ironically displayed), but also it asserts that his celebrated language of love, 'his passionate affectation of intimacy for those who are beautiful', his display of the amorousness of a fashionable perversity, likewise were *ironical*. What it says, in short, is that Socrates was pulling the leg of the Greek *exoletus*,[1] whom he caressed, as much as he was pulling the leg of 'the great market-asses' – or the greater asses, their attic owners. He knew his public only too well, and the simpering but certainly very argumentative epicene young gentlemen of fashion of the time: and 'the great market-asses', he used only as stalking-horses. Similarly, was not the language of love the cynical gilding of the pill? We cannot be surprised that this peculiar and very rare sense of fun should have brought him at last to a violent end – or, at least, an abrupt and involuntary one.

[1] Boy slaves (cf. *The Art of Being Ruled*, Part IX, Chapter VII).

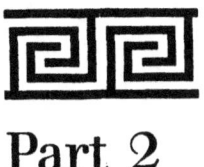

Part 2

Writings on Literature and the Arts

The Caliph's Design
1919

Of Lewis's considerable output of art criticism, we spoke briefly in the Introduction; and if a cause may be furthered by repetition of its merits, we repeat our hope that this lively and intelligent body of comment will in due course receive independent publication. In reproducing the following essay, we depart from the principle of excluding what is available in print;[1] but the departure is justified in this case as enabling us to provide samples of the whole range of Lewis's output. The Caliph's Design, *subtitled 'Architects, where is your Vortex?', is concerned with the author's hopes and fears for art in the post-war world. The target was Impressionism. In opposition to this school, Lewis raised the standard of Vorticism. The Vortex was the symbol of space as opposed to time, classic permanence as opposed to romantic flux. The fate of Vorticism as a movement does not concern us: what is interesting about Lewis's art criticism — and this is as true of* The Caliph's Design *as of the later* Listener *articles — is his capacity to communicate, even in his most critical remarks, a sense of the importance and excitement of what was taking place. The essays, though written with speed, do not betray unseemly haste: there is no searching for the fine phrase, no jargon, but a brisk use of common vocabulary. Lewis has been dead for more than a decade: Picasso is still living. But while the following essay made no pretence to be the last word about Picasso, even in 1919, it is doubtless one of*

[1] The Caliph's Design *is reproduced in* From Blast to Burlington House *(1939).*

the most trenchant of first words; and in the light of the master's later output, there is little that Lewis might have wished to retract.

PICASSO

Pablo Picasso is one of the ablest living painters. It would be impossible to display more ability. In addition to this, he is extremely resourceful and inventive. The back of his talent is too broad to suffer from even an avalanche of criticism. It is the consciousness of this that makes it more easy for me to state plainly his case as I see it.

This is, put pretty directly, what I feel about him.

With remarkable power he has refertilized many extinct modes, and authenticated new and specifically scientific notions. He has given El Greco a new bit of life on the Catalan hills in his painting of Spanish shepherds, oxherds and vagrants. He has revivified a great artist's line there, another's colour combinations here, and has played the skilfulest variations. Since every great creative painter must at the same time have great executive ability – the more dexterity he can command the better – it is always difficult to decide where this hand-training does or should leave off, and where imaginative invention, apart from the delights and triumphs of execution, may or does begin.

Briefly, Picasso's periods are as follows. His earliest work contained a variety of experiments: women sitting in cafés in reds; Daumier-like scenes, but more fragile and rather definitely sentimentalized; then a painting of a poor family standing by the side of a languid and mournful bit of sea, their bones appearing through their clothes, their faces romantically haggard and delicate, and a general air of Maeterlinck or some modern German 'poet-painter' all over it, has been widely reproduced. (Title: 'Pauvres au bord de la Mer!') Then came a period during which Dérain's Gauguinism appealed to him. El Greco was a still more prolonged infatuation and source of study. The portraits of Miss Stein and of Monsieur Sagot are of that time.

African carvings supplied the next step, in conjunction with the Marquesas Islands and André Dérain. These solid and static models, African, Polynesian, Aix, drove out the Grecos, Maeterlincks and

Puvises. Braque appears to be the innovator in Cubism; and obviously in Braquism – the brown brand of mandoline, man's eye and bottle; lately, through Picasso's gayer agency, taking on brighter and purer colours. Futurism once more gave this wandering Jew from not far from the Sierras a further marching order. Off his talent leapt into little gimcrack contrivances – *natures mortes*, in fact, come out of the canvas; little pieces of *nature-morte* sculpture, nature as the artist sees her, in fact; the bottle, mandoline and copy of *La Presse* reappearing out of art transfigured, after passing first through the artist's eye, spending a bit of time in the busy workshop of his brain, and so abiding for a year or so, into the flat world of the artist's canvas. After this series of hairbreadth adventures it is natural that this docile collection of objects should no longer remind the casual observer of any category of objects known to him.

In considering the future of painting, Picasso is the most useful figure on which to fix your attention. This is partly in his favour in as much as it recognizes his activity; but it is the uncertain and mercurial quality of his genius, also, that makes him the symptomatic object for your study and watchfulness. Everything comes out in him perfectly defined. Every influence in his sensitive intelligence burns up and shows itself to good advantage. There is nothing, as I have said, with regard to technical achievement, that he cannot do. He appears to me to have a genius similar to Charlie Chaplin's; a gnome-like child. His watch stopped at fifteen summers (and he has seen more winters than Charles, although Charles is not averse to a Dickens scene of the Poor Orphan in the Snow), with all the shallowness of the very apt, facile and fanciful child, and the miraculous skill you might expect in an exquisitely trained Bambino. These traces of arrested growth are very common in his race. You merely have to consider what sort of child you have to deal with, what moves him most; whether this mercurial vitality, so adaptive as to be flesh-creeping, is preferable to a vertical sense of power, like the sour and volcanic old *crétin*, Cézanne. It is which manner of life you most prize, admire really. You have your critical flight; and I am ready for the moment to suspend you, glide you, spin you, plunge you, or stand you on your head, according to your fancy.

Now, if you are not used to critical flights, and you turn to me as one accustomed to banking, looping and splitarsing, and ask me what I advise, or, to put it another way, what is *my* fancy, I should answer as follows: – 'I consider Pablo Picasso as a very serious and beautiful performer in oil-paint, Italian chalk, Antoine ink, pastel, wax, cardboard, bread – anything, in fact. But he appears to me to be definitely in the category of executants, like Paganini, or today, Pachmann, or Moiseivitch; where Cézanne is clearly a brother of Bach, and the Douanier[1] was a cousin of Chardin.'

That his more immediate and unwavering friends are dimly acquainted with this fact is proved by a statement I have just read, in the current (September 26) number of the *Athenaeum*, by the French painter, M. André Lhote:

> Cézanne embodies, through the romanticism with which he was impregnated, the avenging voice of Greece and Raphael. He constitutes the first recall to classical order. It was necessary, in order that the lesson he gave us might be understood, that an *interpreter* should appear. This was Picasso.
> The young Spanish painter deciphered the multiple enigma, translated the mysterious language, spelt out, word by word, the stiff phrases. Picasso illuminates in the sunshine of his imagination the thousand facets of Cézanne's rich and restrained personality.

What a performer on a pianoforte does in his concerts is to give you a selection of the works of a variety of musical composers. Now, apart from giving us very complete interpretations of Cézanne, Daumier, El Greco, Puvis, as Picasso has done, there are other ways, and far more convincing ones, in which a painter can betray the distinctively interpretative character of his gift. What do all these phases and very serious flutterings of Picasso's imply? To dash uneasily from one seemingly personal mode to another may be a diagnostic of the same highly sensitive but non-centralized talent as you would think that a playing first in the mode of El Greco and then of David probably implied. These are difficult things to decide since painters *are*, through the nature of their art, at the same time composers and executants. And you must usually get at this by consideration of, and sense for, the man's work as a whole.

What happened in this volatile and many-phased career of Picasso's? Has he got bored with a thing the moment it was within his grasp? And he certainly has arrived on occasion at the possessive stage. If it is boredom, associated with so much power, one is compelled to wonder whether this power does not mechanically spring

[1] Henri Rousseau (1844–1910).

from a vitiated and tired source. He does not perhaps believe in what he has made. Is that it? And yet he is tirelessly compelled to go on achieving these images, immediately to be discarded.

But when we consider one by one, and with a detailed scrutiny, the best types of work representing his various periods, we must admit that he had certain reason in abandoning them. However good a pastiche of El Greco may be, it is not worth prolonging indefinitely this exercise. The same applies to his Daumieresque period. Splendid paintings as the Miss Stein and Monsieur Sagot undoubtedly are, they are still pure Cézanne. And although many artists, among his dilettante admirers or his lesser brethren, would give their heads to produce such pure and almost first-hand Cézannes, once you *can* do this as easily as Picasso, it can hardly seem worth while to continue to do it. Very likely, at the present moment, his Ingres or David paintings will induce the same sensations of boredom in him (I can imagine David inducing very dismal feeling in an interpreter), and have a similar fate. All that remains to be considered are the less easily deciphered works of his more abstract periods. I think his effort of initiation and obstinacy in this brand of work showed a different temper to the other set of things that we have been considering. But they, again, are open to question. They reduce themselves to three principal phases. The first, or Cubist, phase, really a dogmatic and savage development of Cézanne's idiosyncrasy (example: 'Dame jouant de la Mandoline') is in a way the most satisfactory. But I am not convinced that Cézanne gains anything by what is a very interesting interpretation of his vision. But on the other hand, the Lady with the Mandolin appears to me as interesting as a typical Cézanne portrait, and it is a powerful and inventive variation on Cézanne. About the next step – fourth dimensional preoccupations and the new syntheses added to the earlier ones ('Dame assise') and the first Braque-like contrivances – you wonder if they are not more important as experiments, and important because of their daring and new nature, than as final works. But the whole character of these things: the noble structure and ascetic quality, the feeling that he must have had, and that he imparted to them, that he was doing something at last worth while, and in fitting relation to his superb painter's gift – this makes them a more serious contribution to painting than anything else done by him. All the admiration you feel for the really great artist in Picasso finds its most substantial footing in the extraordinary series of works beginning with the paintings of the time of the Miss Stein portrait, and finishing somewhere in the beginning of his Braque period.

It has been a critical, and, in intention, destructive analysis.

Men Without Art
1934

Anticipating the theme of the final chapters of Blasting and Bombardiering, *and building up a great body of supporting evidence,* Men Without Art *is Lewis's first major work of literary criticism. It needs to be read in conjunction with* The Writer and the Absolute (1952), *a work equal in power and fortunately still in print. Some of the chapters appeared originally in periodicals. The reader will speedily discover for himself that these essays have not merely worn well but need to be taken out for an airing. For the issues are still very much alive. Meanwhile, the apotheosis of Hemingway and Faulkner may not have proved Lewis wrong; they may prove him to have detected the consequences of a particular trend of taste. Alone among the essays, that on Eliot might have given its author second thoughts: for of all the writers here treated, Eliot remained a consistent upholder of the values Lewis most honoured. There are likewise those who would reject a definition of satire so wide as to identify it with art itself; but Lewis was preoccupied with 'the ethical and political status of these performances', and he was viewing this status in the light of a particular philosophical outlook on human nature. 'It is with man and not with manners that what we have agreed to describe as "satire" is called upon to deal.' He differed from some critics in making this outlook plain instead of concealing it beneath the pose of being analytical – as if analysis were capable of pursuit in an intellectual void.*

The following extracts consist of the Introduction, Chapter II of

Part II, and Chapter VI of Part II. These samples are taken with a view to stressing the general themes of the anthology as well as to preserving continuity of exposition. The choice imposed dilemmas: there was so much worthy of retention. The final extract, shorn of a long quotation, has lost none of its topicality. It is to be hoped that the reader will seek out the volume and make deeper acquaintance with one who dissociated himself 'from all mass-organization, whether aristocratic or demotic'. The book ends with the famous 'taxi-cab-driver test', in which the juxtaposition of two passages of fiction throws light on 'the evil plight of letters'.

INTRODUCTION

In this book I have, not for the first time, proceeded from the particular to the general – from the concrete to the abstract – from the personal to the theoretic. The former is so much more popular than the latter. Better, I thought, to put on what is most popular first. So I have taken the relatively engaging personalities of Messrs Hemingway and Faulkner and used them as an advance-illustration, as it were, of what I have to say. Having given the reader a good run with the popular novelists, I pass, still on the personal plane, into a somewhat chillier field – that of Mr T. S. Eliot – as literary critic, not as poet. Still, that is a figure which has come to be very well known and greatly discussed, greatly influential among the very young. After I have finished with him, and his friend Mr I. A. Richards, I pass over into somewhat less comfortable regions; but still Mrs Virginia Woolf is there to provide a little firm foothold in mere personality for those who prefer persons to ideas. But in fact, beyond a clearly defined, and quickly overtaken limit, you must be prepared to work a little bit, to look an abstract idea in the face and mildly cudgel your brains, if you are going to understand much about books and other products of the artistic intelligence. By this means, at all events, namely that of progressing by easy stages from the particular to the general, it has been my object to lead on the general reader – the 'plain reader' perhaps is better – to an understanding of the absolute necessity of looking behind the work of art for something which is not evident to the casual eye, and which yet has to be dragged out into the light if we are to understand what any work of art is *about*. For that it is *about* something is an axiom for me, and *art-for-art's-sake* I do not even trouble to confute.

'But what is art about anyway?' – Plain Reader asks perhaps, on his mettle at once: 'Except the orderly registration of pleasure? I like (Plain Reader goes on) a nice Medici Society Hobbema on my wall – it gives me a peaceful feeling: or a sporting print of a hunting scene – it makes me think of the good old days, like singing "Old John Peel with his coat so gay – Who lived at Troutbeck once on a day". Then a novel, that is *art*, I suppose. I like a nice novel – I am a youngish Plain Man and I don't mind a spot of love, but I prefer *mystery*: give me a good gory murder all the time! When I was up at Oxford I belonged to the Crime Club – I couldn't get on very well with Mrs Woolf. For me a novel is just a good yarn, or a bad one, about love, crime, romance, adventure: it takes one out of oneself; the author, presumably, is mainly occupied with the problem of taking us out of ourselves – he's a sort of illusionist – making us live for a few hours a more exciting life than our own. When he has satisfactorily achieved that, and paid into his bank the cheque he gets for doing it, his function is at an end as far as I am concerned.'

If you are not so Plain a Reader as all that I apologize for this 'Rugger Blue' interlude (upon the model of Mr I. A. Richards' class of sawneys): but it is just as well to be prepared for the worst!

The above is, however, a true account of ninety-nine novels out of a hundred, which are written, of course, especially for Rugger Blues, Cabinet Ministers, Sporting Girls, and the widows of colonial officials. One novelist in a hundred jacks up his ramshackle, mercenary piece of sensational entertainment on to a more complicated plane. Mrs Woolf has done that, for instance – a little meretriciously; and, in fact, adapted Joyce and Proust and other such things for the salon. But still Mrs Woolf is far too 'highbrow' for the Rugger Blue, and is regarded by Sir Austen Chamberlain probably as a broth of a girl, and right over his head, God bless her! As it is with the novel, so it is with the poem, the picture, the play, the film-play, statue or musical composition. All forms of art of a permanent order are intended not only to please and to excite, believe me, Plain Reader, if you are still there, but to call into play the entire human capacity – for sensation, reflection, imagination, and will. We judge a work of art, ultimately, with reference to its capacity to effect this total mobilization of our faculties. The novel is no exception to this rule. So undoubtedly a work of art, in the full-blooded intellectual sense, is no joke at all, but, from the 'low-brow' standpoint, a rather grim affair; and this in spite of the fact that *Gulliver's Travels* has been a great success as a nursery story-book, because of all the gwate big men and the tiny little chappies!

Implicit in the serious work of art will be found politics, theology, philosophy – in brief, all the great intellectual departments of the human consciousness; even the Plain Reader is aware of that in theory. But what is not so clear to very many people is that the most harmless piece of literary entertainment – the common crime story for instance, or the schoolboy epic of the young of the English proletariat centred around the portly figure of Bunter, 'the owl of the Remove' (see *Magnet Library*, weekly 2d. of all newsagents), is at all events politically and morally influential. How often has it not been pointed out that it is useless to talk of *No more war*, of World Disarmament – while millions of children are being fed with a war-like ideology – the Church Brigade, for instance, and the literature provided for the Church Brigade, in which violence and cruelty play such an important part? And the influence upon the mind of the whole nation, adult and juvenile, of the Hollywood film-factory is terrific: for 'shaping lives' it is obviously an engine comparable to the Society of Jesus. Why people find this and analogous facts so difficult to understand astonishes me. Yet a whole barbarous system of conduct, and judgements to match, is *implied* in every flick of the kinetic novelettes.

But I have not written this particular book in order to demonstrate these important truths. The principles of intellectual *detection* – the injunction to look *behind* everything, however trivial, in the art-field, as a matter of routine, and challenge all 'face values' – merely have to be restated every time, for the benefit of the inattentive, and the chronically 'comfortable' – the inveterately 'cosy'. My present essay is not even for the 'Plain Reader' so much as for the 'Plain Writer'; and not *too* 'plain', even at that, I may as well add. But I will explain, as briefly as possible.

This book has, in fact, been written, to put it shortly, to defend Satire. But to 'Satire' I have given a meaning so wide as to confound it with 'Art'. So this book may be said to be nothing short of a defence of art – as art is understood in the most 'highbrow' quarters today. (How I have been able to identify 'Satire' and 'Art' I argue in Part II.) That there is some occasion to defend art, at the moment at which I write, is pretty generally conceded. Indeed a society of *Men Without Art* is not a mere dream of the future, but a matter of practical politics — many politicians and theologians envisage such a possibility with the most unruffled calm, if not with relish.

For all practical purposes, then, we may describe this book as a defence of contemporary art, most of which art is unquestionably satiric, or comic. And it is a defence against every sort of antagonist, from that deep-dyed Moralist, the public of Anglo-Saxony, down to that nationalist nuisance, which would confine art to some territorial or racial tradition; from the Marxist who would harness art to politics, up to the mystical dogmatism which would harness it to the vapours of the spirit-world.

'But what the devil is art?' somebody may call out again, 'that it should be so elaborately defended as all that? Is it a Church; is it a schism; have we the makings of a political party in the studies and studios?' But that I have not set out to define in these pages. What can be with safety affirmed, however, and at that it can be left, is that if I have here put up a defence of art, it is not for its *beaux yeux*! Anything but that — heaven defend us from the *beaux yeux* of the *beaux arts*! Art is not here defended for its own sake: *art-for-art's-sake*, of Walter Pater, is nothing to do with art — it is a spectator's doctrine, not an artist's: it teaches how to enjoy, not how to perform. I am a performer. It is as a performer that I shall speak.

As a performer, that is to say as an artist, Professor Walter Raleigh (I must quote from a newspaper article) has written about William Blake — 'His work is one prolonged vindication of the cause of all the artists in the world.' That was because Blake was himself a performer; for it was a fine exhibition of *esprit de corps*, as well as of self-help: and he felt that this 'vindication' was imposed on him, and I have no doubt that it was. How much more is not that the case today?

Many books are written concerning the tricks of the performer's trade. Those are useful books (especially for performers): but here is one of a somewhat different type, and perhaps of more interest to the lay reader. It is not a book about the craft of writing or of painting, except incidentally. It is about the ethical or political status of these performances. It is as though an illusionist came forward and engaged us in argument as to his right to make men vanish, to cause rabbits to issue from their breast-pockets, to read their thoughts, and the sound reasons that he had for plunging swords into baskets, and bringing them forth dripping with innocent blood.

Here you have a notorious satirist explaining to you how it comes about that he may with impunity compose disobliging epics, or vignettes, including all and sundry – planting pastiche noses, doubling the dimensions of ears, compressing and elongating anatomies *ad lib* – to confine oneself to the corporeal. These pages will be eagerly read by all satirists – for though you would scarcely believe it, satirists suffer much as a class from an uneasy conscience – are always asking themselves 'how far they may go' – if they may dare say this, or would it not be too brutal to say that. But it should also be read with some attention by many of the satirized. And you do not have to be of much importance today to figure in a work of satire (see later chapter). And there are a vast number of people who come in contact with art and artists who would be glad for a few hints as to how to handle the latter, and how to deliver a *mauvais coup* to the former (for art is not really popular, that is to say, modern art). But in spite of this miscellaneous audience, it is mainly for the satirist, or more generally the artist (have you noticed how today they are one – and can you wonder at it, as one man to another?) that this treatise has been written. Last but not least, it is in the nature of an *Entlastungs offensive*, upon the *personal front*, as it might be called. For that highly ethical proverb, *God helps those who help themselves*, is more true of the satirist than of anybody. No one will exactly rush to the assistance of the satirist, when hard-pressed – he is a sort of Cain among craftsmen – so the satirist is compelled to move swiftly to his own.

But my opening part deals with the work of three people, two novelists and a critic. As artists, of course, all three are satirists. Mr Hemingway, in the rôle he has chosen for himself, is, as it were, a proletarian clown; he satirizes *himself* – but a self that is not his private self at all, but rather a sort of projection of the spirit of Miss Stein into the slow-moving and slow-thinking bulk of a simple-hearted labourer – say an American lumberjack. He is a pseudo-lumberjack, as it were (and so responds to the requirements of the *pseudo* principle of Eliot and Richards). – Mr Faulkner I call 'a satirist with a corn-cob'. He is a fierce moralist, who operates upon the satiric plane, armed with corn-cobs and such-like sardonic weapons of aggression, to insult the victims of his ethical rage.

Mr T. S. Eliot, as a poet, is no exception to the rule that all art is in fact satire today. Sweeney, the enigmatical Mrs Porter, Prufrock, Klipstein and Burbank, are authentic figures of Satire and nothing else. But as a critic he is a very different kettle of fish to what he is as poet. Where he comes in, making a valuable third in this trio of introductory studies, is that he supplies the theological factor lacking in the other two. He is preoccupied with problems of *belief*, as that applies to theologic, as well as to political and other forms, of belief. And as the moralist and the politician are the two chief enemies of the artist today, Mr Eliot's ethical, or rather non-ethical, standpoint, and the *pseudo* principle he has received from Mr I. A. Richards, provide suggestive devices for the better defence of the small garrison of satirist-artists, invested in their cubist citadel.

Although there is nothing written or painted today of any power which could not be brought under the head of *Satire* (if you allow a fairly wide interpretation to that term) yet I could not find a fictionist deliberately dealing in satire – either occasionally or all the time – of sufficient significance to use as one of my illustrations – except myself. Under these circumstances I have been compelled to refer to the work in satire of Mr Wyndham Lewis, 'Personal Appearance Artist' (Part II, Chapter II).

So the three chapters of which Part I is composed – consisting of the work of Hemingway, Faulkner and Eliot (critic) respectively – are intended to supply the sort of information that is required, by a hypothetic reader of this book, about two notable 'creative' writers and a celebrated literary critic. These chapters are intended to demonstrate upon the living model, selecting contemporary figures and so focussing the general argument upon the field of the day-to-day reading of the Plain Reader – *Class* A.I (or A.2) – for I am *fairly* democratic, and in any case eschew as far as possible all that is *too* hereditary-Grand-Duke. To demonstrate *the approach* indicated in such a programme as mine, by showing that programme in operation in three independent critical studies, has been my idea.

I felt that if I did not, somewhere in the course of this study, come down to brass tacks – turn my critical hand-torch upon the inside of a book or two – the reader might only half grasp what all the argument was about. For he might quite well have said to himself: 'Mr Lewis is very concerned with ethical and political pros and cons, and certainly all that *may* apply to some writers (deliberate tract writers like Mr Shaw) but how can it have any bearing upon such mere storytellers as the author of *Farewell to Arms* or *Sanctuary*?' That sort of misunderstanding, I think you will agree, I have cleared up at the start, in my Chapters I and II.

The third chapter of my first part, regarding the *pseudoist* enthusiasms of Mr Eliot, is arbitrarily associated with Chapters I and II. It is intended to supply you, again at the outset, with what appears to me the true view of Mr Eliot, the Anglo-Saxon (and Anglo-Catholic) representative of the continental *thomistic* literary criticism (this is a mouthful, but how else describe it?). The rôle of that type of criticism plays an important part in the argument of my book as a whole. And Mr Eliot himself, in a general way, stands as it were for the marriage of 'the dumb ox' and of Bloomsbury – the 'dumb ox', in this instance, being Aquinas. A strange wedding! – fraught with the oddest consequences both here and in Boston: but that is not the subject of this essay, except incidentally. And I hope it is unnecessary for me to say that I do *not* identify St Thomas Aquinas with the eminent poetic partner of Mr I. A. Richards? The idea is this: that, as we live in a sort of lunatic asylum – or a clinic for the variously 'complexed' – in which it would be quite hopeless to attempt to apply any rational principle in our vital dealings with this seething undergraduate and art-student mob who have become the only audience for the artist and their for the most part clownish masters, it is best to discover how we can use, to the advantage of such light as is vouchsafed us, even the darkest and most fantastic solemnities – even the most inconsequent of pseudo-systems – which, whatever they might be in other times and other places, are very concrete affairs in the world in which we find ourselves.

That all standards of taste and good sense have gone by the board and vanished completely from the popular plane, is generally accepted among us. What I expounded, upon those lines, by the method of verbatim quotation from book or newspaper, demonstrating the affiliation of the sublime and the ridiculous, in my paper *The Enemy*, and in my critical books, is now being expounded by a host of people, from Mr I. A. Richards (and his appendix the Leavises) down to every bottle-washer in Fleet Street. But it is always the *other fellow* – never Number One – who is bereft of criteria and standardless: though it is pretty clear that if things are in a bad way upon one plane of a finely homogeneous, very thoroughly *levelled*, civilization, they are liable to be in a bad way up in the 'highbrow' loft as well as down in the 'low-brow' basement. Is not, however, 'the present writer', as are all other writers, suspect? Certainly he is! Time alone can show which of us, of all these figures engaged in this pell-mell confusion, has preserved the largest store (and at the best it must be modest) of what is rational, and the least affected with rank bogusness.[1]

PART II

II. MR WYNDHAM LEWIS: 'PERSONAL-APPEARANCE' ARTIST

(*The theory of the External, the Classical, approach in Art*)

'Mr Wyndham Lewis could be described as a *personal-appearance* satirist.' Montague Slater, *The Daily Telegraph*.

Making our way back to that statement of Hazlitt's with which we began:[2] the great opportunity afforded by narrative-satire for a *visual* treatment is obvious. To let the reader 'into the minds of the characters', to 'see the play of their thoughts' – that is precisely the method least suited to satire. That it must deal with the *outside*, that is one of the capital advantages of this form of literary art – for those who like a resistant and finely-sculptured surface, or sheer words.

The literary art is not only on the whole less experimental than pictorial and plastic art, but it is also, in the nature of things, possessed of different canons – canons that are inherent both in the nature of the material, and in the fact that the literary art is far more directly involved in life than the pictorial or the plastic. I do not myself believe that anything in the literary field can be done

---

[1] Last paragraph omitted.
[2] 'Shakespeare's characters are men; Ben Jonson's are more like machines, governed by mere routine . . .' (*The English Comic Writers*: Lewis quotes the whole paragraph in the previous chapter.)

that will correspond with what has been called 'abstract design'. But still the art of letters *is* influenced, via life, by the movements in the sister field of painting, sculpture and architecture. So it is not at all beside the point to illustrate my arguments, upon this test of Hazlitt, from parallels in painting or sculpture.

'Shakespeare's characters are men: Ben Jonson's are more like machines,' Hazlitt exclaims. And I have replied – 'Of course they are! – in both cases that is just what they were intended to be.' But 'men' are undoubtedly, to a greater or less extent, machines. And there are those amongst us who are revolted by this reflection, and there are those who are not. Men are sometimes so palpably machines, their machination is so transparent, that they are *comic*, as we say. And all we mean by that is that our consciousness is pitched up to the very moderate altitude of relative independence at which we live – at which level we have the illusion of being autonomous and 'free'. But if one of us exposes too much his 'works', and we start seeing him as a *thing*, then – in subconsciously referring this back to ourselves – we are astonished and shocked, and we bark at him – we *laugh* – in order to relieve our emotion.

Freedom is certainly our human goal, in the sense that all effort is directed to that end: and it is a dictate of nature that we should laugh, and laugh loudly, at those who have fallen into slavery, and still more, those who batten on it. But the artistic sensibility, that is *another* 'provision of nature'. The artist steps outside this evolutionary upward march, and looking back into the evolutionary machine, he explores its pattern – or is supposed to – quite coldbloodedly.

Without pursuing that issue any further at the moment, let us merely consider how that affects these values of Hazlitt – which are, in brief, the *humanist* values – which are starkly opposed to all the plastic and pictorial values in the ascendant today – values which, incidentally, are in general mine.

If you have ever seen and can recall the sculpture of Auguste Rodin – those flowing, structureless, lissom, wave-lined pieces of commercial marble – you will then have the best possible illustration of the in-this-sense *humanist*, the naturalist technique. They are Bergson's *élan vital* translated into marble: the whole philosophy of the Flux is palpitating and streaming in those carefully selected and cleverly dreamified stone-photographs of naked nature.

Now where Hazlitt describes Shakespeare as *'letting us into the minds* of his characters', where we are able to observe 'the play of their thoughts', the humours flowing hither and thither – the Shakespearian creation bubbling and sparkling, and finding its way 'in all directions, like a natural spring', there he is placing before us a great artist of the naturalist, the *humanist* school: he is discovering the same manner of praising the art of Shakespeare that the contemporaries of Auguste Rodin found to exalt that much-overrated master of the Flux – who, it is as well to say, degraded the art of sculpture in stone to the level of confectionery in sugar or icing.

Over against this pretty picture of a happy, guileless, universe, set in the mellow naturalist setting of a not-too-formal park (which, it is implied by Hazlitt, is the bedrock truth about our human life, or 'that is all ye know and all ye need to know') is placed the satiric *machinery* of 'rare Ben Jonson' – *rare* perhaps because he conformed to the type of men-to-come, than to his somewhat happy-go-lucky humanist companions.

If you asked me what I suggest you should place over against the perverted cascades of sleek, white, machine-ground stone of the Bergsonian sculptor, well, there is a wide choice. Neither the Greeks, nor yet the Renaissance masters (except here and there) afford a quite effective contrast. The *naturalist* stream started flowing in Hellas, and it has gone on flowing in the centre of the European consciousness ever since. Only now, at last, has it begun to dry up. I should direct you to Egypt, to China or Japan, to select the monumental counterblast to this last vulgar decadence of the original Hellenic mistake. The Japanese Buddhist sculpture would be as good as any for your purpose – to confront with its opposite principle, 'The Kiss', say of Auguste Rodin – or any of the stream of vulgar ornaments that have gushed out for forty years in its wake, and which still infest the tables or mantelpieces of Kensington and Mayfair, and are to be encountered in great profusion in the shop windows of Bond Street.

At this point I believe I may legitimately make an observation, not without its bearing upon the present critical analysis. It is this: the majority of people who write books of 'criticism' do not write any other books – they prefer to criticize, not to produce: whereas with me you do not have to cudgel your brains as to *why* I should sit down and reduce to some order, in a statement that is a generalization from experience, my opinion of how books of a certain class should be written. I have an obvious interest in what I am writing about! And if you should wish to retaliate upon me, there are the targets standing ready. All you need is to be a practised shot! A 'deliberate theory of life, of nature, of the universe', I do not deny it, is to be found within the crypts and tissues of this criticism: and whether or not it be true that 'the philosopher must ever be, more or less, a partisan', I certainly – deliberately – am that.

This book has derived in the first instance from the notes written in defence of my satire, *The Apes of God*.[1] That book was a fiction-satire, as you may recall, of considerable proportions – a handsome target you will agree: and because of its satiric content it provoked, not an outburst of recrimination – nothing half so frank as that, but what was intended to be a pulverizing hush. The tables were turned upon these malcontents, however, and in the end the satirist had the best of it. If this had not been the history of these notes, and if a good many people did not associate them, as they must do, with the arguments for and against regarding this particular work, I should avoid direct reference to a book of mine. But as it is there is some reason for turning to it for a moment, and that I now will do.

In another book (not a novel, but criticism) the outlook, or the philosophy, from which it derived, was described by me as 'a philosophy of the EYE'. But in the case of *The Apes of God* it would be far easier to demonstrate (than in the more abstract region of philosophical criticism) how *the eye* has been the organ in the ascendant there. For *The Apes of God* it could, I think quite safely, be claimed that no book has ever been written that has paid more attention to the *outside* of people. In it their shells or pelts, or the language of their bodily movements, come first not last. And in the course of the controversy it provoked, I referred to a reader's report on a portion of this book, in which the gentleman in question described it as the work of a *visuel* (de Gourmont's expression). That definition I should certainly accept, as also where he wrote: 'everything is told from the outside. To this extent it is the opposite of, say, James, who sought to narrate from the *inside* the character's

---

[1] The reference is to the pamphlet *Satire and Fiction*, published in 1930 as 'Enemy Pamphlet No. 1'.

mind. James, in short, was a Bergsonian, where you are a Berkleyan!' – there too I am in agreement with this sympathetic publisher's reader.

There was a newspaper article which appeared some weeks after the publication of the *Apes*, which I also quoted at the time, and which, for the light it throws upon the matter in hand, can be used with advantage here – since for an understanding of the creative literature of today and of tomorrow it is very necessary, I believe, to grasp the principles involved in this question of *outside* and of *inside*.

Mr Montague Slater, in an article in *The Daily Telegraph* entitled 'Satire in the Novel', wrote as follows: 'Posted inside the head of a person . . . the novelist informs us of everything that is being enacted upon that inaccessible stage.' Thus posted *within*, the novelist lays bare, for the benefit of the reader, the 'stream of consciousness of the individual'. *The Apes of God* is cited, among others, as one belonging technically to that class of books which melts away the cases and envelopes of human beings, to deal wholly with their 'thought-streams', etc. But such a method, says Mr Slater, 'makes contemporary satiric novels inept'.

I may say at once that I quite agree with this reviewer that the *inside method* does tend to ineptitude, and that many books written during the last decade have been peculiarly inept for that reason. But the particular books he chose – the other two as much as *The Apes of God* – were not examples of that *inner* method at all, as it happened.

That the *inner method* should never be employed at all I should not be disposed to lay down. It has its uses. Nowhere is it indispensable, but can play its part, if it is decided to make use of it, as a sort of comic relief. – The first twenty pages of *The Apes of God*, for instance, is a slow-movement prelude: in the half-light of extreme decrepitude (employed as the illumination for those opening pages) the 'thought-stream' of one of the principal personages, Lady Fredigonde, is revealed to the reader, like the sluggish introspective waters of a Styx. It can scarcely be said that the *outside* of this personage is neglected: but, in her case, the *inside* is there too, that is all. Fredigonde has a special rôle allotted her, however: she appears before the formal raising of the curtain upon the Apes proper. She herself is the *prelude*.

But this aged personage is half out of life, half in. The *interior* method was chosen in that instance as being particularly appropriate. Incidentally, its use (for the purpose of projecting this brain-in-isolation, served only by the senses paralysed with age) is an exposure of the literary dogma of the 'internal monologue', regarded as a *universal* method. Where elsewhere in another satire (with 'Satters' in *Childermass*) I made use of it, I did so with that even more clearly in view.

So what I think can be laid down is this: In dealing with (1) the extremely aged; (2) young children; (3) half-wits; and (4) animals, the *internal* method can be extremely effective. In my opinion it should be entirely confined to those classes of characters. For certain comic purposes it likewise has its uses, especially when used in conjunction with a full-blooded Steinstutter – used, pianissimo, to such good effect, as I have shown, by Ernest Hemingway.

In my criticism of *Ulysses* I laid particular stress upon the limitations of the *internal* method. As developed in *Ulysses*, it robbed Mr Joyce's work as a whole of all linear properties whatever, considered as a plastic thing – of all contour and definition in fact. In contrast to the jelly-fish that floats in the centre of the subterranean stream of the 'dark' Unconscious, I much prefer, for my part, the shield of the tortoise, or the rigid stylistic articulations of the grasshopper.

This can be put in another way. The massive sculpture of the Pharaohs is preferable to the mist of the automatic or spirit picture. Then, the dreamy or disordered naturalism of so much European art is akin to the floating, ill-organized, vapours of the plastic of the spiritist. And just now I selected as an illustration the most anomalous of all these manifestations of extreme naturalism – the floating wave-lined images in stone of Auguste Rodin.

To put this matter in a nutshell, it is *the shell* of the animal that the plastically-minded artist will prefer. The ossature is my favourite part of a living animal organism, not its intestines. My objections to Mr D. H. Lawrence were chiefly concerned with that regrettable habit of his incessantly to refer to the intestinal billowing of 'dark' subterranean passion. In his devotion to that romantic abdominal *Within* he abandoned the sunlit pagan surface of the earth.

But to return again to Satire: Satire is *cold*, and that is good! It is easier to achieve those polished and resistant surfaces of a great *externalist* art in Satire. At least they are achieved more naturally than can be done beneath the troubled impulse of the lyrical afflatus. All the nineteenth-century poetry of France, for instance, from the *Fleurs du Mal* onwards, was stiffened with Satire, too. There is a stiffening of Satire in everything good, of 'the grotesque', which is the same thing – the non-human outlook must be there (beneath the fluff and pulp which is all that is seen by the majority) to correct our soft conceit. This cannot be gainsaid. Satire is *good*!

But so far in these pages we have been accepting the term Satire without stopping to define it. (To define it anew, of course; for the historic definition is far too narrow for what such a definition would have to include today.) Satire in reality often is nothing else but *the truth* – the truth, in fact, of Natural Science. That objective, non-emotional truth of the scientific intelligence sometimes takes on the exuberant sensuous quality of creative art: then it is very apt to be called 'Satire', for it has been bent not so much upon pleasing as upon being true.

No work of fiction, however, is likely to be only 'Satire', in the sense that a short epigrammatic piece, in rhyming couplets (an Epistle of Pope) would be. For again it is necessary to return to the fact that fiction-satire is narrative: a great part of it is apt to be of a most objective nature, cast in a mould very near to the everyday aspect of things. It will only appear 'grotesque', or 'distorted', of course, to those accustomed to regard the things of everyday, and everyday persons, through spectacles *couleur-de-rose*.

But there is the 'truth' of Satire and there is the 'truth' of Romance. – The term Satire suggests off-hand some resolve on the part of the 'satirist' to pick out disobligingly all that is objectionable and ill-favoured in a given system of persons and things, and to make of that a work of art. Certainly such a 'satire' as *The Apes of God* is not that. Indeed often it is nothing but people's vanity that causes them to use that term at all: often they are, in what they call 'satire', confronted with a description of their everyday life as close to the truth as that found in any other artistic formula. It is merely a formula based rather upon the 'truth' of the intellect than upon the 'truth' of the average romantic sensualism.

Must we say, then, that 'Satire' is merely a representation, containing (irrespective of what else may be included in it) many of those truths that people do not care to hear?

What is the 'truth' regarding any person? What is the objective truth about him? – a public and not a private truth? What is that in a person, or in a thing, that is not 'satire', upon the one hand, or 'romance', upon the other? Is there such a purely non-satiric, non-romantic truth, at all? Such questions may at all times with advantage be asked; but the very core of the satiric impulse is of course involved in them.

All men are *some* sort of hero to themselves: equally there is no man who is not, to *somebody or other*, a disagreeable person, as unsightly as a toad, or else a first-class figure of fun. How are we to reconcile these opposites – the seeing-of-ourselves-as-others-see-us, and the self-picture? It is difficult to see how the objective truth of much that is called 'Satire' can be less true than the truth of lyrical declamation, in praise, for instance, of a lovely mistress. There is, in both cases, *another* truth, that is all. But both are upon an equal intellectual footing, I think – only the humanly 'agreeable' is more often false than the humanly 'disagreeable'. That is unavoidable, seeing what we are.

Natural science is a disagreeable study in its way (this was acutely recognized by Leonardo da Vinci, himself a man of science, as well as, in his rôle of plastic artist, a master of vitalist illusion). What interests and delights *the individual*, again, is, *sub specie aeternitatis* far less interesting, much less delightful. The values proper to the specific organism have to be accounted for, that we all know. So, to conclude, do not let us arbitrarily describe as 'Satire' all that is disagreeable to ourselves. That would be a misnomer. For it may not be *satire* at all!

As well as being a satire, *The Apes of God* is a book made of the outside of things. And it is also a book of *action*. By certain critics it was described, even, as an orgy of *the externals* of this life of ours (cf. 'Mr Lewis could be described as a *personal-appearance* satirist', etc.). But that is a compliment. Its author lays great store by that *externality*, in a world that is literally inundated with sexual viscera and the 'dark' gushings of the tides of *The Great Within*. Call him a 'personal-appearance writer' and he is far from being displeased! You please *him* by that, even if *he* displeases so many people (it would appear) by treating of their externals in the way that he does – just by being so *personal-appearance*!

Hazlitt, to return to him again for a moment, must be credited with seeing that 'the fault . . . of Shakespeare's comic muse is . . . that it is too good-natured and magnanimous'. That is the fault also, no doubt, of Hazlitt's *criticism*. And there were, and have been since, many satirists far more apt to bring out this fault in Hazlitt than was 'rare Ben Jonson'. – Shakespeare's comic muse 'does not take the highest pleasure in making human nature look as mean, as ridiculous and contemptible as possible', writes Hazlitt. 'It is in this respect, chiefly, that it differs from the comedy of a later, and (what is called) a more refined, period . . . vanity and affectation, in their most exorbitant and studied excesses, are the ruling principles of society, only in a highly advanced state of civilization and manners. Man can hardly be said to be a truly contemptible animal, till, from the facilities of general intercourse . . . he becomes the ape of the extravagances of other men.'

There must, however, even according to this account, be some first exemplar – some *original* ape! This Rousseauesque picture of man's original perfection does, even in the statement, halt, and seems to point, in spite of itself, to the conclusion that in some form or other that original 'ape' was man!

Again, if you insist, as does Hazlitt, that it is 'when folly is epidemic, and vice worn as a mask of distinction, that all the malice of wit and humour is called out, and justified, to detect the imposture, and prevent the contagion from spreading', the answer you must expect is as follows: At what period of history has folly *not* been epidemic (allowing for ups and downs and for more and less): when has 'vice' not been an advertisement, and virtue a handicap? Certainly Hazlitt's attitude to 'man' is sentimental. The Tudor dramatists were as much surrounded by epidemics of folly as were the later Stuart writers. There was here a seesaw of opinions and of tastes – neither age was quite civilized enough.

But (in conclusion) the justification of 'all the malice of wit' must be more securely grounded than this theory of human corruption succeeding upon a state of original blessedness would allow, so simply stated as that.

It is with man, and not with manners, that what we have agreed to describe as 'satire' is called upon to deal. It is a *chronic* ailment (manifesting itself, it is true, in a variety of ways) not an *epidemic* state, depending upon 'period', or upon the wicked ways of the particular smart-set of the time.

'Period' will not be entirely ruled out, doubtless: only in future it will be *world-period*. The habit of thought of this nation or of that, at a given moment of its discrete history, will sink into the insignificance it deserves. The new world order will possess within it 'periods', but itself will not be a 'period'. Since there is no 'present' properly speaking just now, more than ever the majority of people live in the past. It is impossible in consequence to make them understand the changes that are being effected even inside themselves. Even the chronic *period-tasting* of this time serves to screen and hide away the reality.

Immense and critical revaluations are taking place – an *Umwertung aller Werte*. It is the passing of a world, as it were, not of an empire or of single nations. This will only be manifest to Mr Everyman in the sudden light of cataclysms, exploding in the midst of his comfortable fog. The war was such a cataclysm – but Everyman has already forgotten it!

The present revaluations (operating in every corner of the earth) are of a very different order, both in scale and in kind, to those which changed the 'period' of Elizabeth into the 'period' of Charles II. Those were intrinsically no more important than the mutations of taste within a small German duchy. These facts are of capital importance for literature, of course: but it is quite out of the question to bring many people to an understanding of them. This does not matter: but it makes it difficult to discuss anything of first-rate importance, in literature as much as in politics, with that blind spot always there.

A serious work of art today has a much vaster stage at its disposal, and one far more weighted with fatality, than that possessed by the Elizabethan drama, with its Renaissance motives – upon which, I daresay, it was more easy to be 'good-natured', to be 'magnanimous' and kind. For my part, I am called a rebel, I am called a reactionary, according to which boss at the moment I am facing, or whose dogs are barking at my heels. However that may be, the 'revaluations' I refer to appear to me *good*. But that our drama need be a 'catastrophic' *tragedy of blood* is not true. That is *not* good. To degrade it into something savage and provincial, that cannot be good. The people who are eager to do that – to *sadify* and to ensanguine the noblest of our plots – are the same order of savages who impose those stupid conventions of 'blood' upon the great Tudor dramatists. Like their Elizabethan forerunners, on all hands artists are mixing blood and bombast, more and more, into their inventions, to satisfy this roaring Pit.

Simply in terms of quantity, however, how much more sinister are the reverberations of their thunder! How much more powerful and absolute are the forces involved! What can the artist at present hope for? Only that the gladiatorial phase will pass, and that all the novel perspectives of this universal stage at length may be utilized. An old-fangled Tragedy of Blood could be put on for children on Sundays – as it were a Red Matinée! – as a concession to those ferocious Peter Pans who could not grow up. A few could go up on the stage even and be slaughtered in the Roman fashion, for the delectation of the rest. That would be *good*. What has been called by Mr Roy Campbell the 'Bloomsbury game of ping-pong' will go on to the bitter end, of course: and on the other hand, best-selling writings and paintings will never cease to be poured forth, so long as the present huge democratic societies of the West are organized by astute middlemen into *Book of the Month Clubs*, or into *Royal Academies*. But there is no being 'Elizabethan' or being 'Georgian', any more for the man who is in fact an artist. All *that* is over except for a pretty period-game. An artist who is not a mere entertainer and money-maker, or self-advertising gossip-star, must today be penetrated by a sense of the great discontinuity of our destiny. At every moment he is compelled to be aware of that different scene, coming up as if by magic, behind all that has been familiar for so long to all the nations of the Aryan World. Nothing but a sort of façade is left standing, that is the fact: before which fustian property (labelled *The Past*, a cheap parody of *Ancien Régime*, with feudal keeps in the middle-distance), the Gossip-column Class bask in enormous splashy spot-lights of publicity. It is what is behind the Façade that alone can be of any interest in such a pantomime.

For an understanding of the literature of today and of tomorrow it is very necessary, I believe, to grasp the principles involved in this question; namely, that of the respective merits of the method of *internal* and *external* approach – that statement of mine, made just now, I will return to before concluding the present chapter.

My reasons for believing that the method of *external* approach is the method which, more and more, will be adopted in the art of writing are as follows:

(1) The *external* approach to things belongs to the 'classical'

manner of apprehending: whereas the romantic outlook (though it may serve the turn of the 'transitionists') will not, I believe, attract the best intelligences in the coming years, and will not survive the period of 'transition'.

(2) The *external* approach to things (relying upon evidence of the *eye* rather than of the more emotional organs of sense) can make of 'the grotesque' a healthy and attractive companion. Other approaches cannot do this. The scarab can be accommodated – even a crocodile's tears can be relieved of some of their repulsiveness. For the requirements of the new world-order this is essential. And as for pure satire – there the eye is supreme.

(3) All our instinctive aesthetic reactions are, in the west of Europe, based upon Greek naturalist canons. Of the *internal* method of approach in literature, Joyce or James are highly representative. Their art (consisting in 'telling from the inside', as it is described) has for its backgrounds the naturalism (the flowing lines, the absence of linear organization, and also the inveterate humanism) of the Hellenic pictorial culture. Stein is Teutonic music, *jazzed* – Stein is just the German musical soul leering at itself in a mirror, and sticking out at itself a stuttering welt of swollen tongue, although perhaps, as she is not a pure Teuton, this is not quite fair to the Teuton either – it is the mirror that is at fault.

(4) If you consider the naturalism of the Greek plastic as a phenomenon of decadence (contrasted with the masculine formalism of the Egyptian or the Chinese) then you will regard likewise the method of the 'internal monologue' (or the romantic snapshotting of the wandering stream of the Unconscious) as a phenomenon of decadence.

(5) A tumultuous stream of evocative, spell-bearing, vocables, launched at your head – or poured into your Unconscious – is, finally, a dope only. It may be an auriferous mud, but it must remain mud – not a clear but a murky picture. As a literary medium it is barbaric.

(6) If Henry James or if James Joyce were to paint pictures, it would be, you feel, a very *literary* sort of picture that would result. But also, in their *details*, these pictures would be lineal descendants of the Hellenic naturalism. Only, such details, all jumbled up and piled one against the other, would appear, at first sight, different, and, for the Western Hellenic culture, exotic. Nevertheless, as in

the pictures of most Germans, all the plastic units would be suffused with a romantic coloration. They would be overcharged with a literary symbolism; their psyche would have got the better of their Gestalt – the result a sentiment, rather than an expressive form.

(7) We know what sort of picture D. H. Lawrence would paint if he took to the brush instead of the pen. For he did so, luckily, and even held exhibitions. As one might have expected, it turned out to be incompetent Gauguin! A bit more practice, and Lawrence would have been indistinguishable from that Pacific-Parisian Pierre Loti of Paint.

(8) To turn once more to the renowned critic with whom we started, Hazlitt. In reading Shakespeare, he said, 'we are let into the minds of his characters, we see the play of their thoughts. . . . His humour (so to speak) bubbles, sparkles, and finds its way in all directions, like a natural spring.' And that natural-spring-effect is the Greek *naturalism*, of course, as I have already indicated. That naturalism (whatever else may or may not happen) is bound to be superseded by something more akin to the classic of, say, the Chinese.

Shakespeare is the summit of the romantic, naturalist, European tradition. And there is a great deal more of that Rousseauish, *natural-springishness*, in much recent work in literature than is generally recognized. But especially, in the nature of things, is this the case with the *tellers-from-the-inside* – with the masters of the 'interior-monologue', with those Columbuses who have set sail towards the El Dorados of the Unconscious, or of the Great Within.

(9) Dogmatically, then, I am for the Great Without, for the method of *external* approach – for the wisdom of the eye, rather than that of the ear.

PART II

VI. THE BAD-LANDS[1]

What, then, is this waterlogged stretch of territory, which it is necessary to negotiate, but which has proved a profitable trap to so

[1] The first and last paragraphs are omitted.

many tragical stick-in-the-muds – whose portentous torsos remain, in a distracted immobility, upon all hands, as dark warnings to all and sundry not to engage in this peculiar Slough of Despond? – at once warnings and sly invitations? And what manner of persons are they who compose this gallery of scare-crows, waving (at rare intervals) inarticulately a drooping-arm, as a signal of distress, and emitting unintelligible incantations?

Well, the waterlogged stretch is simply the post-war decade-and-a-half, or rather that period as it is represented in the field of art and letters. And the derelicts that spot it like the legless statues scattered over the landscape of Rapa Nui, are the ladies and gentlemen who have been and are luminaries of Anglo-Saxon art and letters.

But this waterlogged stretch is coeval with the uninterrupted chain of 'crises' which started as soon as the obscene saturnalia of the war came to a close. It is a purely mental bog – at least in so far as the Want-in-the-midst-of-Plenty is artificial, this 'wasteland' is artificial. It is a deliberate inundation, that has become chronic. And, just as in the other case, upon the popular and political plane, a man-made famine is accepted as a visitation of the inscrutable powers of nature – there is no orthodox economist who does not set out from that premise – so in this other field of intellectual endeavour (or its opposite) the same sort of assumption is the order of the day, with only this difference, that occasionally, instead of a terrible natural visitation, it is regarded as a god-sent punishment for mortal wickedness.

Most of the protests, which, from time to time, have broken forth against this policy of despair and of do-nothing, have come from the most compromising quarter possible: some indignant 'hearty' has suddenly 'gone off the deep end' about all this 'spinelessness' – very erect (the *spine* very much in evidence) very red in the face (from a rush of *red-blood* to the head) – very much puffing and snorting with the he-mannish instinct to castigate all these 'slackers' and 'cissies'! That of course has only caused the martyrs-of-the-marsh, as they might be called, entrenched in their inaccessible bog, to titter in their sleeves. That was all excellent advertisement for them – so what we want, in order to shift them, and in order to discredit the bog, is a different approach from that. If you are to discourage these depressing exhibitionists and solemn buffoons of the bad-lands, you must think of something better to do than to puff out your masculine plastron and admonish them to 'be men' or anything idiotic of that sort – or to be womanly-women or mothers of men. You must go about it rather more scientifically than that. You must, in short, analyse *the bog*, the local conditions that promote its continuance. And then, as to the *genii loci* of the bad-lands, or waste-lands, in question, you must psycho-analyse them at once and shoo them out of their pits with unpleasant laughter, rather than with respectful and hortatory wrath. For they are not by any means harmless – men are imitative and they attract a crowd of followers: on the other hand they are not to be taken as anything more serious than as jokes of the Zeitgeist.

A book has been published recently,[1] entitled *The Romantic Agony*, by Prof. Mario Praz. Confronted with this immense mass of intelligent erudition – the harvest of a really first-rate piece of highly selective field-work – there is no one, I believe, who would remain unconvinced, of how, *at every pore*, the post-war period has sucked in the stale and sickly airs which have been hanging over Europe for a century (the putrefaction of the *ancien régime*, guillotined but imperfectly interred) and has fed itself on the same poisons for choice, as those employed for purposes of mental stimulation by the distinguished diabolists – Lord Byron, Huysmans, Baudelaire, Wilde, De Lautréamont, and the rest of them. It is a history of a century of diabolics – of *Fleurs du Mal*, of the *homme fatal* as dramatized by Byron – in his pageant of a (satanic) heart – of *Pen, Pencil and Poison* (the exaltation of the murderer, preceded by de Quincey's), of *Dorian Gray* and the exaltation of the pederast – but the list, both of names and attributes, is endless. It is the carefully-documented historical counterpart of *The Diabolical Principle*, and the sequel to the Machiavelli chapters of *The Lion and the Fox*.

If there is one thing which stands out more clearly than another from this gigantic pile of satanic bric-à-brac, so industriously assembled, under my directions (cf. *The Diabolical Principle*, etc.), by Prof. Praz, it is the astonishing rôle which is played by *morals* – specifically, of course, the Christian, or Judaic, ethic – in all this

[1] (1933).

spectacle of calculated perversity. It is in fact the disintegration of Christendom that we are witnessing in all these outbursts, and the hysteria of Swinburne as much as the hysteria of Huysmans, in their monotonous insistence upon what is 'evil', is patently a consequence of the fact that they are *good* boys gone wrong. They are haunted and terrified by the minatory injunctions of the Mosaic Law. It is the release from two thousand years of suppression and from the reign of an ascetic principle of life. Byron, Wilde, Huysmans (that is to say – incest, pederasty, and homicide) – what is that, at bottom, but the good old melodrama of *The Girl Who Took the Wrong Turning*? And, indeed, how *girlish* are all these intellectual leaders – from the vulgar showing-off propensities of the social pet, the *Childe Harold*, the *Don Juan*, to the same propensities in the yet more feminine figure, Oscar Wilde, with whom the healing gush of tears was never far away and whose strangely disgusting spasms of religiosity matched his bravado as an 'evil-doer'. What would a Greek (brought up in the recognition as 'natural' of what Oscar Wilde regarded as deliciously 'unnatural') what would Alcibiades, as an eminent example, have made of this fat Dublin buffoon, horrifying the mob, and himself into the bargain, by his 'wickedness'! He could have been little else but an object of astonished derision. And yet his silly old 'vice', and the startling advertisement-value attached to it, has upset our society for three decades!

Here surely is an object lesson, if one were needed, in the disadvantages of an excessive development of the ethical will: for by the simple expedient of reversing it, it can be converted into a first-class instrument of farcical self-display, with all the army of false values that marches upon the heels of such an operation.

The enormous part, however, aside from such glaring examples as the author of *De Profundis*, that the moralist-mind played in this century of diabolics can be demonstrated by a brief interrogation, from this point of view, of one or two of the conspicuous participants in the saturnalia in question. Walter Pater, 'the forerunner of the Decadent Movement in England', as Prof. Mario Praz calls him, will serve our turn very well.

We must not, Mr T. S. Eliot warns us,[1] regard Walter Pater as essentially the 'aesthete': for

[1] *Collected Essays*, p. 386.

Pater was ... a moralist ... Even in that part of his work which can only be called literary criticism, Pater is always primarily the moralist. In his essay on Wordsworth he says: 'To treat life in the spirit of art, is to make life a thing in which means and ends are identified: to encourage such treatment, the true moral significance of art and poetry.'

That was his notion: to find the 'true moral significance of art and poetry.'

Or again: 'When we read him on Leonardo or Giorgione, we feel that there is the same preoccupation, coming between him and the object as it really is. He is, in his own fashion, moralizing upon Leonardo or Giorgione, on Greek art or on modern poetry. His famous dictum: "Of this wisdom, the poetic passion, the desire of beauty, the love of art for art's sake has most: for art comes to you professing frankly to give nothing but the highest quality to your moments as they pass, and simply for those moments' sake", is itself a theory of ethics; it is concerned not with art but with life. The second half of the sentence ... is a serious statement of morals.'

And these statements of Mr Eliot's I am sure should satisfy us as to the bona fides of Walter Pater as a moralist. Actually it was this exaggerated development of his ethical will that provided the impulse for his particular contribution to the diabolics of his time. 'Pater had from childhood a religious bent,' Mr Eliot tells us: 'he was "naturally Christian" ': but these happy dispositions, owing to some flaw in the theologic workmanship, cause him to be responsible for what is popularly regarded as the most 'immoral' outburst of any yet in modern England – the 'Naughty Nineties'.

His innovations in the anti-moral line are described as follows by Prof. Mario Praz:

> Walter Pater, the forerunner of the Decadent Movement in England (particularly in his conclusion to *Studies in the Renaissance*, [1873]), the book from which we have quoted the famous passage where the 'Medusan' type of beauty is found incarnate in La Gioconda) shows himself as being 'ready to indulge in the luxury of decay, and to amuse himself with fancies of the tomb' – to use a phrase from *Duke Carl of Rosenmold* – in his tales of the muffled lives of exquisitely meditative youths (see *A Child in the House*, and the characteristic fate of all these youths, Marius the Epicurean, Flavian, Watteau, Duke Carl of Rosenmold), and of beauty devastated by cruelty (Denys l'Auxerrois).
>
> The feminine souls of Pater's 'frail androgynous beings' are already open to all the influences of the Decadence: Duke Carl of Rosenmold is a sensual dilettante in the manner of Ludwig II of Bavaria or of des Esseintes. It is not therefore astonishing that Pater should have

crowned with his approval the *Confessions of a Young Man* (1888) in which George Moore finally succeeded, after various unsuccessful attempts (a few early lines imitated from Baudelaire, *Flowers of Passion*, 1878, *Pagan Poems*, 1881, the novels *A Mere Accident*, 1887 and *Mike Fletcher*, 1889) in presenting to the younger generation in England, already saturated with Pater's aestheticism, a version – which was somewhat superficial, it is true – of the gospel of Mademoiselle de Maupin and *A Rebours*.*

It is perhaps unnecessary to point out how tales of 'the feminine souls', of 'the muffled lives of exquisitely meditative youths', belong to that dim world of the essentially feminine sensibility, with which we have been so closely concerned in the foregoing chapters. The exquisite palsies or languors of decay are – at full strength, if one may so paradoxically express oneself – present in this mid-Victorian moralist aesthete. The fisticuffs of Lord Queensberry are already mobilized in the wings: and to come down to the present time, the droopings and wiltings of Mr Prufrock or, better, the androgynous permutations of *Orlando*, might already have been foreseen.

Next, as a mate for Pater, we can take André Gide – for as Pater stands to Oscar Wilde, so Wilde stands to Gide. So we shall have three consecutive generations of moralists – of moralists-gone-wrong. And let me go to Mr Eliot the critic for help, for a moment too, in the matter of Gide. Yes, Gide is a true moralist, we find, sure enough! 'Certainly, a writer may be none the less classified as a moralist', Mr Eliot lays it down, 'if his moralizing is suspect or perverse. We have today a witness in the person of M. André Gide.' (No wonder Mr Eliot desires to see 'Morals put in their proper place' somewhat!)[1]

. . . People who were not born when André Gide was gathering experiences crystallized in *Si le grain ne meurt*, are today, in their own moralist fashion, producing work, not certainly as important, but at least equally 'romantic', in the sense understood by Mario Praz. It was for instance remarked at the time with considerable astonishment that *Point Counter Point* bore a strange resemblance to Mr Gide's book, which had preceded it by a few years, I think I am right in saying. But it is even unnecessary to be very specific.

* *The Romantic Agony*.
[1] A long quotation from Mario Praz's *Romantic Agony* analysing Gide's diabolism, together with ten lines of commentary by Lewis, are omitted.

When the literary historian of the future comes to cast his eye over our little post-war age, he will not have to go very much to the heart of the matter to detect that he is in the presence of an ethos bearing a very close resemblance to that of the Naughty Nineties: he will see the trial of Wilde as the grand finale of the 'naughty' decade – then fourteen humdrum years of Socialist tract-writing – then the war – and then *more* 'naughtiness'. He will perhaps meditate – 'Here was a people moralist to the core, who only possessed two modes of expression, one childishly rebellious, the other dully dutiful!'

That our bad-lands have been a different sort of bad-lands to that of the scene surveyed by Whistler and by Wilde is evident enough: our bad has not been quite their *bad* – it has been indelibly tinged with what I have called *badtimism* among other things: it has possessed none of the friskiness, the air of irresponsible leisure, nor for that matter the extremism. But such an event as the War, 1914–18, does knock the stuffing out of a people, and already in 1920 the shadows of proletarianization were gathering fast. But all the same, in its dull way, the last decade and a half, our *Only Yesterday*, has kept the Jolly Roger of 'Romance' flying as best it could.

Neither de Quincey nor Wilde could have given us points in veneration for the violent: the headmaster of Eton (Dr Allington) has run a 'Crime Club': the murder-game has been a typical highbrow amusement like the Victorian *charade*: and an immense murder-literature has sprung up (one of our most eminent social reformers, Mr G. D. H. Cole, spends half his time drawing up instructions for salvationist revolution, half in spinning murder plots): one of the principal highbrow papers, Mr Desmond MacCarthy's *Life and Letters*, for some years (the fashion now has passed) 'carried' nothing but news of imaginary crimes of violence: the respective merits of this, that and the other fiction murder-expert were solemnly canvassed. Also, a significant change from Edgar Wallace, the murderer became 'sympathetic' and might have the better of the argument. Then came the immense romance-of-blood of the Gangster: fifteen thousand Sicilians in Chicago demonstrated unchecked their mastery in the art of assassination, and the blood-stained annals of their star killers was greedily perused, or witnessed on the films with gulps of hysterical satisfaction. It was as much a matter of common knowledge that *Aida* was Capone's favourite opera, as with the Yellow Book criminologists it was a matter of history that the poisoner Wainwright adored the *Sogno di Polifilo*. That the second-hand violence of the dime novel, or of Adelphi Melodrama, has always attracted the mob – or in a more openly brutal time, the bear-pit and cock-fight – is true enough: but what has been really peculiar to us (for the Elizabethan man about town scorned the tragedy of blood) has been that the most educated, as well as the least educated, participated in these pleasures, almost to the exclusion of any other. The Cabinet Minister, the philosophy-don, the Harley Street Specialist, the 'rebel' poet, as much as the scullery-maid and office-boy, pored over a long succession of detective-fictions and *nothing else*. This has been one of the features of our proletarianization: our pleasures have become the pleasures of the mob. You have to imagine, for example, a Chesterfield, a Pitt, or a Burke occupied in their spare moments with nothing but books of the order of the 'Crime Club', or the Gem Library, to get the point of this perhaps (for the average man has to resort to artifice to regard a little impersonally his own time, and nothing seems more natural after a year or two than what has the sanction of the will of the majority).

But meanwhile our Theatre has fallen into a state of complete decay: and the commercialization of the book-trade (of publishing, that is) has organized on an unprecedented scale, among educated people, the values and tastes of the cinema mob. And of course all these things hang together, it is a perfect coordination of inferior values – the values of the least gifted and the least educated.

This great decay is, however, a very recent thing: whereas the so-called 'decadence' of romantic art was on the way already at the turn of the eighteenth century. But it really is surprising how few of the famous writers of the last twenty years would not fit into the 'romantic' category, as conceived by Mario Praz. D. H. Lawrence and Ronald Firbank, to take a couple, are almost perfect specimens for his exotic museum. And of course it is pretty certain that the exceedingly low temperatures, the atmosphere of *pompes funèbres* of his *Waste Land*, and his still more *Hollow Men*, qualifies Mr T. S. Eliot for a place in this 'romantic' inferno. These hymns of capitulation breathe an air that, after journeying with Professor Praz for some time, have a somehow familiar sound. Mr Eliot is, I am very much afraid, a 'romantic agony', after all. But everyone must pick their specimens for themselves. There is here a principle of decay, a *suicide club* effect: with all the animal pleasures of life, and borrowing from the intellect a destructive intensity, and dragging the intellect with them down into their frantic maelstrom – 'In the destructive element immerse'!

The Diabolical Principle and The Dithyrambic Spectator 1931

The two essays, 'The Diabolical Principle' and 'The Dithyrambic Spectator', published together, recall the tradition of Elizabethan pamphleteering. Lewis has caught something of the tone of Nash, adapting it to the mood of the twentieth century. Difficult and highly concentrated as they are, the essays represent Lewis at the height of his powers as a polemical journalist, with his finger on the pulse of the intellectual world. They have later parallels in Left Wings over Europe (*1936*) and Count your Dead: They are Alive (*1937*). In reply to those who accused him of dissipating his energies, Lewis observed: 'I fail to see how an artist who is outside the phalansteries, sets, cells or cliques can to-day exist at all, unless he is not prepared to "pamphleteer".'

'The Diabolical Principle' concerned itself with Surrealism. This is defined as a doctrine of life rather than of art. The attack is centred upon the Paris review Transition, foremost among the intellectual 'radical' organs of the time. According to Lewis, the basic ideas of Surrealism derive from the old romantic diabolism. Mario Praz's book The Romantic Agony may have owed something to Lewis, though this was disputed by its author. As we have seen the topic was resumed in Men Without Art. Although Transition came to an end *just prior to the publication of these essays, Lewis remarked that this was only to be expected of a review necessarily in transit; that the very title* Transition *was redolent of time-worship; and that a new* Transition *could confidently be expected to appear at any moment. (The review was in fact resurrected after the war.) Lewis claims that his essay 'will apply to anything that may occur in the coming years in the way of highbrow radical journalism'.*

His comments on the cult of the Naïve and the dawn of the 'New Stein Age' were to apply to much art and literature to follow. There has been the same spurious 'cult of detachment', the same belief that 'only the dream really matters', the same 'deep sympathy with communism' (variously disguised, and often halting on the threshold of commitment). Today, as Lewis confidently predicted, a New Left has arisen. Moreover, the approval extended by intellectuals to the scabrous, disguised as higher art, has its pretensions devastatingly examined in this essay.

'The Dithyrambic Spectator', graced with one of Lewis's best titles, is linked to the first by its analysis of the primitive: a cult not without social implications. As Jolas, the founder and editor of Transition, *observed: 'A certain kind of barbarism is the only solution.' The solution has been tried. It has appeared under several guises, one of which – the 'final solution' – is associated with the name of Eichmann. In* Paleface *(Part II, Section III, 5), Lewis returned to the 'dithyrambic spectator' theme in discussing Lawrence's attitude to the Mexican Indian.*

The essays are such as only a practising artist could have written. Since the comment is highly topical, we reproduce short extracts from both essays. For the history of ideas the two tracts remain relevant.

THE DIABOLICAL PRINCIPLE
PART I, § 5–7

§ 5. THE NEW PHILISTINISM

To the political art reporter I spoke of 'Violences of self-expression, the more tortured the better'. But it has been objected that my own critical writing is full of storm and stress: that I am a counter-storm, merely, and that I do not set an example of olympian calm to my romanticist adversaries.

That I have deliberately used, often, in my criticism, an incandescent rhetoric is true. But then, of necessity, rapidly executed polemical essays, directed against a tireless and innumerable people of termites, can hardly be conducted in any other way. The athenian drafts, at war with Sparta or Persia, did not provide a spectacle of hellenic grace and imperturbability, I think. Such an essay as *Time and Western Man* is not supposed to imitate in its form an attic temple. It is a sudden barrage of destructive criticism laid down about a spot where temples, it is hoped, may under its cover be erected.

But, beyond this, the temple I might design is not a greek temple, as it happens. 'Classical', for me, is not necessarily hellenic. And I am not filled with a deep contempt for Shakespeare because he wrote such a stormy and 'chaotic' piece as *King Lear* instead of a piece observing the classic canon for dramatic art.

I need not go over in this place what I understand by the term 'romantic', since I have devoted a great deal of space to that elsewhere. Also when I come to deal with the 'diabolical principle' it will be clear what I mean by 'romantic' and its opposite, for what the people whose propaganda I am analysing explicitly state is that they wish to promote a *romantic* point of view, nothing less or more.

Next I come to a very serious difficulty for some of my readers. They have taken me, I think, for a 'defender of the faith' in a way that I am not: consequently they have been shocked to find designs and decorations within the covers of the *Enemy* that did not satisfy them as illustrations of what I had to say in my critical text or did not tally with the rôle they had assigned me. Some have believed, I am afraid, that I was disposed to defend, against all that they (but not I) regard as 'ugly' in art, all that is pleasant, innocuous and sweet. That is, of course, not the case. I am afraid that in actual fact my revaluation of the european world, were I given *carte blanche* to build it in conformity with my view of perfection, would be very much more fundamental than that contemplated by *Transition*. And that is even one of my main objections to these particular transitionist radicals. They are, for me, false revolutionaries. They wish for a *transition* into a New Philistinism (smeared over with a debased intellectual varnish) and accompanied with a quite needless material violence, and not a *transition* of a more truly revolutionary order, into an order of things radically different from the 'capitalist state'. For it is precisely a capitalist state of mind of which the Russia of to-day is often with some reason accused. The *violences* of expression I spoke of disparagingly are violences that are deliberately sought and which are artificially entertained and exploited, as *violences*, for violence sake. They always are given an, as it were, physical connotation. It is almost as though, when a persian or chinese artist dislocated the arm or leg of some figure in a composition, for the purposes of his design, a critic had applauded this device on the ground that it symbolized the artist's desire to put upon the rack half the population of Persia or of China, as a punishment for being such terrible *bourgeois*. Whereas, in fact, the artist might not relish his countrymen being such deeply-ingrained *bourgeois*, but, once he started painting, in order to paint well he would have to banish his political sensations altogether, or so I believe.

I do not, of course, suppose that the majority of those people interested in the *Enemy* have fallen into the mistake which led to this further definition of my position. But I have on either hand two sets of interested people, neither of whom I regard as likely to further the interests of art. On the one hand there are the 'radicalist' Philistines, interested in the same things as myself for motives quite alien to those things. Upon the other hand there are the more obvious Philistines, interested in nothing I am interested in, who simply dislike anything that is 'difficult' or 'not beautiful', and who are the average sensual public, defending their vulgar appetites, their sugar-sticks and the gods of their embattled Mediocrity. I can assure any member of that public who has strayed into this discussion that the editorial staff of *Transition*, or of the *Figure on the Carpet*, or any similar organ, are much more of their kidney than am I (and a quotation from Irving Babbitt or from St Thomas Aquinas stuck as an epigraph at the head of their articles does not convince me of the classic composure of their minds).

The doctrinaires that I am thinking of are then, for me, on the side of the 'romantic' – sensual average – majority, and must sooner or later, as the night follows the day, betray the artist whom they use to that majority, for they are as philistine as it. It is not their politics, but this fact, to which I primarily object. And it is owing to this philistine affinity of the professional false-revolutionary (however much disguised beneath a *fard* of intellectualist fashion) that I am the critic of those other Philistines.

§ 6. EVENING DRESS

It is of course at this point that my criticism of what I have called the 'High Bohemia' of the Revolutionary Rich comes in. A Savile Row evening dress suit is the symbol of this absurdity, to which it is always necessary to draw attention. Put across with enough aplomb anything goes: and a Savile Row dinner-jacket in itself supplies all the aplomb that is required for this simple operation. (If any reader immediately would inquire 'Do you object to evening dress?' I shout 'NO!' to him and pass on.) A person in a well-cut twenty-guinea evening dress suit is, as a militant communist, nothing short of a logical monstrosity: the human reason shies at such a spectacle and a laugh bursts or should burst from your throat to greet that walking incongruity.

Lenin in a top hat and frock coat would be a far greater anomaly than the Grand Lama of Thibet or a Zulu chief in that costume. But most communists are not so passionately logical as to be unable to ignore that sort of fundamental propriety of their faith, though Lenin was. The merely symbolical obligations of their religion, or of their 'red' complexions – these tiresome little questions of mere taste – are easily over-ridden. What *anti-noblesse* obliges a man to is the last thing that this new 'proletarian' nobility considers. In the theatres of Leningrad evening dress has once more made its appearance, we learn: but that is not such a striking fact as immaculately dressed persons here in the West, of the same creed. 'Revolution' has become a sort of violent and hollow routine: obviously the less art mixes itself up with such a political machine the better, or else it will run the chance of becoming as unreal as it.

§ 7. MY BILL OF RIGHTS

It is not a political interest at all that drives me to this critical activity. I advance the strange claim (as my private *Bill of Rights*) to act and to think non-politically in everything, in complete detachment from all the intolerant watchwords and formulas by which we are beset. I am an artist and my *mind*, at least, is entirely free: also that is a freedom that I hold from no man and have every intention of retaining. I shall act as a conventional 'radical' at six this evening if that seems to me appropriate to the situation, and at ten a.m. tomorrow I shall display royalist tendencies if I am provoked by too much stupidity or righteous pomp from some other quarter.

Yet if an art has for its function to represent manners and people, I do not see how it can avoid systematizing its sensibility to the extent of showing some figures much as Molière, for instance, did, as absurd or detestable. But the *bourgeois*, or the *bourgeois-gentilhomme*, in the work of Molière, is not an advertisement for 'bourgeois' civilization exactly. So to-day such a creation would be serving a political end, since the 'bourgeois' is the favourite comic Aunt-Sally of the communist.

But here is the point that is essential to my argument. Molière would have done you a *bolshevik* with as much relish as a *bourgeois*, for his *Précieuses* were equally *ridiculous*.

Plomer is probably the best novelist in South Africa to-day. D. H. Lawrence in England and Sherwood Anderson in America are among the very best writers produced by those countries recently: and as to Paris, is it necessary to say that almost all that is good, in formal tendency, or in actual achievement, as either painting or writing (and there is not much), is to be found here and there between the covers of *Transition?* You may not accept this as true, but it is what I believe and it is upon that basis that I am arguing. In the anglo-saxon world, that is to say, all the best artists are engaged in some form or other of political revolutionary propaganda as much as was Tolstoy in Russia in the last century. Almost the only conspicuous exceptions to this rule are to be found among artists of pronounced theological bias.

In anglo-saxon countries to-day then a first-rate or very talented artist or man of letters or philosopher is invariably (with the exception of the theologian) a destructive political revolutionary idealist. In their several ways these persons are as fervent propagandists as was Tolstoy. So it seems to me we get back, in one degree or another, with all of them, to the problem of Tolstoy – of the artist who is at the same time a fanatical politician.

Is it possible to launch and develop this criticism without being accused of bias or an opposite sort – in a word, of being a 'reactionary', of the nature of Thomas Carlyle? My answer is that it is impossible. But that does not make the accusation necessarily true. You may object to Tolstoy, as an artist, on the ground of his politics, without that charge being levelled at you: but it is not possible to make the same criticism of a contemporary without it being said that you are a politician (of opposite sign) as much as the people you arraign.

Yet surely to root politics out of art is a highly necessary undertaking: for the freedom of art, like that of science, depends entirely upon its objectivity and non-practical, non-partisan passion. And surely you should be able to employ the same arguments for a living artist that everyone has always been allowed to employ for one that is dead!

PART II, § 5–8

5. THE 'MERGING' OF DREAM AND REALITY, ALSO OF ART AND OF LIFE

... The actual merging of the dream-condition and the waking-condition (of *the external* and *the internal*) must result in a logical emulsion of the forms and perspectives of life as we know them. Translated into an art-expression, it will approximate most closely to the art of the child. That is, of course, what has everywhere occurred with the theorists of that persuasion.[1] The *infantile* is the link between the Super-realists and Miss Stein, as it is between Miss Stein and Miss Loos.[2]

6. THE OBJECTIVE TRUTH AND THE PRIVATE MENTAL WORLD OF THE ISOLATED MIND

Then if you take more particularly 'the merging of the external and the internal', that dogmatic subjectivism would manipulate the objective truth, of necessity, in favour of some version of the

---

[1] i.e., the 'Romantic Nihilism' of Paul and other members of the *Transition* group.
[2] Author of the best-selling *Gentlemen Prefer Blondes* (1925).

private mental world of the isolated mind. But what, in the super-realist account, is omitted is the fact that all reality is a merging, in one degree or another, of the external and internal. All reality to some extent is one reality, saturated with our imagination. Even more is that the case with the reality of art, or of myth. And this dogmatic *imagism* or dream-doctrine merely wishes to make a sort of official 'reality' of what, in art, is always (in every case in which a great creative fancy is operating) actual.

Super-reality, in short, is not so much a doctrine for art as for life. It is a sort of cheap and unnecessary, popularized *artistic-ness* of outlook that is involved. The creative faculty released into popular life, and possessed by everybody – that is really what 'Super-reality' means. It is merely a picturesque phase of the democratization of the artistic intelligence and the creative faculty. It would result, in practice and in everyday life, in a radical shifting of the normal real towards the *unconscious* pole. If thoroughly effective it would result, even, in a submergence of the normal conscious real in the Unconscious.

But it is not a specifically *art* doctrine, that is a doctrine that issues from the art problems of the arts of expression. For all art worth the name is already *super-real*. To say that it would be more so – or so very much more so as is implied in 'super-reality' – is to pass over into the living material of all art, its ground and what it contemplates, and to tamper directly with the cézannesque apples, for instance, before the painter has started his picture: or to modify the social life which the artist interprets or reflects.

7. THE POLITICAL EXPLOITATION OF THE MAGICAL POWER OF ART

So here again it could be shown that we are not in the presence of an aesthetic phenomenon, but of something else. The dream, indeed the opium dream or the coke-dream, of the super-realists, is to be imposed upon the living material of life. It is 'art' going over into life and changing it, so that it shall conform to its fantasy. But it is *art become life*, as it were, prior to its translation. . . . And as an art it is a feverish, untrue, dehumanized, exceedingly artificial art. And it is artificial because it has fed upon a life falsified with doctrine, and merged in dream. Or, if we call it *a dream* instead of *an art*, then, as a dream, it is evidently a sort of static nightmare, of the *Maldoror*[1] order. It is its avowed programme 'to evoke the logic of pathological terror' and to shock human society 'to its foundations'. And that is also one of the avowed objectives of the communists in their Films. But horror, or 'pathological terror', however useful in politics, is not of the same standing in art.

It is in formulas and arguments of the most superficial sort . . .[2] that such a movement clothes itself. The more shallow and obvious they are, of course, the better they serve the propagandist purpose. But this subject is of great importance for a full understanding of the various affiliated theoretic groups involved in this analysis. The 'reality' in question is a religious or semi-religious reality – the *religion* behind it in the case of the Super-realists being the religion of Communism. It is not a 'reality' of art. Indeed it is the opposite of that. For it must have for its result not the 'merging' of the external in the internal, but the *merging of art in life*. And by 'art' here is meant something much more generally important than mere current watercolour paintings or polite fiction.

Art at its fullest is a very great force indeed, a magical force, a sort of *life*, a very great 'reality'. It is *that* reality, that magic, that force, that this 'dream-aesthetic' proposes to merge with life, exactly on the same principle as the Producers at the Moscow theatres to-day merge audience and performer, stage and auditorium.

8. THE INFINITY-PHOBIA OF SUPER-REALITY

There is another aspect of the dream-psychology that it will be worth investigating a little further. I refer to the sort of scale-madness that finds expression in a sentimentally expansive attitude towards *Infinity* – 'Infinity' in its most mellow, popular and sentimental significance, that is.

In the midst of the decadence (the result of war and unremitting social disturbances of every nature – a decadence that would justify any number of hundred-million-dead wars, followed by civil wars even more catastrophic, Jolas assures us) there are 'a few men' here and there, who 'create a universe of their own in dreams and evocations of infinity. In a mediumistic trance, a new mythos is

---
[1] *Le Chant de Maldoror*, by Lautréamont (1846–70), pseudonym for Isidore Ducasse.   [2] A parenthesis omitted.

hammered out that is definitely a revolt against the burden of orthodox prejudices, and that creates a solitude of immense splendours'.

This is at the start of *Enter the Imagination*, leading up of course to the latter-day romantics, the Lautréamonts. But this ecstatic dream-language, describing 'evocations of infinity' and 'solitudes of immense splendours', bears a striking resemblance to Spengler. Already in my earlier notes on Miss Stein and her friends I have insisted that their vein is peculiarly germanic, in the bad sense of that term. But Spengler also can be made to provide, from his *Decline of the West*, excellent descriptions of *transitionists*, who are in any case so much at one with him. Paul and Jolas are perfect 'faustians', in the spenglerian idiom. I will quote a few passages from Spengler's account of the 'infinity-worship' of 'Faustian Man', and you will at once recognize these affinities – even to the translation into slovenly english of a bad and clumsy post-war german book.

> Everything that is Classical is comprehensible in *one* glance, be it the doric temple, the statue, the Polis, the Cults; backgrounds and secrets there are none. . . . Consider what it means that every one of our epoch-making works of poetry, policy and science has called forth a whole literature of explanations. . . . (These) are in fact symptoms of Western life-feeling, viz, the 'misunderstood' artist, the poet 'left to starve', 'the derided discoverer', 'the thinker who is centuries in advance of his time', and so on. These are types of an esoteric Culture. Destinies of this sort have their basis in *the passion of distance in which is concealed the Desire-to-infinity and the Will-to-power*. . . . What does it mean that no german philosopher worth mentioning can be understood by the man in the street, and that the combination of simplicity with majesty that is Homer's is simply not to be found in any Western language? The Nibelungenlied is a hard reserved utterance. . . . We find everywhere in the Western what we find nowhere in the Classical – the exclusive form.

There is no occasion to accept this account of Spengler's; I have gone to him for evidence because he belongs to the same side of the argument as Paul or Jolas, and to use him is like convicting Paul or Jolas out of his own mouth. Spengler, for instance, attributes to some mysterious, radically *different*, Western soul (which he names 'Faustian soul') what I should attribute to various systems of habit. The urge to the 'faustian' Infinite is exemplified in

Lautréamont, and, says Jolas, in all writers to-day worth considering.

This 'Desire-to-infinity' Spengler associates with the 'Will-to-power', quite correctly, no doubt. And a mind entranced with power, or possessed of a 'power-complex', is surely revealed in the *Lay of Maldoror*, if anywhere. That is the main reason why other people, themselves in the grip of the power complex, like him so much. And what takes more 'inhuman' forms than this hungry appetite for 'power'? It is by way of the more recent and most chilling analysis of the Nietzsche 'Will-to-power' conception that you can best arrive at an understanding of the highly emotional nature that bathes voluptuously in the maledictions of a Lautréamont.

THE DITHYRAMBIC SPECTATOR

INTRODUCTION

If, in response to an immediate need, some industry requiring great skill comes into existence; and if the need is then removed, and the industry languishes, there is mostly no excuse for perpetuating that craft, however elaborately it has been developed in the process of meeting this vital demand. Most of the Fine Arts are today in that position; only with the difference that their exercise is in itself so enjoyable that their various techniques, it is felt, should be perpetuated *for their own sake*.

That is what was realized by the 'Aesthete' of the Nineties, he who coined the expression *ART for ART'S sake*. The arts had then for a century been in competition with industry, and it had come to be generally recognized that they could not survive, except as a group of privileged activities disassociated from the needs of life, which they no longer met so satisfactorily as many of the industries that had substituted mechanical process for manual dexterity and emotional formulae. But these ancient and superseded industries were still superstitiously entrenched in men's conceit about their *civilization* (their way of referring to the exceptional activities of a handful of their kind, whose efforts their malice delights to embarrass, but the results of which efforts they appropriate) and the devolution of these practically obsolete technical traditions was still in the hands of a specially-trained professional class.

As, however, we recede from the time when these arts were the only substitutes for nature – before machinery went straight to nature and eliminated the middleman, Man – the position of this 'professional' nucleus becomes more and more precarious.

In the great readjustment in the sensibility of the world which is in progress there are very powerful factors whose instincts will hardly allow the survival of a purely ornamental human fringe of 'professional' *playing*. The human conceit that made it possible for this small privileged guild of specialists to claim the protection of 'Civilization' has received many rebuffs. The scandal of man's 'Origins' was the first; and the scandal of the recent gigantic war is the last scandal, from which it is doubtful if the fair name of 'Civilization' will ever recover. The course that has been taken is not 'to live it down', but rather to 'brazen it out'. 'Civilization' having become brazen in her new rôle of Whore of Babylon, she has a malignant squint for her traditional retainers and wears her high-brow ornaments with an unconcealed impatience. When she was a Madonna and claimed her descent from Simon Magus, she was the friend of every art. But as a tart she has her living to make; as she ages she becomes more practical.

The Fine Arts to-day survive on the same basis (or that will soon be the case) as the Art of the hunter or *sportsman*. Hunting, the supreme art and business of primitive life, survived in our civilization as the most delightful pastime and coveted privilege. So the fine arts, corresponding to no present need that a variety of industries cannot answer more effectively, the last survivals of the *hand* against the *machine*, but beaten by the machine in every contest involving a practical issue, must, if they survive at all, survive as a sport, as a privilege of the wealthy, negligently indulged in – not any longer as an object of serious devotion.

The sport of hunting either large or small game is the symbol of an idle and strictly useless life; and to-day the foxhunter and the painter or poet are in the same category. All that is necessary is for the fox-hunter to take to painting pictures and writing verse, and the close association of these two occupations in the public mind will be effected.

Had the primitive hunter been presented suddenly with machine-guns, with which he could mow down his game in droves, he would not have troubled to practise his lonely and difficult art any more.

Similarly, had the peruvian potters been accommodated with the resources of a Staffordshire factory for producing pots, they would have immediately abandoned their archaic wheel. Since men in the aggregate, however, are made by their occupation, both the potter and the hunter would deteriorate, become parasitic on their machines, and upon the engineer and inventor. But in neither case would that appear to them as a consideration of an order to appeal to a man or woman of the world.

A business that survives as a sport does so only when it has some pleasure-value or vanity-value. Shooting or trapping other animals has these values. Also the pictorial representation of objects, the composing of music and performing on musical instruments, singing, literary composition, verbal dexterity, and so forth, possess great pleasure-value and great vanity-value.

In future, probably what are now still 'artists' by profession (for there are still people who on identity cards describe themselves in that way) will form a class similar to that of gamekeepers, huntsmen, horse trainers, sculptors' ghosts and printers' devils. They will be the people who will keep the game, but not shoot at it – rear the horse, but not ride it. The actual *act of art* (whereby a picture is finally produced with delight, or a song sung with unction) will become of the same character as the laying of a foundation-stone, or let us say the ceremonious fixing of the last tile upon the roof, or the driving of the last rivet into the flank of the beflagged ship.

The act of art will be performed 'while one is dressing for dinner'. There will have to be a class of experts, in short, in the various arts, non-performers themselves (for there must be no professional competition): these will coach and encourage with flattering remarks the wealthy performers.

The *pleasure-value* of such performance will probably be regarded as considerable enough to make it worth while to preserve it. But its *money-value* (in the sense of its value to the man doing it, its value as an expensive pastime – not, of course, the value of what is produced, that ultimately must come to be recognized as a zero quantity, with the monied magnate as an art-monopolist) will also assure it the status of an exclusively privileged pastime. Also, it will be definitely recognized *as a pastime only*, with none of that unseemly competition with the agent-principle to which Lord Byron so rightly objected – that adulation lavished in his time upon a man of letters (as though he had won a naval engagement) or upon a musician (as though he had been the head of a noble house); or that competition that our present-day industrial magnate so justly resents in the Intelligence – as though it were a slight upon the beauty of his magnate-power, an insult to Mammon: or of that competition with 'life' against which the vitalist philosopher of the egalitarian interregnum finds it his duty to protest.

Whether it is your opinion that these conditions would or would not promote the grandest and severest forms of artistic expression is immaterial, for there is clearly no alternative. In the Civilization into which we are moving the fine arts can only survive upon these terms. And whether in the upshot they should, from your standpoint, deteriorate or improve, they must undergo a very great transformation.

The money-value of *leisure* – which is a condition of much artistic production – is now economically assessed. The 'Man of Genius' was formerly respected, by a public more rustic than ours. That simple public had no incentive to compete with genius, as its interests were of such an opposite order; it never dreamt how their dissimilar interests might be combined to the advantage of the lesser. Then the leisure that the 'Man of Genius' enjoyed was accepted as part of the natural order of things.

But with a better sense of values, people to-day have *valued* leisure. And they price it very high. Simultaneously, they do not regard the fine arts as the preserve of 'genius', but as an activity with a pleasure-value and vanity-value by no means negligible. But up to the present this pleasure-value and this vanity-value have selfishly been monopolized by 'geniuses' and other specialists. Instead of this dirty *professional* workshop (they say), the fine arts should constitute a sort of grown-up nursery, where the rich can be kept young – dabbling and dreaming in studios and galleries.

In this way these two valuable things, *leisure* and the *satisfaction of artistic performance*, should not go begging, and waste their sweetness (or rather their money-value) upon people who already have more genius than they have any right to, or need for, or money to support – who possess, that is, something for which they have not paid in cash. Indeed, do not these malefactors *unlawfully secrete* almost something at which it is impossible to get, or of which it is impossible to supervise the issue?

> '*Saint-Amant n'eut du ciel que sa veine en partage,*
> *L'habit qu'il eût sur lui fut son seul héritage.*'

Yes, but that *vein* is auriferous! Why should not 'genius' be taxed? It is all very well to call it 'genius'! A very pretty and disarming name! But is it not in fact the most insidious form of *property*?

Yes. That heroic immaterial wealth bombastically described by Boileau, with the leisure that it has always claimed just as other forms of wealth claim leisure, is to-day to all intents and purposes illegal. Is it not a reactionary possession? And the only thing that is recognized as entitled to put the egalitarian law at defiance in contemporary society is money – no other possession takes that or any other privileges with it. Therefore the spoils of 'Genius' in the revolution of our taste is very strictly the perquisite and preserve of the wealthy.

None of the furniture of jewellery or other dazzling possessions of 'Genius' goes to the crowd, in whose name 'Genius' is proscribed and dispossessed. The portion of it that it is impossible to despoil (until Science has discovered some means) must be as far as possible ignored – that is the most generally accepted procedure. This is, of course, upon that principle that establishes a blind spot in the brain where it is liable to come in contact with those other tricks of nature so disconcerting to the civilized – irreducible standing outrages, such as the lavatory or as war. The only difference is that those time-honoured scandals tend to be rescued from obscurity and dishonour: there is a strong feeling that they have been misunderstood or treated with unnecessary superiority by the ape-like creature who depended upon them for his existence or for his virility; whereas those so much vaunted intellectual qualities of his, on whose account his more animal functions suffered a prolonged eclipse, are (with the natural tact of revenge) consigned to the oubliettes and dustbins to which formerly he banished his 'animal' functions!

In short, there is a price upon the man-ape's *head*. Contrariwise, his more specialized organs receive many flattering attentions.

The standard of workmanship when a Fine Art is one of the 'arts of life' is necessarily high and exacting. But none of the pictorial and plastic arts, at least, are today any more than an adjunct to the critical and historical faculty. The contemporary audience is essentially an audience of critics. They are, that is to say, as active as the performer – who, indeed, exists chiefly in order that the critic may *act* – as a Critic.[1]

[1] The last six paragraphs are omitted.

Madness in Shakespearian Tragedy (Preface) 1929

The author of The Lion and the Fox (1927) *was well equipped to tackle the subject of alienation in the characters of Shakespeare. Indeed, as Dr H. Somerville remarked in his own Introduction, Lewis was 'deeply impressed by the vast amount of madness' to be found in Shakespeare's plays. The following is his interesting Preface to Dr Somerville's book* Madness in Shakespearian Tragedy, *published in 1929.*

How far a person, whose only existence is what he derives from the text of a play, is amenable to diagnosis by a doctor, must depend, I suppose, upon the degree of reality with which he has been endowed by his creator. No literary artist has ever been more competent than William Shakespeare to achieve this intense reality. It confers upon the least remark of the persons we find in the great plays a remarkably authentic air, that produces an illusion of nature.

Dr Somerville takes advantage of this: he treats the characters of Shakespeare as though they were breathing persons in our midst. Indeed Pirandello himself could not approach, say, Othello with more of the respect due from one creature to another than that displayed by Dr Somerville. Desdemona becomes a young lady like another – a bright though rather weak girl: he even feels that her end, painful as it undoubtedly was, still is hardly to be regretted; her life would not have been a happy one, poor girl, with an impotent husband! Or one is reminded of the professional credulity of the evangelical divine, who will chat familiarly about the movements of Judas or of Jesus on the morning of the latter's apprehension, or the probable antecedents of the Woman of Samaria, as if he were 'reminiscing', and he and Judas had been 'college chums', who had lost sight of each other latterly, or as though he had been born and reared upon the borders of Samaria. But Dr Somerville has a quite different professional axe to grind from that of the priest: he is the mad-doctor, and he has been called in to clear up the problem of the sanity of this shakespearian world. He is concerned in short purely with the question as to whether, had these people come individually beneath his care, he would have certified them or not. His answer is that in most cases he would have done so: at all events, in the fifth Act of any shakespearian tragedy all the principal characters would, were he called in, go straight to Colney Hatch, and that most have the seeds of madness long before their entrance in Act I.

Meanwhile, Dr Somerville has done me the honour to say that my book, *The Lion and the Fox*, is the only place where he has seen it stated that Shakespeare was particularly prone to the description of demented persons. That will explain my rôle as 'Announcer' on this occasion. I will venture to make a few remarks as to the conduct of the very interesting examination at which it has been my privilege to assist: but the last word must remain, naturally, with the physician.

First, then, I should myself be inclined to think that his report upon Timon of Athens as a clear case of syphilitic poisoning involved too technical an explanation of the behaviour of that character: the necessity of judging him, as a certifiable person, *before* and *after* his social downfall, presents a serious difficulty: for if it is true of the syphilitically insane that they are at once exceedingly lavish and full of the milk of human kindness, and that irritability is the last thing to be expected of them, then, although certainly Timon's liberality might have been the result of mania resulting from syphilis, his subsequent undeniable irritability would suggest that the infection was wearing off: you would be left with nothing more than the violence involved in loss of temper and the degree of insanity that goes with it. The alleged pathologic ground would be snatched from under the feet of the person submitted to our curious judgment. Mad liberality often exists without the intervention of syphilis, but, on the other hand, frantic irritability is not met with in that conjunction, we learn from Dr Somerville. This would seem to absolve Timon of Athens of the charge of having contracted syphilis (especially as Shakespeare, his creator, does not mention anywhere that he had had it, though as Dr Somerville points out, he is prone to suspect it in others, and that is a little suspicious). But it leaves his insanity, presumably of some other order, intact.

It is with the greatest deference to the distinguished physician who is the author of this book that I tentatively advance this suggestion, not in order to criticize, but merely to illustrate the nature of my own difficulties in reading this doctor's certificate of the various shakespearian star-figures with whom we are all familiar. I do think that their dementia has not been enough remarked upon; but I dare say that, able only to build up his diagnosis from their utterances in the shakespearian text, it may be that there is really not enough material to go upon to affirm with such absolute certainty what the particular disease was, as in the instance of his treatment of Timon.

Othello as a eunuch, and Hamlet as a homosexual, on the other hand, appear to me to offer us a plausible explanation of some of the eccentricities of those characters. Desdemona, as she appears on the modern stage, answers to what one would imagine would be the attitude of a woman wedded to an impotent negro pugilist, say, in love with his muscles and his championship-belt, but a little wistful on account of his unfortunate shortcomings as a bedmate. As to Hamlet's behaviour towards Ophelia it is, in fact, rather suggestive of homo-sexuality, and the bosom-friend Horatio certainly supplies a valuable clue. If Hamlet was in love with his gentleman of the bed-chamber, then his persiflage where the rather over-simple piece of femininity for whom the *bon papa bourgeois* Polonius was responsible would, I suppose, be explained.

Many readers I dare say will find, as I have, in Dr Somerville's account of Macbeth, the most notable contribution in this book to the problem of the mental condition of this formidable set of people, the giants of shakespearian tragedy. He is particularly happy in his emphasis upon the fact that Macbeth was a good man gone wrong, indeed that it was 'the milk of human kindness' that was his downfall, once allowance is made for Lady Macbeth. But even with Macbeth, I think, Dr Somerville tends to interpret the text too realistically in places, as where, for instance, he quotes the lines 'Will all great Neptune's ocean,' etc. That is rhetoric, and scarcely bears the realistic interpretative burden placed upon it.

I thoroughly agree with Dr Somerville where he says 'the whole question of the correct interpretation of the plays is involved' – namely, in whether you decide that the characters are mad, or just possess 'such trifling insanity' as Dr Bradley allows them. But, on the other hand, *more* of them are mad for Dr Somerville than for me.

'The question of sanity or insanity is a relative one. The border of demarcation is broad and ill-defined,' Dr Somerville writes. The 'mad' of Polonius is a very crude counter, naturally, and even the possibility of being 'nothing else but mad' (or its opposite, for that matter, to be 'nothing else but sane') we can reject. Still, some further definition is probably necessary.

What is most generally meant, no doubt, when the average man employs the word 'mad', is something that could most accurately be applied to himself: for if to be the victim of a constant indestructible delusion is to be insane, then certainly we all are fairly insane: and further than that, those most 'normal' are the most mad. The greater part of men and women live plunged in the depths of the great naïf hallucination that causes them to struggle passionately for what, regarded dispassionately, would be strictly nothing, and that passion is surely insanity, if anything is. To accept every appearance without question (in the sense of those questions asked by the philosophic man), to ask your butcher to give you a 'nice' porkchop or your restaurateur a 'nice' beefsteak, to refer to yourself as 'noble' when you are engaged in the most unbecoming and indeed (if that may be said, as between sane individuals) the most insane actions of murderous violence; for it to be your tendency, unless corrected and disciplined by some impulse exterior to yourself, to exalt all that is meanest, and to seek to circumvent and to disintegrate all that is finest – are not these things, taken at random, characteristic of our nature, and are they not the actions and impulses of 'dementia'? To be *quite* sane we should all have to vomit at the sight of a side of beef or some nice giblets, should we not? – as to those small frilled pigs in the windows of provision merchants, I have surprised a look of slight disgust upon the face of even the most hardened 'normal' fellow, as he gazed at one of them: we should have, I am afraid, even to laugh outright whenever we met a two-legged animal like ourselves: and as for those very gallant gentlemen who engage themselves to be the pilots of military aeroplanes, destined to drop colossal bombs upon the houses of sleeping families (of whatever nationality at the moment labelled 'enemy') – from them, if we were really entirely 'sane', we should turn in amazement and horror, and as members of the electorate of an enlightened democracy, we should arrange that they be apprehended immediately and sent to some suitable reformatory, where their abominable coarse childishness might, after prolonged treatment, be charmed out of them, when they might be returned to civilized society provisionally. Life, as the average live it, who can doubt, is 'A tale told by an idiot, full of sound and fury, signifying *nothing*', that is the 'normal' life.

This is not the sense however in which we could use the word 'insane' for so many of the great figures of shakespearian tragedy. Most often they are a higher type of man, 'maddened', perhaps, by conflict with the herd, or in a combat of wits with some of the more cunning of the demented average – that is the case of Othello. With them, when they become mad, it is rather the isolation of one idea, the *idée fixe*, in short, that marks them down as 'insane'. Whether syphilis or shell-shock has been the proximate cause of this is really the subject of Dr Somerville's book: and that of course he cannot definitely tell us: all he can say is that the symptoms have an analogy to this lesion or to that, to this disease or that. His statement at the outset, in his introduction, is to this effect.

The isolation, in the mind, of one idea (to the exclusion of everything that surrounds and modifies it in the universe) is characteristic of most madness. But there is such a thing, I should like to contend, as *shakespearian madness*, as it might be called, on the analogy of 'midsummer madness': for the idea that is isolated can obviously be either a stupid idea or an intelligent one, a bad one or a good one; and what certainly characterizes 'shakespearian madness' is that almost invariably it is a noble and generous one. There is certainly a 'decay of altruism' in the case of most of these 'heroes' – the heroism does not take the form of an exaggeration of altruism: the impulses of his Hamlets, Timons, Antonys, Othellos, Lears, are, so far as is consistent at all with human conditions, the reverse of mean or stupid. This is as much so with his great creations as it is in the case of Cervantes' Don Quixote. And this madness is the result, usually, of their realization of some besetting depravity of falseness in the general world of men, which threatens, or condemns to futility, some specific hope, or 'wish', of their more ardent, more sensitively equipped natures. In short, they are as much 'heroes' as the canons of the most conventional drama could require. Nothing, I think, in Dr Somerville's book contradicts this view of the shakespearian hero, and it is even an attempt to supply a scientific basis for it.

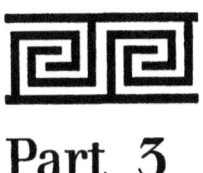

Part 3

Autobiographical Writings

Blasting and Bombardiering 1937

Lewis's first volume of autobiography is one of his most entertaining pieces. 'In art as in war,' he remarks, 'I was extremely lighthearted.' Indeed, much of this book is written in high spirits and in a tone of deliberately contrived chattiness. Like The Old Gang and The New Gang *and the appendix to* Hitler, *however, it uses a light touch, even flippancy, for the communication of a serious message. Twenty-five years after its publication, it remains diverting and relevant.*

The period of the author's childhood is not covered; for that we must go to The Letters. *The later years are the subject of* Rude Assignment.

Beginning with Lewis's pre-war experiences as leader of the Vorticist movement, Blasting and Bombardiering *continues with an account of his service as a Bombardier and Battery Officer. It culminates with a survey of the post-war period, ending with the General Strike of 1926. This was an important year for Lewis. It was then that, emerging from semi-retirement, he published his major works. Moreover, the narrative of the satiric novel* The Apes of God *concludes in that year. A most interesting chapter deals with T. E. Lawrence. There is an amusing account of an early meeting with James Joyce (introducing T. S. Eliot and – off-scene – Ezra Pound); and a series of sketches, all too brief, of some of his famous sitters. In more sober vein, Chapters II and III of Part V discuss the generation of writers and artists to which Lewis lent such distinction, and the prospects of an Artless Society. Forming some of his best essays in eristic, and culminating in the arresting phrase: 'We are the first men of a future which has not materialized', these two chapters are here reproduced in their entirety.*

PART V

II. THE PERIOD OF 'ULYSSES', 'BLAST', 'THE WASTE LAND'

The men of 1914 were a 'haughty and proud generation', I quote Mr Ford Madox Ford: the Joyces, the Pounds, the Eliots, my particular companions. Nineteen-fourteen is the year I have selected for the commencement of this history, and as observed by Mr Madox Ford, who had seen the generation of James, Conrad, and Hudson, this new 'generation' was remarkable for its 'pride'.

If Mr Ford was correct, what was the origin of this arrogance? We were of course a youth racket – oh yes! among other things. This may have contributed to that impression of 'haughtiness', experienced at contact with us by the middle-aged observer.

It was scarcely our fault that we were a youth racket. It was Ezra who in the first place organized us willy nilly into that. For he was never satisfied until everything was *organized*. And it was he who made us into a youth racket – that was his method of organization. He had a streak of Baden Powell in him, had Ezra, perhaps more than a streak. With Disraeli, he thought in terms of 'Young England'. He never got us under canvas, it is true – we were not the most promising material for Ezra's boyscoutery. But he did succeed in giving a handful of disparate and unassimilable people the appearance of a *Bewegung*.

It was Pound who invented the word 'vorticist': it was Pound who introduced Joyce to Miss Harriet Weaver – indeed thrust him down her throat – and thereby made a great many things possible which would not otherwise have been so: it was Pound who tirelessly schooled and scolded Eliot (as the latter is the first to recognize) and his blue pencil is all over *The Waste Land*. Ezra was at once a poet and an impresario, at that time an unexpected combination.

Benjamin Disraeli was of course the first 'Youth' racketeer to make his appearance in England. But that was a political racket. It was named by him 'Young England', and he used it as an emotional lever to oust Peel, and to hoist himself into power. When Peel fell, Disraeli said that it was Young England that had done it, though in fact it was his own cunning old fingers and resourceful tongue that had done the trick. But Ezra was not a politician *de métier*, and his racket was merely an art-racket.

All politics to-day, and all the 'Youth-racket' elements in politics, are put across by means of men-of-letters, journalists, *philosophes*, or the propaganda of intellectualist sects, groups and phalansteries, rather than via the Clubs or on the floor of the House of Commons. And as I have already indicated, earlier in this book, there was a tidy bit of political contraband tucked away in our technical militancy. But I was not the responsible party.

However, the fact that we were a Youth-racket it is not amiss to remember: not the first in England, that was Disraeli's, and perhaps Rossetti ran another one, but still we were the first one in this century. And although there have been hundreds since — there is a new one every month or so — ours was much the most important.

But it was not that that made us 'proud' — as, of course, it is nothing to be proud of. But since people saw us somewhat as Ezra presented us — and as *he* of course, was *very proud* of us! — it may be that the adjectives of Mr Madox Ford which I have quoted have after all something to do with this circumstance.

I have said 'the men of 1914'. But we were not the only people with something to be proud about at that time. Europe was full of titanic stirrings and snortings — a new art coming to flower to celebrate or to announce a 'new age'.

In retrospect already one experiences a mild surprise. In future this surprise will increase, year by year. What will become of those stern and grandly plastic glimpses of a novel universe, which first saw the light in the Western capitals immediately before the war, it is impossible to say. Some of it has been taken up into everyday life. Though one Kauffer does not make an Underground summer, poster art is somewhat more alive than it was, and a few shop-fronts, here and there, give a 'modern' flavour. One thing however is certain. Apart from the gallant rear-guard actions spasmodically undertaken in the British Isles by literary sharpshooters steeped in the heroic 'abstract' tradition, usually still termed 'avant-garde' for want of a more appropriate word; and save possibly for the rather untidy sunset, for a few years yet, in the 'new' American Fiction, by the end of this century the movement to which, historically, I belong will be as remote as predynastic Egyptian statuary.

To the English eye – and I am of course speaking here of how these things are seen from London – the period of *Blast*, of *Ulysses*, of *The Waste Land* will appear an island of incomprehensible bliss, dwelt in by strange shapes labelled 'Pound', 'Joyce', 'Weaver', 'Hulme'. With an egoistic piety I have made it my business to preserve in these pages something of the first-hand reality. My reporting may, who knows, serve to trip up one or two of the Ludwigs and Stracheys of a future time. I have even gone so far as to put down a barrage of gossip about Joyce's little beard, and Eliot's great toe, to make things less easy for these distant scribblers.

Yet Mr Joyce, Mr Pound, Mr Eliot – and, for I said that my piety was egoistic, the Enemy, as well – the Chiricos and Picassos, and in music their equivalents – will be the exotic flowers of a culture that has passed. As people look back at them, out of a very humdrum, cautious, disillusioned society (I am assuming here that the worst will have happened and the world bled itself white; so that the Europe of that time has become like modern China, culturally extinct), the critics of that future day will rub their eyes. They will look, to them, so helplessly *avant-garde*! so almost madly up-and-coming!

What energy! – what impossibly Spartan standards, men will exclaim! So heroically these 'pioneers' will stand out like monosyllabic monoliths – Pound, Joyce, Lewis. They will acquire the strange aspect of 'empire-builders', as seen by a well-levelled and efficiently flattened out Proletariat, with all its million tails well down between its shuffling legs!

Even, people may ask themselves if such creatures ever in fact existed, or did not rather belong to the family of the phoenix, or if dragon-blood did not flow in their veins. How otherwise could they find it worth-while to make these efforts, or to believe so bravely in the future of the world, which by then every schoolboy will know is a bughouse and leave it at that. But 'biographies' will still be written. Whatever happens, there will be plenty of biographies. So let me step in at once, and make it as difficult as possible for the distant biographer to do his usual uncannily inaccurate work.

I will fix for an alien posterity some of the main features of this movement. No one is better fitted than I am to do so, in all humility I may asseverate. I was at its heart. In some instances I was *it*.

However, I may seem to sweep on too fast and far, and to speak as if Mr Eliot were not there, alive although no longer kicking, to write a morality next year, to be played in the Chapter of some venerable Close; or his melancholy ex-lieutenant Mr Read, to write yet another dashing but dull rear-guard book, about the 'abstract' arts; or Mr Henry Moore to polish a whole necklace of fine abstract stones. Of course I have not forgotten that. And I do not mean to say that all the masterpieces of this school have yet been penned, painted, or planned. But what I do say is that whatever happens in the world during the next century or so, there will be no society present upon the globe to think, live, and speculate in a manner conducive to the production of such works as *Bouvard and Pécuchet*, *Ulysses*, *The Hollow Men*, *The Ambassadors*, *The Portrait of Carlyle*, to name a few of the sort of productions that I mean, and to mix my times and arts a little too. The last society likely to do anything of that sort vanished with the War. It is a case of good-bye to all that, and for good. And one has to be no great prophet to foresee that whichever of the forces confronted upon the political stage to-day may get the upper hand, the Red or the Black, any detached artistic effort, on the grand scale, will be quasi-impossible. There will not be present the will, the psychological incentive, the time, or *the peace*, that are requisite for that. This applies to Germany as much as to Russia, to America as much as to Japan. Martial law conditions have come to stop. The gentler things of life are at an end.

We are not only 'the last men of an epoch' (as Mr Edmund Wilson and others have said): we are more than that, or we are that in a different way to what is most often asserted. *We are the first men of a Future that has not materialized.* We belong to a 'great age' that has not 'come off'. We moved too quickly for the world. We set too sharp a pace. And, more and more exhausted by War, Slump, and Revolution, the world has *fallen back*. Its ambition has withered: it has declined into a listless compromise – half 'modern', half Cavalcade!

The rear-guard presses forward, it is true. The doughty Herbert (he of 'Unit One') advances towards 1914, for all that is 'advanced' moves backwards, now, towards that impossible goal, of the pre-war dawn. At his back struggles a thin militia – except for one little giant, the last of the Mohicans, Mr Moore, the sculptor. But it is in vain. We are all taking in each other's washing. Soon as a society we shall none of us have any money to pay the laundry bill, but that is the fact of the matter.

The above statement, unsupported by data and by argument, might appear at first sight a mere outbreak of irresponsible pessimism. So let us see how one can arrive at such a discouraging estimate of the chances of the arts at the present time; and why it is quite reasonable, with all proper detachment, to believe that they have not the chance of the proverbial Chinaman in the 'new' age of which they were so naïf as to allow themselves to appear the clamorous harbingers.

III. TOWARDS AN ART-LESS SOCIETY

The Arts with their great capital A's are, considered as plants, decidedly unrobust. They are the sport, at the best, of political chance: parasitically dependent upon the good health of the social body.

The most robust-*looking* art by a long way is sculpture. Yet it is just snuffed out by a change of wind – or to pursue the parasitic image, by a brusque change of position on the part of the human dreamer. The frailest-looking of the visual arts, drawing, possesses far greater endurance. Mere scraps of paper that it is, in this respect it has more vitality than basalt.

This book and especially this section of it is mainly concerned with the art of writing. There is always a lot of writing, of sorts, going on at any period. If quantity meant anything, to-day would be a golden age for the art of writing. You cannot snuff out penmanship by upsetting a régime. The crash of a great religion does not diminish the output of the written word. But writing as an *art* is very susceptible to shock. That gets upset by almost anything. And to-day it is as an art in as great a decline as its sisters.

A few arts were born in the happy lull before the world-storm. In 1914 a ferment of the artistic intelligence occurred in the west of Europe. And it looked to many people as if a great historic 'school' was in process of formation. Expressionism, Post-impressionism, Vorticism, Cubism, Futurism were some of the characteristic nicknames bestowed upon these manifestations, where they found their intensest expression in the pictorial field. In every case the structural and philosophic rudiments of life were sought out. On all hands a return to first principles was witnessed.

Such a school as was then foreshadowed would have been of far more significance than the schools based on a scientific naturalism *à l'outrance* which filled the galleries and mansions of the Nineteenth Century, and would have had equally little in common with the elegancies of the Eighteenth. And in literature a purgative almost equally radical was undertaken.

The natural sciences which had been responsible for the Industrial Age had acquired maturity, it seemed, and the human mind was to indulge, once more, its imagination. Scientific still, essentially, it was to go over from the techniques of the sciences into the field of art. There it was to create a novel world, free from the sloppiness of the impressionist.

These arts were not entirely misnamed 'new' arts. They were arts especially intended to be the delight of this *particular* world. Indeed, they were the heralds of great social changes. Then down came the lid – the day was lost, for art, at Sarajevo. World-politics stepped in, and a war was started which has not ended yet: a 'war to end war'. But it merely ended art. It did not end war.

Before the 'great War' of 1914–18 was over it altered the face of our civilization. It left the European nations impoverished, shellshocked, discouraged and unsettled. By the time President Wilson had drawn up his famous Fourteen Points, the *will to play* had been extinguished to all intents and purposes forever in our cowed and bankrupt democracies.

The great social changes necessitated by the altered conditions of life were not to come about, after all, rationally and peacefully. They were to come about 'catastrophically' instead (that is to say, after the Marxian prescription). And the great social changes which with such uncouth and wasteful violence started to get themselves born, in that tragical atmosphere, extinguished the arts which were to be their expression, and which had been their heralds.

No one, it is true, ever supposed that some bigoted theorist of the mass-life, or some Brasshat, either – much less the 'Financial Wizard' who controlled the Brasshat and subsidized the bigot – would ever feel drawn towards *an art*. That would be the last thing he would favour. No one imagined that such figures would give a row of pins, under any circumstances, for the sort of question in which the artist, or philosopher, is interested. But then, although he had in a sense announced, the artist did not foresee, these interminable convulsions of War, Revolution, Economic Nationalism and Slump.

That the artist of 1914 was no seer is of little importance, since it would have made no difference if he had been. Yet the artist is, in any society, by no means its least valuable citizen. Without him the world ceases to see itself and to reflect. It forgets all its finer manners. For art is only manner, it is only style. That is, in the end, what 'art' means. At its simplest, art is a reflection: a far more mannered reflection than that supplied by the camera.

Deprived of art, the healthy intellectual discipline of well-being is lost. Life instantly becomes so brutalized as to be mechanical and devoid of interest. Further, there is a worse thing than no art at all (no manner, no style) – the saccharine travesty of art, namely, of the kind supplied by the Hollywood magnate.

In considering art here I am not complicating the matter by going on to consider how life also is brutal and empty without the heightening it acquires through the metaphysical or religious values. We need go no farther than art; and for the purpose of this discussion art can be isolated, conventionally, from those values. For it is possible to have life with a minimum of metaphysics; the age of Lord Shaftesbury and Pope is there to prove it, though I do not say it is the best life. But *without art* – then life is utterly impossible. And there is unquestionably less and less *art* in life at the present time – and less and less in what passes as art, too.

The activities of the artists of 1914 did foreshadow all that has come to pass in the meanwhile. But those events obviously could, by a kinder fate, have been arranged differently, so that they would have been productive of less unpleasant and stultifying results. Great changes *could* have been achieved – indeed greater changes – with less destructive haste. Passchendaele and the 'Thirty days that shook the world', that was not the *only* way to adapt ourselves to the novelties of the Power House and the internal combustion engine and consummate the revolution that the Luddite Riots began.

In the event, what has looked like a speeding up, brought about by the very violence of the methods employed, has at the same time involved a remarkable retrogression. To match the mechanical advance, there has been a backsliding of the intellect throughout the civilized world. And this backsliding is glaringly demonstrated in the continued impoverishment of artistic expression, not in one art, but in every art.

Rude Assignment 1950

Subtitled 'A Narrative of my Career Up-to-Date', this second volume of memoirs lacks the gaiety and verve of Blasting and Bombardiering. It reflects the post-war era, with its austerity and drabness, as faithfully as the collection of short stories Rotting Hill (*1951*). Some of it would appear to have been written in rage and frustration. There are signs of haste; the humorous banter and the delicious ridicule are absent; it bears the one title which disappoints. Nevertheless, the book is indispensable for a true assessment of Lewis, chiefly by virtue of its sober and objective account of its own literary achievement.

The following excerpts are from Part I, Section A, 'The Intellectual', which deals with the theme of the Two Publics, or the 'binary system of two cultures', in a manner more profound than that recently discussed; for, as Lewis remarks, 'the two publics is the beginning of no public at all'. With complete lack of pretentiousness, Lewis reverts to the theme of declining standards; the erection of bad taste 'into a position where it becomes above criticism'; the 'isolation and stultification of society's most intellectually energetic and imaginative individuals'; and the forcing of artists into Reservations, culminating in 'a crisis of respect for human kind'. An additional reason for preserving this sustained argument is that, like much else of Lewis's, it stated plainly what others have said obscurely, and it did so a good deal earlier: which may account for its having been in large part overlooked.

II. THE HIGHBROW, AND THE TWO PUBLICS

I am what is described as a 'highbrow'. That is the first thing about me; it underlies, and influences, all the other things that I am – all the things that it is not desirable to be. And this part of my book is to take the form exclusively of a catalogue of my personal handicaps.

But this term – half abuse, half of derision – is not *me*, it is not an attribute of mine, or anything personal to me. It is just something that happens to any writer or other artist, to be described in this ridiculous fashion – one who is not a best-selling or potboiling hack.

There are two distinct kinds of writing, or of any other art, at the present time. Such conditions have never existed before, and will perhaps never be present again; we are uniquely cursed. The 'highbrow' is one of these two divisions into which humanity has been cut – for the use of these terms extends beyond the artist to the Public catered for. It has come to describe a human category – the 'highbrow' and the 'lowbrow'.*

This clownish American term, 'highbrow', is more than just a label. It is a *uniform,* as much as the garment stamped with arrows worn by the convict. For a man is a 'highbrow' all over, from head to foot, or not at all. He is somebody set apart from other men – for thinking in a peculiar way. He cannot mix with them without their at once detecting the difference, and feeling embarrassed. Even he uses a dialect – long and funny words and expressions – as unpopular with the solid citizen as is thieves' slang. He is regarded as 'standoffish', but people stand off him, his company as much wanted as that of an escaped budgerigar by a cluster of sparrows.

The Philistine once felt diffident in the presence of the 'clerk' or *Gelehrter* – of his intellectual betters. But he knows now that they are only 'intellectuals', or 'highbrows' – *jokes*! He knows too that the Philistines are really the Chosen People: the Nineteenth Century was the 'Century of the Philistine'. The Twentieth is called 'the Century of the Common Man': but it is turning out to

---

* This classification does not extend beyond the bourgeoisie. The working class, of course, do not count. The typical 'lowbrow' would not like to think he shared his brow with *them*. They might, if it came to the point, be described as the 'no-brows'.

be the Century of the Philistine again, just the same as the last. (Someone meant to go to town with the Common Man, but they lost him on the way.)

Why on earth should an intellectual, however, wish to associate with the Philistines? Surely that would be the most uncongenial company for him! – He does not, of course, wish to do that. The best variety of intellectuals, on the other hand, are by no means enamoured of the Ivory Tower. They do not want to speak to the stars, but to men. They merely object to their being Philistines: especially they resent people deriving merit from their barbarity: their social conscience recognizes in them a vast infected area, which should not be permitted to remain as it is. They object to being denied (by means of the branding described above) the missionary's privilege to go amongst the Philistines and bring civilization to these modern middle-class savages. And, then, if as seems very probable, this badly-infected middle class is economically wiped out: if golf-courses are put under the plough, bridge clubs converted into something more useful, the commercial theatres turned over to the State, the culturally destructive monopolies controlling them dissolved – what then? Will the Philistine perish with the Bourgeoisie?

A danger that is patent enough is that the 'lowbrow' will infect the working mass underneath it, into which Philistia will sink – if the virus is not there already, transmitted by the Moving Picture industry. The division into 'low' and 'high' would thus be perpetuated, with an added militancy: or what is derisively labelled 'high' be wiped out. – The unity thus obtained would be a cultural zero as injurious to the social body as any other organic atrophy. For the Anglo-saxon is not the Slav, or even the Celt: he does not dance or sing for *preference*, he is strong but he is silent, and we have the most conclusive evidence, in certain parts of the world, of what he is capable when left to his own devices, in the way of a cultural desert.

Do not let us be distracted, however, by speculations as to what may come to pass in the fullness of time: it is what is here now, irrespective of what may be here tomorrow, that is the subject of this and the succeeding chapters. *The Two Publics* I have collectively named them. And for a writer the Public is of critical importance as it is for the actor.

Though already in Dickens' day the Public was too big, it has now broken into two very unequal parts: a 'popular' and a 'highbrow', the latter being so insignificant in size as to be practically a private audience, such as a group of friends and relatives would provide.

As the cities grew, and privilege gave ground, the Public altered, from the compact, alert, educated Public of moderate size, that of the aristocracies, to the swelling mass of readers of the Victorian shopkeeping and mercantile classes. It became so large that writers were a little uncertain for whom they were writing. The focussing became blurred. The immediate result was a falling off in quality. The beautifully written books of the Eighteenth Century were succeeded by books the style of which was coarser and looser. To come down to our own day, such writing as that of H. G. Wells (I am not speaking of the matter, only of the manner, if one can make such a distinction) could not have been handed by any bookseller to the Public which currently read *The Sentimental Journey* or *The Tale of the Tub*.*

It was hoped by good-hearted people that 'popular education' would elevate the new multitudinous society to a plane where it would equal in understanding and appreciation that of the privileged classes. Because 'popular education' was a sham, if for no other reason, this did not occur. There was another deadly factor: the flattery of the 'sovereign people' by politicians tended to erect bad taste, or no taste, into a position where it became above criticism: and as I have remarked, the word 'highbrow' was coined slightingly and damagingly to describe those who persisted in employing their critical faculties.

Then the commercial gentleman, at a certain moment, stepped into the picture. He had been held in check under the aristocracies. (I have written somewhere that the only conceivable use I could think of for the fox-hunter was to keep the businessman in his place.) This predatory money-spinner saw very clearly that the multitude was a goldmine. The fact that it was uninstructed, sentimental, greedy of sensation, did not trouble *him*. The 'What the Public wants' principle, it was called. – He, too, assisted in confirming the zero-mind (which is what the human mind is like until you have

* In comparing, as I am about to do, these two types of Public, although certainly I would agree that the aristocratic Public was the better of the two, no *partipris* for that social order need be surmised, for it is not there I, no more than de Tocqueville, would recommend a return to that, or anything like it.

put something into it and trained it to function) in its position of cultural arbiter. Hollywood is the most perfect expression of this.

One might have supposed that among the political class – I speak of the era which ended with the advent of the present social democratic administration – however rotted it might be by Victorian philistinism through which it had passed, something would remain of the better earlier standards: the popular press, the many temptations to illiteracy, notwithstanding. Anything but that happened. Except in a few cases, nothing whatever was left. There are no throwbacks to the habitués of Button's Coffee-House among Twentieth Century London Clubmen.

Detective fiction has for long been the cabinet minister's habitual reading, with Mr Wodehouse's ghastly butler as an alternative to Poirot and Lord Peter Wimsey. In the States it is much the same. One of my personal experiences which have a bearing upon the question of the cultural level at which the politically or socially prominent live relates to the young wife of a multi-millionaire. Wishing to display her cultivation, she informed me she had been reading *Forever Amber*. She did not seem to know any other book of the same cultural range, although I could see she was trying to remember one or two. As her chauffeur drove me back to my hotel, he, too, I learned, had been reading *Forever Amber*. There was a note of self-importance in his voice, as there had been in hers, as he alluded to it. – Then Herr Hitler, according to reporters accompanying him, was wont upon long plane journeys to read crime stories – Another illustration of these tendencies: in Public Libraries in the New World 'Western Stories' occupy whole blocks of bookshelves. This for adult reading.

But the roster of backslidings into juvenilia, or related phenomena, is endless. Nor of course do I say that there is any harm in 'mystery' and murder, our debased form of Arabian Nights Entertainments (nor the literary sex stimuli which could come under the same head) except when it represents a literary monopoly. W. B. Yeats once told me that he never used detective fiction until he was forty: but he assured me that all men at forty did so. Yeats read other books as well, however.

The Majority Public, to return to that, is not one solid mass, ten million strong. There are layers, as it were. But even the top layer is far too low for, say, *The Way of all Flesh*. Contemporary man is allergic to the masterpiece. He is allergic, that is, to other than superficial matter between the covers of a non-technical book. One way of gauging by analogy the extent of his literary toleration is to observe how much, if any, of serious matter he will suffer on the radio, before switching off. In practice he never is obliged in Great Britain to switch off anything, however, unless by mistake he should tune in to the Third Programme. All his cultural allergies are locked away in the so-called Third Programme, which, because of the wave-length reserved for it, can only be heard in London and its neighbourhood. So, in Manchester or Nottingham he is perfectly safe.

Our present-day Minority public, is not a half, probably only a tenth, of the Eighteenth Century Public. It is the Public of the Intelligentsia. Although much smaller, this Public of the Intelligentsia might be expected to compare favourably with the public of the aristocratic era. That is, however, not the case. It is too specialized: an unrepresentative fraction of the whole. And it *is* the whole, in some form or another, that is required by a writer.

III. THEY STEAL THE HALOES FROM THE STATUES OF THE SAINTS

The existence of two distinct communities, such as those of Highbrowland and Lowbrowland, owing their origin, as distinct entities, to irreconcilable differences of taste and of opinion, cannot but involve hard feelings: and hard feelings there are. The smaller community is so small that what in the end this must lead to is the suppression, the liquidation, of the intellectual groups altogether. It will come about as the result of pressure on the feebler to conform. Let us start, however, by imagining what must be the sensations of a gilded hack, as he watched the degraded products of his nasty brain being contemptuously trampled underfoot by the seedy but conscientious critic. This occurs every time, his latest bestseller having appeared, he peruses his press-cuttings.

Critics of books, pictures, or plays, are as often as not 'Highbrows': but many of the books, pictures, or plays they are paid to write about are 'lowbrow'. As might be anticipated, sometimes they say wounding things about them. The general Public regards critics as a pernickety and spiteful class. It shuts its eyes and ears as far as possible to what the critics say. With the lowbrow writer, painter, or actor it is another matter. Their lives are often embittered by ridicule and censure, for although they sell their books by the hundredweight they are respected by nobody: or though a play has a run of six hundred nights, the critics are apt to provide an opprobrious chorus. A film gets such terrible press notices (especially if it is American) that one would think the Public would stop away. Mercifully, from the standpoint of the box-office, the average movie-lover is not in the habit of looking at newspapers, much less the weekly periodical press.

Before the war there was scarcely an art-critic who did not reprove, ridicule, or scold the Royal Academy Exhibition, when every Spring it displayed, according to its custom, its meretricious wares – its glittering diamonds, its juicy satins, its glittering brass hats, and sketchy peeps at nature. (An institution of the same order and quality as Madame Tussaud's – though this is rather unfair to the waxworks, where waxen effigies have a certain Douanier-like charm.)

If in the book world, or in the theatrical profession the critic can be to some extent disregarded, this has not proved to be the case with painting, sculpture and design. Perhaps because oil-paintings cost much more than books, bad pictures have almost ceased to sell.

The intellectualist barrage of the last thirty years has had a great effect in the sale room, and, in the matter of the visual arts, the Minority has won the day in that sense. In literature, even when the writer has had every critic in the press acclaiming him, it has made very little difference financially – until by some extraneous means, he came to the attention of the Public. Since the establishment of the two water-tight Publics this has been a fairly rare occurrence.

The author of *Lady Chatterley's Lover* only reached the Plain Man of today by way of the bedroom window. In all his attempts prior to that, Lawrence remained outside, an intellectual's hero, that was all. And the bedroom or lavatory window is the intellectuals' best bet (or, I should say, was). Hemingway showed the children how to play at a 'stick-up' and how to strap their popguns under their arm-pits: *he* got in that way. Neither Lawrence nor

Hemingway departed from their high standards as writers. It was a question of subject-matter, not of style.

Enter by the front-door and you go dressed accordingly. And it is a very cheap outfit indeed that you will wear; or a cowboy get-up, or masked and with an ill-concealed Smith-Wesson. If a woman, with a tiara and a haughty stare, or as a 'womanly woman', with Mrs Beeton's Cookery Book under your arm or with a story of how you were seduced. There is no dignified or decent way of going in.

The invisible line separating the two Publics cannot be crossed with impunity by one of the Minority. So fine a preraphaelite painter as Millais ended his career with 'Bubbles' and a baronetcy.* As to the dangers that beset the Minority Writer, it is enough if he transgresses in his heart. So fine a mind as Hudson's (I suppose toying with thoughts of popularity) was guilty of *Rima*. To produce anything so sickly there must, I suppose, have been some native rot. There are very few cases, if any, however, of a great artist like Henry James committing intellectual suicide.

The advocate of 'highbrow' values, as against the values of the good easy man, who 'knows what he likes', must always appear pernickety. The label 'highbrow' contributes to this impression. Whereas the two-party character of criticism gives to the opinion of the *outs* – the permanent Minority – a suspect and merely partisan appearance.

There is another result of this separation of the bright from the dull, the intellectual from the non-intellectual, namely the exclusive encouragement of opposite orders of extremism. Thus in the United States Frank Salisbury, R.A., was to be official artist. At the other extreme stands picassoan or other extremism. Nothing gets much chance in the gulf that yawns ever wider between these extreme positions. If there were no gulf and the extremes drew together, then many artists who are not by nature extremists (of whichever kind) would produce what is the finest and maturest type of work.

The gulf widens and deepens, however, and the conditions favourable to the production of the best intellectualist extremism

* A poster advertising Pears' Soap, showing a curly-headed boy blowing bubbles.

(such as Paris provided for those mercurial masters who are now old) disappear. In writing, the same shrinkage of opportunity may be recorded. One day soon all of *that* kind of extremism will be engulfed. But what an extremism will meanwhile have been built up at the other end of the scale!

A hundred years ago, or even half as long, it was a generally accepted belief that the poet or philosopher, shivering in his garret, was a better man than the sleek bestseller, basking on his terrace at Cannes. What the latter produced had no value except in terms of L.S.D., whereas the former was 'loved of the gods' and would no doubt 'die young' – but *how glorious*! It was almost like dying in battle, for England, Home and Beauty. Browning expressed all this type of feeling on numerous occasions. 'What porridge had John Keats,' he exclaims with dramatic emphasis – and all his readers, invariably well-fed and well-heeled, applauded.

Apart from the fact that there was an unmistakable tendency to let everybody die of starvation who displayed any unusual talent, and much talent must have been lost through hunger and neglect, nevertheless the respectful attitude was *something*. It was better than being sneered at as a 'high-brow', and starving just the same, or living on charity. The emergence of socially valuable personalities at least was not obstructed: for their values were not questioned. Those valuations are today under attack: even a tendency exists – a primitive Christian impulse – to say that what has been considered high is really low, and what has been thought low is high. It is the democratic levelment that de Tocqueville foresaw, extending far beyond merely social particulars.

I would now like, having prepared the way, to draw attention to a distinction which is perhaps the key to what is novel in the situation I have been describing. – Changing values, representing a see-saw of taste from decade to decade, affecting the reputations of the inhabitants of our pantheon – from Shakespeare downwards – is one thing. Such movements are going on continually. They are changes that emanate from reactions within the ranks of the small Minority groups alone. These are the keepers of the pantheon, as it were. They engage in arguments constantly about the relative importance of their idols.

These changes affect very slightly, if at all, the great Public. The early Victorian romantic poets lose standing: Shelley and Keats decline, Dryden and Crabbe go up. The Majority is unaware of such fluctuations among the unread authors dustily huddled upon the library shelves.

The values involved in these periodic adjustments are of a totally different order from those which distinguish a contemporaneous 'highbrow' and 'lowbrow' work. And this is the fundamental distinction to which I referred above. In the latter case it is *a difference in the essential nature* of the respective works. The difference between something self-evidently trivial or shoddy, and something self-evidently engaging all the energies of a considerable mind and sensibility. And there measurement is possible – as much as it would be possible to measure and compare the brain of Isaac Newton and that of a fieldmouse. Taste is not really involved at all. Only the cash-nexus blurs the verdict: only that and the automatic reflection in our department of life from violent political readjustments elsewhere.

The word 'self-evident' uncovers the essential humbug in the position. For the two Publics would never have come into being; there would be no labelling 'highbrow' what is work seriously undertaken – in order to distinguish it offensively from what is *not* serious – were *the self-evident inferiority* of work done to soothe the tired businessman, or to provide sensations for the bored matron, not disputed. And there is today unquestionably, in however veiled a form, this novel dispute. In America I have heard the matter openly canvassed, and bold claims made for the purely commercial article.

No dispute should ever have developed as to *ultimate* values: for that is what it means. Were the potboiler and bestseller content with the purely monetary reward all would be well. But he, and even more his promoter, wishes to enhance still more the profits accruing, by gilding the notoriety obtained in this (quite legitimate) traffic, by stealing the haloes from the statues of the saints: by appropriating the homage formerly reserved for great achievements of the mind, and putting it to commercial uses. In this way the cash-value of what they have to sell is notably augmented: and our binary system of two cultures, with distinct Publics, came into being. And gradually the 'low' Public – the commercially promoted Majority – has come to claim that it is the real, the best, and the only, one.

IV. THE CRISIS OF MANAGERIAL CONCEIT

What is to be predicted of a civilization that has cut itself in two, and driven into an abusively labelled pen (the minor and despised one of the two unequal parts) all that is most creative and intelligent in it? Any member of this 'intelligentsia' who challenges the justice and the wisdom of this division, collects bad marks against himself, as *extra-pernickety*. Yet all the population suffers (since no man gains anything from misusing, or not using, his mind) because of the isolation and stultification of its most intellectually energetic and imaginative individuals. Were these not relegated to what is little better than a concentration camp, and condemned to impotence in this way, the cultural standards of the English-speaking societies would be very different from what they are.

Responsibility for the Majority Public must in the first place be laid at the door of monopoly-capital and mass-production. Then there is a psychological explanation, too. The ubiquitous power-bug has a part in this herding, and in the low quality of the herd. – To deny to other people the means of understanding obviously gives great satisfaction to many, as is sufficiently demonstrated by the orgy of unnecessary censorship, when war comes. *They* know what is going on: 'The Public' does not.

Again, to keep other people in mental leading-strings, to have *beneath* you a broad mass of humanity to which you (although no intellectual giant) can feel agreeably superior: this petty and disagreeable form of the will-to-power of the average 'smart' man counts for much in the degradation of the Many. And there is no action of this same 'smart' man that is more aggravating than the way in which he will turn upon the critic of the social scene (who has pointed out the degradation of the Many) and accuse him of 'despising the People'.

The instinct to be 'big' at the expense of the Many, to acquire superiority by means of impoverishing others mentally, turned the other way round – upwards instead of downwards – accounts for much of the hatred of the 'intellectual'. – In a thoroughgoing analysis a number of minor causes would have to be considered: but these two factors, with all their ramifications, are the decisive ones: namely (1) the perennial instinct of man to feel superior, and

(2) the discovery by monopoly-capital of this novel eldorado, the democratic mass-public.

So people have deteriorated. They have neither the will nor commonsense of the peasant or guildsman, and are more easily fooled. This can only be a source of concern and regret, to all except 'the leader of men'.

The Russian people, who have never had to pass through the cheapening process to which for a hundred years the English and Americans have been subjected, respond to art stimuli of a more severe and serious order – plays, ballets, books – than would be possible for our Public.

It is not our Public that is to blame, then – any more than it is the fault of the English labouring man, of the navvy type, that he is like an artificially preserved prehistoric creature. He no longer signs his name with a cross – as he still did when first permitted to vote. But they were very careful in giving him the vote not to give him at the same time the mind (which education supplies) to use it with understanding.

The mind of the 'petit-bourgeois' Public (and in this we must include the rank and file professional man) is not much above the labouring man. This bourgeois Public have been denied education as much as he has—or, better, cultivation: that most valuable part of education, such as is provided by good books or good plays, beautiful buildings, intelligent recreations, travel and leisure. These it does not possess – because it has been supplied with 'what it wants'. And 'what it wants', its mentors and purveyors decided, was what is most banal and platitudinous, the sugary and the violent. – It would be wholly absurd if it were held responsible for being what it is: for remaining in the low I.Q. category. How could it be otherwise, seeing that it has been locked up in that category by the purveyors of cheap sensation, sob-stuff, 'glamorous' sex? Just as the 'highbrow' – in his compulsory divorce from the People – has been locked up in his 'high' attic, or in his Ivory Tower.

Thus prepared, we may now speak of what may grow into a crisis of respect for human kind – let alone a crisis of altruism, for altruism cannot survive in the existentialist atmosphere of these times, pervading the ruins of Europe. But this crisis is in part the outcome of the existence of the 'lowbrow' mass, whose origins I have been considering. Also playing its part, is the deliberate brutalization of the 'lower-orders' by the Victorian, and the post-Victorian. The new men as a rule are intellectuals. Whereas their opposite numbers in Russia, whatever may be said of stalinism, do not suffer from a *lady and gentleman* complex. There are few Englishmen who do not. Will the new men here since 1945 retain a decent respect for the 'little man' of the capitalist cartoon; the small suburbanite, the football and dog racing crowds, the antlike swarms on the summer beaches, suddenly become his clients?

I will digress in order, in passing, to examine the specifically *national* factor. Men who make revolutions are, through it all, Frenchmen, Russians, or Englishmen. The worst blemish in the English character is not, as many people would have it, hypocrisy: it is that the Englishman is a congenital snob. This fact seems to me of importance to socialism – though I am often told that it is not. Will the Englishman divest himself of his snobbery, as he passes over into the new social order: or will he take it with him – assuming, in its new environment, horrible and unexpected forms? Will the Stalin of England insist that he is of awfully good family, and will it be high treason to remind him that his papa hawked fish in the New Cut? Will the shoddy genius of the Old School Tie go hand in hand with this British version of the Commissar?

There has been 'Labour', but in England socialism has mostly existed as salon-socialism, up till now; a middle-class monopoly. I know and have met great numbers of socialists but only two or three issuing from the working-class. – You would think that a young middle-class man, when he has decided to dedicate himself to the emancipation of the working-class, would lay aside for good the old school tie, and with it the degrading emotions of idiot-pride in the not very interesting fact that his people floated at a respectable middle-class distance above the gutter. You would think he would dump all that in the trash-can and try to be serious.

But this as a rule does not happen: among Popular Front acquaintances I have met with more straight social snobbery than anywhere else. Where one had thought only to find a passion for social justice, one so often discovers nothing but an unlovely little power-complex. Snob and socialist are not regarded as mutually exclusive terms in England. And this feudal atavism, or, as it usually is, hangover from the Servants-hall, has not been by any means confined to the small-fry. – When, many years ago, I met Prince Kropotkin, I detected no sign that he remembered that once he had been a Prince. That he had left behind, along with his fortune, when he went into a most honourable exile. Perhaps this is easier for an aristocrat: it is easier to leave a good deal, possibly than to turn your back upon something insignificant.

It is abashed that we learn – in the book of her friend and biographer – that Beatrice Webb could not manage to like the working-class. Was she just an interfering middle-class Victorian lady, then, troubled with a power-complex? That great Irish gentleman, Mr Bernard Shaw, in his obituary notice of H. G. Wells (*New Statesman*, Aug. 17, 1946) goes on like some snobbish schoolboy about Wells's parents, who, it seems were not so rich as Mr Shaw's. Oh dear me!

Now I will return to the crisis of respect for human kind – present, or rapidly developing. In politics this can have terrible results: for those in power then begin pushing men around as if they were chessmen, not of flesh and blood. The 'managerial' type are exponents of an advanced inhumanity. Some have seen in the present social democratic administration in England examples of the 'managerial' type. – With that view I am not in agreement, though it is too early to come to any final conclusion. All government is management. Because these more honest men do not govern in a smart underhanded way like their predecessors, they expose themselves to partisan misrepresentation as *over* governing, that is all.

James Burnham gave a name to a class to which he belonged himself, by temperament. And no feudal class ever acquired so superior an attitude towards its dupes and dependents as the 'new managerial' type shows towards its prospective, or actual, clients, the multitude. Herr Hitler (picked by Burnham as a heroic and *successful* 'manager') produced, in his notorious treatise, what was among other things a handbook as to how scientifically to fool the Many. In it he studies with chuckling rapture the demagogy of Lloyd George – whose speeches he regarded as models of demagogic perfidy and sleight of hand.

The crisis of respect for humanity is only assuming universal proportions today. But with world war I and its sequel it began already to appear. It has been immeasurably aggravated by world war II and *its* sequels. The cheapening of human life – until we all have grown rather like doctors in our necessary callousness about the human animal, whose 'ideals' look sillier at every fresh homicidal outburst: the lowered standards of life ensuing upon war – all of this conspires to dethrone homo sapiens and to put in his place homo stultus, or the Yahoo of Swift. No one is to blame for this. It is human nature accomplishing its destiny. – The enemies of man do not point these things out, since they profit by them. And the friends of man get called his enemies.

Those engaged in publicity services or in popular entertainment – to go on with the catalogue of dehumanization – cannot retain much respect for the million-headed Baby, whose mouth it is their job to make water, or from whose big blue eyes their job it is to extract buckets of tears. (Only a hypocritical propagandist would dispute the accuracy of this account of the mind of the publicist, or entertainer, always hard-boiled and professionally sardonic.) It is difficult to see how politicians, whose function it is to feed and clothe it – to the accompaniment of howls for more food and more silk-stockings – can feel as warmly as they should towards it. And the people who best sell and potboil for it feel much the same. The pressman studies with entire detachment his paper's clients, whom he baits with titbits of highly-flavoured news. And now, since the shortages in consumer goods and foodstuffs, there is yet another division of our society, namely that between shopman and customer. In England the queueing herds of shoppers, receiving their tiny ration or being fleeced for some absurdly over-valued article of household necessity, or illfitting preposterously priced garment, do not inspire respect, and certainly do not receive it. I speak particularly of the English scene and Europe generally.

There are, when you come to think of it, great numbers of people almost obliged to feel little respect for man in the mass: respect for what I have called – not out of disrespect but as a means of obliging the reader to focus the situation in all its horrible bleakness – the million-headed Baby.

It is impossible, Renan believed, *d'aimer 'le peuple' tel qu'il est* – to love the people the way they are. They have first to be trained. But training has not been forthcoming for the one class, and has been taken away from the other – for the professional classes once shared in the cultivation of their rulers. Rather than cure the great big Baby, 'the Public', as is done with children, of its worse habits, it has deliberately confirmed it in them. And just now its stocks are lower than at any period since its birth – lip service notwithstanding. The puny minority of creative men too, let me repeat, enjoy less consideration than at any former time. How identical are the destinies of these two categories of men, separated seemingly by an abyss.

V. THE THICKENING TWILIGHT OF THE ARTS

Had Milton or Voltaire been born in Carthage, they would never have given literary expression to their thoughts. Only the State spoke there. It did not speak of social justice, either, or of the sanctity of the human soul. No one had ever heard of the individual in the city of Hannibal. And this would apply of course to Tartary and Turkestan, and many other places.

A 'public' is a feature of Graeco-roman civilization. – But *two* Publics is the beginning of no Public at all.

With my account of the Two Publics – not a parable but a fact – I have explained the great fundamental handicaps with which all creative intelligences in the Twentieth Century are born. It may be compared to a physical disability, lameness or curvature of the spine. It affects them as radically.*

Had Lord Byron been writing *à cœur ouvert* about himself he most likely would have started by speaking of his lameness – and how in spite of it he swam the Hellespont. H. G. Wells (seeing that this is England, where there are things worse than a hump or a club-foot) would begin with the poverty of his father and mother. With the author of *The Idiot* it would be his epilepsy. – These are first things. So I began by showing you the English writer or artist finding himself restricted to a Public not much larger than that possessed by the research worker, or that existing in the academic field. A botanist's audience is no smaller or more specialized than the author of *The Way of All Flesh* secured, or *Dubliners*, or an early Lawrence.

If a writer complains of this situation, the retort is as follows: 'If you say your Public is unrepresentative and small, write books

* The troubles of the man of science take a rather different form, and with them I leave it to someone better qualified than I am to deal.

like Daphne du Maurier and you will have a Public as representative as that of Dante.' If it is a painter, here is what is said: 'Paint pictures like Brockhurst and you will have a Public as wide and representative as Titian's.' – All this is something not of our making: our will is not engaged. I wanted to begin by getting down the things that are as remote from the individual volition as being English or being such and such a height in your 'stocking-feet'. The Public influences everything: Joyce's *Finnigan's Wake* was conditioned by it, or the pictures of Paul Klee.

The two artists I happen to have mentioned suggest a postscript to what I have been saying regarding the two Publics. The first named is a specialist's book, the second are a specialist's pictures. Neither has any organs for the outer atmosphere of the market-place, or where 'the brute male force of the wicked world which marries and is given in marriage' has its being. Both inhabit the thickening twilight of the arts, both are creatures adapted to that twilight: or call it if you like an interior or a subterranean world. For specialists in literature and painting they exist for no one else, except students who hear them lectured about by highbrow professors, and a few dozen curious minds here and there. Yet is one to pretend that the audience that rocked and wept in the Attic Theatres in response to works by Aristophanes or Aeschylus were in the presence of an inferior truth: and is a work of art more profound because its meaning is mysteriously wrapped up in however dexterously packed a verbiage?

There are many intellectuals who say that the artist should inhabit the same world as the saints, or at least one as secluded from 'the brute male' extroversions of the human average. It is but another case – although they would not admit it – of shyness of the 'common man', of the market-place. For these the Two Publics arrangement does not seem amiss. They might perhaps say that what I am describing as a 'reservation' would be justified if only because it enabled the cultivation of such esoteric beauties, in the half-lit antechambers of the Unconscious, as those produced by Joyce in the last phases of his life, or those for which the precious and exquisite *petit-maître* of the Bauhaus was responsible.

Enjoying as I do this kind of work (being a specialist), I am as alive as any pundit to the fact that this exclusive 'highbrow' workshop, catering for a small Public, has something remarkable to show for itself. Out of its very limitations and frustrations, it has created something. Its little dark and stony desert has flowered. Like a prison-art or the introspection of the recluse, or the strange genius of the demented, it will survive in some form, as an integral part of our cultural expression. Some people would treat it as a permanent institution; and why not?

These considerations, however, in no way cause me to qualify my indictment of the Two Publics. The Russians are correct when (for their own purposes) they condemn the art of the *avant-garde* in Western countries – 'unrealistic, romantic and mystical' – for its 'separation from the people'. But it should be recognized that the 'people' here has been degraded by commercial standards, or lower down, by its relegation to the status of a beast of burden; and indeed that the artist has been, in the manner described above, *kept away* from them.

Art of the first order must be lost in this cul-de-sac. A whole society, not an unrepresentative fragment, is demanded by great gifts of speech and great interest in public affairs such as Dante or Milton possessed, for instance. The public stage, with live actors – in contrast to the private Mystery, staged in a rich patron's cellar, for an audience of cognoscenti of shadow pictures of an obscure emotional underworld – is what now stands empty. With his architectonic appetites, requiring air-filled spaces, for Buonarotti there would be no place today, nor would there be for most of the so-called 'great masters' of the past.

The artist has not 'escaped', or 'fled from', the outer world of men in general, he has been *driven* from it. There the philistine business-man and his satellites have it all to themselves. A materialism such as Rome at its worst never knew has invaded everything: we only speak of 'culture', as of religion, when engaged in a world-war now: and then it is only the bureaucrats brought into being to promote 'culture' who get anything out of it, not the artist.

Before leaving the subject of the Two Publics I should like to say something with reference to life within the small highbrow compound, or, better, Reservation; more especially that part of it inhabited by the painters. Traditionally impecunious, it exercises a fatal attraction of a social order for moneyed outsiders. Then it offers an excuse of idleness and temperamental behaviour too. All of which represents a most unwelcome complication for more serious artists.

We artists do rather live like an Indian tribe, the relics of another civilization, in a Reservation. Rich visitors can come among us: they are initiated into the tribal mysteries, becoming 'bloodbrothers' – just the way it happens with the Indians of Taos, or some other dusty centre of exotic tourism.

The Indians, you will recall, from what you have read of such resorts, begin to turn out art-objects for sale to these seasonal intruders. When they do that naturally the work so produced loses greatly in artistic value. So long as a totemic object is carved or painted in response to the demands of a tribal cult, it has the power inherent in all belief. Producing it for sale to tourists – or to 'bloodbrothers' who had bought their way in – is another matter. And so it is with the 'Highbrow' tribe.

It has always been my feeling that these patrons are a curse. I have not concealed my feelings, much to the rage of the patrons. These people intrigue, too, and interfere in tribal affairs. – As if without such extra irritations it were not bad enough being little better than a motheaten Indian, and living in the equivalent of an Indian Reservation!

But the choice of this 'romantic' imagery, for some readers perhaps, clothes with a misleading glamour what is in fact very squalid. The patron now is apt to live – as a privileged member of that small impecunious society – among his protégés. As may be conceived, in a calling so depressed and impoverished, he exercises much power. Quite small sums of money, expended in the purchase of pictures, have an action like dynamite. Even, in certain cases, the rich intruder becomes a sort of dictator, which is not only undemocratic but undesirable for many reasons.

The indulgence of these instincts, on the part of a wealthy dilettante, might be beneficial if it were not for the fact that, unlike the dealer, his social preferences enter into it. As a rule these direct him, as do his other tastes, to what is second-rate, and to a lavish advertisement of what is not very good. The introduction of the less exacting values of the potboiling world outside may accompany such a régime: in Anglo-saxon countries this always is the danger.

Since, as I have said, he *lives* with those he supports, our Mæcenas is repelled by personality, and attracted by the lack of it. So rebarbative a genius as Cézanne, or so uncomfortably intense a one as Van Gogh, or so arrogant a master as Whistler, would not make the ideally subservient dinner-guest. So, in such a little world, the handicap upon any over the light-weight class is formidable.

Renaissance patrons, who are the models generally for ours, were more robust. But what is involved is completely different. That was a great public matter, this a small private one. The patrons of other centuries were popes and princes, whose patronage altered the whole appearance of the world they lived in. Ours are small-time collectors.

Another troublesome feature is the hundreds of idle people who are drifting around, with or without money. Displaced persons, in truth, who find it convenient to live with the artists. They have swollen to unnatural proportions the ranks of Bohemia. The fact that during the last decades this has come to be recognized as normal does not make it any better. It has again to be put on record to complete the picture here.

It is not yet quite a 'World Without Art': but Art is flickering out among these unrealities. A small body of people are still attempting to produce fine art and good literature; but it is impossible to exaggerate the difficulties. The artistic impulse, with no outlet in the public life of the community, has been consigned to what is, as I have called it, nothing but a Reservation: not of Indians still supplicating ancestral divinities, but of writers and other artists persisting in their devotions – very substantial sacrifices demanded of them, with terrible consequences if withheld – as under happier circumstances commanded the devotion of those who are now our 'classics', the great humane intelligences of the past.

Part 4

Travel

Filibusters in Barbary 1932

In flight from what he termed 'our dying European Society', Lewis paid a visit to Morocco in the summer of 1931. The result was a book of considerable merit, as anyone who had occasion to visit that country during the colonial epoch will confirm. With his capacity for extracting from a new experience everything on which his mind could fasten, he exchanged years of sedentary toil for what was to prove in itself something of a filibuster exploit.

Travel books tend towards one of two extremes: the over-impressionistic and the over-scholarly. The one is all atmosphere; the other is all fact and gloss. In Filibusters in Barbary, *Lewis successfully steered a middle course.*

Owing to certain remarks on a compatriot, a writ was served and the book had to be withdrawn. (This brought to three the number of Lewis's books which foundered before and after publication: Filibusters in Barbary, The Doom of Youth *and* The Roaring Queen, *a novel which did not progress beyond page-proof.) The scarcity of* Filibusters in Barbary *more than justifies the salvaging of two extracts. The first is an account of Casablanca, and the second is a description, spiced with comment in the 'field worker' vein, of a visit to the* Bled *of a French film troupe.*

Lewis once informed the Editor that he intended to write an illustrated book on Moroccan castles. *Unfortunately, the project was never realized.*

PART I

XII. CASA

Casablanca is a huge marine outpost of Europe. It is the last city of the coast to have a railway this side of Senegal – beyond it, travelling south, you must go by car. It is the Queen of the Atlantic for the *Vieux Morocain*, it is *Casa la Blanche* – or so its corps of journalists invariably refer to it. It is a hell of a stink-fein city in fact, and deserves more than a passing mention. Casablanca was the first town of the French Protectorate: the moroccan conquest started there. As it appears today, it is pointed to as the city Lyautey built – it is the last place he saw when he left Morocco for good in the *Anfa* – it is 'the pearl of the French Renaissance', emblematic of the precarious post-war power of France. It is perhaps the place that holds the secret of the destiny of this astonishing latter-day colonial conquest.

The history of Casablanca, or Dar el Beida, is not important. It is an ancient settlement, for some reason – the *Anfa* of the Phoenicians; though why it is difficult to see, since it is the world's worst natural harbour, with nothing to distinguish it from any other point of unidentified coastline south of Rabat. It is cursed with an abnormal surf: it has an abordage calculated to prejudice any mariner against it.[1]

A *Vieux Marocain* – which means a 'colon' of a dozen years standing – told me that when being a small boy he landed at Casablanca for the first time (in 1914, I think) he and his parents, sisters and brothers, were carried ashore through the breakers on the backs of boatmen. And today at Safi ships are loaded in the same manner: chains of men, standing up to their waists in the surf, pass from hand to hand the cargoes coming in or going out, which are then rowed in open boats to the anchored ship.

The Casablanca, or Dar el Beida, of 1870 is described by Dr Leared[2] as 'the dirtiest, most tumble-down place ever seen'. A still more emphatic observer, writing in 1889, describes it as follows:

> Casablanca occupies a flat low-lying piece of ground close to the sea; the houses have not a single feature worth remarking; the principal

---

[1] A paragraph with a long quotation omitted.
[2] Author of *Morocco and the Moors*.

street is a running sewer of filth . . . the people are more ugly and dirty, the donkeys worse treated and more mangy, the dogs more numerous and repulsive, and the beggars in greater numbers and decidedly more importunate and loathsome, than in any of the other places we had yet seen. (Thompson.)

At that time it was a township of 4,000 inhabitants, surrounded by walls of *tabia*, or mud concrete, twenty feet high, well supplied with water, but often visited with cholera and plague – the former killing as many as a dozen Jews a day. Owing to the uncomfortable harbour-bar at the mouth of the river upon which Rabat stands, a good deal of the export trade of Rabat – wool, carpets and wax – was shipped from Casablanca.

There is one respect in which the Dar el Beida of 1870 is reminiscent of the *Casa la Blanche* of today, and that is in the prevalence of the dwellings of an auxiliary population of nomads. Thus Dr Leared writes: 'There are also many waste spaces. Of these not a few are covered with reed huts, in bad repair, in which, when we saw them, many Arabs, wretchedly poor, were encamped.' These *encampements* of reed huts, or their equivalent, are still everywhere to be met with, wherever there is an open space.

But whereas the physician who visited it in 1870 said of it that 'The worst climate on the african coast could hardly show a higher rate of mortality', it must today possess one of the lowest deathrates in the world, for its climate is in fact excellent, and of course Europe has brought its drains and lavatories with it, all stinks are banished and middens frowned upon.

Dr Leared describes 'an arab village' outside Mazagan, 'made up of conical huts, which resembled the barley-stacks of an english homestead'. These are the *nouala*: but they are black cones of a coarse thatch of sticks or of reeds, and remind the traveller at the first blush much more of equatorial Africa than of Sussex or Kent.

Drawing into the station of Fedhalla, which is a small port between Rabat and Casa, upon the Rabat side, the traveller finds himself in the midst of an enormous *nouala*-village of this sort; and, with its cactus hedges and the naked squalor of its dusky infants, he would not have to be very fanciful to imagine himself in Guinea or the Congo, rather than in a North African nomadtown. Nothing indicates that this is not Fedhalla itself: coming from Fez or Tangier the traveller will have seen nothing of the sort, except here and there (associated with tents) one or two of these thatched cabins: and he certainly could be excused for jumping to the conclusion that either the activities of the Colonial Exhibition had shuffled the African colonies in some manner (was not this perhaps an equatorial village bodily on its way to Paris, which had got left behind, or settled down en route, finding itself too late?) or else that a different race dwelt here – perhaps a stray community of the Harratin, that is, the negritic stocks of the desert or Anti-Atlas?

The black beehive-villages, built in orderly rows, are met everywhere in the south of Maghreb el Aksa: unquestionably they have something to do with the prevalence of negro blood. That a thatch cabin of the order found in the Upper Volta should occur in central Morocco is as natural as that a Zenetic tent should turn up South of Tchad among the Massas.

The Negro shades into the Moor everywhere south of this. The famous white Touaregs even, of the Hoggar, have a delicate measure of negro blood – just enough to put a shadow in the White. The greatest of the Lords of the Atlas (the Glaoui, the M'Tougi) have it more plainly still. Many villages in the Anti-Atlas are already definitely negritic, and all the saharan oases are populated by the Harratin, a negroid race (descendants perhaps of the most ancient people in the Sahara, the peculiar Blacks whose last retreat is Tibesti).

No bones are made about this inky blood. The Sultans, and the great cherifian families (their descent from the Prophet notwithstanding) all sport it without a thought. They have been visibly blackened with the blood of slaves – for this there is no help, in a society run upon the basis of the use of the Black *Untermensch* to do the hard manual work: and it has never occurred to anyone to call his neighbour 'nigger' (in the way that one *rasta* will say of another 'Es Indio!') for the excellent reason that in their vocabularies there is no such word. In the Berber and Arab tongues of Morocco there is no word expressing in any way what we mean by Negro. Apparently the shading-off has been so effectively *nuancé* that no such idea as that of a White and a Black, starkly contrasted, has ever presented itself to a Moor or Berber. They must surely have noticed the enormous ethical difference between a 'buck-nigger' and a typical Berber. But if so they have been so little preoccupied with it as to find it unnecessary to make a new word for the phenomenon. — Indeed in the plain of Marrakech ('the Plain of Morocco' for the men of the last century) and the valley of the Sous, the Soudan is already there — already you have entered the Saharan World of the great steppes and deserts between the Noun or Tafilalelt and the Niger.

In contradistinction to all this, however, the Soudanese are conscious of *Whiteness*, as a thing differing from the Soudanese norm. They have their words to indicate a person upon the other side of the Colour Line — not necessarily a European. A Berber for them would come under that head (unless, it is assumed, particularly negritic).

The *Nouala* (or *Kabbousah* — 'caboose') is technically a cylindrical mud hut, with a conical thatch roof. Often the roof extends to the ground: then it is a ten-feet-high or more, dark conical dwelling, made of branches and sticks, secured at intervals with hoops of the same material.

This *nouala*-town, which you see from the train, is, however, not Fedhalla, which lies out of sight of the station. It is merely an important nomad or semi-nomad settlement composed of many hundreds of families, come there to work, They come from anywhere, they are always moving around: it is the works going on in the port, or the fish factories, that attract them. First they pitch their tents. It is the low-slung black roof of coarse home-spun cloth, made of camel and goat hair, palmetto and other vegetable fibre — high enough for squatting but not standing — that you see all over Maghreb. Next they prowl round and smell out the work and the money. If it is all right, they build a *nouala*. Others build *noualas*. If hundreds of hands are wanted, soon there is a Caboose-city. If these sources of employment fail or slack off, or if they get tired of the place, they abandon the *nouala* (or course without the slightest hesitation — no one would regret a dark insanitary *caboose*): they load their ass and move on to any point of the compass they fancy. Then the same thing happens again.

These people come under the head of semi-nomad, I expect. They are of the same nomadic category as the *transhumant* — those who alternate between pastoral tent-dwelling, and highland village life.

The Berber is a foot-nomad. The Berber is a matchless walker. Mr Cunningham Graham scoffs at this born foot-slogger, comparing him unfavourably with the Arab (whom he pictures as always mounted upon a priceless and high-spirited steed). But I think it is a great pleasure to watch these romantic athletes, in Indian file, undoubtedly setting up, daily, desert records.

They should be trained for Marathons. They cover prodigious distances, it is said. It is nothing for a family, starting in the Sous, to go and do some harvesting in Tunis. Their brains are like those of animals, they photograph the desert landmarks; doubtless they know too, the smells, and the characteristic geology of the soil – that must be their embossed map, which they feel with their feet, since they all go barefoot. Flint and broken glass means no more to a Berber (especially 'transhumant') than to a good solid shoe. (The feet of dead Berbers should be utilized for shoe-leather.)

Everywhere, throughout the thousand miles from Oran to Casa, groups of nouala, or most often the low, dark brown, nomadic tent, are met with incessantly. It is a chain of encampments – or strings of wandering families, pressing forward, in indian file, with loaded asses.

Wherever there are mines, or farms, there are groups of tents, and occasionally rough *cabooses*. And, in this country where the day labourer is a nomad, who pitches his tent against the field or mine he is to work in, the question that presents itself to the statistician is no doubt whether these people are 'transhumant', 'nomads', or on the other hand, uprooted 'sedentaries', in search of work. No one I suppose can quite say, in such a fluid life. The 'sedentary' is always apt, upon the slightest provocation, to become a 'transhumant'. And the 'transhumant' is more than likely to develop into a nomad. So what is the ratio of nomadism, what of settlement, must remain uncertain.

In Casablanca, for instance, there is a vast settlement that the French have named 'Bidonville'. It is a city within the city, in fact. It consists of small huts mainly composed of petrol-tins. 'Petrol-tin Town' (a blemish in *Casa la Blanche*) is again a mushroom settlement of nomads, attracted by the dollars to be picked up in this Babylon of the Nazarene half-finished. Thousands of these petrol-tin dwellings already exist, day by day they are added to: they have streets and squares.

Bidonville is quite 'sedentary'. It lies in a hollow. Above its tower the dazzling white palaces of the *Quartier Reservé* – which could be called 'Brothel-Town' or, to make a joke to show you the idea,

'Strumpetville'. Let us call it 'Strumpetville' to match 'Bidonville'.

By the 'Petrol-tin Town', or 'Bidonville', of Casablanca, one is irresistibly reminded of another excrescence of the same sort, recently described in english newspapers, namely the sub-city, or shack-town growing up outside Chicago. *Capitalism and Barbary breed the same forms* – but how odd! The world slump that hit America with the velocity of a tornado, strewed out on to the streets millions of decent people, not necessarily passionately nomad. So many have gone to live in the 'Bidonville' of Chicago, we are told: they are sardonic, they name the principal boulevards of their Hobo-city 'Prosperity Avenue' or 'War-debt Drive'. Their hovels are numbered, like the dwellings of any other town; they have their letters addressed to, say,

Mr So-and-So,
No. 486 Hoover Road.

So the enthusiastic Frenchmen, who point to Casablanca as 'the pearl of the French Renaissance', and emphasize that it is a great city upon the latest transatlantic model, could even, if they wished, adduce the existence of Bidonville, to make the flattering comparison even more apposite! It is a parallelism which is, however, in no way dishonourable for the French, for *their* 'Hobo-town' is the creation of born nomads, who are, by choice, the inhabitants of a tent or a caboose. No capitalist laws could drive them out of these hovels. It is different in the case of *War-debt Drive*, in the Hobo-town upon the shores of Lake Michigan. *There* our White stock is being forced down into a semi-savage sub-world of the down-and-out, or Untermensch. It is being thrown back into Barbary – not invited to issue out of Barbary into the advantageous plane of the civilized european life.

Strumpetville is of course another matter. Both 'Bidonville' and 'Strumpetville' are typical of Casablanca, itself a mushroom city. When I described the houses of its *Quartier Reservé* as palaces, I was not dealing in hyperbole. I do not suppose that any *Quartier Reservé* on earth is so sumptuous. With its own shops, gardens and so forth, it is situated, by some irony, cheek by jowl, with 'Bidonville'. Yet considering the two together – the cloud-capped towers and gorgeous palaces of the one, and the kennel constructed of petrol-tins (looking like a savage congeries of small barbaric shields) of the other, it is difficult to decide which in fact looks the more impermanent.

Casablanca itself is an enormous whitewashed fungus-town. Fifteen or twenty years ago it did not exist. One of its old-established hotels – its premier-hotel, a place about the size of the Strand Palace – the *Excelsior*, a decade or so ago was not there. The *Excelsior* was built upon the bed of a river. This may have been the river that turned the wheel of the little flour-mill in the days of Dr Leared. The river was in a ravine, and all 'ravines' in Moroccan cities are shoots for refuse. So it was built, also, no doubt, upon a refuse heap. There is a pump in the basement of the hotel: every day they have to go down and pump it out. Not many London hotels provide as good a dinner as the *Excelsior* table d'hôte: there is a first-rate American Bar, lounges, great and small. Upstairs, in the passages, as full of incense as a Caid's palace (as a result of the cigarettes of guests thrown into the escupidors or ash-trays filled with sawdust, igniting the aromatic cedar wood), storey above storey, are luxurious bedrooms with bath, douche, etc. As a hotel it is in every way more 'modern' than most London or Berlin hotels, beneath the Ritz class. But in the basement the water of the *oued* is flowing, and it has to be pumped out daily, else, presumably, this Grand Babylon would tumble down, or the subterreanean waters would rise and submerge the guests and their Porto Flips in the American Bar.

Casablanca is a city upon the american model then. It is semi-skyscraping, 'Block'-built, as modern as modern. An impression of kaleidoscopic unreality of the same order as that that disengages from the 'canyons' of Manhattan, assails you as you enter it for the first time, a passenger from Europe (all allowances made for the inferior importance of this french colonial fungus, as against the staggering impressiveness of the externals of New York, seen from a Cunarder's decks in the early night by a London visitor). From both emanate the same unmistakable sensations of violent impermanence. But in Casa it is in some ways more striking, since the civilization it apes, namely the Mediterranean, is traditional, whereas the american is frankly upstart – it is the uprush of a New World. The 'forcing' operation whereby Casa has suddenly come to be, is, upon all hands, starkly apparent. Its shell, the dazzling balanced plaster walls, what are they, the suspicious traveller asks, but a gigantic architectural confectionery? Tap them, they must be hollow, or filled with *marsh mallow* – certainly of a mushroom flimsiness, porous rag-pulp or paper-mulberry-heated. In fact no one has been there long enough to saturate any cubic foot of it with his presence. There is no personality in its hasty palaces: this densely-peopled city might still be empty, for all the human aura with which it is charged. Organically it is a hoax: here is not an organism, but a preposterous assemblage of discrete and self-sufficing cells, which would collapse at a touch, administered with force enough, almost anywhere.

All its inhabitants, too, are a huge scratch population, blown together by a big newspaper puff from the four ends of the earth, gold-diggers in posh city-quarters, ten-a-penny filibusters in plaster palaces: the 'big noises' in this mushroom metropolis are adventurers of a decade's standing at the longest – not like the old and crusted harpies of Tangiers and Tunis: the biggest 'men of substance' here, you feel, would, anywhere else, be straw-magnates, with big question-marks against their names. So this half-caste, ex-legionary citizenry, is, again, racially unreal. Its cohesion, such as it is, is its tongue, which is kitchen-french, little more (and even that will shortly grow to be a mere *saber*, full of German and Berber). What is it doing there all of a sudden then, *Casa la Blanche*, in the midst of an ancient piratic empire – pretending to be a european 'conqueror' – with all the white, impressive power it has brought together, or that has been brought together for it (that is nearer the mark, I think!). Will it not all as suddenly disrupt, escape perhaps with the hiss of a puncture, one fine night – one of the Thousand and One Nights of arabian phantasy! Meanwhile the pseudo-Paleface is far outnumbered by the dark faces come out of the *Bled*: Casa is swarming with nomads, just as half its *soi-distant* permanent population are nomads of some kind as well: it was built by nomads: perhaps it will be destroyed by nomads!

PART II

II. FILM-FILIBUSTERS

Before going south of the Atlas into 'the mysterious' Sous – a land so pregnant with plots and so overrun with lawless outsiders as to

TRAVEL

make a mere tourist's hair stand on end – before rushing for four hundred miles up and down the sides of mountains in a mighty bus, and at last dropping with a dull roar into the ocean valley of Santa Cruz de Cap d'Ager, the very home-soil and breeding ground of the essential Filibuster (whose filibustering is the principal industry of the place), I will give some account of an important Filibuster met with farther north – not in the Sous – namely the Film-Filibuster. I fell in with a huge caravan of them at Fez. And then (in more aristocratic surroundings and in a much grander form – juvenile-lead and magnate rolled into one) at Marrakech.

But if I take it upon myself to refer to the Film-pro or screen-king as a 'Filibuster', it must be understood that I am casting no reflection upon his rectitude. At least, the ramp is elsewhere. The gulls are in the distant theatres, in such centres of civilization as Chicago or Glasgow, much more than among the natives of Barbary – among whom the Ufa and Pathé magnates send their troupes (not troops) merely to afford their sham-sheiks a hispano-mauresque photographic setting. The whispering masses in the Film-palaces – it is for them that this description of filibuster filibusts – throwing up shoddy mirages, with his photographic sausage-machine of the desert-life – so falsely selected as to astonish into suspicion sometimes even the tamest Robot. As to the filmable populations – true, this mechanical Vandal degrades them as he does everything he touches, but for the rest he puts many a lightly-earned *peseta* in their pockets, and is a pure benefactor as far as that goes. And as to the Italian hotels of Barbary, it is difficult to see what they would do at all if it were not for those truck-loads of queer fish brought from Paris and quartered on them by the gross. The touring film-rabble make up for the absent tourist – the latter a rarer bird every minute, with every fresh oscillation of the world's Exchanges and every fresh currency ramp or tariff wall.

At Fez, the *Hotel Transatlantic* was closed – it is open only for a few months in the cool season. Similarly all over Morocco these huge hotels were shut down – they are the 'follies', as in other days they would have been called, of a Steamship Company, I believe. The *Grand Hotel*, that, when I arrived, was open, but it was very large and it languished – it had been conceived to meet the booming requirements of a 'Renaissance Marocaine' which has not materialized, and for a volume of sightseers and filibusters far in excess of what can now ever again be expected. The enormous dining-room adjoining the café, with its numerous staff of white-jacketed Algerian waiters, its Italian managers, was perhaps a quarter full upon the first evening. Then upon the second day the train came in with all its compartments packed with a super sheik-film company. Its fifty-odd personnel poured in for lunch, and immediately the winter of our discontent was turned, at one blow, into glorious summer. These fifty dumb characters in search of an author dumb enough to concoct a plot and text for them (accompanied by the sharp-shooters of the mechanical staff) swarmed forward, vociferous and replete with a strident reality that was so thin as to stamp them anywhere as screen-folk – creatures, that is, at one remove from the shadow picture. With all the prestige of this idiotic industry (as practised in our Western savagery) they gave the hotel-staff something to live for, and a scene of great animation was the result.

They swung (if of the Mix-class) – danced, shuffled, dashed, sidled, stalked or tottered in, each according to his kind: noticeably *two-by-two* (as if picked out into sex-pairs by an official Cupid) like the animals entering the Ark – for of course each of these Stars, however impotent a one-candle-power washout (even according to Box-office canons) must, off the Screen, move in a triangle of bloodshot adultery – to satisfy the business-end of the racket – in order to suggest the bombardment of an anguished fan-mail (if to no one else, to their fellow-actors). Only one or two dared to be solitary for however brief a time.

This company had come to Fez to enact a rather elaborate arabesque of kiss-stuff, crime and contraband of arms, to be called 'The Three Unlucky Travellers'. My informant was a half-caste waiter – pock-marked and with the scars of several other epidemics as well to underline his attractions. But he felt himself nearer to the great dynamic heart of the universe than ever before with these people – he told me that he had been remarked at once by the Filmboss. At sight he had been engaged for a minor part. What part? Oh, that of a blind mendicant, not an important part! They had *wanted* him to take a more important part, but he hadn't time. He wished in a way he had! They had asked him to go away with them. Yes, they desired him to become one of them. But he did not see his way to do that. He could not be spared just then, so must remain at Fez. At that moment one of the Three Unlucky Travellers (the polish one, the least lucky of the lot) clapped his hands impatiently in our direction, and shouted for a straw for his ice-water. When the waiter returned to me (after watching for some minutes the Star make use of the straw) he informed me that the one he had just obliged – who had just asked him to help him about a straw – was the first of the three to fall a victim to the spells of the magician's daughter (who was the leading lady) and to fall over a cliff. The cliff as it happened (by this time everything was ship-shape – Fez had been ransacked scenically), was the other side of the Medina. It was a very big rocky lump, which the Fési has accounted for by attaching it to a local legend – it is supposed to be the colossal detritus of an indignant divinity, who was disgusted with the people of Fez, and took this rather objectionable way of showing it.

The Unlucky Traveller, Number One, was French, as was right and proper in a parisian film. His were the almost matchlessly empty histrionic blend of attractions of the french Music Hall – those throaty troubadours of the Third Republic who mouth with a mealy sweetness the songs that are hawked in broadsheets afterwards by tenoro-guitarists in the provinces. Only I had been accustomed always to see that figure in a *tuxedo*. Therefore at first I was somewhat puzzled, for he considered an Aertex vest and canvas slacks sufficient clothing even for dinner in these sporting tropics, and in that form he was at once terribly familiar and yet absolutely strange. Of course in that way his athletic proportions stood revealed, but they were pallid (as one would suppose the city songster's to be in spite of his cavemanly cawing and basso-profundo cooing). He looked in fact not unlike those half-naked bakers who occasionally emerge in pastry cooks' at the times the hot cottage loaves are brought up from the subterranean ovens.

When this clumsy Hearty, the first juvenile-lead, entered the restaurant, he *swung* himself over to his place at table, as if in the atmosphere a system of massive ropes had been secreted – his torso, which was flat but very wide, swung in one direction, his arms (which were a clerk's and not a blacksmith's – but large-boned at least, if innocent of muscle), swung in the other direction. And he remained at all times a Man-of-the-hour, although he would not be 'released' for a twelve-month. If he went over to the kiosk, which stood in front of the hotel, to buy a newspaper or packet of cigarettes, he inflated his chest beneath the proud fabric of the

Aertex beforehand – *then* he started: he swung across the road, again as if ropes upon either side of him, suspended in a fluid medium, led direct from café to kiosk. 'Unfortunate Traveller' for six weeks (the troupe was to remain there for at least as long as that, they said), he was a most melancholy gymnast, his existence a footlight one, overshadowed by an epic struggle on the other side of the Medina – on the Tarpeian Rock, then out in the pitiless *bled* with a bloodthirsty Sheik – never off-duty, compelled to remain stripped (to his Aertex) for the fray, by the etiquette of his profession. Did the poor chap ever relax? Did he in his bedroom relax, and become the clumsy, slouching clerk of his early youth once more – or did he sleep bolt upright, even in his sleep an 'Unlucky Traveller', with his chest stuck out three inches beyond the norm of its recumbent silhouette?

These simple universal problems (for the onlooker) are provided in common by all those who live by impersonating 'unlucky' characters, cast for abnormal episodes, of great physical violence. But it occurred to me as I watched these film cattle, that the stage actor, the backgrounds for whose work are the scenes of everyday, though they have much in common, must differ very widely in important particulars. The stage actor, for instance could at all times be spotted out of the theatre, in his non-public life. Likewise the film-actor, but less so. For on the whole with the latter the actorishness must be of a more insidious sort. His artificiality has to be more intense, since the demands of the *real* everyday background are more exacting. In his professional displays the Screen-worker in the nature of things is the last word in *naturalism* at the opposite pole to a formal art. His actorishness therefore (the stigmata of the trade of Makebelieve stamped into his features and attitudes) must be rather a distortion of a very common-or-garden norm, rather than the reflections of a transcendent, an abnormal, existence. The Film-man will tend to be a very intense, very slightly heightened Everyman: whereas the Garricks and Irvings would carry about with them in private the impress of successions of great Individuals of the Imagination – separated by all the arts of the formal stage-play from that everyday nature of Everyman, which is the particular province of Film-photography.

The huge company that came to the Cherifian capital to reproduce the great dime-drama of the *Three Unlucky Travellers*, was polyglot. One of the luckless heroes was a German, but there was every nationality represented, even English. The spectacle of this cosmopolitan social organism taking shape beneath one's eyes was a mild diversion. They arrived as a mere chaos of personalities, upon the scene of the *Grand Hotel*. But at the end of three or four days they had separated out into well-defined classes. The Leading Parts (irrespective of nationality, age, salary, or looks) sat at a smaller table. This became a sort of High Table. There was a second table for those not quite so eminent. But from this second table people were occasionally promoted to the first. This was usually as a consequence of successful love-passages with a male or female of the first rank. This necessarily brought them into the charmed circle of Stars (if the love-passages lasted above twenty-four hours, that is). But upon the first day of one of these adventures the couple involved in the new intrigue would separate on arrival in the restaurant, and would go to their respective tables, according to class. Sometimes after a day or two at the High Table, a Second-Classer would have to return to Table Number Two, upon being superseded in the affections of the Star in question. There was therefore a constant going and coming. It was an evolutionary pattern, supervised by Cupid, the *motif* divorce, of course.

After four or five days a new phenomenon was to be remarked. A pair of important Stars would roughly break away from the central tables, and go off into a corner by themselves – to a table à deux. At the end of the sixth or seventh day most were back again where they had started, in their original groupment. Others had, meanwhile, broken away, and were to be seen with their heads together alone at a table, even perhaps going so far as to order a half-bottle of rather better wine (say two francs worth of Sauterne) than was supplied gratis with each meal.

As two would come in – and, instead of going to their usual seats, according to class, at a common board, were observed to pass down the room and establish themselves in a distant spot – all the other tables would be in a fulsome momentary ferment – people would turn round and point, chatter and signal from one table to the other. In short, the attitude of all these people to their own actions – of 'passionate' couplement and precipitate divorce, and then new couplement and further violent separation – was exactly the same as though they had been a crowd of *fans*, instead of a crowd of pros.

They acted the *fan* for each other! Their shop was as much, or a great deal more, *publicity*, than it was the art of acting, that goes without saying. The good-looker, not the good actor, would become the Star. It may be regarded as certain that each morning a *fan-mail* would come up with the principal's breakfast. It would be composed and dispatched over-night by lesser members of the flattersome company. And from the camera such attentions would come particularly well no doubt. All day long the individuals of this herd were showing off to each other, attempting to convince the rest that they were 'coming' Stars, or if already by way of being Stars, that *this* show would give them a place in the centre of the world-spotlight, with semi-Garbo-like laurels – or recall the days of Valentino, when Stars were Stars indeed.

The quality of the female élite of the company, I regret to say, was exceedingly low according to any standards. They were all undersized, almost like another species, and their intense artificiality took the form of an odd degenerescence. In *forcing* the normal everyday reality, as it were – in compelling it to conform to what was certainly a vulgar average, but a particularly odd variety of the vulgarest commonplace – they suggested the exact opposite of the *heightening* said to characterize the finest art. Theirs was *lowering*: but it was a descent so much *below* the *average* level as to be eccentric and extraordinary. Here were indeed the authentic *depressed* levels of the universe of the *Untermensch*, in all their blatant pretentiousness. Seeing that their departure from the norm was in the direction of a dwarfishness, an eccentricity, an air of impaired health – with the demented self-assertiveness of the *Asphalt*-folk that they of course are, and the demented concentration upon *effect* – an impression (even necessarily) of a *degeneration* – from power, law, dignity, and sense – was conveyed by their presence. It was as if some patently *inferior* – some less healthy, less excellently balanced, less beautiful – some half-mad midget people, were, father to son, Film-pros. In Maghreb all the acrobats come from a particular tribe in the Sous – all the builders and masons come from a particular tribe in the Great Atlas – in the same way all the personnel of this Film-world might come from a certain district – say in Galicia or in Czecho-Slovakia. One could imagine them as a diminutive, phthisic, gutter-people, who had started in gutter-theatricals, prospered, spread over the world (as the —— have done), caricaturing any eccentricity, or imitating any particularly brutal behaviour on the part of the full-grown, 'normal', master people by whom they were surrounded – falling in and out of love, to show that they were *real* and not just puppets, and even taking their desperate pretence of reality so far at times as to blow their papier-maché brains out – a small vampire, or vampish, kohl-lidded, heterosexed clan, an important subdivision of the Untermensch, selecting for their imitations for preference Crime – some specializing in gangster parts, some in coke-addict parts, some in lesbian rôles – some partial to blackmail, some to arson, some sticking to 'straight' Murder-Club stuff, some having patent side-lines of fancy homicide – but all violent – all guaranteed to be intelligible to the least talented, to the most adenoid-stifled gutter infant, or to the lowest average level of City-serfdom – always the crudest Box-office 'appealed' to – everything imitated by them to be violent *de rigueur*. So, restless and keyed up to jazz-concert-pitch, this swarm moved about the hotel: to overhear a dialogue in the elevator was to be let into a secret of the heart of a Star. At the mere presence beside them of a stranger (a potential *fan*) they began talking feverishly so that you should feel that when they passed out of sight a pistol would be fired – a pipe of opium resorted to – an illegal operation consummated – or (at the mildest and meekest) a fruity adultery be instantly forthcoming. This *atmosphere of climax* in this great hotel became somewhat oppressive at last. It blotted out the Arabs finally, and made the Berber a little dim – I was, of course, grateful for the eclipse of the hispano-mauresque Babs and Minarets, Medersas and Mosques! They certainly cast a spell over the 'capital of the Islamic World', as the Sultan's good town of Fez is often called. They swarmed everywhere, they whispered in the passages, danced in the café, wrote masses of letters and cards (to languishing *fans*) in the writing-rooms, monopolized the Bars.

The three he-men and their three he-friends were the principal American Bar guests – one in puggaree and pipe, two walking ads. for underwear – and then the three understudies of course to match, though exaggerating the absurdities of their principals – dressed in an inferior quality of men's vests, and with even an inferior quality of skin – though the latter was in fact somewhat of a feat, in the way of subordination!

The younger officers of the Fez garrison mingled on terms of equality and patronage with the Film-folk – not of course sitting at their tables, but occasionally inviting one or two to theirs – or often a Film-man would come up and sit down with them unasked, and they suffered this with a good grace.

I take it that this big Film-troupe was a second-rate french one, dispatched to Fez on the cheap, on a Lunn Tour basis – probably 'done' by the hotel at ten francs per day per head, for six weeks – everything found, the least choice algerian wine thrown in and glad to get rid of it. Trade was at an abnormal ebb – the Economic Blizzard must have emptied every hotel from the Bermudas to Bombay – and this ill-favoured herd certainly filled up the hotel and gave it a spurious air of prosperity.

Part 5

America

America and Cosmic Man 1948 and America, I Presume 1940

Lewis spent a number of years in North America. He first visited the U.S.A. in 1927, and he was resident there for part of the Second World War. Some of the difficulties he encountered during his longer stay were presented movingly and in thinly fictional guise in the novel Self-Condemned (*1955*).

His two works about America, together with the war pamphlet, Anglo-Saxony (*published in Toronto in 1942*), contain some of his best satiro-comedy, his ablest analysis of national character, and his most successful straightforward reporting. It is regrettable, and somewhat surprising, that America and Cosmic Man (*1948*), with its mastery of American history and government, is not better known, as it might form an excellent textbook. It is in fact based on lectures delivered at Assumption College (later University), Ontario. The 'asides' are often admirable: witness the acute pen-picture of Franklin Roosevelt, and the designation of Harry S. Truman as 'Rotarian Caesar'. (*These match the earlier sobriquet of G. K. Chesterton as 'a Toby Jug', and of Gertrude Stein as 'a whale out of water'.*)

Lewis elaborated the view, first outlined in Paleface, *that America was the melting-pot of the future cosmopolis; and although he found much to criticize in that country, he retained for it an overall*

373

admiration. His appraisals and many of his prognostications have been justified, despite the rapid changes in American life.

The extract immediately following consists of the Conclusion to Part I of America and Cosmic Man. This is a valuable piece of writing, not only for its comments upon the underlying ethos of American society, but also for its occasional applicability to countries other than the United States.

The second extract is from America, I Presume (*1940*), Chapter VI. Lewis was in personal difficulties when he wrote this book, but the approach is balanced and direct, and full of acute observation. Despite its fictitious guise, it is included here as being based upon personal experiences.

AMERICA AND COSMIC MAN: PART I

CONCLUSION

As a witch says her prayers backwards, I have moved from that superlative political conjuror, Franklin Roosevelt, back to the alien English 'foundation' of a nation not destined to remain English, in an age that was more remote from the twentieth century than it was from the Rome of Cicero. Endeavouring madly, as at moments he was, to break out into the open – into the universal America of tomorrow, we met Roosevelt first. Going backwards, we at last found ourselves with one of the earliest representatives of reactionary America, hobbling round the tottering boudoirs of the *ancien régime*, inhaling the last fragrance of an epoch in which America had been born.

Atomic or nuclear energy apart – which puts in question everything – the permanent revolution which scientific techniques entail makes our politics look absurd, like an archaic buggy upon an autobahn. What figure we can find to describe our *economic* system I hardly know. An ox-drawn cart making its way up Fifth Avenue will have to serve, though really that is far too snappy a conveyance at all adequately to represent what is meant. Gold is the archsymbol of the barbarous nature of our twentieth-century institutions. All that is not technique stands still. Not only science, but scientific thinking, stops at the doors of our banks, and at the gates of our parliaments.

Human societies are engaged in a perpetual struggle to disengage themselves from a chaos of superannuated laws. The accelerated tempo of mechanical evolution makes things much worse. We suffer from no superstitious attachment to a primitive type of automobile. But it is quite a different matter where government is concerned. A bundle of old statutes, or the medium of exchange hallowed by long use, has us bewitched. There a superstitious fixation makes of our political and economic life one vast 'bottleneck'.

We raise temples, even, like redoubts against change. 'Be sure wherever you see an ancient temple it is the work of error,' Voltaire asserted. And if you look inside and discover a bronze politician instead of a cross-legged idol, enthroned there, you can be no less positive of that. Error he may not have represented at the time, but you may be sure the deified politician does so now.

Revolutions are required, to satisfy the sanitary requirements of our social life. Yesterday's refuse has to be expelled generally with *brio*. It is idiotic, but we have discovered no more practical and orderly method. What should be discarded at brief intervals is allowed to accumulate, because of sloth, greed, or superstition. So the explosions have to be so big they shatter our society.

Could a new body of laws be enacted every week-end, and the old ones thrown out, that would guarantee the efficient functioning of the national body. For a law is after all not a thing of beauty. It is of no more than transitory usefulness. As a rule, it is a mediocre prescription given us by a none too gifted doctor. Obviously the more often we change the laws, and the less superstitious confidence we develop regarding the law-maker, the better for the body politic. In a free society of men competent to govern themselves (assuming such a society to be possible) a politician would not be a person of any great importance. The machinery of justice, civil and criminal, is there functioning daily, without our taking any more notice of those engaged in it than we do of the dustmen who remove the rubbish twice a week. We do not make heroes of those sort of magistrates, nor ideally should we of the politician, or that other kind of magistrate, the Chief Executive himself.

When kings and queens were superseded by politicians, the understanding was that importance of that kind was at an end. The

People became the King, and politicians were the People's servants. The politician's task was supposed to be a quite humble one. Otherwise why not have carried on with the kings and queens, emperors and empresses? So, if you notice that a superstitious veneration is shown for politicians, you may be quite sure that undue power is once more being exercised; is vested in the ruler or rulers. That is, of course, if you believe in the possibility of 'popular sovereignty', and do not regard that as just a beautiful phrase.

In effect we know – however much we may believe in the ultimate possibility of full 'popular sovereignty' – that at present to say that 'men are competent to govern themselves' (see my above proviso) does not agree with the facts.

A law made in a free society by a quite unimportant functionary – a mere politician – would be a day-to-day affair. Our society admittedly does not quite answer the description of free. Nevertheless, with conditions altering all the time, as is the case just now, and with such rapidity, laws require to be overhauled incessantly. This is not subservience to our techniques; the radio, television, the flying machine, and now atomic energy are not easy to ignore. It probably saves time to conform – be 'subservient'. And the most portentous of statutes is only a technique which should be scrapped with as little compunction as we do an obsolete mode of locomotion, or a lighting and heating system.

Yet the stark contradiction remains between more and more rapidly modified conditions of life – vastly multiplied power of production, etc., on the one hand, and the inherited rigidity of law on the other.

Men move into a new country or continent and take their laws with them, as they do their personal belongings. Yet if a man is moving from a very hot country to a very cold one, he provides himself if possible with warmer garments, and *vice versa*, should it be from the subarctic to the subtropic. Not so with laws. They never change until they drop off us in a state of advanced decomposition.

America offered to start with, and still provides in many important particulars, a striking example of these contradictions. It may be recalled that I quoted de Tocqueville, who bestowed much attention upon this subject. He discovered in New England an inherent contradiction: these people quite unconsciously had brought over from England in their baggage a full complement of reactionary laws. The brutal property laws of the English penal code came over side by side with Trial by Jury, the Writ of Habeas Corpus. Good and bad, there was all the bag of tricks by which the English were governed. When they surprised one of their fellow-colonists in the act of stealing a horse, embezzling, or committing bigamy, the lawyer who had come with them was consulted, and naturally went to work on the culprit with the legal tools he was used to handling.

But I will again quote de Tocqueville: 'The . . . religion and the customs of the first immigrants undoubtedly exercised an immense influence on the destiny of their new country. Nevertheless, they could not found a state of things originating solely in themselves: no man can entirely shake off the influence of the past; and the settlers . . . mingled habits and notions derived from their education and the traditions of their country (England) with those habits and notions that were exclusively their own.' With these latter habits and notions, of course, they began to build up a new personality, which eventually emerged as that of the American.

'Laws and customs are frequently to be met with in the United States which contrast strongly with all that surrounds them. These laws seem to be drawn up in a spirit contrary to the prevailing tenor of American legislation; and these customs are no less opposed to the general tone of society.' You will, perhaps, remember that the cause of such anomalies was to be sought, de Tocqueville believed, in the fact that only lawyers knew anything about the law; and it was to their interest 'to maintain them as they are, whether good or bad', simply because these men had, with much expense of time and energy, acquired a knowledge of this particular set of rules, and had no wish to be compelled to acquire a new set.

But if this is the case with law, and with lawyers, so is it also with economy, and with economists: though with these latter a factor is present of a quite different order. Monopolistic interests, with all the great power of which such interests dispose, set their face against any change in an antiquated system which has served their purpose so well, and has so many advantages from their standpoint over a new model.

This fairyland of bank capital and grandiose universal usury, out of which region a dense fog of unreality for ever drifts over into politics, and makes them even more unreal than otherwise they might be, is an arcanum, of the very existence of which the average educated man is ignorant. It is relatively of recent date: for in the eighteenth century you or I would not be paying the monthly tradesman's bill by cheque, for then such things did not exist. The fairyland of Credit had not yet been built.

Only passing reference is being made here to this subject: it throws light upon the puzzling question of the seeming impossibility of bringing back rational standards into politics, so it cannot be left out. If politics came out of the bow-and-arrow stage, obviously economics would have to do so as well – to abandon its golden cave. So many interests, alas, prefer to confine us to a primitive and childish plane, whether in politics, or economics, or even in art. It is preferred that Alice in Wonderland should remain as she is, with her sublime candour unimpaired – rather than that she should grow up into a strong-minded political woman, such as the political hostesses with whom Gouverneur Morris had such difficulties in the Paris of the Revolution: that same Paris that is witnessing today the transfer of the banks from private hands to the guardianship of the State, the French being the first European government to take that obvious and necessary step.

Before very long all nations, such are the portents, will, as did the Reich, divest themselves of the competitive system of so-called 'free enterprise'. (This does not in any sense involve their turning to Communism.) It is no longer of such importance, therefore, to pay special attention to the casual trail where it is found to disappear into the massive portals of a bank.

All that need be said is that the great artificiality of politics, which in these pages I have been endeavouring to describe, is at least equalled, if not outdone, by the artificiality of economics. That is true of England as much as of America, though the United States is now the headquarters of the world of finance. The meaning of Bretton Woods was sufficiently aired in the Press, and the general public must have gained some insight, however slight, into these mysteries.

Is it possible that that inertia, or superstition of which I have been speaking – which results in the political capacity of mankind seeming to be so feeble, compared with its scientific and technological aptitude – is imposed upon the majority? Is there sabotage, in other words, where political techniques are concerned? To answer that question would be very complicated. But we are not obliged to do so here. The 'sense of the State' is, as Professor Laski has said, one of the rarest of attributes; although it might be objected that in a free society – or where people are persuaded they form part of such a society – men tend to take no further notice of the activity of their politicians. They take it for granted they are doing their job to the best of their ability; as political technicians. They trust their lawyer and their plumber, not because they regard lawyers or plumbers as necessarily very trustworthy, but they have not time to acquire those techniques themselves. So with the techniques of statecraft. Perhaps in a 'free society' people have less 'sense of the State' than in an unfree one.

Even if the extent of the political paralysis (the prostration before obsolete formulas, the growing unreality of all ostensible government) may sometimes, in its fatuity, seem deliberate, it is undeniably a true image of mass conservatism and confused thinking.

As to the backwardness of politics, millions of people ruling themselves (in so far as that exists) is an operation of a different order to one man designing an aeroplane, or bombarding the atom in his laboratory. In the nature of things, 'science' is more efficient than politics. We hate the sacrifice of 'popular sovereignty' it involves, the curtailment of liberty: but necessarily a Council of Ten, or a Politburo, or any small group of men controlling a state, work faster and better than where the machinery of power is very much more complex. Whatever the type of government, social engineering has for its material human beings, not steel, aluminium, or wood. It is the view of the democrat that when the statesman begins to compete with the automobile manufacturer, or to treat men as if they were electrons, he has failed. And the sign that a human society was approaching its vital perfection would be the disappearance of government altogether.

Were I to return to this earth five centuries hence, and discovered a country the size of Great Britain ruled by a 'Premier' and half a dozen secretaries, I should know that the 'free society' so often said to be there, was at last in actual being. But its citizens would have to be very differently trained from those composing any national group today. It should be our endeavour to assure the eventual arrival of such an ideal society. But we should never pretend it exists when it does not: for that is the way to postpone its arrival indefinitely and to encourage the exercise of lawless power, as mischievous as hypocritical.

We have seen how the United States was born out of the Whig revolution in England, and the Whigs were men of rank and influence under the Stuarts who availed themselves of that great reservoir of political power in the domain of religion represented by the Sectaries, Non-jurors, Quakers, Brownists and the rest, to overwhelm the kingly power, which power they proposed to transfer to themselves. Swift's account of the Whig Lords – whose clients were the black-garbed hosts who had originally sprung from Wycliffe's Bible, and at last had set up a 'Bible religion' against a 'Church religion' – is very illuminating. They were a much more clever set of Lords than their Tory confrères.

The fidelity of Americans to the Whig formula of defiance of authority has confined the American mind in a conventional mould, though the mould was expanded and adapted to accommodate the bitterness of the Irish immigrant mind, inflamed by that last great injustice, the Potato Famine; a mind for which the name of Cromwell held a very different connotation from what it did for the Puritan. So Rome and Geneva appeared finally clamped into the same formula of 'rebel' religiosity, under a flag that imitated the firmament.

The incubation of America in these revolutionary ferments when the Renaissance and Reformation had refashioned England; and especially the perfervid *fixity* which is such a characteristic of the traditional in America, has tended to freeze Americanism in an unprogressive 'progressiveness'. To start life as a rebel, knowing nothing else than attitudes of defiance and disrespect – perfectly expressed in 'the American at the Court of King Arthur' – the vicious side of which is a kind of wilful vulgarity, and aggressive common-mannishness, is probably not so good as the inductive road, of direct reaction against presumption and abuses of authority.

We must, I think, attribute the rather old-fashioned type of attitude, the sentimental radicalism among Americans, to the fact that their vision has been narrowed down, because of their political pieties, to one set of pictures in the past: a manner of Jack the Giant-killer fairy-tale. For the Puritanism has faded out, but the rather musty rebellion remains. Not in order to weaken impulses to combat injustice naturally, but to render the mind more elastic, some benefit might be derived from a study of an iconoclastic philosopher of the days when America was being born, but who was extremely reactionary where it came to questions of government.

David Hume was a great eighteenth-century philosopher who became also a notable historian. He was as far removed from a Whig as a man may get and still remain on the earth. Everything that made a man a Whig he heartily detested, and the authoritarian principle, of which the Stuarts were such pedantic but ineffectual exponents, recommended itself to his intellect. It was in its support that he turned to history. As he stated so unequivocally: 'I must confess that I shall always incline to their side who draw the bond of allegiance very close.'

(Incidentally, had a Stuart king been there in place of George III, the revolt of the American colonies would have occurred, if anything, earlier.)

The fact that the United States of America was born in Whiggery could not but 'incline' it to the opposite extremity of the political compass to that occupied by David Hume. It must for ever 'incline to their side' who are violently divesting themselves of all authority: to the 'rebel' side, in short. The beauty of Authority (for it has its appeal, not only for Hume, but many intelligent men in every age) is, in the abstract, for the average American something inconceivable. Yet, *in practice*, there is no country in which so authoritarian a type of government has flourished (apart from openly despotic states), and because, in America, kings have been *elective* they have none the less been kings. The 'rebel' fixation of the American has prevented him from seeing that he was ruled in that way, that is all: or that demands upon his allegiance often have been excessive.

We now all of us know – and even many Americans share this knowledge – what students of politics have of course always known, that the problems of 'liberty' and 'authority' are not so simple as they have seemed to the majority in America, and, with less blind emphasis, here in England. Everybody (or perhaps I should say a lot of people) is now aware that the King (traditionally the tyrant, for an American or, more mildly, an Englishman) is not the *only* kind of tyrant in the world. Under Western governments as at present constituted, we still enjoy more liberty than we could be certain of enjoying beneath a single ruler invested with divine right. But the old simple-hearted democratic picture is no longer intact.

It was, for instance, in the course of struggles against the encroachments of the Crown and of personal power, that Englishmen evolved such historic safeguards as Habeas Corpus. So powerful an instrument the Writ of Habeas Corpus has proved, that no mere king or queen would, for three hundred years, have dared to defy it. But we have found that what a king or queen would not have ventured to do, a 'people's government' has never thought twice about doing, in years of 'national emergency' – namely, when indulging in the 'sport of kings', or when against their will obliged to engage in it.

In the atmosphere of messianic politics, which have in Europe, as much as in America, prevailed everywhere during this century, the puny safeguards of democratic liberty have been swept down beneath the impact of emotional tides, either of nationalism or class-conflict, from the Right or from the Left. The legal barricades erected by the Weimar Republic against the despotism traditional in Germany were disposed of by National Socialism in the twinkling of an eye. And arrived at power, Socialism, with us, even seeks to govern as a Trade Union, and Trade Union government would remove the ability to strike. As likewise, if that government assume authoritarian powers, the guarantees of civil liberty, of which Habeas Corpus is the supreme example. This is, of course, because there is supposed to be no need for them any longer, any more than you would feel nervous, I imagine, about your valuables while staying with a clergyman.

No one today, or very few, would place themselves at the side of David Hume, in his veiled advocacy of the Stuart view of government. As between Charles Stuart and such determined individualists as Hampden and Eliot, or Holles, or Selden (the 'great dictator of learning of the English nation') or Benjamin Valentine, there would be no hesitation. We are all against tunnage and poundage: all of us loathe onerous taxes, to the imposition of which Charles Stuart was so prone. Yet we cannot but notice that the twenty shillings odd which John Hampden was asked to pay (and which led to his famous legal battle with King Charles I) is a bagatelle to the kind of taxation which today we are burdened with, in spite of the fact that we have long ago got rid of despotic kings and queens, and enjoy what is described as 'popular government'.

Or again, who would hesitate – unless they really enjoyed being fleeced and soaked by rapacious governments, and welcomed the fining and jailing which ensued in the event of non-payment – who would not place himself immediately at the side of Pym, or Coke, or Rudyard, rather than beside Charles Stuart, and promptly set his signature to the Petition of Right, which makes memorable the year 1628?

Where in that Petition the King is reminded that 'your people have been in divers places assembled, and required to lend certain sums of money unto your Majesty', and that when the money was not forthcoming, these same people had been 'imprisoned, confined, and sundry other ways molested' – why, it is plain enough to everyone that these gentlemen were thoroughly justified in exacting from a man of that sort a promise to desist from interfering with his subjects, and to refrain from asking them to part with their good money – however beautiful a war the said monarch might be contemplating against France, or against Spain, which could not be launched without additional revenue.

We are all against Charles Stuart, and understand how such behaviour should in the end have led to his losing his head: and it is difficult to understand how David Hume should waste a tear over so extortionate a person (whose execution, it is generally considered, was decreed by the City of London, whose hard-boiled capitalists resented these tendencies of Charles more deeply even than the squirearchy). But today our great sympathy with the strongminded gentlemen who so successfully defended their pocketbooks is even exceeded by our amazement at the mildness of this tyrant, and his lack of all real power. For our contemporary tyrants are made of so much sterner stuff. In our times, Hampden's head would 'roll in the dust' with great dispatch; the twentieth-century tyrant would not wait for Hampden, or his friends, to strike *his* off.

It was easier for a man of 1913, say, than for anyone today, to feel strongly about kings and queens. Their royal wars, which more often than not were comparable to very expensive and ornate football matches, costing a fraction of what ours do (which leave us utterly ruined), their clippings and debasings of currency – seeing how debased is our own: their arbitrary imprisonment, where with us justice loses more of its beautiful impartiality every day: about all these things in retrospect we are acquiring a sense of proportion.

The American, off on his lonely continent, is probably too far away for his reactions to have been brought very much up to date. He has not suffered as have we in Europe either: even compared with Canada, his taxes are inconsiderable. So he does not feel as otherwise he would, that kings have been overrated, as historical bugbears. They have been a sort of childhood obsession of his: as the symbol of arbitrary power they so monopolized the emotional field that in arming his soul against that particular monster he has left other parts exposed to the great variety of new monsters, nearer home perchance, with which the modern age is so well stocked.

As to his Presidents, they have been no tyrants, certainly. Yet his attitude towards them would have been entirely different had they been dressed differently. Eliminate all the glittering paraphernalia of kingship, and everything is different. A king in a seersucker suit, who is called a 'chief executive', is completely disarming to the romantic 'rebel' mind. He could do all the nasty things that kings do – levy taxes and make war – and no objection would be taken.

For the above-mentioned glittering paraphernalia, if I may speak for myself, I feel a considerable distaste. I am very glad that that barbaric type of ruler, with his tiresome crown and sceptre puppetry, is extinct. I am impatient to see the title 'lord' dispensed with as a reward for very doubtful services to society: and the fewer Lady Jingle Joneses there are kicking around the better pleased I shall be. This brutal statement I trust will carry conviction – but I am speaking of today. Three centuries ago, I think that a king – even poor Charles Stuart – was not necessarily a worse type of ruler than a number of Whig lords: it is difficult to see how men who had grown rich by pillage of Church lands, or later by robbing the peasantry of their common lands, perpetuating their criminal eminence by a law of primogeniture, and, impressively tilted, exercising a snobbish mesmerism over their dupes – how such are, ideally, a great improvement on a king, no more prone to taxation than they would be. All rulers are taxers.

If modern politics are to be understood, superstitious thinking has of course to be superseded by a more objective type, which takes no count of how much, or of how little, gold braid the potentate displays. And intelligent Americans by their use of such expressions as 'economic royalists' reveal a clear understanding of the essentials of the problem. What it remains to do, in order to go to the heart of the problem of political liberty, is – having grasped the fact that the title 'king', 'mogul', 'shah' or 'tsar' is not important, nor the clothes a man wears, nor the weighty incrustations of gold and lace – to go on from that to a further bitter truth: namely that when great *wealth* is eliminated, but great *power* remains, human liberty is no way advanced. It is power, not money, that is important.

The object of these observations, since that point where I introduced the Whig-hating figure of David Hume, has been to show how difficult it is to bring political thinking up-to-date if a foundation of emotional prejudice underlies the national mind. In America, that, unfortunately, is what we find, in spite of the great numbers of emancipated intelligences – more, I dare say, than are to be met with in England – who counteract, on the fringes, the archaic fixity of tradition.

Because the Americans have embalmed their Whiggery, along with their 'Bible religion'; because they make exhibition of so noisy, if superficial, a radicalism, they look more progressive than they in fact are.

AMERICA, I PRESUME

VI. CLASS DISTINCTIONS

Nineveh N.Y., is, I believe, a very typical American city. Of its seven hundred thousand inhabitants a few thousand are Anglo-Saxon. They are the old inhabitants. The rest are Poles, Italians, Negroes, Germans, Jews, Swedes, Chinese and Czechs. In this city the Poles are the most numerous. There are three or four hundred thousand of them. You can walk for a half-mile through Nineveh and hear nothing but Polish spoken. The Italians are in almost as great numbers, and in their districts it is Little Italy.

The Germans have been pretty much absorbed, though there are still German-language theatres and cinemas. But other nationalities are as yet unassimilated.

A great barrier to assimilation, here as elsewhere, is religion. The Poles, Italians, and Germans are for the most part Catholic.

Nineveh swarms with Catholic churches, seminaries, convents, clubs and schools.

And in America *Catholic* is synonymous with *foreign*. I believe that the average descendant of the original Puritan feels nearer to the Jew than he does to the Catholic. And spiritually, of course, he *is*; for Puritanism, in its emphasis upon *righteousness*, is the child of the Judaic ethos. Morals are the great gift of the Jew, as Science is the legacy of the Hellene.

How powerful this feeling about the Catholics can be is easier to understand if one remembers what the fathers of these people felt upon the subject. A prominent citizen of Nineveh once told me how his grandfather would sit on his house-porch of an evening, and if a Catholic priest passed down the street he would stamp loudly with his stick in blind sectarian rage at the sight of this Papist interloper.

Now the religious cleavage, with its connotation *foreign*, where it concerns the Roman Catholic (Rome is after all the capital city of the Italian Mediterranean world) takes with it something else which every would-be student of modern America must note. Catholic also spells *socially inferior*. This must not be taken too far, but it is a tendency worth stressing.

To explain how this operates let me record a conversation I had with Jane Greenacres, the married daughter of one of the Grahame Brothers. Mrs Jane Greenacres has her troubles, and one of them distinctly is her adolescent daughter, Popette. Frowning, she confided in me one day how Popette was causing her anxious perplexity by going around with a couple of Catholics. Very nice persons, both of them: she had nothing whatever against them – *except*: oh, well, she didn't know! There it was – she just didn't like the idea of *Catholics*!

'But what is the objection? Really that they are *Catholics*?' I asked, out of idle curiosity.

'Uhugh,' she nodded. 'I guess so.'

'But the Catholics are very excellent people as a rule. Lot to be said for a good Catholic!'

'I know it,' she agreed. 'I know there is.'

'They take their moral responsibilities very seriously. Jolly straightlaced lot!'

'I know they do,' Jane assented very ruefully. She couldn't deny it, she wished she *could*. There was nothing she resented so much as their undeniably high principles, which she seemed inclined to regard as part of a Popish plot. 'I know many people who have been converted to Catholicism even.'

'It is "the Old Religion", as they used to call it,' I reminded her. 'Has much in its favour. Pretty ritual.'

'But I was brought up a Unitarian!' Jane complained. 'I just would not stand for it if Popette married a *Catholic*. Why, the children would be brought up as Catholics. No!' She shook her head in vigorous rejection of such a sordid picture.

'Is it religious prejudice on your part?' I asked. For I wanted to get to the bottom of this. My curiosity was aroused.

'I'm afraid in the last analysis it's *snobbery*,' Jane answered, laughing at herself.

'*Social* snobbery?' I persisted. 'Not social snobbery!'

'Well, yes – I suppose it *would* be that. Social snobbery.'

This was quite beyond me at the time.

'But is there then a social stigma attached to Catholicism?' I asked her, as wide-eyed as my eye-glass allows. Here was something entirely novel. For the Duke of Norfolk is a Catholic, and so of course are many of the European crowned heads. The King of Sweden does not put on dog with the King of Spain because the latter goes to Mass.

'Well, Nineveh is a city with a large foreign population,' Jane explained.

Then I saw light.

'I see,' I said. 'And the foreign element is predominantly Catholic?'

'That is it,' said Jane. 'We have half a million Poles and Italians!'

'Ah ha. I see.'

I did not take this any farther, nor inquire what was the matter with the Poles and Italians. Even I knew what the social status of the Polacks and the Wops was perfectly well. The Wop is regarded as a creature of another clay. He's almost in the same class as the Negro. Wops are a servant and workman class. But whereas there are many cranks eager to assist the Negro to improve his status, there is no one who has given any thought to the social handicap that afflicts the Italian, in this strictly 'Nordic' land.

In Nineveh a Wop can be a waiter, but nothing else in the better part of the town. In the large grocery store where later on we bought our provisions, the assistant who took your order was strictly un-Latin. But the errand boy or errand man – the fetcher and carrier – was Italian. No one would buy shirts and collars, pants and overcoats, meat, or cough lozenges from a Wop. All the heavy rough work is done by the countrymen of Dante. And they intermarry outside their own people only with Poles or sometimes Jews – though the latter have just as strict rules about that sort of thing as the Anglo-Saxons. There is another barrier there.

In New York the Jew and the Italian have an uneasy racial alliance. This is symbolized by the Mayor, La Guardia, who is half Italian, half Jew, and incidentally much the best Mayor New York has ever known. On the other hand the situation dramatized in 'Abie's Irish Rose' (a play of 20 years ago) does not seem to have been very successful. A Jewish cop, for instance, shot and killed *his* 'Irish Rose' the other day, in New York, so incompatible did he find this fragrant Celtic blossom. Both the Jew and the Irishman have their virtues: but they are not virtues that are complementary. So it seems. In Nineveh there are no Irish, so *that* problem does not arise.

In the United States of America, Class takes two forms. First, there is *money*. A million dollars is the great patent of nobility. Next to *money*, is *race*. An Italian or a Jew is a 'second-grade citizen' in the U.S.A., every bit as much as is the Jew in Grossdeutschland.

There is another form that Class has recently taken. In Livingston County, N.Y., I have heard certain families settled there for four generations, and always enjoying a moneyed status, described as 'aristocrats'. With more and more unction this term is used in the press about such families as the Roosevelts and Vanderbilts. Or there are families that for a hundred years or longer have owned a canning factory, say, in a small New England *bourgade* and been bosses there; they would now undoubtedly describe themselves as 'aristocrats'.

When I seemed puzzled by the term 'aristocrat' on one occasion, a man eyed me severely and proceeded to instruct. 'Oh, yes, we *have*,' he said, 'our *aristocrats* here in America too.' (He did not mean 'we've got 'em as well', he meant 'don't run away with the idea that we are such plain folk that we haven't got that class of people as much as you!')

But, aside from this somewhat fancy category of citizen, money and race, respectively, provide the main ingredients for class stratification in most parts of the United States.

Very oddly, other nationalities outside the English and Scotch – to which the ruling class is supposed by descent to belong* – are graded according to some mental process it is not always easy to follow. For instance, a Spaniard is a 'Dago', certainly. But he is a higher grade Dago than an Italian. It is considered all right to have a Spanish grandmother. It is not quite so romantic in the States as it is in England to have 'Spanish blood'. But it is by no means a disgraceful departure from the Anglo-Saxon norm. The Spaniards are a 'proud', if distinctly dirty and dark-skinned, race. It is quite okay to be a quarter Spanish. To be entirely Spanish is another matter. That involves being *Catholic*, of course. That is not so good.

German and Irish origin, racially, is in a class apart. The Germans and Irish run neck and neck for second place to the Anglo-Saxon. The Rockefellers and Clark Gable are of Germanic stock: and though the Rockefellers are not absolutely *first*-class millionaires (though – again a paradox – as rich as any), they are quite respectable folk. Clark Gable of course is a first-class Star and racially quite all right.

The Irish have been under a cloud for so long, the discrimination against the Irish socially is so ingrained in American social tradition, that even today people shrink from admitting too overwhelming an admixture of Irish blood.

A Nineveh hostess, hailing from New Haven, Connecticut, is the possessor of an extremely long upper lip. This is a pure bog-trotting lip, if I have ever seen one. And she has a wit and common sense as well, that are hardly Anglo-Saxon. Having occasion to refer to this lip one day, she said (looking at me hard in the eye), 'This obstinate Scottish upperlip of mine.' But I smiled: I would have none of that nonsense.

'That lip, Madam,' said I, 'is an *Irish* lip – as you know quite well!'

* Dutch, too, is of course very chic. But that is confined to New York State, and the Seventeenth or Eighteenth Century. It would not be at all chic, for instance, to be a last century Hollander much less a mere Dutchman of today. 'Van' or even 'Ten' is as much an index of nobility in the U.S.A. as 'Von' is in Germany. But it is the whole of the States, about which I am writing here, not of the Hudson Valley, where most of the *Vans* survive.

Being absolutely one of the most intelligent women in Nineveh, and also one of the nicest, she pulled her big lip down and her eyes had a friendly sensible twinkle. 'Well . . . perhaps it *is*!' she assented, and had a little laugh at being traced by me to the Lakes of Killarney, in the act of trying to lead me off along the shores of the Firth of Forth.

Today, Ireland is on the upgrade in the U.S.A. The attitude in popular fiction, in the press, in city or state politics, to all that is Irish, is increasingly respectful. In the pages of the fictionist the Irish characters are often as not highly sympathetic: even, sometimes, serious and noble (if always impetuous and unfortunate). In several of the most important cities of the East the Irish have big powerful political machines. New Haven has an Irish mayor for the first time in history. Boston is entirely controlled by the immense Irish majority party. But what I am stressing here is that in every-day social life it is getting to be not such a blemish as it was even a decade ago to have a name beginning with O. To have a name beginning with Mac is *better*. But an O-something can now meet a Mac-something *almost*, if not quite, on equal terms.

English and Scottish are the two really swagger things to be. Nothing is quite so good as to be English or Scottish – or Welsh. (Welsh is almost equally good – Pierpoint Morgan, all said and done, is Welsh.) But there is a small point to be noted here. You may think me fussy, but it is as well to get these things shipshape while we are at it.

Formerly to be English was *best of all*. Today that is no longer the case. The prestige of the Scot stands very high indeed. This is partly owing to the fact that tweed suitings and golf come from Scotland. But there is another factor: undeniably the English have, ever so little, lost caste.

Epilogue

On his Blindness
1951

We conclude with the article, published in The Listener *for May 10, 1951, which brought to an end Lewis's art criticism, and, so far as his personal life was concerned, put other people on 'the other side of the partition'. To the Literary Editor of* The Listener, *J. R. Ackerley, he wrote in April: 'I am afraid I depressed you by my account of the dark room in which I am going to be locked. But there is an* interval. *And we are all going into some dark room after all: we none of us ever give a thought to that, so why should I anticipate my more limited black-out?'*

THE SEA-MISTS OF THE WINTER

It became evident quite early that it was going to be a deplorable winter. The cold was unvarying, it had purpose, it seemed. Usually in a London winter it forgets to be cold half the time; it strays back to autumn or wanders dreamily forward to spring, after a brief attempt at winter toughness, perhaps, squeezing out a few flakes of snow. But *this* winter though it experienced its usual difficulty in producing anything but a contemptible snowfall there has been an un-British quality, an unseemly continuity.

Speaking for myself, what struck me most was the veil of moisture like a sea-mist which never left my part of the town. I remember

EPILOGUE

first remarking this just before Christmas. I said to Scott, my journalist-newsagent-friend, that these perpetual mists must slow him down in the morning; he drives up to business in his car, from his home in the outer suburbs. He did not seem to mind a light sea-mist for he shook his head absent-mindedly. Another time I was talking to him over the magazine counter of the shop and indicating the street outside, with its transparent film of blue-grey. I protested, 'Another mist!' He looked out and said, a little sharply, 'There is no mist.' I did not argue, I suppose that he meant it was not up to the specification of what *he* called 'a mist'.

But you may have seen through my innocent device. The truth is that there was *no* mist. The mist was in my eyes: there was no sea-mist in nature. In spite of conditions which, one would have supposed, would have made it quite clear what these atmospheric opacities were, it took me a considerable time to understand. It was not, you see, like this that I had imagined my sight would finally fade out. 'You have been going blind for a long time,' said the neuro-surgeon. And I had imagined that I should go on going blind for a long time yet: just gradually losing the power of vision. I had never visualized mentally, a sea-mist.

In such cases as mine there always arrives a time when normal existence becomes impossible, and you have to turn towards the consultant who has made a speciality of your kind of misfortune. When I started my second portrait of T. S. Eliot, which now hangs in Magdalene College, Cambridge, in the early summer of 'forty-nine', I had to draw up very closely to the sitter to see exactly how the hair sprouted out of the forehead, and how the curl of the nostril wound up into the dark interior of the nose. There was no question of my not succeeding, my sight was still adequate. But I had to move too close to the forms I was studying. Some months later, when I started a portrait of Stella Newton, I had to draw still closer and even then I could not quite see. So I had to have my eyes examined again. This was the turning-point, the date, December 1949. What, in brief is my problem, is that the optic nerves, at their chiasma, or crossing, are pressed upon by something with the pleasing name of cranial pharyngeoma. It is therefore a more implacable order of misfortune than if I had a jolly little cataract. There has been a great acceleration of failure of vision during the last seven months or so. Of course I was told that I should first lose my 'central vision', which would mean that I should no longer be able to read or write. Already I was obliged to read with a magnifying glass. Then I found I could no longer read the names of streets, see the numbers on houses, or see what stations I was passing through on the railway. About that time everything except banner headlines was invisible: then I found I could no longer read the letters inside the finger-holes of a telephone-dial. At present, if I wish to dial a number, I count the holes with my fingertips until I reach the opening where I know the letter I have to locate is situated. Thus seven is P.R.S. five is J.K.L. I know what letters the holes near the beginning and end of the half-circle contain, and what the figures are as well.

As to typing, it is some time ago now that I ceased to see distinctly the letters on the keys. I still write a certain amount with a pen or pencil, but I write blind. However much I write on it the page before me is still an unsullied white: and sometimes the lines I have written distressingly amalgamate. The two books on which I am at present working, one a novel, the other an art book, will proceed quite smoothly, but the method of their production will be changed. A dictaphone, or 'recorder' as the Americans call it, will supersede the pen or the typewriter, at least as far as the first stages of composition are concerned. Many American writers I am informed employ the recorder, although possessing ordinary visual powers.

As to the sea-mist, that is now too pretty a name for it. Five or six weeks ago I still went to my newsagent to have a talk with Scott and make some purchases. He of course would move about as a fresh customer would come in and demand attention. At any given time I found it extremely difficult to decide whether he was there before me or not, for he would come back and stand silently near me, and often it was only because of the tobacco he was smoking, and a slight movement in the mist before me, or at my side, that I knew that he had returned. Recently he has told me that he realized that half the time I did not know he was there. I went to other shops as well, as long as it was possible: but when for me the butcher became nothing but a white apron, and the skinned back of a bullock protruding, as it hung, seemed to me a fleshly housewife, I ceased to be a shopper. Now I take my exercise arm-in-arm with some pleasant companion, and it's surprising how easily one can

EPILOGUE

thread one's way in and out of the shadowy pedestrians, very slightly steered by another but sharp-eyed person.

Sometimes I am still at large solo, though increasingly rarely. I may go out, for instance, and some twenty yards away look for a taxicab. In these cases I will stand upon the edge of the pavement, calling imperiously 'Are you *free*?' to owner-drivers, who probably observe me coldly from behind their steering wheels as if I were the Yonghi-Bongi-Bo. I signal small vans, I peer hopefully at baby-trucks. At length I get a response. It *is* a taxi! But I assure you that it is one thing to hail a taxi-cab, another to get into it. This is quite extraordinarily difficult. I try to force my way in beside the indignant driver. He or I will open the door. But as I see everything so indistinctly I attempt to effect a passage through the wood of the door itself, in Alice Through the Looking Glass fashion, rather than take advantage of the gaping hole in the side of the taxi produced by the opening of the door. It is with a sign of relief that I at last find my way in, after vainly assaulting the stationary vehicle in two or three places. This I realize must be extremely difficult to understand for a person with rude eyesight and piercing vision. It is also difficult for the acquaintance who comes up, as I am staring through the slabs of dark grey at darker slabs, which I hope may be taxis, who addresses me with familiar cordiality. For he is just another slab of nondescript grey, at which I stare, inquiring a little unceremoniously, 'Who are you?'

When visited by friends, which will be usually in the evening, in a room lit by electric light properly shaded (for I have not removed these obstacles to sight, belonging to an era out of which I am passing) I see them after a fashion, but fragmentarily, obliquely, and spasmodically. I can see no one immediately in front of me. But I sit and talk to them without embarrassment, of course, just as if I could see them. It is rather like telephone conversations, where the voice is the main thing. But an awareness of the bodily presence is always there, and as one turns one's head hither and thither, glimpses constantly recur, delivering to one's fading eyesight a piece of old so-and-so's waistcoat or bald head, or dear Janet's protruding nose. These token odds and ends of personality are really just as good as seeing them whole, and their voices have an added significance.

The failure of sight which is already so advanced, will of course become worse from week to week until in the end I shall only be able to see the external world through little patches in the midst of a blacked out tissue. On the other hand, instead of little patches, the last stage may be the absolute black-out. Pushed into an unlighted room, the door banged and locked for ever, I shall then have to light a lamp of aggressive voltage in my mind to keep at bay the night.

New as I am to the land of blind-man's-buff I can only register the novel sensations, and not deny myself the enjoyment of this curious experience. It amuses me to collide with a walking belly; I quite enjoy being treated as a lay-figure, seized by the elbows and heaved up in the air as I approach a kerb, or flung into a car. I relish the absurdity of gossiping with somebody the other side of the partition. And everyone is at the other side of the partition. I am not allowed to see them. I am like a prisoner condemned to invisibility, although permitted an unrestricted number of visitors. Or I have been condemned to be a blind-folded delinquent, but not otherwise interfered with. And meanwhile I gaze backward over the centuries at my fellow condamnés. Homer heads the list, but there are surprisingly few. I see John Milton sitting with his three daughters (the origin of this image, is to my shame, it seems to me, a Royal Academy picture), the fearful blow at his still youthful pride distorting his face with its frustrations. He is beginning his great incantation: 'Of Man's first Disobedience and the Fruit of that Forbidden Tree', while one of the women sits, her quill-pen poised ready to transcribe the poetry. Well, Milton had his daughters, I have my dictaphone.

This short story of mine has the drawback of having its tragedy to some extent sublimated. Also, we have no ending. Were I a dentist, or an attorney I should probably be weighing the respective advantages of the sleek luminol, or the noisy revolver. For there is no such thing as a blind dentist, or a blind lawyer. But as a writer, I merely change from pen to dictaphone. If you ask, 'And as an *artist*, what about that?' I should perhaps answer, 'Ah, sir, as to the artist in England, I have often thought that it would solve a great many problems if English painters were born blind.'

And finally, which is the main reason for this unseemly autobiographical outburst, my articles on contemporary art exhibitions necessarily end, for I can no longer see a picture.

For Product Safety Concerns and Information please contact our EU
representative GPSR@taylorandfrancis.com
Taylor & Francis Verlag GmbH, Kaufingerstraße 24, 80331 München, Germany

www.ingramcontent.com/pod-product-compliance
Lightning Source LLC
Chambersburg PA
CBHW052139300426
44115CB00011B/1439